BOTTLE PRICING GUIDE

by Hugh Cleveland

- Over 4,000 old and new bottles, alphabetically listed and priced.
- About 2,500 pictures
- 19 Catagories; Avons, Medicine, Jim Beam, Bitters & Others
- How to sell and buy.

On The Cover: Reproduction of Madonna Bottle from Mexico, $5.00-7.50; Bromo Bracer Jar, $25.00; Green Soda Water Bottle, $5.00-10.00; Avon Car, $6.00-9.00.

The current values in this book should be used only as a guide. They are not intended to set prices, which vary from one section of the country to another. Auction prices as well as dealer prices vary greatly and are affected by condition as well as demand. Neither the Author nor the Publisher assumes responsibility for any losses that might be incurred as a result of consulting this guide.

Table of Contents

Tips On Identifying Bottles

Imperfections

Most old bottles have imperfections, which are dents in the glass, crooked necks, bubbles, etc. They are most valuable for every imperfection and most desired by collectors.

Three Piece Molds

These bottles were made in three different pieces; the bottom below the shoulder in one piece, above the shoulder in two pieces. You can identify these rare bottles by the mold marks.

Inside Thread Marks

The threads are on the inside of the top of this bottle. Usually a whiskey bottle, there was a hard rubber cork that went into the bottle.

Applied Lip

Glass makers called this "laid on ring" because it actually was a ring of glass laid and pressed onto the cracked-off neck of a bottle or jar.

Kick-up Bottom

Glass makers called it push-up. The bottoms of certain bottles, wine bottles in particular, were deliberately pushed up to make them easier to ship. The neck of one bottle was nestled into this pushed-up bottom of another, making them easier to pack.

Blob Seals

Blob seal bottles are very popular because they have a raised seal or blob of glass with the company name, product name, dates, etc.

Whittle Marks

These marks were caused by blowing glass that was too cold to flow smoothly into the mold, and can be produced even by modern machinery by starting the line moving while the molds are still cold.

Sheared Lip

This occured when blown glass bottles and jars were cracked off the blowpipe, usually by applying a few drops of water to the hot glass. The neck was then reheated or firepolished and hand tooled.

Tips On Buying and Selling Bottles

Limited Editions

How large is the issuing company and does it keep its word? Any company that promises to issue 100 bottles and then issues several thousand will probably do so in all situations where a bottle sells well. Established collectors will usually have knowledge about what companies can be depended on.

Token Issue

These are usually manufactured in small scale for an event or a commemorative issue for an obscure but graphic happening. But, watch out for issues of bottles on a world interest scale, such as one commemorating the the first moon landing. They are made in great abundance and are worthwhile only if the buyer is not planning to resell.

Brief Issues

Bottles honoring an outlet for the issuing company that are quality bottles depicting dramatic scenes or eye-grabbing names are hard to lose on.

Figural Bottles

Bottles that look nothing like what they are supposed to represent will usually have very little resale value. Animals, birds and nostalgic subjects retain their worth rather consistently, but the shape must appeal to collectors all over the continent. Too often, bottles are made that are nostalgic only for one small part of the country, such as the cable car in San Francisco, and will never attain a high resale value.

Mold Seams

Mold seams indicate the age of a bottle:

Mold seam stops at shoulder . . . . about 1800
Mold seam stops between shoulder and top of neck . . . about 1875
Mold seam stops nearly at top of neck . . . . about 1890
Mold seam stops at top of neck . . . . about 1900
Mold seam stops at top of bottle . . . . 1910 and later

Low mold seams are not the perfect sign of collectibility because they can be reproduced. But, when a bottle of this kind is dug up, the item is pretty sure to be collectible.

Unusual shape, color or former contents

Sun-colored amethyst bottles are fairly old, for the glass was made with manganese, which will turn when exposed to the sun, or will even eventually turn in dark places. Aqua, amethyst, yellowish tints and pinks (in that order of age) are usually collectible.

Unfinished Spots

Unless machine-made, bottles will show small, obviously unfinished spots on their bases, from just circular rings to open, small pits. These wounds are usually rough, or at least less finished than the balance of the bottle. This is where the glass blower pontil stick was abruptly broken off, and it is a point to seek for the antique quality of a bottle.

Ground Stopper

The ground throat with a ground stopper is also a clue to antiquity. These bottles, as in the apothecary jars and bottles and some fine perfumes, usually have a fine quality glass. Each inserting part of a stopper, and each inside throat of a bottle that has been re-ground identifies this category. Each stopper was carefully ground to fit the individual bottle throat it belonged in, so it is very difficult to find another bottle that an excavated stopper will properly fit.

Labels and Embossings

Bottles with labels or embossings that say cure will be old, because federal directives against this have been in effect so long. Some bottles have a permanent "in-the-glass" label as an integral part of the bottle and are highly desireable in any collection. Enameled lettering on some old bar bottles, many with verifiable old pictures are also acceptable.

Recent Bottles

All bottles bearing the legend FEDERAL LAW PROHIBITS THE RE-USE OR RE-SALE OF THIS BOTTLE are contemporary, and are not generally desirable.

Prices

Bottle prices have not stabilized, and certainly shall not for several decades. They cannot until a suitable grading system is invented to cover all variants, conditions and vintage years. This is always a delicate subject and an author should advise on possible highs and lows only, as has been done in this book. The in-between range is the dickering radius.

Acknowledgements

The inspiration for writing this book came from Mrs. Paul L. (Bessie) Jenses, of San Angelo, Texas. She knows bottles and is more than willing to help anyone who is interested in collecting bottles and other kinds of antiques. Many of the pictures in this book came from her collection.

Other help on this book came from Mr. Ed Bartholomew in Fort Davis, Texas, a writer and publisher of many books on the West as well as old bottles of all kinds. Mr. Bartholomew has a really nice collection of bottles and deals in them as well as writes about them. His books should be a must in your library.

The fine Avon ladies of this area have been a lot of help by bringing in their collections for me to photograph, as well as helping me in the description of a lot of the Avons. One in particular—Mrs. Marvin Motl of San Angelo—has given me much of her time and service.

Our thanks go to Mr. J.K. Talley of San Angelo for his great help with Jim Beam bottles, and Mrs. Alex Von Gotten, also of San Angelo, for her help with numerous assorted bottles.

One never knows how many friends he has until he gets out and looks for them. It seems that the bottle collectors are one of the finest groups of people there is.

The prices in this book are average prices as advertised in the trade journals of bottles, and are not construed to be the correct price for your area, only a guide to go by in buying and selling.

AVONS

1.   1964 AFTER BATH FRESHENERS, Clear glass container with a knob screw-on lid. Lilac lid-Lilac, Pink lid-Rose Geranium, Yellow lid-Jasmin. 8 ozs. 8½" high.... $ 3.00- 4.00
2.   1971 ALADDIN'S LAMP, Foaming bath oil, 5 fragrances, green glass, gold cap. 6 ozs. 7½" long. PP $7.00 .... $ 7.50- 10.00
3.   1971 THE ARISTOCAT, Non-tear shampoo - Walt Disney's Aristocat. Gray plastic container & pink band around neck. 6½" high. 4 ozs. PP $3.00............. $ 3.00- 4.00
4.   1972 ARMOIRE, foaming bath oil decanter. 4 fragrances, white glass, gold screw-on lid. Floral trim, 5 ozs., 7" PP .... $ - 4.00

5.   1936 ASTRINGENT, Clear glass container with aqua screw-on lid. Came with small paper label. 4 ozs. 5½" PP $12.50 .... $ 12.00- 15.00
6.   1971 AVONSHIRE BLUE COLOGNE, 4 fragrances, blue opaque glass vase, white trim, 8" high, stopper top, 6 ozs. PP $10.00................................... $ 10.00
7.   1960 BABYOIL, White plastic bottle, blue lettering, dark blue screw-on cap. 6 ozs. PP $.98............... $ 5.00- 6.00
8.   1970 BABY PRODUCTS, The following came in white, blue and pink plastic containers with blue plastic screw-on lid: BABY POWDER (9 oz., 7" tall), BABY LOTION (6 oz., 5½" tall), BABY SHAMPOO (6 oz., 5½" tall), BABY CREAM (2 oz., tube, 5¾"), BABY SOAP (3 oz.). PP $.25 to $1.00 each .... $ .25- .50

1

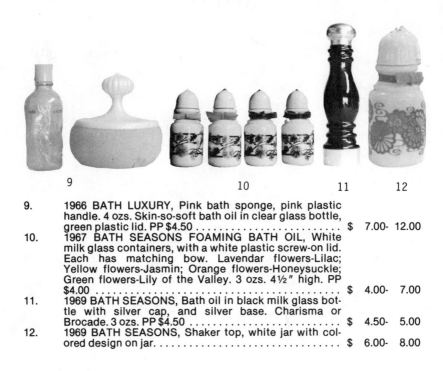

9   10   11   12

9.   1966 BATH LUXURY, Pink bath sponge, pink plastic
      handle. 4 ozs. Skin-so-soft bath oil in clear glass bottle,
      green plastic lid. PP $4.50 . . . . $ 7.00- 12.00
10.   1967 BATH SEASONS FOAMING BATH OIL, White
      milk glass containers, with a white plastic screw-on lid.
      Each has matching bow. Lavendar flowers-Lilac;
      Yellow flowers-Jasmin; Orange flowers-Honeysuckle;
      Green flowers-Lily of the Valley. 3 ozs. 4½" high. PP
      $4.00 . . . . $ 4.00- 7.00
11.   1969 BATH SEASONS, Bath oil in black milk glass bot-
      tle with silver cap, and silver base. Charisma or
      Brocade. 3 ozs. PP $4.50 . . . . $ 4.50- 5.00
12.   1969 BATH SEASONS, Shaker top, white jar with col-
      ored design on jar. . . . . $ 6.00- 8.00

14   15   16

13.   1971 BATH URN, White milk glass container, with a
      gold lid. White ball on top. 6" high. 5 ozs. PP $4.00 . . . . $ 4.00
14.   1969 BIRD OF PARADISE BATH OIL, Clear glass bottle
      with a gold cap. 6 ozs. 6" high. PP $5.00 . . . . $ 2.00- 4.00
15.   1969 BIRD OF PARADISE COLOGNE, Clear glass bot-
      tle with gold cap. Comes in 2 other sizes. 4 ozs. PP
      $5.00 . . . . $ 2.00- 3.00
16.   1970 BIRD OF PARADISE, ½ oz. cologne. Clear glass
      bottle, gold screw-on lid. 2½" high. PP $1.50 . . . . $ 1.00- 3.00

2

17   18   19   20

17. 1969 BIRD OF PARADISE COLOGNE FLUFF, 5½"
high, Aqua plastic coated over glass bottle, Gold
designed cap. Gold rope around cap. PP $5.00 .... $ 3.00-   4.00
18. 1970 BIRD OF PARADISE COLOGNE MIST, Aqua
plastic coated bottle with a gold cap & neck tag. 3 ozs.
5" PP $6.00 .... $ 2.00-   3.00
19. 1969 BIRD OF PARADISE CREAM SACHET, Aqua jar
with gold cap. .66 ozs. PP $3.00 .... $ .50-   1.00
20. 1970 BIRD OF PARADISE DECANTER COLOGNE,
Clear glass with a gold plastic bird-head cap. 5 ozs. 8"
high. PP $6.00 .... $ 6.00-   8.00

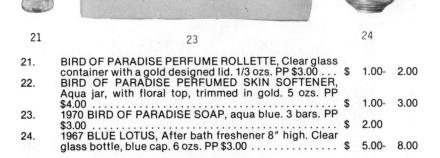

21   23   24

21. BIRD OF PARADISE PERFUME ROLLETTE, Clear glass
container with a gold designed lid. 1/3 ozs. PP $3.00 ... $ 1.00-   2.00
22. BIRD OF PARADISE PERFUMED SKIN SOFTENER,
Aqua jar, with floral top, trimmed in gold. 5 ozs. PP
$4.00 .... $ 1.00-   3.00
23. 1970 BIRD OF PARADISE SOAP, aqua blue. 3 bars. PP
$3.00 .... $ 2.00
24. 1967 BLUE LOTUS, After bath freshener 8" high. Clear
glass bottle, blue cap. 6 ozs. PP $3.00 .... $ 5.00-   8.00

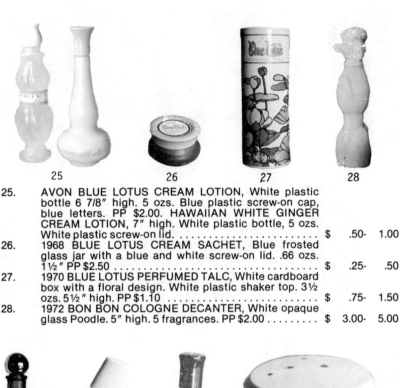

25   26   27   28

25.	AVON BLUE LOTUS CREAM LOTION, White plastic bottle 6 7/8" high. 5 ozs. Blue plastic screw-on cap, blue letters. PP $2.00. HAWAIIAN WHITE GINGER CREAM LOTION, 7" high. White plastic bottle, 5 ozs. White plastic screw-on lid. .... $	.50-	1.00
26.	1968 BLUE LOTUS CREAM SACHET, Blue frosted glass jar with a blue and white screw-on lid. .66 ozs. 1½" PP $2.50 .... $	.25-	.50
27.	1970 BLUE LOTUS PERFUMED TALC, White cardboard box with a floral design. White plastic shaker top. 3½ ozs. 5½" high. PP $1.10 .... $	.75-	1.50
28.	1972 BON BON COLOGNE DECANTER, White opaque glass Poodle. 5" high. 5 fragrances. PP $2.00 .... $	3.00-	5.00

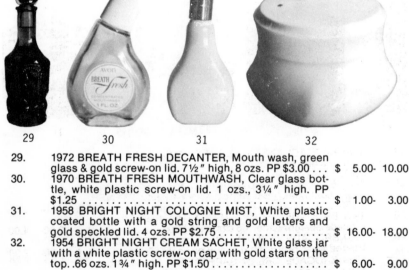

29   30   31   32

29.	1972 BREATH FRESH DECANTER, Mouth wash, green glass & gold screw-on lid. 7½" high, 8 ozs. PP $3.00 ... $	5.00-	10.00
30.	1970 BREATH FRESH MOUTHWASH, Clear glass bottle, white plastic screw-on lid. 1 ozs., 3¼" high. PP $1.25 .... $	1.00-	3.00
31.	1958 BRIGHT NIGHT COLOGNE MIST, White plastic coated bottle with a gold string and gold letters and gold speckled lid. 4 ozs. PP $2.75 .... $	16.00-	18.00
32.	1954 BRIGHT NIGHT CREAM SACHET, White glass jar with a white plastic screw-on cap with gold stars on the top. .66 ozs. 1¾" high. PP $1.50 .... $	6.00-	9.00

4

| | 33 | 34 | 35 | 36 |

33. 1954 BRIGHT NIGHT POWDER SACHET, White milk glass container with a white plastic screw-on lid with gold stars on top. White & gold paper label on the front. 9 ozs. 2½" PP $1.50 .... $ 10.00- 20.00

34. 1955 BRIGHT NIGHT TOILET WATER, Clear glass bottle with a gold speckled cap and gold neck tag. 2 ozs. PP $2.00 .... $ 17.00

35. 1967 BROCADE COLOGNE, Tan ribbed oval shaped glass container with a tan and white brocade designed screw-on lid. 4 ozs. 4½" high. .... $ 2.00- 3.00

36. 1970 BROCADE COLOGNE, .5 ozs. 2 5/8" high, clear glass bottle, gold screw-on lid...................... $ 2.00- 3.00

| | 37 | 38 | 39 | 40 | 41 |

37. 1967 BROCADE COLOGNE MIST, (Refillable) Tan ribbed container, plastic designed lid. 3 ozs. 6½" high. PP $6.00 .... $ 3.00- 6.00

38. 1967 BROCADE COLOGNE SILK, Tan frosted ribbed glass container, gold ribbed screw-on lid. 3 ozs. PP $4.50 .... $ 3.00- 5.00

39. 1967 BROCADE CREAM SACHET, Tan glass jar with a brocade designed top. .66 ozs. PP $3.00 .... $ 3.00- 4.00

40. 1967 BROCADE PERFUME OIL, .5 ozs., 2 5/8" high. Tan frosted glass bottle, gold screw-on lid. PP $5.00 ...... $ 4.00- 7.00

41. 1969 BROCADE CREAM SACHET, Tan frosted ribbed glass oval shaped jar, tan & white designed screw-on lid. .66 ozs. 1¾" high. PP $3.00................... $ 3.00- 4.00

5

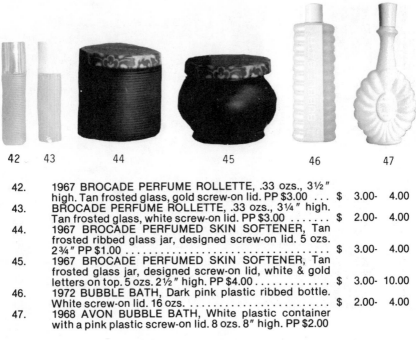

42 43 44 45 46 47

42. **1967 BROCADE PERFUME ROLLETTE, .33 ozs., 3½"**
    high. Tan frosted glass, gold screw-on lid. PP $3.00 . . . $ 3.00- 4.00
43. **BROCADE PERFUME ROLLETTE, .33 ozs., 3¼" high.**
    Tan frosted glass, white screw-on lid. PP $3.00 . . . . $ 2.00- 4.00
44. **1967 BROCADE PERFUMED SKIN SOFTENER, Tan**
    frosted ribbed glass jar, designed screw-on lid. 5 ozs.
    2¾" PP $1.00 . . . . $ 3.00- 4.00
45. **1967 BROCADE PERFUMED SKIN SOFTENER, Tan**
    frosted glass jar, designed screw-on lid, white & gold
    letters on top. 5 ozs. 2½" high. PP $4.00 . . . . $ 3.00- 10.00
46. **1972 BUBBLE BATH, Dark pink plastic ribbed bottle.**
    White screw-on lid. 16 ozs. . . . . $ 2.00- 4.00
47. **1968 AVON BUBBLE BATH, White plastic container**
    with a pink plastic screw-on lid. 8 ozs. 8" high. PP $2.00

50

48 49 51 52

48. **1966 BUD VASE COLOGNE, Clear glass bottle with a**
    glass top with gold trim. Comes in 8 fragrances. 4 ozs. . $ 7.00- 9.00
49. **1967 BUNNY'S DREAM SOAP, Orange carrot soap on a**
    green rope. PP $1.35 . . . . $ 10.00
50. **1972 BUTTERFLY COLOGNE, 5 fragrances. 3½" high.**
    1.5 ozs. Clear glass bottle, gold head as lid. PP $3.00 . . $ 4.00- 7.00
51. **1962 CAMEO CREAM SACHET, Pink glass jar, 2½"**
    high on gold stand, with white screw-on metal lid, with
    lady's face on pink background. 1.5 ozs. PP $3.25 . . . . . $ 8.00- 10.00
52. **1968 CHARISMA COLOGNE, 2½ ozs. Gold cap on red**
    glass bottle. . . . . $ 2.00- 4.00

6

53   54   55   56   57

53.	1968 CHARISMA COLOGNE MIST, Red plastic coated bottle with gold trim. 3 ozs. 8¼ " high. PP $8.00	$ 2.00-	3.00
54.	1969 CHARISMA COLOGNE SILK, Frosted glass bottle with a gold ring around the top and a red screw-on cap. 3 ozs. PP $4.50	$ 3.00-	4.00
55.	1968 CHARISMA PERFUME ROLLETTE, Red container with a gold ring and matching lid. .33 ozs. 4¼ " PP $4.50	$ .50-	1.00
56.	1968 CHARISMA CREAM SACHET, Red jar with gold trim. .66 ozs. PP $3.00	$ .50-	1.00
57.	1970 CHARISMA POWDER SACHET SHAKER, Red glass container with crisscross impressions on it. A silver salt shaker top and a red bow around the neck. 1½ ozs. 2¾ " high.	$ 3.00-	4.00

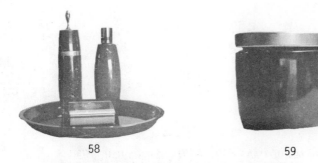

58   59

58.	1968 CHARISMA SET, Red plastic tray, gold edge. 3 ozs. perfumed bath soap. 4 ozs. cologne. Foaming bath oil, red plastic bottle, gold screw-on cap. 6 ozs. 6½ " high. Tray $2.00-4.00; Soap $.50; Cologne $2.00-4.00; Bath Oil $1.00-3.00		
59.	1968 CHARISMA SKIN SOFTENER, 5 ozs. Gold trim on red glass jar. PP $4.00	$	2.00
60.	1969 CHIEF SCRUBBEM, Red plastic Indian head container with yellow markings, black brush bristles on top. 5½ " tall. 4 ozs. Liquid soap. PP $2.50	$ 2.00-	4.00

7

62

61

63

61. 1969 CHRISTMAS COLOGNE, Christmas ornament, 4
fragrances, 3 ozs. each. PP $3.50 . . . . $ 3.00- 7.00
62. 1967 CHRISTMAS ORNAMENTS, Bubble bath. Round
bottle came in silver, gold, red, and green, painted on
clear glass, silver cap. 4 ozs. PP $1.75 . . . . $ 4.00- 6.00
63. 1968 CHRISTMAS ORNAMENTS, Bubble bath. Came in
silver, blue, and green. Gold caps, indented on both
sides of bottles, painted on clear glass. 4 ozs. PP $2.50 $ 3.00- 7.00

64

65

64. 1970 CHRISTMAS ORNAMENT, Bubble bath. Orange,
red, and green plastic ornaments, silver plastic screw-
on cap. 5 ozs. PP $2.50 . . . . $ 2.50- 5.00
65. 1968 CHRISTMAS TREE, Bubble bath. 4 ozs. Gold,
silver, green and red, painted on clear glass. PP $2.50 . . $ 5.00- 7.00
66. 1970 CLARENCE THE SEA SERPENT, Sponge and
soap. Orange, red, and yellow sponge with 3 ozs. soap,
13" long. PP $2.25 . . . . $ 3.00- 5.00

67.   **1970 CLEAN SHOT**, Orange basketball sponge rests in a orange plastic hoop with a yellow net. 3 oz. bar of soap. .... $ 4.50-   5.00

68.   **1951 CLEANSING CREAM**, White glass jar, with green screw-on lid, and green label. .... $ 2.00-   4.00
ALSO HARMONE CLEANSING CREAM & RICH SUPER CREAM, came in same kind of jar. .... $ 2.00-   5.00

69.   **1971 AVON CLEAR SKIN FACIAL MASK**, White plastic tube with blue lettering & a silver screw-on top. 3 ozs. 4½" long. .... $ .50

70.   **1959 AVON CLEAR SKIN LOTION**, White plastic container with black plastic screw-on lid. 3 ozs. 4½" high. PP $.79 .... $ 2.50

71.   **1966 COLOGNE**, Clear glass bottle, four embossed leaves. Gold screw-on lid. .5 ozs. 3¾" high. PP $3.00 .. $ 3.00-   7.00

72.   **1967 COLOGNE GEMS**, Clear glass bottle, clear and gold plastic screw-on lid. 1 oz. 3" high. PP $1.75 ...... $ 3.00-   7.00

73.   **1967 COLOGNE CLASSIC**, Clear ribbed glass bottle with a gold cap. Comes in all fragrances. 4 ozs. 9" high. PP $3.50 .... $ 5.00-   7.00

74.   **1963 COLOGNE MIST**, Came in 7 fragrances, colored band for each fragrance, gold cap. Avon ensignia embossed in clear glass. .... $ 4.00-   8.00

75.   **1968 COLOGNE MIST**, clear glass, ribbed bottle. Plastic gold lid, gold & white decorations below lid. 5 7/8" high. 2 ozs. Came in 8 fragrances. PP $2.50 ..... $ 1.00-   2.00

76.   **1969 COLOGNE MIST**, Frosted glass bottle, gold cap. 2 ozs. Came in 4 fragrances. PP $4.00 .... $ 1.00-   2.00

| | 77 | 78 | 79 | 80 |

77. 1971 COLOGNE MIST, 4 fragrances. 2 ozs. Clear cut looking glass silver top, with black cast on top. PP $2.50 .... $ 2.00- 4.00

78. 1968 COLOGNE RIVERIA, Clear glass bottle with silver trim and cap. All fragrances, 4 ozs. Unscrew bottom of bottle & reverse metal to make a stand for the bottle. PP $6.00 .... $ 6.00- 8.00

79. 1970 CONCERTINA, Yellow & blue plastic accordion container with a pink handle. 8 ozs. of bubble bath. 5" tall.. $ 2.50 3.00

80. 1971 CORNUCOPIA SKIN-SO-SOFT DECANTER, Foaming bath oil. 5½" high, white milk glass. 6 ozs. PP $5.00 .... $ 5.00- 6.00

| | 81 | 82 | 83 | 84 | 85 |

81. 1957 COTILLION COLOGNE, Clear glass container with a paper label, and white plastic screw-on lid. Came in a bath set. 2 ozs. 3¼" high. Cologne bottle only..... $ 10.00- 14.00

82. 1957 COTILLION COLOGNE, Clear glass bottle with a pink top. 4 ozs. PP $4.95 .... $ 18.00- 20.00

83. 1961 COTILLION COLOGNE, Frosted glass bottle, gray or white cap. 4 ozs. PP $3.00 .... $ 1.00- 2.00

84. 1970 COTILLION COLOGNE, Clear glass bottle with gold lettering and a white plastic screw-on lid. 5 ozs. 4 1/8" high. PP $1.50 .... $ .75- 1.00

85. COTILLION COLOGNE MIST, Plastic coated glass container. Some have white bottom with a white snap-on plastic top. Some have a yellow bottom with a white top. The white top turns grey with age. 3 ozs. 7½" high. PP $4.00 .... Solid White $ 1.00- 2.00
Yellow bottom $ 7.00- 10.00

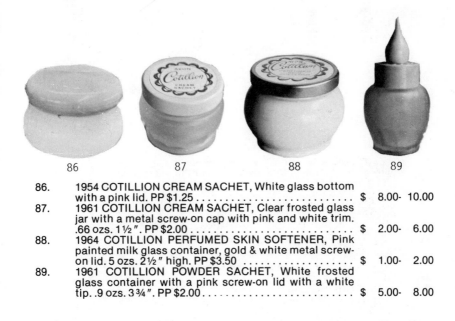

86   87   88   89

86.	1954 COTILLION CREAM SACHET, White glass bottom with a pink lid. PP $1.25	$ 8.00-	10.00
87.	1961 COTILLION CREAM SACHET, Clear frosted glass jar with a metal screw-on cap with pink and white trim. .66 ozs. 1½". PP $2.00	$ 2.00-	6.00
88.	1964 COTILLION PERFUMED SKIN SOFTENER, Pink painted milk glass container, gold & white metal screw-on lid. 5 ozs. 2½" high. PP $3.50	$ 1.00-	2.00
89.	1961 COTILLION POWDER SACHET, White frosted glass container with a pink screw-on lid with a white tip. .9 ozs. 3¾". PP $2.00	$ 5.00-	8.00

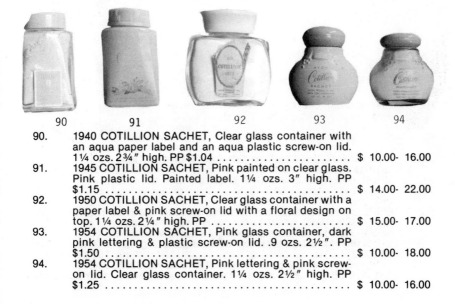

90   91   92   93   94

90.	1940 COTILLION SACHET, Clear glass container with an aqua paper label and an aqua plastic screw-on lid. 1¼ ozs. 2¾" high. PP $1.04	$ 10.00-	16.00
91.	1945 COTILLION SACHET, Pink painted on clear glass. Pink plastic lid. Painted label. 1¼ ozs. 3" high. PP $1.15	$ 14.00-	22.00
92.	1950 COTILLION SACHET, Clear glass container with a paper label & pink screw-on lid with a floral design on top. 1¼ ozs. 2¼" high. PP	$ 15.00-	17.00
93.	1954 COTILLION SACHET, Pink glass container, dark pink lettering & plastic screw-on lid. .9 ozs. 2½". PP $1.50	$ 10.00-	18.00
94.	1954 COTILLION SACHET, Pink lettering & pink screw-on lid. Clear glass container. 1¼ ozs. 2½" high. PP $1.25	$ 10.00-	16.00

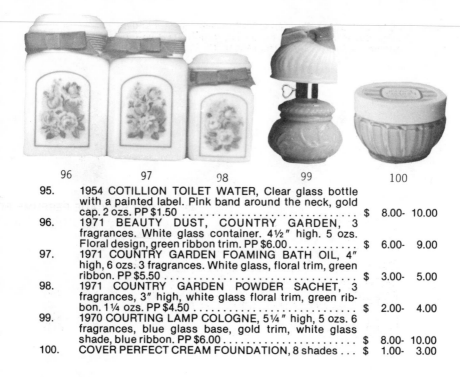

96   97   98   99   100

95.   1954 COTILLION TOILET WATER, Clear glass bottle
       with a painted label. Pink band around the neck, gold
       cap. 2 ozs. PP $1.50 .... $ 8.00- 10.00
96.   1971 BEAUTY DUST, COUNTRY GARDEN, 3
       fragrances. White glass container. 4½" high. 5 ozs.
       Floral design, green ribbon trim. PP $6.00 .... $ 6.00- 9.00
97.   1971 COUNTRY GARDEN FOAMING BATH OIL, 4"
       high, 6 ozs. 3 fragrances. White glass, floral trim, green
       ribbon. PP $5.50 .... $ 3.00- 5.00
98.   1971 COUNTRY GARDEN POWDER SACHET, 3
       fragrances, 3" high, white glass floral trim, green rib-
       bon. 1¼ ozs. PP $4.50 .... $ 2.00- 4.00
99.   1970 COURTING LAMP COLOGNE, 5¼" high, 5 ozs. 6
       fragrances, blue glass base, gold trim, white glass
       shade, blue ribbon. PP $6.00 .... $ 8.00- 10.00
100.   COVER PERFECT CREAM FOUNDATION, 8 shades ... $ 1.00- 3.00

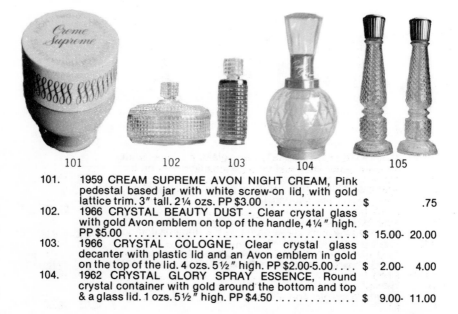

101   102   103   104   105

101.   1959 CREAM SUPREME AVON NIGHT CREAM, Pink
       pedestal based jar with white screw-on lid, with gold
       lattice trim. 3" tall. 2¼ ozs. PP $3.00 .... $ .75
102.   1966 CRYSTAL BEAUTY DUST - Clear crystal glass
       with gold Avon emblem on top of the handle, 4¼" high.
       PP $5.00 .... $ 15.00- 20.00
103.   1966 CRYSTAL COLOGNE, Clear crystal glass
       decanter with plastic lid and an Avon emblem in gold
       on the top of the lid. 4 ozs. 5½" high. PP $2.00-5.00 .... $ 2.00- 4.00
104.   1962 CRYSTAL GLORY SPRAY ESSENCE, Round
       crystal container with gold around the bottom and top
       & a glass lid. 1 ozs. 5½" high. PP $4.50 .... $ 9.00- 11.00

12

105.   1970 CRYSTALLITE COLOGNE, Clear glass candle
         stick decanter, gold screw-on lid, which serves as a
         candle holder. 8″ high. 6 fragrances. PP $5.50 . . . . $ 5.00- 7.00

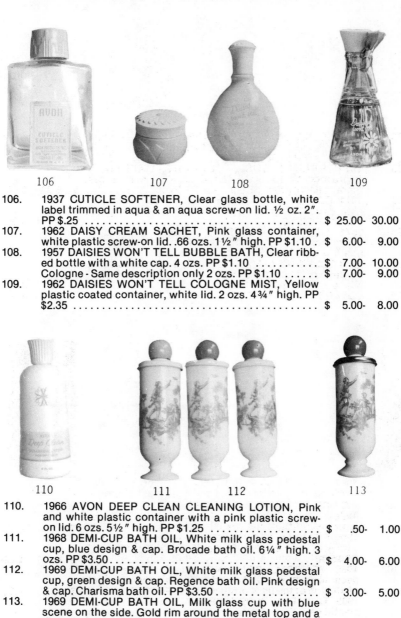

106   107   108   109

106.   1937 CUTICLE SOFTENER, Clear glass bottle, white
         label trimmed in aqua & an aqua screw-on lid. ½ oz. 2″.
         PP $.25 . . . . $ 25.00- 30.00
107.   1962 DAISY CREAM SACHET, Pink glass container,
         white plastic screw-on lid. .66 ozs. 1½″ high. PP $1.10 . $ 6.00- 9.00
108.   1957 DAISIES WON'T TELL BUBBLE BATH, Clear ribb-
         ed bottle with a white cap. 4 ozs. PP $1.10 . . . . $ 7.00- 10.00
         Cologne - Same description only 2 ozs. PP $1.10 . . . . . . $ 7.00- 9.00
109.   1962 DAISIES WON'T TELL COLOGNE MIST, Yellow
         plastic coated container, white lid. 2 ozs. 4¾″ high. PP
         $2.35 . . . . $ 5.00- 8.00

110   111   112   113

110.   1966 AVON DEEP CLEAN CLEANING LOTION, Pink
         and white plastic container with a pink plastic screw-
         on lid. 6 ozs. 5½″ high. PP $1.25 . . . . $ .50- 1.00
111.   1968 DEMI-CUP BATH OIL, White milk glass pedestal
         cup, blue design & cap. Brocade bath oil. 6¼″ high. 3
         ozs. PP $3.50 . . . . $ 4.00- 6.00
112.   1969 DEMI-CUP BATH OIL, White milk glass pedestal
         cup, green design & cap. Regence bath oil. Pink design
         & cap. Charisma bath oil. PP $3.50 . . . . $ 3.00- 5.00
113.   1969 DEMI-CUP BATH OIL, Milk glass cup with blue
         scene on the side. Gold rim around the metal top and a
         blue plastic screw-on lid. 6¼″ high, 3 ozs. PP $3.50 . . . $ 4.00- 6.00

13

114   116   117   118

114.   1970 DUTCH TREAT DEMI-CUP, Cream lotion, plays 2 roles. 3 ozs. Pink knob on top, white cup. Pink flowers-Hawaiian White Ginger. Yellow flowers-Honeysuckle. Blue flowers-Blue Lotus. PP $3.50 . . . . $ 3.00- 6.00

115.   1969 ROSE DEMI-CUP BATH OIL, White milk glass cup, with red and yellow roses on sides, metal top with rose colored plastic screw-on lid. 6¼" high. 3 ozs. PP $3.50 . $ 4.00- 8.00

116.   1969 SKIN-SO-SOFT DEMI-CUP, White glass, with colored design, and colored lid. . . . . $ 5.00- 7.00

117.   1951 DEODORANT, FLOW-ON, White plastic container, green letters, green circle on front, white plastic screw-on lid. 3½" high. . . . . $ 2.00- 4.00

118.   1960 DEODORANT, FLOW-ON, 4¾" high, aqua painted on clear glass. 1.75 ozs. Aqua screw-on lid, flow-on in white letters. . . . . $ 2.00- 4.00

119   120   121   122

119.   1967 DEODORANT, PERFUMED, 3¾" high, clear glass bottle, with aqua paper label and aqua plastic screw-on lid. 4 ozs. PP $.79 . . . . $ 3.00- 6.00

120.   1972 DEW GLOW MOISTURIZER, for protection. 2.25 ozs. frosted glass jar, metal screw-on lid, pink floral design on top. Contents pink. . . . . $ 3.50- 5.00

121.   1960 DEW KISS, Clear bottle, Pink plastic screw-on lid. Came with a pink & gold tag, held by a gold string. 1.5 ozs. 4¼" high. . . . . $ 5.00- 6.00

122.   1966 DEW KISS, Clear glass container with dew drop shaped paper labels, white plastic screw-on lid. 4¾" high. 3.5 ozs. . . . . $ 2.00- 3.00

14

123   124   125   126

123. 1971 NEW COLOGNE ELEGANT, 4 ozs. gold plastic
     coated bottle, red rose stopper. 12" high. PP $8.50 .... $ 10.00- 14.00
124. 1970 EIFFEL TOWER COLOGNE, Clear glass with a
     gold cap. 6 fragrances. 3 ozs. 9" high. PP $4.00 .... $ 4.00- 7.00
125. 1972 ELIZABETHAN FASHION FIGURINE, 6" high
     decanter, pink plastic top. 4 fragrances of cologne. PP
     $5.00 .... $ 6.00- 9.00
126. 1969 ELUSIVE, ½ ozs. COLOGNE, Lavender ribbed
     glass bottle. PP $1.75 .... $ 1.00- 2.00

127   128   129   130   131

127. 1969 ELUSIVE COLOGNE MIST, Lavender plastic
     coated bottle with a gold and lavender cap. 3 ozs. 5½"
     high. PP $6.00 .... $ 1.00
128. 1969 ELUSIVE CREAM SACHET, Lavender glass jar,
     gold and lavender trim cap. PP $3.00 .... $ 1.00
129. 1970 ELUSIVE POWDER SACHET, Crystal-like glass
     bottle with a plastic screw-on lid with gold trim. White
     paper label on bottom. 1¼ ozs. 3½" high. .... $ 2.00- 3.00
130. 1969 ELUSIVE ROLLETTE, Lavender glass container
     with a gold and lavender cap. PP $3.00 .... $ 1.00
131. 1969 ELUSIVE SKIN SOFTENER, Lavender glass jar,
     gold trim on top. PP $4.00 .... $ 1.00- 2.00

132	134	135
	136	137

132. 1971 EMERALD BUD VASE, Cologne, 5 fragrances, 9″ high, 3 ozs. Green glass with stopper. PP $5.00 .... $ 2.00- 5.00
133. 1964 EYE & THROAT OIL, Clear glass bottle, gold letters and screw-on gold lid. 1 ozs. PP $2.50 .... $ 1.00- 2.00
134. 1969 EYE CREAM, White glass jar, 1¾″ high, metal screw-on lid, letters in blue with eye on top of lid. .58 ozs. PP $1.50 .... $ 1.00- 2.00
135. 1971 FASHION FIGURINE-VICTORIAN COLOGNE DECANTER 6″ high, 4 fragrances, 4 ozs., white china, plastic top slips off. PP $4.00 .... $ 5.00- 8.00
136. 1950 FASHION FILM, Clear glass container with a white plastic screw-on lid with pink lettering on the lid. Paper label. 1 ozs. 1 5/8″ high. PP $.75 .... $ 6.00- 7.00
137. 1971 FIELD FLOWERS COLOGNE MIST, Green plastic coated bottle, 3 ozs., yellow flowers, raised design cap, screw-on. PP $6.00 .... $ 1.00- 2.00

138	139	140	141

138. 1967 FINISHING FACE POWDER, Pink cardboard box with stripes around the sides and a gold ring around the top & bottom. Avon emblem on the top. 2.5 ozs. PP $1.50 .... $ 1.00- 2.00
139. 1967 FIREWORKS NAIL ENAMEL, ½ oz. clear bottle, blue label, orange label, also came in three other colors. 3¼″ high. White plastic screw-on cap, with brush. PP $4.50 .... $ 1.00- 3.00
140. 1971 FLAMINGO DECANTER, Clear glass figural decanter with a gold screw-on lid. 4 fragrances. 5 ozs. PP $4.50 .... $ 4.00- 7.00
141. 1972 FLORAL CREAM SACHET, Violet, carnation, gardenia, clear glass container, screw-on lid. Each has its on floral design on lid. .66 ozs. PP $1.25 .... $ 2.00- 4.00

16

| 142 | 143 | 144 | 145 | 146 |

142. 1970 FLORAL DEMISTICKS, Blue-Lotus, Hawaiian White Ginger, Honeysuckle, Lilac. PP $1.50 .... $ .50
143. 1949 FLOWERTIME SACHET, Clear glass container with a paper label and pink screw-on lid. 1¼ ozs. 3" PP $1.19 .... $ 10.00- 13.00
144. 1951 FLOWERTIME SACHET, Clear glass container with a paper label & a pink screw-on lid with a flower on top. 1¼ oz. 3" high. PP $1.19 .... $ 10.00- 13.00
145. 1915 CALIFORNIA PERFUME CO. FOOD COLORING, Yellow and brown stoppered bottles. Also came in other colors. PP $.85 .... $ 30.00- 40.00
146. 1950 FOREVER SPRING CREAM SACHET, Milk glass container with a green floral designed screw-on lid. .66 ozs. 1 3/8" high. PP $1.25......................... $ 9.00- 10.00

| 149 | 150 |

147. 1956 FOREVER SPRING CREAM SACHET, Yellow painted glass container, yellow metal screw-on lid. Floral design on top. 1 3/8" high. .66 oz. PP $1.25 ...... $ 7.00- 11.00
148. 1956 FOREVER SPRING POWDER SACHET, Yellow painted glass container, yellow metal screw-on lid. Floral design on top. .9 oz. 2¼" high. PP $1.25 .... $ 9.00- 11.00
149. 1950 FOREVER SPRING TOILET WATER, Clear glass bottle with green lettering and a yellow bud-shaped screw-on lid. 2 ozs. 4½" high. PP $1.50 .... $ 18.00- 20.00
150. 1960 AVON FOUNDATION DEMONSTRATOR, Liquid powder samples, 12 one-dram clear glass bottles, white screw-on lids. Plastic & cardboard case. Sets.... $ 10.00

17

151 152 153 154

151. 1965 FRAGRANCE BELL COLOGNE, Clear glass bell shaped bottle and plastic screw-on lid. 4 ozs. 5½" high. PP $3.50 .... $ 15.00- 20.00
152. 1968 FRAGRANCE BELL COLOGNE, Bell rings, clear glass bottle and gold plastic handle. 9 fragrances. 1 ozs. PP $2.00 .... $ 2.00- 5.00
153. 1968 FRAGRANCE FLING COLOGNE, 13 fragrances, clear diamond-cut glass bottle. Gold ball screw-on cap. 3¾" high. 5 ozs. PP $3.00 .... $ 4.00- 10.00
154. 1964 FRAGRANCE GOLD TRIP, ½ oz. heart-shaped clear glass bottles. 1966 glass tray - $8.00-10.00 ... Set $ 16.00- 20.00

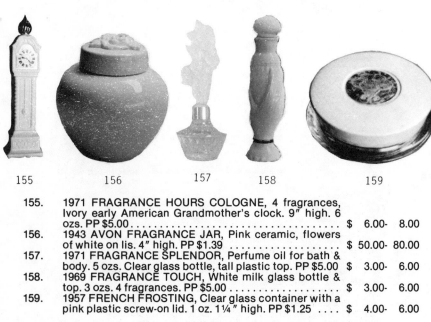

155 156 157 158 159

155. 1971 FRAGRANCE HOURS COLOGNE, 4 fragrances, Ivory early American Grandmother's clock. 9" high. 6 ozs. PP $5.00 .... $ 6.00- 8.00
156. 1943 AVON FRAGRANCE JAR, Pink ceramic, flowers of white on lis. 4" high. PP $1.39 .... $ 50.00- 80.00
157. 1971 FRAGRANCE SPLENDOR, Perfume oil for bath & body. 5 ozs. Clear glass bottle, tall plastic top. PP $5.00 $ 3.00- 6.00
158. 1969 FRAGRANCE TOUCH, White milk glass bottle & top. 3 ozs. 4 fragrances. PP $5.00 .... $ 3.00- 6.00
159. 1957 FRENCH FROSTING, Clear glass container with a pink plastic screw-on lid. 1 oz. 1¼" high. PP $1.25 .... $ 4.00- 6.00

18

| 160 | 161 | 162 | 163 |

160. **1971 FRENCH TELEPHONE**, 6 ozs. of foaming bath oil. ¼ oz. of perfume in handle. 4 fragrances. Base is white milk glass. Gold trim, 5" high. PP $20.00 .... $ 20.00- 25.00

161. **1936 GARDENIA PERFUME**, 1/8 oz., 1 7/8" high. Clear glass bottle, with gold screw-on lid. .... $ 35.00- 39.00

162. **1969 GIFT COLOGNE**, 4 ozs. Clear glass bottle with gold screw-on cap. 6¾" high. PP $4.00 .... $ 4.00- 6.00

163. **1948 GOLDEN PROMISE SACHET**, Clear glass jar, gold metal screw-on cap. 1¼ ozs. PP $3.95 .... $ 15.00- 20.00

| 164 | 165 | 166 | 167 |

164. **1972 GRECIAN PITCHER**, Skin-So-Soft bath oil. White opaque glass pitcher, 6½" high, 5 ozs. Greek inspired. PP $5.00 .... $ 3.00- 6.00

165. **1967 HAIR CONDITIONER**, 6 ozs. White jar, pink metal screw-on cap. PP $2.50 .... $ 2.00- 4.00

166. **1970 HANA GASA COLOGNE**, 5 ozs. 2 1/8" high. Clear glass bottom, yellow plastic screw-on lid. PP $2.00 .... $ 2.00- 4.00

167. **1970 HANA GASA COLOGNE MIST**, Yellow glass container with pink flowers and a yellow lid. 3 ozs. 5½" high. PP $6.00 .... $ 1.00- 2.00

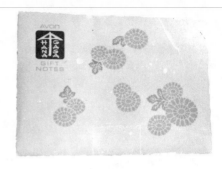

168   169

168. 1970 HANA GASA CREAM SACHET, Yellow glass jar with green and red designs.Yellow plastic screw-on lid. .66 oz. 1½ " high. PP $3.00 . . . . $ 1.00- 2.00

169. 1970 HANA GASA GIFT NOTES, Yellow envelope with pink flowers. Contains note paper which can be folded and used as the envelope too. Included are gold Hana Gasa stamps to seal the envelope. . . . . $ 1.00- 2.00

170. 1970 HANA GASA PERFUME ROLLETTE, .33 oz. 2½ " high. Yellow plastic screw-on lid. . . . . $ 1.00- 2.00

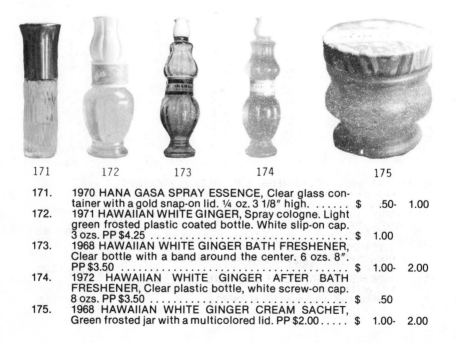

171   172   173   174   175

171. 1970 HANA GASA SPRAY ESSENCE, Clear glass container with a gold snap-on lid. ¼ oz. 3 1/8" high. . . . . . . $ .50- 1.00

172. 1971 HAWAIIAN WHITE GINGER, Spray cologne. Light green frosted plastic coated bottle. White slip-on cap. 3 ozs. PP $4.25 . . . . $ 1.00

173. 1968 HAWAIIAN WHITE GINGER BATH FRESHENER, Clear bottle with a band around the center. 6 ozs. 8". PP $3.50 . . . . $ 1.00- 2.00

174. 1972 HAWAIIAN WHITE GINGER AFTER BATH FRESHENER, Clear plastic bottle, white screw-on cap. 8 ozs. PP $3.50 . . . . $ .50

175. 1968 HAWAIIAN WHITE GINGER CREAM SACHET, Green frosted jar with a multicolored lid. PP $2.00 . . . . . $ 1.00- 2.00

20

176   177   178   179

176.   1969 HER PRETTINESS BRUSH & COMB SET, for girls. Yellow. Brush 6½″ long, comb 5″ long. PP $3.50 . . . . . . $ 5.00

177.   1969 HER PRETTINESS COLOGNE MIST, Enchanted Tree Cologne. Green see-thru bubble top on brown tree base. Bird spray button. 3 ozs. 6¾″ PP $5.00 . . . . $ 3.00-   6.00

178.   1970 HER PRETTINESS CREAM SACHET, Blue frosted glass container with a plastic screw-on lid that represents a fountain. .66 oz. 5″ high. . . . . $ 1.00-   2.00

179.   1969 HER PRETTINESS FLOWER BELL COLOGNE MIST, Yellow plastic coated glass bottle, blue plastic lid. 2 ozs. 5¼″ high. PP $2.50 . . . . $ 2.00-   4.00

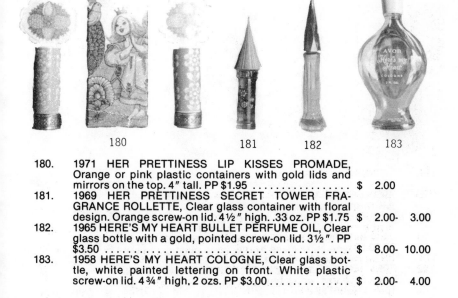

180   181   182   183

180.   1971 HER PRETTINESS LIP KISSES PROMADE, Orange or pink plastic containers with gold lids and mirrors on the top. 4″ tall. PP $1.95 . . . . $ 2.00

181.   1969 HER PRETTINESS SECRET TOWER FRA-GRANCE ROLLETTE, Clear glass container with floral design. Orange screw-on lid. 4½″ high. .33 oz. PP $1.75 $ 2.00-   3.00

182.   1965 HERE'S MY HEART BULLET PERFUME OIL, Clear glass bottle with a gold, pointed screw-on lid. 3½″. PP $3.50 . . . . $ 8.00- 10.00

183.   1958 HERE'S MY HEART COLOGNE, Clear glass bottle, white painted lettering on front. White plastic screw-on lid. 4¾″ high, 2 ozs. PP $3.00 . . . . $ 2.00-   4.00

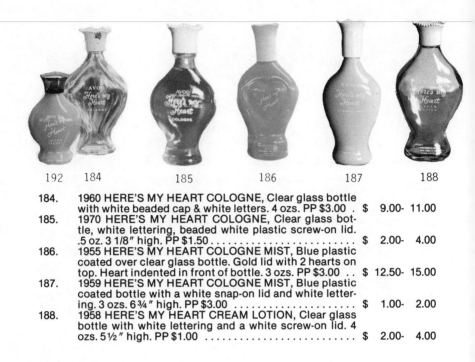

192 184 185 186 187 188

184.	1960 HERE'S MY HEART COLOGNE, Clear glass bottle with white beaded cap & white letters. 4 ozs. PP $3.00 . $ 9.00- 11.00
185.	1970 HERE'S MY HEART COLOGNE, Clear glass bottle, white lettering, beaded white plastic screw-on lid. .5 oz. 3 1/8" high. PP $1.50 . . . . $ 2.00- 4.00
186.	1955 HERE'S MY HEART COLOGNE MIST, Blue plastic coated over clear glass bottle. Gold lid with 2 hearts on top. Heart indented in front of bottle. 3 ozs. PP $3.00 .. $ 12.50- 15.00
187.	1959 HERE'S MY HEART COLOGNE MIST, Blue plastic coated bottle with a white snap-on lid and white lettering. 3 ozs. 6 ¾" high. PP $3.00 . . . . $ 1.00- 2.00
188.	1958 HERE'S MY HEART CREAM LOTION, Clear glass bottle with white lettering and a white screw-on lid. 4 ozs. 5½" high. PP $1.00 . . . . $ 2.00- 4.00

189 190 191

189.	1959 HERE'S MY HEART CREAM SACHET, Blue jar with a white beaded top. .66 ozs. PP $2.00 . . . . $ 1.00- 2.00
190.	---- HERE'S MY HEART EAU DE COLOGNE, Diamond shaped clear glass bottle with a gold cap. $ 7.00- 8.00
191.	1958 HERE'S MY HEART LOTION SACHET, 2" high, ½ oz. Fan type clear glass bottle, aqua plastic screw-on lid. Also comes in Persian Wood. PP $8.00 . . . . $ 6.00- 9.00
192.	1959 HERE'S MY HEART LOTION SACHET, Blue plastic coated white beaded cap. (Wrong cap in picture) 1 oz. PP $2.00 . . . . $ 8.00- 15.00

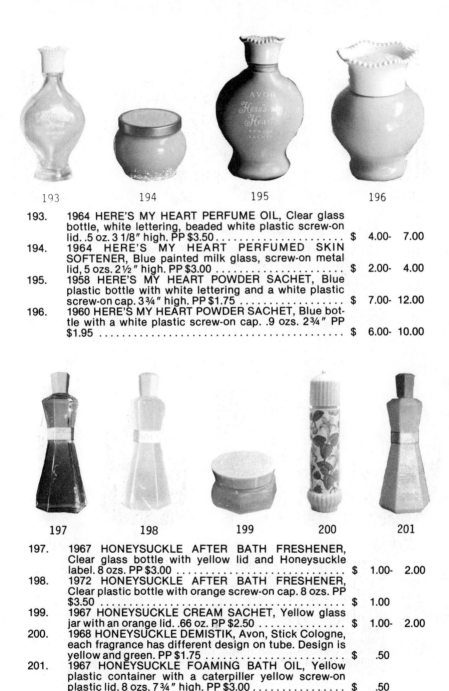

193.

194.

195.

196.

193.	1964 HERE'S MY HEART PERFUME OIL, Clear glass bottle, white lettering, beaded white plastic screw-on lid. .5 oz. 3 1/8" high. PP $3.50	$ 4.00- 7.00
194.	1964 HERE'S MY HEART PERFUMED SKIN SOFTENER, Blue painted milk glass, screw-on metal lid, 5 ozs. 2½" high. PP $3.00	$ 2.00- 4.00
195.	1958 HERE'S MY HEART POWDER SACHET, Blue plastic bottle with white lettering and a white plastic screw-on cap. 3¾" high. PP $1.75	$ 7.00- 12.00
196.	1960 HERE'S MY HEART POWDER SACHET, Blue bottle with a white plastic screw-on cap. .9 ozs. 2¾" PP $1.95	$ 6.00- 10.00

197   198   199   200   201

197.	1967 HONEYSUCKLE AFTER BATH FRESHENER, Clear glass bottle with yellow lid and Honeysuckle label. 8 ozs. PP $3.00	$ 1.00- 2.00
198.	1972 HONEYSUCKLE AFTER BATH FRESHENER, Clear plastic bottle with orange screw-on cap. 8 ozs. PP $3.50	$ 1.00
199.	1967 HONEYSUCKLE CREAM SACHET, Yellow glass jar with an orange lid. .66 oz. PP $2.50	$ 1.00- 2.00
200.	1968 HONEYSUCKLE DEMISTIK, Avon, Stick Cologne, each fragrance has different design on tube. Design is yellow and green. PP $1.75	$ .50
201.	1967 HONEYSUCKLE FOAMING BATH OIL, Yellow plastic container with a caterpiller yellow screw-on plastic lid. 8 ozs. 7¾" high. PP $3.00	$ .50

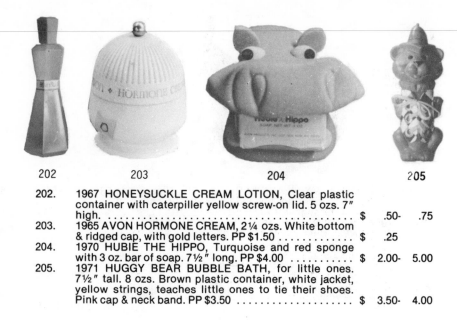

| | | 202 | 203 | 204 | | 205 |

202. 1967 HONEYSUCKLE CREAM LOTION, Clear plastic container with caterpiller yellow screw-on lid. 5 ozs. 7" high. .... $ .50- .75
203. 1965 AVON HORMONE CREAM, 2¼ ozs. White bottom & ridged cap, with gold letters. PP $1.50 .... $ .25
204. 1970 HUBIE THE HIPPO, Turquoise and red sponge with 3 oz. bar of soap. 7½" long. PP $4.00 .... $ 2.00- 5.00
205. 1971 HUGGY BEAR BUBBLE BATH, for little ones. 7½" tall. 8 ozs. Brown plastic container, white jacket, yellow strings, teaches little ones to tie their shoes. Pink cap & neck band. PP $3.50 .... $ 3.50- 4.00

| 206 | 207 | 208 | 209 | 210 |

206. 1963 HUMPTY DUMPTY BUBBLE BATH, Blue plastic bottle with lid. 8 ozs. 4¾" high. .... $ 5.00- 7.00
207. 1969 MODELING SOAP, Cardboard container. 6 ozs. 4¾" high. PP $1.98 .... $ 5.00
208. 1967 ICICLE PERFUME, Clear bottle, gold top. 1 dram of perfume. 9 fragrances. .... $ 4.00- 5.00
209. 1963 INSECT REPELLENT, 2 ozs. Clear bottle, with white or red screw-on lid. PP $2.50 to $4.00.......... $ 4.00- 7.00
210. FOREIGN AVON-JAO DE PARIS, Clear glass with gold metal casing around the container and a gold lid. 1 oz. 4¾". .... $ 10.00- 12.00

211   212   213   214

211.   1946 JASMINE POWDER SACHET, Clear glass jar.
       Black metal cap & black label. 1½ ozs. PP $1.19 ...... $ 15.00- 22.00
212.   1969 JUMPIN' JIMMINY, Green plastic container for
       the body with an orange vest. Yellow hat is the screw-
       on lid. Sits on a green wagon with yellow wheels &
       green string. Contains 8 ozs. of bubble bath. 6" tall. PP
       $3.50 .... $ 1.00- 4.00
213.   1970 KEEPSAKE CREAM SACHET, Frosted base
       jewelry tree with a gold lid. 5 fragrances. PP $3.00 ..... $ 3.00- 5.00
214.   1971 KEEPSAKE CREAM SACHET, 5 fragrances cream
       sachet, 6½" high, .66 oz. white base, gold screw-on lid
       & tree. PP $3.50 .... $ 4.00- 6.00

215   216   217   218

215.   1972 KITTEN LITTLE COLOGNE, White glass, 4
       fragrances. 3½" high. 1.5 oz. PP $2.00 .... $ 2.00
216.   1971 KOFFEE KLATCH DECANTER, 4 fragrances, 5½"
       high, 5 ozs. Yellow klatch, gold lid, floral design on
       front. PP $5.00 .... $ 5.00- 7.00
217.   1970 LAVENDER COLOGNE, White milk glass bottle
       with lavender flowers and a bow around the neck.
       White cap. 1.7 oz. .... $ 3.00- 4.00
218.   1961 LAVENDER POWDER SACHET, Clear glass jar &
       top. Pink and white label and a neck band. PP $2.00 ... $ 6.00- 10.00

25

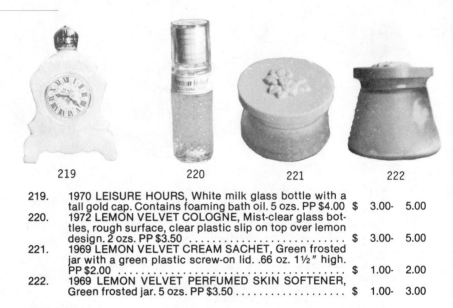

219	220	221	222

219.   1970 LEISURE HOURS, White milk glass bottle with a tall gold cap. Contains foaming bath oil. 5 ozs. PP $4.00 $ 3.00- 5.00
220.   1972 LEMON VELVET COLOGNE, Mist-clear glass bottles, rough surface, clear plastic slip on top over lemon design. 2 ozs. PP $3.50 . . . . $ 3.00- 5.00
221.   1969 LEMON VELVET CREAM SACHET, Green frosted jar with a green plastic screw-on lid. .66 oz. 1½" high. PP $2.00 . . . . $ 1.00- 2.00
222.   1969 LEMON VELVET PERFUMED SKIN SOFTENER, Green frosted jar. 5 ozs. PP $3.50 . . . . $ 1.00- 3.00

223	224	225	226

223.   1969 LIGHTS & SHADOWS COLOGNE, Shadows Cologne has a smoked glass cap and container. Lights has a clear glass container with a gold cap. 2 ozs. PP $4.00 . . . . Set $ 3.00- 5.00
224.   1961 LI'L FOLKS TIME BUBBLE BATH, White and yellow plastic figural. 8 ozs. 5" high. PP $1.79 . . . . $ 7.00
225.   1963 LILAC AFTER BATH FRESHENER, Clear glass bottle with an orchid cap. 8 ozs. PP $2.50 . . . . $ 2.00- 3.00
226.   1963 LILAC CREAM SACHET, Orchid frosted glass jar, gold & white metal screw-on lid. Orchid letters. .66 oz. PP $2.50 . . . . $ 1.00- 2.00

26

227	228	230

227. 1968 LILAC PERFUMED SOAP, Three cakes of purple colored soap. 3 ozs. each. PP $.59 .... $ 3.00- 5.00
228. 1968 LILY OF THE VALLEY CREAM SACHET, Green frosted glass container, gold & white metal screw-on lid. .66 oz. 1½" high. PP $2.50 .... $ 1.00- 2.00
229. 1968 LITTLE RED RIDING HOOD BUBBLE BATH, Yellow plastic bottle with Little Red Riding Hood on front. Red flower screw-on lid. Red plastic glasses. 5" high. 4 ozs. PP $1.50 .... $ 3.00- 5.00
230. 1970 LOOKING GLASS COLOGNE, Frame holds 1½ ozs. cologne. Clear glass mirror, gold lid and handle. PP $3.50 .... $ 4.00- 6.00
231. 1964 LOTION LOVELY, Clear glass bottle and top. Gold letters. 8 ozs. PP $4.00 .... $ 6.00- 8.00

231	232	233	234

232. 1969 LOVE BIRD PERFUME, Frosted glass as the body of the bird with a silver cap as the head. ¼ oz. PP $6.25-7.50 .... $ 2.00- 4.00
In box $ 5.00- 8.00
233. 1971 LOVELY TOUCH BODY LOTION DECANTER, 12 ozs. Rich Moisture or Vita-Moist Body Lotion. 9" high, clear glass with dispenser. PP $4.00 .... $ 3.00- 4.00
234. 1970 MAD HATTER BUBBLE BATH, Gold plastic figural with red, green, and pink clock, and a pink top hat. 6 ozs. 8" high. PP $3.00 .... $ 3.00- 4.00

235. 1966 MANICURE KIT, Tan & white patterned vinyl, plastic case holds 1 bottle enamel set, 1 bottle long-last base coat, & 1 bottle of nail polish. The kit also contains 1 tube of cuticle remover, cream & tube of Nail Beauty. Enamel remover pads, emery board, orange stick 6¾" wide, 3¾" high. PP $8.50 .... $ 8.00- 14.00

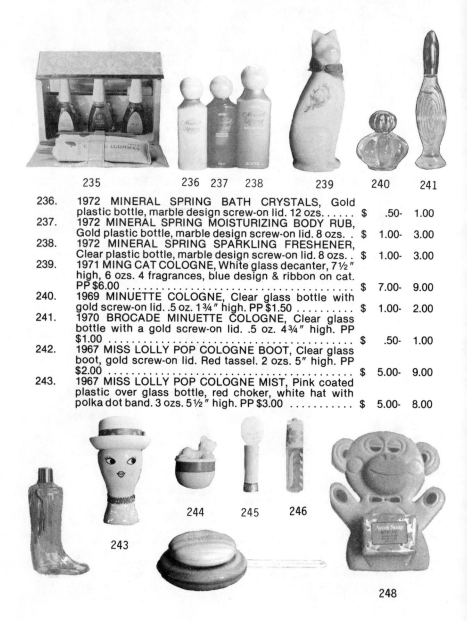

235   236 237 238   239   240   241

236. 1972 MINERAL SPRING BATH CRYSTALS, Gold plastic bottle, marble design screw-on lid. 12 ozs. ...... $ .50- 1.00
237. 1972 MINERAL SPRING MOISTURIZING BODY RUB, Gold plastic bottle, marble design screw-on lid. 8 ozs. . $ 1.00- 3.00
238. 1972 MINERAL SPRING SPARKLING FRESHENER, Clear plastic bottle, marble design screw-on lid. 8 ozs. . $ 1.00- 3.00
239. 1971 MING CAT COLOGNE, White glass decanter, 7½" high, 6 ozs. 4 fragrances, blue design & ribbon on cat. PP $6.00 .... $ 7.00- 9.00
240. 1969 MINUETTE COLOGNE, Clear glass bottle with gold screw-on lid. .5 oz. 1¾" high. PP $1.50 .... $ 1.00- 2.00
241. 1970 BROCADE MINUETTE COLOGNE, Clear glass bottle with a gold screw-on lid. .5 oz. 4¾" high. PP $1.00 .... $ .50- 1.00
242. 1967 MISS LOLLY POP COLOGNE BOOT, Clear glass boot, gold screw-on lid. Red tassel. 2 ozs. 5" high. PP $2.00 .... $ 5.00- 9.00
243. 1967 MISS LOLLY POP COLOGNE MIST, Pink coated plastic over glass bottle, red choker, white hat with polka dot band. 3 ozs. 5½" high. PP $3.00 .... $ 5.00- 8.00

244   245   246

243

248

28

244. 1967 MISS LOLLY POP CREAM SACHET, Yellow painted glass jar, orange plastic lid. .66 oz. 2½" high. PP $2.00 .... $ 3.00- 6.00
245. 1968 MISS LOLLY POP LIP POP LIPSTICK, Pink plastic tube, gold holder. PP $1.75 .... $ 3.00
246. 1968 MISS LOLLY POP ROLLETTE, Clear glass container, yellow plastic screw-on lid. .33 oz. 3 3/8" high. PP $1.50 .... $ 2.00- 4.00
247. 1967 MISS LOLLY POP SOAP AND SPONGE, Pink sponge with white plastic handle and pink & white soap. Sponge and handle is 9" long. PP $2.50 .... $ 8.00- 12.00
248. 1969 MONKEY SHINES, Gold, pink, and brown sponge and 3 oz. bar of soap. 8½" high. PP $2.50 .... $ 3.00

249   250   251   252

249. 1971 MOONWIND COLOGNE MIST, Royal blue plastic container, silver trim. 6¼" high, plus silver tip on lift off top. 3 ozs. PP $7.50 .... $ 6.00- 7.50
250. 1971 MOONWIND CREAM SACHET, Royal blue container, silver trim. .66 oz. PP $4.00 .... $ 3.00- 4.00
251. 1972 MOONWIND FOAMING BATH OIL, Royal blue ribbed design, in plastic, silver trim, screw-on lid. 6 ozs. $ 1.00- 5.00
252. 1971 MOONWIND ROLLETTE, Royal blue plastic container, silver trim. 4¼" high. .33 oz. PP $4.00 .... $ 4.00- 10.00

253   254   255   256   257   258

253. 1959 ANTISEPTIC MOUTHWASH & GARGLE, Clear glass bottle, grey & white paper label, red lettering, white screw-on lid. 5 5/8" high. 7 ozs. PP $.59 .... $ 7.00- 12.00

29

254.	1968 MOUTHWASH & GARGLE, Clear glass bottle, gold paper label, white plastic screw-on lid. 10 ozs. 7¼" high. PP $1.25	$ 1.00- 3.00
255.	1967 MR. LION BUBBLE BATH, White plastic bottle, brown lion on front. Red bubble blower with white stick. 4 7/8" high. 4 ozs. PP $1.50	$ 5.00- 6.00
256.	1970 FREDDY THE FROG MUG, White milk glass mug with an orange metal lid and a white knob on top. Green frog with blue lettering on the front. 5 ozs. 4½" high. PP $3.50	$ 5.00
257.	1970 GAYLORD THE GATOR MUG, White milk glass mug with a yellow metal lid and a white knob on top. Green alligator & yellow and orange lettering. Contains 5 ozs. non-tear shampoo. 4½" tall. PP $3.50	$ 5.00
258.	1968 BREATH FRESH, 10 ozs., 7¼" high, white paper label, clear glass. PP $1.25	$ 1.00

259 360 261 262 263

259.	1954 NEARNESS COLOGNE, Back see-thru label, clear bottle, blue mingled screw-on cap, 4 ozs. PP $2.50	$ 15.00- 20.00
260.	1954 NEARNESS CREAM SACHET, Aqua glass container, 1 3/8" high. Blue designed metal screw-on lid. .66 oz. PP $1.50	$ 7.00- 10.00
261.	1954 NEARNESS POWDER SACHET, Aqua glass container with a blue designed label, blue plastic screw-on lid. .66 oz. 2½" high.	$ 8.00- 12.00
262.	1956 NEARNESS POWDER SACHET, Aqua glass jar & cap with a darker label. 1¼ ozs. PP $1.50	$ 12.00- 15.00
263.	1971 NEW HONEY LAMB SOAP-ON-A-ROPE, Sculptured soap 5" high, 5 ozs., yellow, with blue rope and gift box. PP $2.00	$ 2.00- 4.00

264   265   266   267   268

264. 1963 OCCUR COLOGNE, Clear glass bottle with gold
     lettering and a rhinestone under the exclamation point.
     Gold screw-on lid. 2 ozs., 3¼ " high. PP $1.50 . . . . $ .50- 1.00
265. 1970 OCCUR COLOGNE, Clear glass bottle, gold letter-
     ing, gold plastic screw-on lid. .5 oz. 2¼ " high. PP $1.50 $ 2.00
266. 1963 OCCUR COLOGNE MIST, Black plastic coated
     container with gold painted lettering. Rhinestone
     under the exclamation point. Gold cap. 3 ozs. 5¾"
     high. PP $2.75 . . . . $ 2.00- 6.00
267. 1964 OCCUR COLOGNE MIST, Frosted glass bottle,
     gold lettering & black plastic snap-on lid. 5″ high. 2
     ozs. PP $5.00 . . . . $ 2.00- 6.00
268. 1964 OCCUR CREAM LOTION, Clear glass bottle, gold
     screw-on cap, gold letters. 4 ozs. 4¼ " high. PP $1.75 . . $ 4.00- 5.00

269   270   271   272

269. 1963 OCCUR CREAM SACHET, Black painted milk
     glass jar, black lid, rhinestone under the exclamation
     point. Gold letters. .66 oz. 1 3/8″ high. PP $2.50 . . . . $ 2.00- 4.00
270. 1965 OCCUR FOAMING BATH OIL, Black plastic bottle
     with gold lettering and gold screw-on lid. 6 ozs. 5″ high.
     PP $3.50 . . . . $ .50
271. 1964 OCCUR PERFUMED TALC, Black can & cap. Gold
     letters. 2¾ ozs. PP $1.00 . . . . $ .50
272. 1964 OCCUR PERFUME OIL, Clear glass bottle, gold
     lettering, gold plastic screw-on lid. Imitation diamond
     set in glass. .5 oz. 2¼ " high. PP $5.00 . . . . $ 6.00- 8.00

31

273   275   274   276   277

273.	1964 OCCUR PERFUMED SKIN SOFTENER, Black painted milk glass jar, black & gold lid. 2½″ high, 5 ozs. PP $1.75	$ 2.00- 5.00
274.	1964 OCCUR POWDER SACHET, Black glass container with gold lettering and a rhinestone under the exclamation point. Black plastic screw-on lid. 2½″ high. 9 ozs. PP $2.50	$ 6.00- 9.00
275.	1969 OCCUR TRAY, Black plastic trimmed in gold. 10″ in diameter.	$ 2.00- 4.00
276.	1968 AVON OILY ENAMEL REMOVER, 3 ozs. Clear bottle, screw-on white cap. PP $.90	$ 2.00
277.	1960 AVON OILY POLISH REMOVER, 2 ozs. Clear glass bottle, white screw-on cap. PP $.75	$ 4.00

278   279   280   281   282   283

278.	1969 ONE-TWO, LACE MY SHOE BUBBLE BATH, Pink plastic shoe with an orange chimney for a screw-on lid. Green roof, orange covering with orange shoe lace. 8 ozs., 6″ tall. PP $2.98	$ 5.00- 7.00
279.	1971 PARLOR LAMP, Yellow base, shake talc, 2.5 ozs. Lift-off top has 3 ozs. cologne, 5 fragrances, gold trim, on base, top is carnival glass, with gold screw-on lid. PP $7.00	$ 7.50- 11.00
280.	1969 PATTERNS COLOGNE MIST, Black and white designed bottle. 6½″ high. 3 ozs. PP $6.00	$ 3.00- 6.00
281.	1969 PATTERNS CREAM SACHET, Black and white designed jar with a black lid. PP $3.00	$ 1.00- 2.00
282.	1969 PATTERNS LIP STICK, Black and white designed metal container. PP $1.50	$ .50- 1.00
283.	1969 PATTERNS PERFUME ROLLETTE, Black and white designed container with metal lid. .33 oz. PP $3.00	$ 1.00- 3.00

284   285   286

284. 1970 PEEP A BOO SOAP-ON-A-ROPE, Yellow chick
     soap on pink rope. PP $1.35 . . . . $ 3.00- 6.00
285. 1962 ONE-DRAM PERFUME, Clear glass container in
     ribbed design on inside and outside. Gold screw-on lid.
     2½" high. PP $2.50 . . . . $ 5.00- 6.00
286. 1971 PERFUMED SOAPS, 3 ozs. Blue Lotus,
     Honeysuckle, Silk & Honey, Hawaiian White Ginger. PP
     $.75 each . . . . $ .75
287. 1969 PERFUME HALF OUNCE, Clear cut glass bottle
     comes in a pink, round box with a pink ribbon and bow
     on top. Bottle is 4" high. 10 fragrances. PP $11.00 . . . . . $ 10.00- 14.00

287   288   289   290   291

288. 1970 PERFUME, One dram, clear miniature bottle, gold
     screw-on cap. 12 fragrances. 1/8 oz. . . . . $ 2.00- 4.00
289. 1963 PERFUME CREAM ROLLETTE, Small round bot-
     tles with embossing on the clear glass bottle. Gold
     cap. Came in 6 fragrances. . . . . $ .50- 1.00
290. 1964 PERFUME OIL, Frosted glass container with a
     white plastic screw-on lid. .5 oz. 4" high. . . . . $ 5.00- 6.00
291. 1969 PERFUME OIL FOR BATH & BODY, Clear bottle
     with gold lid, that has designs on the entire surface, ½
     oz., 4 fragrances. PP $6.00 . . . . $ 2.00- 4.00

33

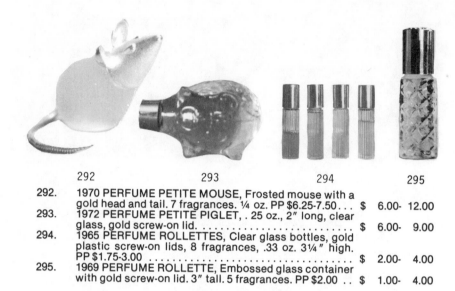

292	293
294	295

292. 1970 PERFUME PETITE MOUSE, Frosted mouse with a gold head and tail. 7 fragrances. ¼ oz. PP $6.25-7.50... $ 6.00- 12.00
293. 1972 PERFUME PETITE PIGLET, . 25 oz., 2″ long, clear glass, gold screw-on lid. .... $ 6.00- 9.00
294. 1965 PERFUME ROLLETTES, Clear glass bottles, gold plastic screw-on lids, 8 fragrances, .33 oz. 3¼″ high. PP $1.75-3.00 .... $ 2.00- 4.00
295. 1969 PERFUME ROLLETTE, Embossed glass container with gold screw-on lid. 3″ tall. 5 fragrances. PP $2.00 .. $ 1.00- 4.00

296	298
299	300

296. 1966 PERRY THE PENGUIN, Black & white plastic soap dish with a yellow beak, White soap. 3 oz. 6¾″ long. PP $1.98..................................... Penguin $ 5.00
Set $ 9.00- 11.00
297. 1957 PERSIAN WOOD CREAM SACHET in 1960 CLEAR PLASTIC HOLDER, Holder can be used with any Avon cream sachet. .66 oz. 1¾″ high................... $ 8.00- 15.00
298. 1957 PERSIAN WOOD MIST, Red plastic coated bottle with a gold cap. 3 ozs. PP $3.00 .... $ 3.00- 15.00
299. 1959 PERSIAN WOOD COLOGNE MIST, Red plastic-coated spray bottle with a gold slip-on cap. 6 1/8″, 3 oz. PP $3.00 .... $ 3.00- 10.00
300. 1957 PERSIAN WOOD CREAM LOTION, Clear glass bottle with gold lettering and a gold screw-on lid. 5″ high. 4 ozs. PP $1.25 .... $ 5.00- 7.00

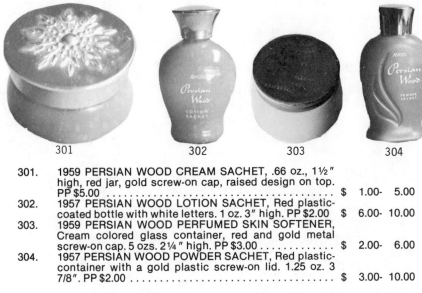

301.   302.   303.   304.

301.	1959 PERSIAN WOOD CREAM SACHET, .66 oz., 1½" high, red jar, gold screw-on cap, raised design on top. PP $5.00	$	1.00- 5.00
302.	1957 PERSIAN WOOD LOTION SACHET, Red plastic-coated bottle with white letters. 1 oz. 3" high. PP $2.00	$	6.00- 10.00
303.	1959 PERSIAN WOOD PERFUMED SKIN SOFTENER, Cream colored glass container, red and gold metal screw-on cap. 5 ozs. 2¼" high. PP $3.00	$	2.00- 6.00
304.	1957 PERSIAN WOOD POWDER SACHET, Red plastic-container with a gold plastic screw-on lid. 1.25 oz. 3 7/8". PP $2.00	$	3.00- 10.00

305   306   307   308

305.	1960 PERSIAN WOOD TOILET WATER, Clear glass bottle with a gold cap. 2 ozs. PP $2.50	$	5.00- 12.00
306.	1969 PETITE FLOWER COLOGNE, Clear glass bottle with a gold cap. Shaped as a flower, 4 fragrances. 10 ozs. 2¾" PP $2.50	$	3.00- 5.00
307.	1970 PICTURE FRAME COLOGNE, Gold picture frame with a gold lid. Displays Avon's "Girl in Brown". 4 fragrances. PP $8.00	$	7.00- 9.00
308.	1956 PINE BATH OIL, Clear glass bottle, dark green screw-on lid. 4" high, 4 ozs. PP $1.25	$	22.00- 27.00

309	310	311	312		313

309. 1970 PLUTO NON-TEAR SHAMPOO, Yellow plastic figural. 4 ozs. 6¾" high. PP $3.50 . . . . $ 3.50- 5.00
310. 1970 POLLY PARROT PUPPET SPONGE & SOAP, Green orange, and blue sponge with 3 oz. bar of soap. 9½" long. PP $3.00 . . . . $ 4.50- 6.00
Sponge and Soap   2.50- 3.00
311. 1972 POWDER SACHET SHAKER, White milk glass bottle, gold screw-on shaker lid. 1.25 oz. 3½" high. 4 fragrances. Avon 64th anniversary creation. PP $4.50 . . $ 2.00- 5.00
312. 1972 PRECIOUS OWL CREAM SACHET, White glass, 1.5 ozs. 3" high. 4 fragrances. PP $3.00-5.00 . . . . $ 1.00- 4.00
313. 1964 PRETTY PEACH COLOGNE, 2 ozs. Clear glass bottle with yellow, peach-shaped lid. 4" high. . . . . $ 5.00- 8.00

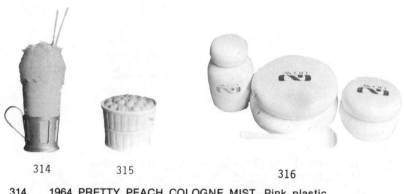

314	315	316

314. 1964 PRETTY PEACH COLOGNE MIST, Pink plastic coated, over glass bottle, bubble top. 2 blue straws, white daisies, gold metal stand. 2 ozs. 5" high. PP $7.00 $ 12.00- 16.00
315. 1964 PRETTY PEACH CREAM SACHET, Yellow glass container with peaches on the plastic screw-on lid. PP $1.00 . . . . $ 3.00- 7.00
316. 1971 PRIMA NATURA, Cleansing Formula. 5" high, 4 ozs. Moisturizing Freshener, 4¾" high, 4 ozs. Toning Freshener, 4¾" high, 4 ozs. White milk glass jars & screw-on caps, gold trim & letters. . . . . Each $ 1.00- 4.00

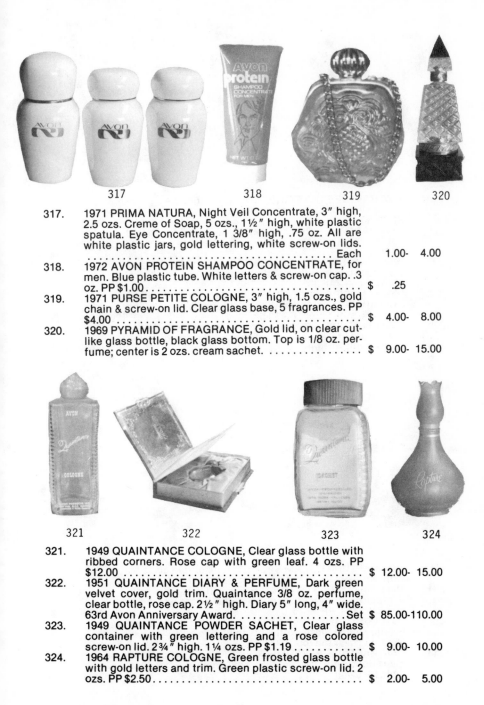

317   318   319   320

317.   1971 PRIMA NATURA, Night Veil Concentrate, 3″ high,
        2.5 ozs. Creme of Soap, 5 ozs., 1½″ high, white plastic
        spatula. Eye Concentrate, 1 3/8″ high, .75 oz. All are
        white plastic jars, gold lettering, white screw-on lids.
        .... Each   1.00-   4.00
318.   1972 AVON PROTEIN SHAMPOO CONCENTRATE, for
        men. Blue plastic tube. White letters & screw-on cap. .3
        oz. PP $1.00 .... $ .25
319.   1971 PURSE PETITE COLOGNE, 3″ high, 1.5 ozs., gold
        chain & screw-on lid. Clear glass base, 5 fragrances. PP
        $4.00 .... $ 4.00-   8.00
320.   1969 PYRAMID OF FRAGRANCE, Gold lid, on clear cut-
        like glass bottle, black glass bottom. Top is 1/8 oz. per-
        fume; center is 2 ozs. cream sachet. .... $ 9.00- 15.00

321   322   323   324

321.   1949 QUAINTANCE COLOGNE, Clear glass bottle with
        ribbed corners. Rose cap with green leaf. 4 ozs. PP
        $12.00 .... $ 12.00- 15.00
322.   1951 QUAINTANCE DIARY & PERFUME, Dark green
        velvet cover, gold trim. Quaintance 3/8 oz. perfume,
        clear bottle, rose cap. 2½″ high. Diary 5″ long, 4″ wide.
        63rd Avon Anniversary Award. ....Set $ 85.00-110.00
323.   1949 QUAINTANCE POWDER SACHET, Clear glass
        container with green lettering and a rose colored
        screw-on lid. 2¾″ high. 1¼ ozs. PP $1.19 .... $ 9.00- 10.00
324.   1964 RAPTURE COLOGNE, Green frosted glass bottle
        with gold letters and trim. Green plastic screw-on lid. 2
        ozs. PP $2.50 .... $ 2.00-   5.00

37

325 326 327 328 329

325. 1970 RAPTURE COLOGNE, .5 oz. 3¼" high. Clear glass bottle with gold lettering. Green plastic screw-on cap. PP $1.50 .... $ 1.00- 3.00

326. 1964 RAPTURE COLOGNE MIST, Aqua plastic coated bottle with a plastic lid and gold lettering. 3 ozs. PP $5.00 .... $ 3.00- 4.00

327. 1966 RAPTURE COLOGNE MIST, Light blue frosted glass container with plastic lid and gold trim. 2 ozs. 4¾" high. PP $5.00 .... $ 3.00- 4.00

328. 1966 RAPTURE COLOGNE MIST, Aqua frosted glass container with gold trim. White doves on paper label on lid. 2 ozs. 5 1/8" high. PP $3.50 .... $ 4.00- 6.00

329. 1964 RAPTURE CREAM LOTION, Blue plastic bottle with gold lettering and a bud-shaped matching screw-on lid. 4 ozs. 6" high. .... $ 3.00- 4.00

330 331 332 333

330. 1964 RAPTURE CREAM SACHET, Dark purple glass jar with white doves on the lid. .66 oz. PP $2.50 .... $ 1.00- 2.00

331. 1968 RAPTURE FOAMING BATH OIL, Aqua plastic container with a bud-shaped matching screw-on lid. 6 ozs. 6½" tall. PP $2.75.............................. $ 1.00- 3.00

332. 1964 RAPTURE PERFUME OIL, .5 oz., 3¼" high. Green plastic coated glass bottle, green plastic screw-on top. Gold ring near the top. PP $3.75 .... $ 5.00- 8.00

333. 1967 RAPTURE PERFUME ROLLETTE, Green carnival glass bottle with vertical ribs, gold screw-on cap. 3¼" high. PP $2.50 .... $ 3.00- 7.00

38

334   335   336   337   338

334.   1964 RAPTURE PERFUMED SKIN SOFTENER, Blue & gold lid on an aqua glass jar, 5 ozs. PP $2.50 . . . . $ 1.00- 3.00

335.   1965 RAPTURE PEFUMED SKIN SOFTENER, Aqua painted milk glass jar, metal screw-on lid. White doves painted on. 5 ozs. 2½" high. . . . . $ 2.00- 4.00

336.   1964 RAPTURE RHAPSODY TRAY, Gold trimmed tray, aqua velvet top. Mirror in center, two doves on the back. Tray 8" long, held Rapture powder sachet, perfume & cologne. . . . . $ 40.00- 60.00

337.   1936 REFRESHING COLOGNE, Clear glass container with a green plastic screw-on lid. Paper label. 4 ozs. 5½". PP $.52. . . . . $ 30.00- 35.00

338.   1966 REGENCE BATH OIL, Clear glass bottle, gold screw-on cap. 6 ozs. . . . . $ 3.00- 5.00

339   340   341   342   343

339.   1966 REGENCE COLOGNE, Clear glass container with gold plastic screw-on lid. 2 ozs. 5" high. PP $3.00 . . . . . $ 3.00- 4.00

340.   1970 REGENCE COLOGNE, .5 oz. 3¼" high, clear glass, gold designed screw-on lid. PP $1.75 . . . . $ 2.00- 4.00

341.   1969 REGENCE COLOGNE MIST, Green metal container with gold trim. 7¼" high. PP $4.00 . . . . $ 6.00

342.   1968 REGENCE COLOGNE SILK, Clear frosted glass container with a gold screw-on lid. 3 ozs. 5½" high. PP $4.50 . . . . $ 2.00- 3.00

343.   1966 REGENCE CREAM SACHET, Green designed jar, green & gold plastic screw-on lid. .66oz. 1½" high. PP $3.00 . . . . $ 2.00- 4.00

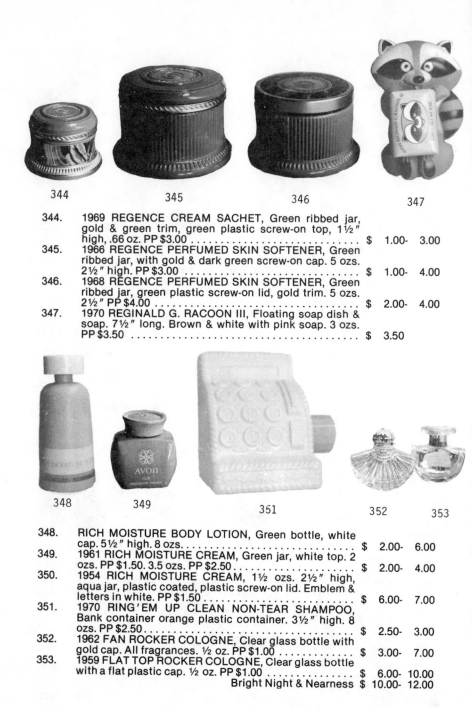

344. **1969 REGENCE CREAM SACHET,** Green ribbed jar, gold & green trim, green plastic screw-on top, 1½" high, .66 oz. PP $3.00 .... $ 1.00- 3.00

345. **1966 REGENCE PERFUMED SKIN SOFTENER,** Green ribbed jar, with gold & dark green screw-on cap. 5 ozs. 2½" high. PP $3.00 .... $ 1.00- 4.00

346. **1968 REGENCE PERFUMED SKIN SOFTENER,** Green ribbed jar, green plastic screw-on lid, gold trim. 5 ozs. 2½" PP $4.00 .... $ 2.00- 4.00

347. **1970 REGINALD G. RACOON III,** Floating soap dish & soap. 7½" long. Brown & white with pink soap. 3 ozs. PP $3.50 .... $ 3.50

344. 345. 346. 347.

348. 349. 351. 352. 353.

348. **RICH MOISTURE BODY LOTION,** Green bottle, white cap. 5½" high. 8 ozs. .... $ 2.00- 6.00

349. **1961 RICH MOISTURE CREAM,** Green jar, white top. 2 ozs. PP $1.50. 3.5 ozs. PP $2.50 .... $ 2.00- 4.00

350. **1954 RICH MOISTURE CREAM,** 1½ ozs. 2½" high, aqua jar, plastic coated, plastic screw-on lid. Emblem & letters in white. PP $1.50 .... $ 6.00- 7.00

351. **1970 RING'EM UP CLEAN NON-TEAR SHAMPOO,** Bank container orange plastic container. 3½" high. 8 ozs. PP $2.50 .... $ 2.50- 3.00

352. **1962 FAN ROCKER COLOGNE,** Clear glass bottle with gold cap. All fragrances. ½ oz. PP $1.00 .... $ 3.00- 7.00

353. **1959 FLAT TOP ROCKER COLOGNE,** Clear glass bottle with a flat plastic cap. ½ oz. PP $1.00 .... $ 6.00- 10.00
          Bright Night & Nearness $ 10.00- 12.00

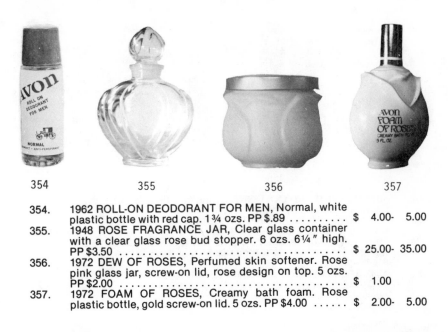

354	355	356	357

354. 1962 ROLL-ON DEODORANT FOR MEN, Normal, white plastic bottle with red cap. 1¾ ozs. PP $.89 .... $ 4.00- 5.00
355. 1948 ROSE FRAGRANCE JAR, Clear glass container with a clear glass rose bud stopper. 6 ozs. 6¼" high. PP $3.50 .... $ 25.00- 35.00
356. 1972 DEW OF ROSES, Perfumed skin softener. Rose pink glass jar, screw-on lid, rose design on top. 5 ozs. PP $2.00 .... $ 1.00
357. 1972 FOAM OF ROSES, Creamy bath foam. Rose plastic bottle, gold screw-on lid. 5 ozs. PP $4.00 ...... $ 2.00- 5.00

358	359	360	361

358. 1972 MIST OF ROSES, Pink plastic coated bottle, gold slip-on cap. Spray bottle. 3 ozs. .... $ 6.00- 8.00
359. 1972 SACHET OF ROSES, Cream sachet. .66 oz. Pink glass, screw-on lid. Roses painted on top. PP $3.00 .... $ 3.00- 5.00
360. 1972 SCENT OF ROSES COLOGNE GELEE, 3 ozs. Rose colored glass jar. PP $2.00 .... $ .75
361. 1954 ROYAL JASMINE BATH SALTS, 8 ozs. N.Y. & Pasadena, 4¼" high, clear glass, yellow metal screw-on cap. Dark green label. Yellow letters. .... $ 20.00- 25.00

362   363   364   365

362.   1971 ROYAL SWAN COLOGNE, White milk glass swan, 6 fragrances. 1 oz., 3″ high. .... $ 2.00-   3.00

363.   1970 ROYAL VASE DECANTER COLOGNE, Blue vase trimmed in gold, 4 fragrances, 3 ozs. .... $ 4.00-   5.00

364.   1970 RUBY BUD VASE COLOGNE, Red glass vase container with a round cork stopper. 6 fragrances, 3 ozs. 8¼″ high. .... $ 3.00-   5.00

365.   1962 SALES AWARD, Blue glass jar, sits on gold stand. PP $12.00 .... $ 12.00-   15.00

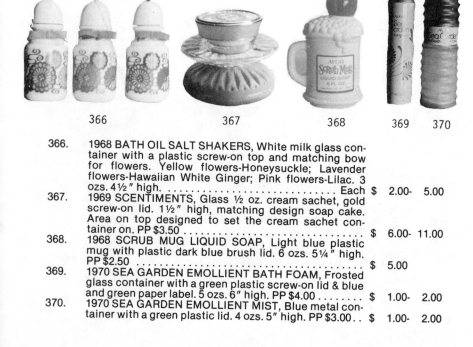

366   367   368   369   370

366.   1968 BATH OIL SALT SHAKERS, White milk glass container with a plastic screw-on top and matching bow for flowers. Yellow flowers-Honeysuckle; Lavender flowers-Hawaiian White Ginger; Pink flowers-Lilac. 3 ozs. 4½″ high. .... Each $ 2.00-   5.00

367.   1969 SCENTIMENTS, Glass ½ oz. cream sachet, gold screw-on lid. 1½″ high, matching design soap cake. Area on top designed to set the cream sachet container on. PP $3.50 .... $ 6.00-   11.00

368.   1968 SCRUB MUG LIQUID SOAP, Light blue plastic mug with plastic dark blue brush lid. 6 ozs. 5¼″ high. PP $2.50 .... $ 5.00

369.   1970 SEA GARDEN EMOLLIENT BATH FOAM, Frosted glass container with a green plastic screw-on lid & blue and green paper label. 5 ozs. 6″ high. PP $4.00 .... $ 1.00-   2.00

370.   1970 SEA GARDEN EMOLLIENT MIST, Blue metal container with a green plastic lid. 4 ozs. 5″ high. PP $3.00 .. $ 1.00-   2.00

42

371	372	373	374	375

371. 1971 SEA TREASURE, Foaming bath oil. Carnival glass, gold screw-on lid. 7″ high, 5 ozs. PP $5.00 . . . . $ 6.00- 7.00
372. 1972 SECRETAIRE FOAMING BATH OIL, Pink glass, gold screw-on lid. 4 fragrances. 7″ high. 5 ozs. PP $6.00-7.50 . . . . $ 7.50- 10.00
373. 1969 SILK & HONEY BATH GELEE, Honey colored frosted glass bottom, with gold top & gold spoon Bee on top. Shaped like a bee hive. 4.5 ozs. 3¼ ″ high. . . . . . $ 2.00- 6.00
374. 1969 SILK & HONEY CREAMY MASQUE, Honey colored, ribbed jar with a darker honey-colored screw-on lid with a bee on top. 3 ozs. 2½ ″ high. PP $2.50 . . . . $ .50- .75
375. 1970 SILK & HONEY MILK BATH, Miniature milk can with powdered milk bath inside. Bronze plastic container, trimmed in yellow. 6½ ″ high. 6 ozs. PP $5.00 . . . $ 3.00

376	377	378	379

376. 1969 SILK & HONEY SOFTALC, Ribbed plastic bottle, gold color, gold plastic screw-on lid. Yellow paper label. 5½ ″ tall. 3 ozs. PP $1.50 . . . . $ .50- 1.00
377. 1971 SITTING PRETTY COLOGNE, White milk glass, rocking chair, 6″ high. 4 ozs. 5 fragrances, gold cat screw-on lid. PP $5.00 . . . . $ 6.00- 9.00
378. 1954 SKIN FRESHENER, SAMPLE, Clear glass bottle, white letters, aqua screw-on lid. 1 oz. 3¼ ″ high. . . . . . . $ 4.00- 7.00
379. 1956 AVON SKIN FRESHENER, Normal skin, clear glass bottles with aqua label, aqua plastic screw-on lid. AVON ASTRINGENT Moisturized, clear glass, same lid and label. AVON SKIN FRESHENER, moisturized, same bottle, label, and cap as above. 4 ozs. 4¾ ″ high. . $ 2.00- 5.00

43

380	381	382	383	384

380. 1967 SKIN FRESHENER, for oily skin, normal skin, and moisturized. Each clear glass bottle, gold letters & gold avon emblem. One has peach tinted band and peach colored cap, one yellow, and one aqua. 4¾" high, 4 ozs. PP $1.25 .... $ 2.00- 4.00

381. 1962 SKIN-SO-SOFT, Clear glass bottle with a gold neck tag. Round clear glass cork stopper. 5¼ ozs. PP $3.50 .... $ 6.00- 9.00

382. 1964 SKIN-SO-SOFT, Clear glass bottle with a gold screw-on lid. Gold neck tag. 6 ozs. 10½" high. PP $3.50 $ 7.00- 12.00

383. 1966 SKIN-SO-SOFT, 3½" high, gold painted leaf, gold plastic cap. PP $2.00 .... $ 4.00- 8.00

384. 1967 SKIN-SO-SOFT, Clear glass urn with the handle made into the bottle. Cork stopper has a crystal tear-drop top. 8 ozs. 11" high. PP $2.25 .... $ 5.00- 9.00

385	386	387	388	389

385. 1968 SKIN-SO-SOFT, Frosted glass dolphin. Gold plastic tail and lid. 8 ozs. 10" high.................. $ 6.00- 7.00

386. 1969 3 S' SKIN-SO-SOFT, Clear plastic bottles. 2 sizes, 4 ozs. 5¾" high. PP $1.00. 8 ozs. 6¾" high. PP $2.00. Green plastic screw-on cap. .... $ .50- 1.00

387. 1969 SCENTED SKIN-SO-SOFT BATH OIL, Clear glass container with a clear plastic screw-on lid. 2 ozs. 4¾" high. PP $2.50 .... $ 2.00- 4.00

388. 1963 SKIN-SO-SOFT BATH URN, White milk glass cruet jug type handle. 7 fragrances. 8 ozs. ...... $ 10.00- 12.00

389. 1966 SKIN-SO-SOFT CRUET DECANTER, Clear glass container with an arched shelf handle. Latticed bulb type lid. 8 ozs. 10" high........................... $ 8.00- 10.00

390.   391.   392.   393.   394.   395.

390.	1969 SKIN-SO-SOFT GREEK GODDESS, Milk glass figural decanter. Gold cap. 8 ozs. 11″ high............ $	5.00-	7.00
391.	1970 SKIN-SO-SOFT SEA HORSE, Clear glass figural bottle with a gold cap. 9″ high...................... $	5.00-	8.00
392.	1971 SKIN-SO-SOFT SEA MAIDEN, Clear glass figural decanter with a gold screw-on lid. 6 ozs. 10″ high...... $	4.00-	7.00
393.	1965 SKIN-SO-SOFT URN, Clear glass bottle with a metallic gold floral band and a gold lid. 10 ozs. 9½″ tall. 2¾″ in diameter................................. $	7.00-	10.00
394.	1970 SMALL WORLD COLOGNE, Amber and white glass, bottle, black & pink plastic. Pink daisy necklace 4¼″ high, 2 ozs. ISLAND MISS. PP $2.50 .... $	5.00-	6.00
395.	1970 SMALL WORLD COLOGNE MIST, 5″ high, 3 ozs. Purple dress with white trim and blonde hair. PP $5.00 . $	5.00-	7.00

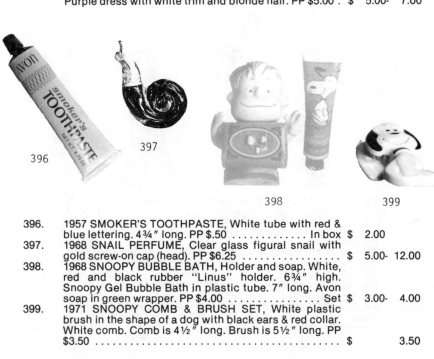

396.   397.   398.   399.

396.	1957 SMOKER'S TOOTHPASTE, White tube with red & blue lettering. 4¾″ long. PP $.50 .... In box $	2.00	
397.	1968 SNAIL PERFUME, Clear glass figural snail with gold screw-on cap (head). PP $6.25 .... $	5.00-	12.00
398.	1968 SNOOPY BUBBLE BATH, Holder and soap. White, red and black rubber "Linus" holder. 6¾″ high. Snoopy Gel Bubble Bath in plastic tube. 7″ long. Avon soap in green wrapper. PP $4.00 .... Set $	3.00-	4.00
399.	1971 SNOOPY COMB & BRUSH SET, White plastic brush in the shape of a dog with black ears & red collar. White comb. Comb is 4½″ long. Brush is 5½″ long. PP $3.50 .... $		3.50

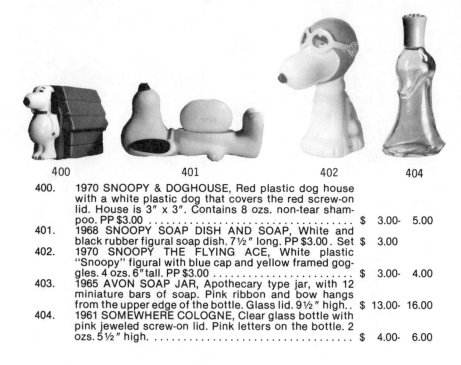

400	401	402	404

400. 1970 SNOOPY & DOGHOUSE, Red plastic dog house with a white plastic dog that covers the red screw-on lid. House is 3" x 3". Contains 8 ozs. non-tear shampoo. PP $3.00 .... $ 3.00- 5.00
401. 1968 SNOOPY SOAP DISH AND SOAP, White and black rubber figural soap dish. 7½" long. PP $3.00 . Set $ 3.00
402. 1970 SNOOPY THE FLYING ACE, White plastic "Snoopy" figural with blue cap and yellow framed goggles. 4 ozs. 6" tall. PP $3.00 .... $ 3.00- 4.00
403. 1965 AVON SOAP JAR, Apothecary type jar, with 12 miniature bars of soap. Pink ribbon and bow hangs from the upper edge of the bottle. Glass lid. 9½" high.. $ 13.00- 16.00
404. 1961 SOMEWHERE COLOGNE, Clear glass bottle with pink jeweled screw-on lid. Pink letters on the bottle. 2 ozs. 5½" high. .... $ 4.00- 6.00

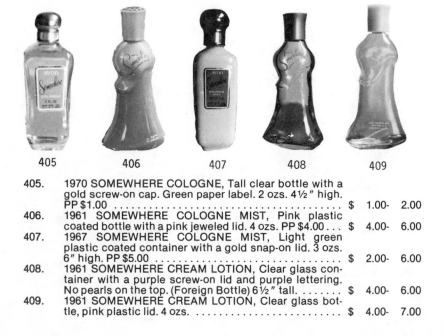

405	406	407	408	409

405. 1970 SOMEWHERE COLOGNE, Tall clear bottle with a gold screw-on cap. Green paper label. 2 ozs. 4½" high. PP $1.00 .... $ 1.00- 2.00
406. 1961 SOMEWHERE COLOGNE MIST, Pink plastic coated bottle with a pink jeweled lid. 4 ozs. PP $4.00 ... $ 4.00- 6.00
407. 1967 SOMEWHERE COLOGNE MIST, Light green plastic coated container with a gold snap-on lid. 3 ozs. 6" high. PP $5.00 .... $ 2.00- 6.00
408. 1961 SOMEWHERE CREAM LOTION, Clear glass container with a purple screw-on lid and purple lettering. No pearls on the top. (Foreign Bottle) 6½" tall. .... $ 4.00- 6.00
409. 1961 SOMEWHERE CREAM LOTION, Clear glass bottle, pink plastic lid. 4 ozs. .... $ 4.00- 7.00

410   411   412   413   414

410.   1961 SOMEWHERE CREAM SACHET, Jeweled lid on a
        pink glass jar. .66 oz. . . . . $ 2.00-   3.00
411.   1966 SOMEWHERE CREAM SACHET, White glass jar
        with a green design trim and gold trim around the lid.
        .66 oz. PP $2.00 . . . . $ 1.00-   3.00
412.   1966 SOMEWHERE FOAMING BATH OIL, Green
        plastic bottle with gold letters and gold screw-on cap. 6
        ozs. 6". PP $3.50 . . . . $ 3.00-   6.00
413.   1963 PERFUME OIL FOR THE BATH, .5 oz. 3¾" high,
        clear glass bottle, pink plastic screw-on lid. PP $4.00 . . $ 10.00- 15.00
414.   1966 SOMEWHERE PERFUME OIL, Clear glass bottle
        with a gold cap and green label. 5 ozs. PP $4.00 . . . . $ 2.00-   6.00

415   416   417   418

415.   1961 SOMEWHERE PERFUMED SKIN SOFTENER,
        Pink painted milk glass jar, gold & pink metal screw-on
        lid. 2½" high, 5 ozs. PP $3.25 . . . . $ 3.00-   6.00
416.   1964 SOMEWHERE PERFUMED TALC, 2¾ ozs. Pink
        can with white lettering. 5¾" high. PP $.89 . . . . $ 2.00
417.   1966 SOMEWHERE PERFUMED SKIN SOFTENER,
        Green glass jar, gold & green metal screw-on lid. 5 ozs.
        PP $3.25 . . . . $ 3.00-   5.00
418.   1961 SOMEWHERE POWDER SACHET, Pink glass jar
        with a pink plastic screw-on lid. White paper label on
        bottom. 1¼ ozs. 3" high. . . . . $ 5.00-   8.00

47

| 419 | 420 | 421 | 422 |

419. 1966 SOMEWHERE POWDER SACHET, White milk glass container with a green paper label and a white plastic screw-on lid. The lid has a gold rim around the bottom. .9 oz. 2¾" high. SCARCE PP $2.00 . . . . $ 5.00- 10.00

420. 1968 SOMEWHERE SOAP, 3 white bars of soap in a green box. PP $3.00 . . . . $ 9.00- 12.00

421. 1971 SONGBIRD COLOGNE, 5 fragrances, clear glass, gold screw-on base. PP $3.00 . . . . $ 4.00- 6.00

422. 1968 SPICY TALC FOR MEN, Cardboard with plastic bottom & shaker top. 3½ ozs. PP $.98 . . . . $ 1.00- 2.00

| 423 | 424 | 426 |

423. 1970 SPLASHDOWN BUBBLE BATH, White space capsule with an orange nosecone & a yellow base. Yellow, orange & blue rings around the middle. 8 ozs. 6" tall. PP $4.00 . . . . $ 4.00
Bottle only $ 1.00- 1.50

424. 1968 SPLASH 'N' SPRAY COLOGNE, Clear glass bottle, gold screw-on cap. Gold spiral design around the center section of the bottle. 2½ ozs. PP $7.00 . . . . . Set $ 15.00- 20.00

425. 1959 SPRAY ESSENCE, Black plastic coated bottle, gold cap. Came in 7 fragrances. 7 ozs. PP $4.00 . . . . $ 3.00- 5.00

426. 1971 SPRING FLOWERS, CREAM SACHET, Green glass jar. Orchid flower raised design, screw-on cap. .66 oz. . . . . $ 3.00- 5.00

427   428   429

427. 1970 S.S. SUDS, Blue & white plastic boat with a blue plastic screw-on lid. Contains 8 ozs. non-tear shampoo. 7″ long. PP $3.00 .... $ 2.00- 4.00

428. 1969 STEPPING OUT, Foot care cream, blue jar, white screw-on lid. 4 ozs. PP $2.00 .... $ 1.00- 2.00

429. 1970 STRAWBERRIES & CREAM, Bath foam, pitcher-shaped container, white milk glass, red strawberries on front. Round red stopper cap. 4 ozs. 5¼″ high.PP $3.50 $ 3.00- 6.00

430   431   432   433

430. 1971 STRAWBERRY BATH FOAM & STRAWBERRY SOAP, 4 ozs. Red glass pitcher, with stopper. 6″ high. 3 bars of soap, strawberry shaped, red. PP $4.00 Bath foam $ 5.00- 9.00
                        Soap $ 4.00- 5.00

431. 1971 STRAWBERRY BATH GELEE, 4″ high, red glass jar, gold cap and ladle. 4½ ozs. PP $2.00 .... $ 7.00- 8.00

432. 1956 STRAWBERRY COOLER CREAM, Round white frosted glass jar with white screw-on lid. Strawberries in 2 shades of red on lid. PP $1.50 .... $ 3.00- 5.00

433. 1954 SUN LOTION, with insect repellent, clear glass bottle, white plastic screw-on lid. Brown & white paper label. 4½″ high, 4 ozs. .... $ 7.00- 11.00

434   435   436   437

434. 1972 SWAN LAKE COLOGNE, White milk glass. 8″
     high. 3 ozs. 4 fragrances. PP $5.00 . . . . $ 2.00- 5.00
435. 1960 TEMPLE OF LOVE, Topaze cream sachet comes
     in a yellow container with a yellow screw-on lid with a
     topaze stone on top. .66 oz. 1¾″ high. Yellow and
     white plastic temple is 2″ tall. Comes in a yellow and
     gold cardboard box. 2½″ tall. . . . . $ 15.00- 18.00
436. 1966 THREE HEARTS ON A PIN CUSHION, Perfume oil
     petites, three heart-shaped glass containers, rest on
     red velvet. Gold cardboard container has a red felt
     cushion on top. . . . . $ 34.00- 42.00
437. 1967 TIC TOC TIGER, Orange plastic clock with yellow
     plastic screw-on lid. 8 ozs. 5″ tall. PP $1.75 . . . . $ 4.00- 5.00

438   439   440   441

438. 1969 TIC TOC TURTLE BUBBLE BATH, Green turtle
     with a pink mouth on its stomach is a yellow plastic
     clock face with pink hands and blue numbers. 8 ozs.
     5¾″. PP $2.50. . . . . $ 6.00- 7.00
439. 1954 TO A WILD ROSE BODY POWDER, Milk glass
     container with a white screw-on lid. Roses around the
     bottom on a paper label. 4¼″ high. 3 ozs. PP $1.79 . . . . $ 8.00- 12.00
440. 1960 TO A WILD ROSE COLOGNE, White milk glass
     bottle with a pink screw-on knob lid and a painted label.
     2 ozs. 4¾″ high. PP $2.50. In box $25.00. . . . . $ 4.00- 5.00
441. 1963 TO A WILD ROSE COLOGNE, White bottle with a
     pink cap and pink letters and trim. 2 ozs. PP $2.50 . . . . . $ 3.00- 5.00

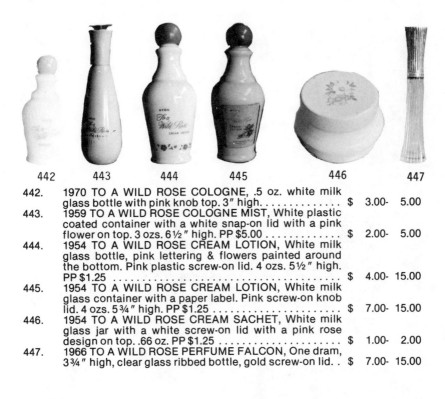

442 443 444 445 446 447

442. 1970 TO A WILD ROSE COLOGNE, .5 oz. white milk glass bottle with pink knob top. 3″ high. . . . . $ 3.00- 5.00
443. 1959 TO A WILD ROSE COLOGNE MIST, White plastic coated container with a white snap-on lid with a pink flower on top. 3 ozs. 6½″ high. PP $5.00 . . . . $ 2.00- 5.00
444. 1954 TO A WILD ROSE CREAM LOTION, White milk glass bottle, pink lettering & flowers painted around the bottom. Pink plastic screw-on lid. 4 ozs. 5½″ high. PP $1.25 . . . . $ 4.00- 15.00
445. 1954 TO A WILD ROSE CREAM LOTION, White milk glass container with a paper label. Pink screw-on knob lid. 4 ozs. 5¾″ high. PP $1.25 . . . . $ 7.00- 15.00
446. 1954 TO A WILD ROSE CREAM SACHET, White milk glass jar with a white screw-on lid with a pink rose design on top. .66 oz. PP $1.25 . . . . $ 1.00- 2.00
447. 1966 TO A WILD ROSE PERFUME FALCON, One dram, 3¾″ high, clear glass ribbed bottle, gold screw-on lid. . $ 7.00- 15.00

448 449 450 451

448. 1964 TO A WILD ROSE PERFUME OIL, .5 oz. 3″ high. White milk glass bottle, pink knob top. PP $3.50 . . . . . . $ 6.00- 15.00
449. 1964 TO A WILD ROSE PERFUMED SKIN SOFTENER, White glass jar and pink & white metal screw-on lid. 5 ozs. 2½″ high. PP $3.50 . . . . $ 2.00- 4.00
450. 1962 TO A WILD ROSE PERFUMED TALC, 2.75 ozs. 5¾″ tall. White can green & pink letters, pink plastic cap. Roses painted around bottom of can. PP $.69 . . . . $ 1.00- 2.00
451. 1950 TO A WILD ROSE POWDER SACHET, Clear glass container, blue paper label, blue plastic screw-on cap. 1¼ ozs. 3″ high. PP $1.25 . . . . $ 7.00- 10.00

452 453 454 455 456

452.	1954 TO A WILD ROSE POWDER SACHET, White jar with a white metal screw-on lid with roses on the top. Band of roses around the bottom of the jar. .9 oz. 2½″. PP $1.25	$ 6.00-	8.00
453.	1961 TOPAZE COLOGNE, Clear glass bottle. 4 ozs. PP $3.00	$ 7.00-	14.00
454.	1970 TOPAZE COLOGNE, Clear glass bottle, gold lettering, gold plastic screw-on lid. .5 oz. PP $1.50	$ 4.00-	5.00
455.	1959 TOPAZE COLOGNE MIST, Yellow plastic coated bottle with a yellow jewel on the lid. 3 ozs. PP $4.00	$ 5.00-	6.00
456.	TOPAZE CREAM LOTION, Tall clear glass bottle with gold lettering and a yellow snap-on lid over a white screw-on lid. 4 ozs. 8″ high. PP $1.50	$ 2.00-	8.00

457 458 459 460 461

457.	1960 TOPAZE CREAM SACHET, Yellow cap with a jewel on the top and a yellow glass bottom. PP $2.50	$ 1.00-	3.00
458.	1966 TOPAZE FOAMING BATH OIL, Yellow plastic bottle with gold lettering and a yellow screw-on lid. 6 ozs. 8¾″ high. PP $2.75	$ 1.00-	2.00
459.	1962 TOPAZE PERFUMED TALC, 2.75 ozs. Yellow can and cap. PP $1.00	$ 6.00-	8.00
460.	1964 TOPAZE PERFUME OIL, Clear glass bottle, gold lettering and a gold plastic screw-on lid. .5 oz. 2 5/8″ high. PP $4.00	$ 7.00-	8.00
461.	1959 TOPAZE POWDER SACHET, Yellow glass container with a yellow plastic screw-on lid. .9 oz. 3½″ high. PP $2.00	$ 7.00-	9.00

462

463

464

462. 1964 TOPAZE SKIN SOFTENER, Yellow glass jar, 2½″
high, gold & white metal screw-on lid. 5 ozs. PP $3.50 . . $ 1.00-   4.00
463. 1971 TREASURE TURTLE, 14 fragrances, amber glass
gold screw-on lid (as head). 3½″ long, 1 oz. PP $3.50. . . $ 3.50-   5.00
464. 1971 THE TWEETSTERS BATH SOAPS, Three pink
birds figural soaps. 1.5 oz. each. PP $2.00 . . . . $ 3.00-   6.00

465

466

467

465. 1970 TWO LOVES, GIFT SET, Bird of Paradise, 1 cream
sachet. .66 oz. 1 perfume rollette, .33 oz. Gold box, gold
lining. PP $6.00 . . . . $ 5.00- 10.00
466. 1970 TWO LOVES, GIFT SET, Charisma, 1 cream
sachet, .66 oz. 1 perfume rollette, .22 oz. Gold box, red
lining. PP $6.00 . . . . $ 5.00- 10.00
467. 1970 TWO LOVES, GIFT SET, Elusive, 1 cream sachet,
.66 oz. 1 perfume rollette, .33 oz. Gold box, pink lining.
PP $6.00 . . . . $ 5.00- 10.00

| 468 | 469 | 470 | 471 | 472 |

468. **1970 ULTRA-SHEER UNDER MAKEUP MOISTURIZER,** Came in three shades of cream; aqua, apricot and mavine. 2 ozs. White jar & cap. PP $3.00 . . . . $ 1.00- 2.00

469. **1969 UNFORGETTABLE PERFUMED POWDER MIST,** Orange can trimmed in gold with gold lettering. Orange plastic snap-on cap. 7 ozs. 5½" tall. PP $3.75 . . . . $ 1.00- 3.75

470. **1965 UNFORGETTABLE POWDER SACHET,** Orange painted glass container with a gold metal neck and gold plastic screw-on lid. 2¼" high. PP $2.50 . . . . $ 7.00- 10.00

471. **1970 UNFORGETTABLE COLOGNE,** Clear glass bottle, gold plastic screw-on lid. .5 oz. 2 1/8" high. PP $1.75 . . . $ 1.00- 5.00

472. **1965 UNFORGETTABLE COLOGNE MIST,** Orange plastic coated glass bottle with gold metal neck and gold plastic lid. 3 ozs. 4¼" high. PP $3.50 . . . . $ 2.00- 5.00

| 473 | 474 | 475 | 476 | 477 |

473. **1966 UNFORGETTABLE COLOGNE MIST,** Orange plastic coated bottle with a gold cap and lettering. 3 ozs. 4½" high. . . . . $ 3.00- 4.00

474. **1966 UNFORGETTABLE COLOGNE SILK,** Frosted glass bottle with a gold cap, blue or pink band around the neck. 3 fragrances. 3 ozs. 6" high. 2.50 . . . . $ 2.00- 3.00

475. **1966 UNFORGETTABLE CREAM LOTION,** Orange plastic bottle with a gold cap and lettering. 4 ozs. 4" high. 1.75 . . . . $ 2.00- 4.00

476. **1965 UNFORGETTABLE CREAM SACHET,** Orange painted milk glass container, gold trimming & plastic screw-on lid. .66 oz. . . . . $ 3.00- 10.00

477. **1965 UNFORGETTABLE PERFUME OIL,** Clear glass container, gold screw-on lid. Gold collar. .5 oz. 2 1/8" high. . . . . $ 6.00- 8.00

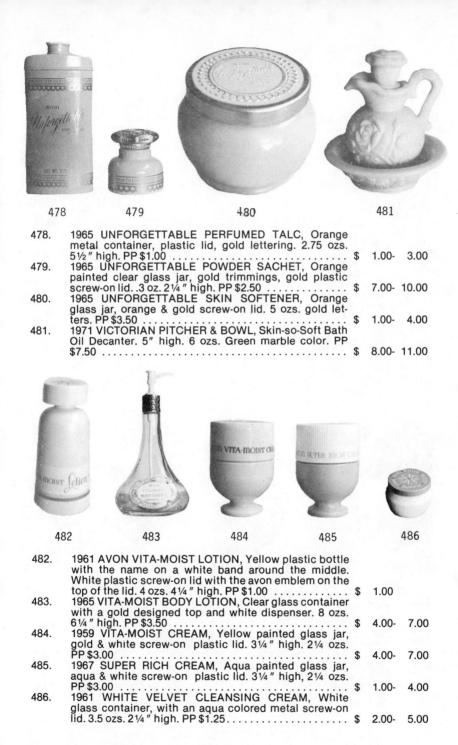

478　　　479　　　　480　　　　481

478. 1965 UNFORGETTABLE PERFUMED TALC, Orange
metal container, plastic lid, gold lettering. 2.75 ozs.
5½" high. PP $1.00 .... $ 1.00- 3.00
479. 1965 UNFORGETTABLE POWDER SACHET, Orange
painted clear glass jar, gold trimmings, gold plastic
screw-on lid. .3 oz. 2¼" high. PP $2.50 .... $ 7.00- 10.00
480. 1965 UNFORGETTABLE SKIN SOFTENER, Orange
glass jar, orange & gold screw-on lid. 5 ozs. gold letters. PP $3.50 .... $ 1.00- 4.00
481. 1971 VICTORIAN PITCHER & BOWL, Skin-so-Soft Bath
Oil Decanter. 5" high. 6 ozs. Green marble color. PP
$7.50 .... $ 8.00- 11.00

482　　　　483　　　　484　　　　485　　　　486

482. 1961 AVON VITA-MOIST LOTION, Yellow plastic bottle
with the name on a white band around the middle.
White plastic screw-on lid with the avon emblem on the
top of the lid. 4 ozs. 4¼" high. PP $1.00 .... $ 1.00
483. 1965 VITA-MOIST BODY LOTION, Clear glass container
with a gold designed top and white dispenser. 8 ozs.
6¼" high. PP $3.50 .... $ 4.00- 7.00
484. 1959 VITA-MOIST CREAM, Yellow painted glass jar,
gold & white screw-on plastic lid. 3¼" high. 2¼ ozs.
PP $3.00 .... $ 4.00- 7.00
485. 1967 SUPER RICH CREAM, Aqua painted glass jar,
aqua & white screw-on plastic lid. 3¼" high, 2¼ ozs.
PP $3.00 .... $ 1.00- 4.00
486. 1961 WHITE VELVET CLEANSING CREAM, White
glass container, with an aqua colored metal screw-on
lid. 3.5 ozs. 2¼" high. PP $1.25 .... $ 2.00- 5.00

487 488 489 490

487. 1963 WISHING COLOGNE, Clear bottle with a white
top. White wishbone around the neck. 2 ozs. PP $1.75 . $ 5.00- 8.00
488. 1963 WISHING COLOGNE MIST, White plastic coated
container with a gold neck trim and gold and white
plastic lid. 2.5 ozs. 4¼" PP $3.50 . . . . $ 3.00- 5.00
489. 1963 WISHING CREAM SACHET, White glass jar with a
white plastic screw-on top with a gold wishbone on the
top. .66 oz. 1½" high. PP $1.75 . . . . $ 3.00- 10.00
490. 1963 WISHING PERFUME OIL, Clear glass container
with a white plastic screw-on lid and a metal wishbone
on a string around the neck. PP $3.50 . . . . $ 10.00- 12.00

491 492 493

491. 1964 WISHING PERFUMED SKIN SOFTENER, White
glass jar, white & gold metal screw-on cap. 5 ozs. 2½"
high. PP $3.00 . . . . $ 1.00- 4.00
492. 1963 WISHING POWDER SACHET, White milk glass
bottle with a yellow plastic screw-on lid. Gold metal
wishbone on the top of the lid. .9 oz. 3" high. 1.75 . . . . . $ 8.00- 12.00
493. 1970 WRIST WATCH BUBBLE BATH, Orange and white
plastic watch with a blue plastic screw-on lid. 2 ozs.
3½" high. PP $3.00 . . . . $ 4.00- 5.00

MEN'S AVONS

| 494 | 495 | 496 | 497 |

494. 1957 AFTER SHAVE FOR MEN, ½ oz. sample bottle. . . . $ 5.00- 7.00
495. 1962 AVON AFTER SHAVE LOTION, Spicy, clear glass container, red plastic screw-on lid. Paper label. 4 ozs. 3¾" high. PP $1.78 . . . . $ 6.00- 10.00
496. 1951 AFTER SHAVE SAMPLE, Clear glass bottle, red plastic screw-on lid. ½ oz. 1¾" high. . . . . $ 4.00- 10.00
497. 1971 AMERICAN EAGLE DECANTER, 6" high, amber glass, gold screw-on lid. .5 oz. 2 fragrances. After shave. PP $5.00 . . . . $ 5.00- 6.00

| 498 | 499 | 500 | 501 |

498. 1966 ALPINE FLASK, After shave lotion. Gold chain and green label on a dark brown glass bottle. Gold cap. 8 ozs. PP $4.00 . . . . $ 40.00- 55.00
499. 1969 THE ANGLER, Blue glass container shaped like a fishing reel. Silver screw-on cap. 3" high, 4½" long. PP $5.00 . . . . $ 4.00- 6.00
500. 1972 THE AVON OPEN AFTER SHAVE, Green see-thru glass cart, two golf bags and clubs. 5½" long. 5 ozs. PP $6.00 . . . . $ 3.00- 6.00
501. 1963 BARBER BOTTLE AFTER SHAVE, White milk glass bottle with gold letters and white cap and gold around the neck. 8 ozs. . . . . $ 25.00- 30.00

502   503   504   505

502.   1962 BAY RUM JUG, Paper label on the side of a green and white jug. 8 ozs. PP $2.50 . . . . $ 10.00- 15.00

503.   1965 BAY RUM KEG, After Shave Lotion. Brown and silver painted container with a silver label and brown cap. 8 ozs. PP $2.50 . . . . $ 10.00- 20.00

504.   1969 BRAVO AFTER SHAVE, Clear glass container with black plastic screw-on lid. 4 ozs. 3¾" high. PP $2.00 . . . . $ 4.00

505.   1971 BUCKING BRONCO, 8" high, 6 ozs. after shave in 2 fragrances. Gold removeable plastic man. PP $3.00 . . $ 6.00- 10.00

506   507   508   509

506.   1971 BUFFALO NICKEL DECANTER, 2 fragrances of after shave, or liquid hair lotion. Silver coated, screw-on cap. 5 ozs. 5" high. PP $4.00 . . . . $ 5.00- 8.00

507.   1968 CANDY AFTER SHAVE, Bottle fits in a wood carved type plastic case with a silver top. 6 ozs. . . . . $ 12.00- 15.00

508.   1970 CAPITOL AFTER SHAVE, Amber glass container with a gold cap. 5 ozs. 5" high. PP $5.00 . . . . $ 4.00- 5.00

509.   1964 CAPTAIN'S CHOICE AFTER SHAVE, Round captain's ship bottle in smoke green with a gold screw-on lid. 8 ozs. 4¼" high. PP $2.50 . . . . $ 8.00- 10.00

510   511   512   513

510.   **1970 CAPTAIN'S PRIDE,** Avon's ship-on-the-bottle. Windjammer or Oland after shave lotion. 6 ozs. 8″ high. PP $5.00 .... $ 5.00- 7.00

511.   **1966 CASEY'S LANTERN AFTER SHAVE LOTION,** Gold coated over glass with a red window. 10 ozs. Gold handle prongs. PP $6.00. 10 ozs. .... $ 20.00- 22.00
Amber window $ 24.00- 26.00
Green window $ 24.00- 26.00

512.   **1969 AVON CLASSICS BOOKS AFTER SHAVE,** Yellow, blue, dark amber & clear containers with black tops. 6 ozs. .... $ 4.00- 8.00

513.   **1949 COLOGNE FOR MEN,** Clear glass container with a silver and white label and an orange plastic screw-on lid. 2 ozs. 2½″ high .... $ 5.00- 6.00

514   515   516   517

514.   **1969 COLOGNE TRILOGY,** Brown case with gold and brown designed inserts. 3 - 1½ oz. cologne bottles inside. Hexagonal shaped. 6¼″ high. PP $8.00 .... $ 8.00- 17.50

515.   **1970 COVERED WAGON AFTER SHAVE,** Amber glass with white top and gold cap. 6 ozs. 4½″ high. PP $4.00 . $ 3.00- 6.00

516.   **1968 DAYLIGHT SHAVING TIME,** Clear bottle with gold painted surface and a white face and black numbers. 6 ozs. 6″ high. PP $5.00 .... $ 6.00- 8.00

517.   **1965 DECISIONS AFTER SHAVE,** Clear glass container with a black plastic base. Black plastic screw-on lid with red "Panic Button". 8 ozs. 7½″ high. PP $2.50 .... $ 25.00- 27.00

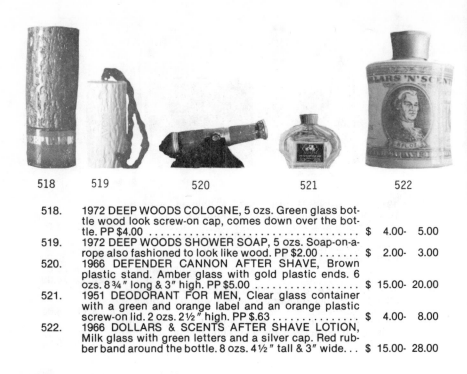

518   519   520   521   522

518. 1972 DEEP WOODS COLOGNE, 5 ozs. Green glass bottle wood look screw-on cap, comes down over the bottle. PP $4.00 .... $ 4.00- 5.00
519. 1972 DEEP WOODS SHOWER SOAP, 5 ozs. Soap-on-a-rope also fashioned to look like wood. PP $2.00 .... $ 2.00- 3.00
520. 1966 DEFENDER CANNON AFTER SHAVE, Brown plastic stand. Amber glass with gold plastic ends. 6 ozs. 8¾" long & 3" high. PP $5.00 .... $ 15.00- 20.00
521. 1951 DEODORANT FOR MEN, Clear glass container with a green and orange label and an orange plastic screw-on lid. 2 ozs. 2½" high. PP $.63 .... $ 4.00- 8.00
522. 1966 DOLLARS & SCENTS AFTER SHAVE LOTION, Milk glass with green letters and a silver cap. Red rubber band around the bottle. 8 ozs. 4½" tall & 3" wide... $ 15.00- 28.00

523   524   525

523. 1971 DUNE BUGGY, Bracing lotion or liquid hair lotion, 5 ozs. Blue glass container. 6" long. PP $5.00 .... $ 5.00- 8.00
524. 1970 ELECTRIC CHARGER AFTER SHAVE, Black glass with red paper stripe on both sides. 5 ozs. 5½" high. PP $4.00 .... $ 2.00- 4.00
525. 1962 ELECTRIC PRE-SHAVE LOTION, Spicy, Clear glass bottle, with a red plastic screw-on lid. 4 ozs. 3¾" high. .... $ 6.00- 10.00

526	527	528	529

526. 1967 ELECTRIC PRE-SHAVE LOTION. 4 ozs. 3¾" high. Clear glass bottle, white screw-on cap. . . . . $ 2.00- 3.00

527. 1969 EXCALIBUR AFTER SHAVE, Clear glass bottle, gold cap, indented like rocks in bottom. 6 ozs. PP $5.00 $ 2.00- 5.00

528. 1970 FIRST CLASS MALE AFTER SHAVE LOTION, Blue glass mail box with red cap and white letters. 4 ozs. 4¼". PP $3.00 . . . . $ 2.00- 4.00

529. 1970 FIRST DOWN DECANTER, A football filled with Wild Country after shave or Sports Rally bracing lotion. White stand. 5 ozs. 4½" tall & 2½" wide. PP $3.00 . . . . $ 2.00- 5.00

530. 1967 FIRST EDITION BOOK AFTER SHAVE, Clear bottle with gold lettering. 6 ozs. PP $3.50 . . . . $ 6.00- 8.00

531	532	533	534

531. 1971 FIRST VOLUNTEER, 2 fragrances, cologne. 5" long, 6 ozs. PP $8.50 . . . . $ 8.00- 10.00

532. 1965 MEN'S FRAGRANCE WARDROBE, After shave. Clear glass bottle, black cap, 4¼" high. 2 ozs. Comes in 8 different labels, also after shower cologne. Sold in sets of 3 & 4, also single. PP $3.50 each. . . . . Each $ 10.00- 14.00

533. 1969 FUTURA COLOGNE FOR MEN, Silver coated bottel with a silver cap. 5 ozs. 8" high. PP $7.00 . . . . $ 12.00- 16.00

534. 1967 GAVEL AFTER SHAVE LOTION, Dark amber glass with brown plastic handle. 5 ozs. 10¾" long, 4" wide. PP $4.00 . . . . $ 12.00- 15.00

535	536	537

535. 1971 THE NEW GENERAL 4-4-0, 7" long. 5½ ozs. after shave in 2 fragrances. Blue glass. PP $7.50 .... $ 7.50- 10.00
536. 1969 GENTLEMAN'S CHOICE AFTER SHAVE, Clear glass bottle with a silver plastic lid. 2 ozs. 2½" high. PP $1.75 .... $ 3.00- 6.00
537. 1970 GENTLEMEN'S SELECTION, Avon Leather cologne. 2 ozs. Clear bottle with gold screw-on lid. 5 other fragrances. 3½" high. PP $1.75 .... $ 1.00- 3.00

538	539	540	541

538. 1969 GOLD CADILLAC AFTER SHAVE, Gold painted glass container. 6 ozs. 7" long. PP $5.00 .... $ 3.00- 8.00
539. 1966 GOLD TOP BOOT AFTER SHAVE, Dark amber glass container. 8 ozs. 6½" high. PP $5.00 .... $ 4.00- 5.00
540. 1966 LIQUID HAIR LOTION, 5¼" high, clear glass bottle, white screw-on lid. Paper label, 4 ozs. .... $ 1.00- 3.00
541. 1970 INDIAN HEAD PENNY AFTER SHAVE LOTION, Round bronze coated bottle with bronze cap. 4 ozs. PP $4.00 .... $ 3.00- 4.00

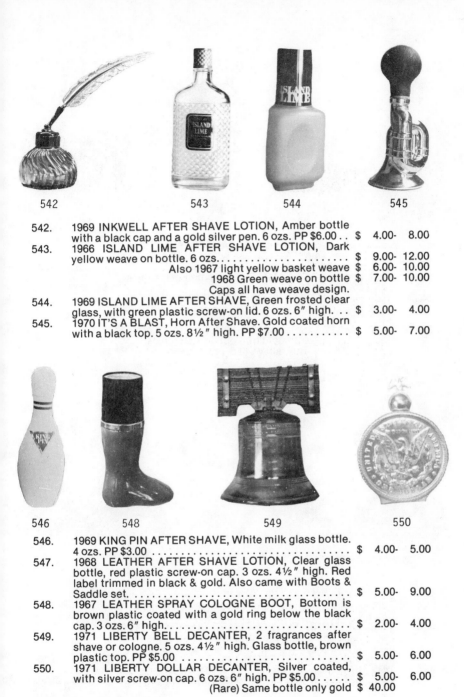

542   543   544   545

542.	1969 INKWELL AFTER SHAVE LOTION, Amber bottle with a black cap and a gold silver pen. 6 ozs. PP $6.00 ..	$ 4.00-	8.00
543.	1966 ISLAND LIME AFTER SHAVE LOTION, Dark yellow weave on bottle. 6 ozs.	$ 9.00-	12.00
	Also 1967 light yellow basket weave	$ 6.00-	10.00
	1968 Green weave on bottle	$ 7.00-	10.00
	Caps all have weave design.		
544.	1969 ISLAND LIME AFTER SHAVE, Green frosted clear glass, with green plastic screw-on lid. 6 ozs. 6″ high. ..	$ 3.00-	4.00
545.	1970 IT'S A BLAST, Horn After Shave. Gold coated horn with a black top. 5 ozs. 8½″ high. PP $7.00	$ 5.00-	7.00

546   548   549   550

546.	1969 KING PIN AFTER SHAVE, White milk glass bottle. 4 ozs. PP $3.00	$ 4.00-	5.00
547.	1968 LEATHER AFTER SHAVE LOTION, Clear glass bottle, red plastic screw-on cap. 3 ozs. 4½″ high. Red label trimmed in black & gold. Also came with Boots & Saddle set.	$ 5.00-	9.00
548.	1967 LEATHER SPRAY COLOGNE BOOT, Bottom is brown plastic coated with a gold ring below the black cap. 3 ozs. 6″ high.	$ 2.00-	4.00
549.	1971 LIBERTY BELL DECANTER, 2 fragrances after shave or cologne. 5 ozs. 4½″ high. Glass bottle, brown plastic top. PP $5.00	$ 5.00-	6.00
550.	1971 LIBERTY DOLLAR DECANTER, Silver coated, with silver screw-on cap. 6 ozs. 6″ high. PP $5.00	$ 5.00-	6.00
	(Rare) Same bottle only gold	$ 40.00	

551   552   553   554

551.   **1970 ABRAHAM LINCOLN DECANTER,** Avon spicy or tribute after shave. Clear glass with a gold cap. 4 ozs. 5½". PP $3.50 . . . . $ 3.00-   4.00

552.   **1967 MALLARD DECANTER,** Dark green glass duck. 6 ozs. 6" high. PP $5.00 . . . . $ 7.00-   9.00

553.   **1969 MAN'S WORLD GLOBE AFTER SHAVE LOTION,** Gold coated bottle with a brown plastic stand. 6 ozs. 4½". PP $5.00 . . . . $ 5.00-   7.00

554.   **1970 MASTER ORGANIZER,** Plastic wood grained case. Red lining with gold trim outside. Contains: 1 cologne (3.5 oz.) 1 after shave (3.5 oz.) 1 bar of soap. PP $25.00 . . . . $ 27.00- 35.00

555   556   557

555.   **1972 MODEL "A" AFTER SHAVE,** Yellow painted car. Fueled with 2 fragrances of after shave. 5½" long. 4 ozs. PP $4.00 . . . . $ 4.00

556.   **1968 OPENING PLAY HELMET AFTER SHAVE,** Decanter is shaped like a football helmet. Either blue glass with gold helmet or black and gold. Both have screw-on lids. 4 ozs. PP $4.00 each. . . . . $ 14.00- 25.00

557.   **1949 ORIGINAL AFTER SHAVE LOTION,** Clear glass bottle, red cap, with green & red label. 4 ozs. 3" high. . . $ 4.00-   9.00

558   559   560   561

558.   1970 PACKARD ROADSTER, 2 fragrances. 6 ozs. 6½".
PP $6.00 .... $ 5.00- 6.00
559.   1972 PIANO DECANTER, 2 fragrances after shave. 4"
high. 4 ozs. Amber glass container, white screw-on lid.
PP $4.00 .... $ 3.00- 5.00
560.   1967 PIPE DREAM AFTER SHAVE LOTION, Dark amber
glass with tan plastic base and black top. 6 ozs. 5" long
& 5¾" high. PP $5.00 .... $ 14.00- 20.00
561.   1971 PIPE FULL DECANTER, 3 fragrances, after shave.
Amber glass base, silver & black trim. 6½" long. 2 ozs.
PP $3.50 .... $ 2.00- 3.00

562   563 564 565   566

562.   1971 AVON PONY EXPRESS, 2 fragrances after shave.
5 ozs. 6" high. Amber glass, gold man riding. PP $4.00 . $ 5.00- 6.00
563.   1966 TALL PONY AFTER SHAVE, Green glass with a
gold cap. 8 ozs. PP $4.00 .... $ 7.00- 8.00
564.   1968 SHORT PONY HEAD AFTER SHAVE, Green glass
with a gold top. 4 ozs. PP $3.50 .... $ 3.00- 4.00
565.   1972 PONY POST DECANTER, Bronze color, 2
fragrances after shave. 8" high, 5 ozs. PP $5.00 .... $ 2.50- 6.00
566.   1970 POT BELLY STOVE, Black glass bottle with a
black top. 5 ozs. 5" high. PP $4.00 .... $ 3.00- 6.00

| 567 | 568 | 569 | 570 |

567. **1972 REMEMBER WHEN RADIO DECANTER,** After shave or liquid hair lotion. 5" high. 5 ozs. Brown glass. Gold trim. .... $ 3.00- 5.00

568. **1972 REO DEPOT WAGON,** Amber glass body with black plastic cab and roof. Tai Winds or Oland After Shave. 5 ozs. 5" long. PP $6.00 .... $ 3.00- 6.00

569. **1965 ROYAL ORB AFTER SHAVE,** Clear round container, with gold screw-on lid. Red lettering on front and back. 8 ozs. PP $3.50 .... $ 18.00- 25.00
White letter on left $ 75.00

570. **1968 SCIMITAR AFTER SHAVE LOTION,** Red coated jewels on a gold coated container. 6 ozs. 10" high. PP $6.00 .... $ 10.00- 22.00

| 571 | 572 | 573 | 574 | 575 |

571. **1970 SILVER DUSENBERG,** Silver painted 1933 model auto. 6 ozs. 7½" long. PP $6.00 .... $ 4.00- 7.00

572. **1965 SILVER STEIN AFTER SHAVE LOTION,** Silver coated finish with embossed sides. Screw-on plastic lid. 8 ozs. 6¼" high. PP $4.00 .... $ 9.00- 12.00

573. **1968 SILVER STEIN AFTER SHAVE LOTION,** Embossed sides. 6 ozs. 5½" high. PP $4.50 .... $ 6.00- 10.00

574. **1971 SMART MOVE COLOGNE,** Amber glass bottle, silver head as cap, 2 fragrances. 6" high. 3 ozs. PP $4.00 .... $ 4.00- 8.00

575. **1969 SNOOPY SURPRISE AFTER SHAVE,** White glass figural with black plastic ears and a blue plastic baseball cap. 5 ozs. 5¾" high. PP $4.00 .... $ 2.00- 4.00

576   577   578

576.   1967 SPICY AFTER SHAVE, Amber glass container, with black plastic screw-on lid. 4 ozs., 4¼" high. PP $1.50 .... $ 1.00-   2.00

577.   1970 SPIRIT OF ST. LOUIS, Silver coated plane with a silver cap. 6 ozs. 7½" long & 3" high. $8.50 .... $ 6.00-   8.50

578.   1960 EMBOSSED STAGE COACH AFTER SHAVE LOTION, Clear glass container with a stage coach embossed on the front. Came in three sizes: 2 ozs. with red or white plastic lids; 4 ozs. with a white plastic lid; 8 ozs. with a gold metal lid. PP $1.25 .... Each $ 20.00- 25.00

579   580   581

579.   1970 STAGE COACH AFTER SHAVE LOTION, Amber glass in the shape of a stage coach with embossed wheels and doors and windows. 5 ozs. 4½" high. PP $3.50 .... $ 3.00-   5.00

580.   1970 STAMP AFTER SHAVE, Amber glass with black cap and pink rubber "Paid" stamp on bottom. 4 ozs. PP $4.00 .... $ 3.00-   5.00

581.   1971 STATION WAGON, 6 fragrances after shave. Green glass, plastic top. 7" long. PP $6.00 .... $ 6.00-   7.00

582   583   584

582.   1971 STEAM BOAT SIDE WHEELER, After shave decanter, 5 ozs. 2 fragrances. 6″ long. Amber glass, gold trim. PP $6.00 .... $ 6.00- 8.00

583.   1968 STERLING SIX CAR, The container is shaped like a roadster. Black screw-on cap. Various shades of amber. PP $4.00 .... $ 6.00- 9.00

584.   1969 STRAIGHT EIGHT CAR AFTER SHAVE, Amber glass container with a black twist-on cap. 5 ozs. PP $3.50 .... $ 2.00- 4.00

585   586   587   588

585.   1969 STRUCTURED FOR MEN, Black plastic base holds three bottles of cologne: Blue glass with a silver plastic cap. Clear glass with clear plastic cap. Amber glass with wood grained plastic cap. Each holds 3 ozs. 3¾″ high. PP $8.50. Bottles $2.00-3.00 each. ...... Set $ 12.00- 15.00

586.   1971 SUPER CYCLE AFTER SHAVE, or bracing lotion. 7″ long, green glass. 4 ozs. PP $5.00. Clear test $35.00. Black $18.00. .... $ 6.00

587.   1969 SWINGER GOLD BAG AFTER SHAVE, Black glass and clubs with a red plastic top. 5 ozs. 7¼″ high. PP $5.00 .... $ 5.00- 7.00

588.   1969 TELEPHONE AFTER SHAVE LOTION, Gold coated glass bottle with a black plastic ear piece which contains mens talc. 6 ozs. 8¾″ high. .... $ 6.00- 8.00

589. 1969 TOURING "T" CAR AFTER SHAVE LOTION, Black glass container with a black plastic top. 6 ozs. 6½" high. PP $6.00 .... $ 4.00- 6.00
590. 1968 TOWN PUMP AFTER SHAVE, Figural of an old pump, in black glass, with a gold plastic pump handle. 6 ozs. PP $5.00 .... $ 4.00- 7.00
591. 1963 TRIBUTE AFTER SHAVE, Clear glass container with silver metal shoulder and blue and silver plastic cap. 6 ozs. 4" tall. PP $2.50 .... $ 5.00- 9.00
592. 1968 TRIBUTE AFTER SHAVE, Clear glass container, paper label & blue and silver plastic cap. 4 ozs. 4½" high. PP $3.00 .... $ 2.00- 3.00
593. 1966 TRIBUTE AFTER SHAVE LOTION, 1 oz. Blue glass container silver plastic lid. Came in set of 4 different fragrances, chest like container, called THE FRA-GRANCE CHEST AFTER SHAVE SET. .... Each bottle $ 4.00- 7.00
Complete Set $ 30.00- 40.00

594. 1971 TRIBUTE COLOGNE, Warrior head, ribbed design clear glass. 6 ozs. PP $4.50 .... $ 4.00- 8.00
595. 1963 TRIBUTE COLOGNE FOR MEN, 4" high, clear glass bottle, blue letters, silver metal cover & shoulder, silver & blue plastic screw-on lid. 4 ozs. PP $3.00 ...... $ 5.00- 12.00
596. 1971 TWENTY DOLLAR GOLD PIECE, 2 fragrances after shave or electric pre-shave lotion. 6" high, gold plastic coated. PP $5.00 .... $ 5.00- 6.00
597. 1967 TWENTY PACES COLOGNE, Wood grained case with red felt lining. 2 gold pistol figural bottles with screw-on lids. Each pistol is 10" long. PP $10.00 ...... $ 25.00- 27.00

| 598 | 599 | 600 |

598. 1966 VIKING HORN AFTER SHAVE, Dark amber glass with a gold knob on the end and a gold designed top. 7 oz. 7" high & 6" wide. PP $5.00 .... $ 12.00- 20.00

599. 1970 VOLKSWAGON, Black glass bottle. 4 oz. 5½". PP $2.00 .... $ 4.00- 5.00

600. 1971 RED VOLKSWAGON, 2 fragrances after shave or bracing lotion. 5½" long. 4 ozs. PP $3.00 .... $ 4.00- 5.00

| 601 | 602 | 603 | 604 |

601. 1968 FROSTED WARRIOR HEAD, Silver cap. Pale green frosted bottle. 6 ozs. 6" high. .... $ 3.00- 5.00

602. 1967 SILVER WARRIOR HEAD, Silver coated container. 6 ozs. 6" high. .... $ 9.00- 15.00

603. 1970 GEORGE WASHINGTON DECANTER, Clear bottle with a gold cap. 4 ozs. 5½" high. PP $3.50 .... $ 3.00- 4.00

604. 1969 WEATHER VANE AFTER SHAVE, Figural weather vane in dark amber glass. Gold screw-on cap. 5 ozs. 8" high. PP $5.00 .... $ 4.00- 5.00

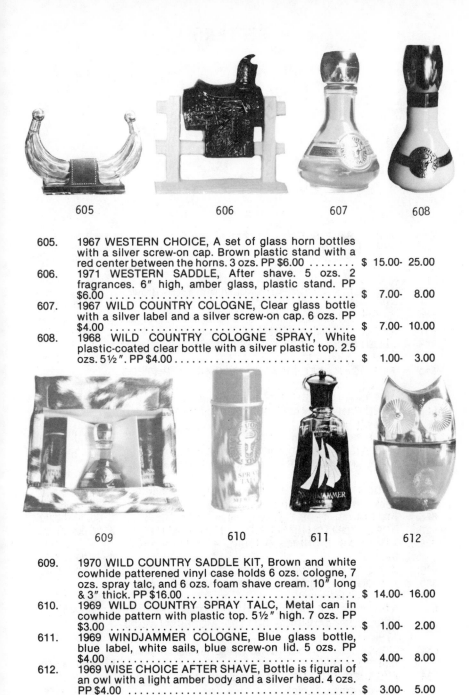

605   606   607   608

605.   1967 WESTERN CHOICE, A set of glass horn bottles with a silver screw-on cap. Brown plastic stand with a red center between the horns. 3 ozs. PP $6.00 . . . . $ 15.00- 25.00

606.   1971 WESTERN SADDLE, After shave. 5 ozs. 2 fragrances. 6″ high, amber glass, plastic stand. PP $6.00 . . . . $ 7.00-   8.00

607.   1967 WILD COUNTRY COLOGNE, Clear glass bottle with a silver label and a silver screw-on cap. 6 ozs. PP $4.00 . . . . $ 7.00- 10.00

608.   1968 WILD COUNTRY COLOGNE SPRAY, White plastic-coated clear bottle with a silver plastic top. 2.5 ozs. 5½″. PP $4.00 . . . . $ 1.00-   3.00

609   610   611   612

609.   1970 WILD COUNTRY SADDLE KIT, Brown and white cowhide patterened vinyl case holds 6 ozs. cologne, 7 ozs. spray talc, and 6 ozs. foam shave cream. 10″ long & 3″ thick. PP $16.00 . . . . $ 14.00- 16.00

610.   1969 WILD COUNTRY SPRAY TALC, Metal can in cowhide pattern with plastic top. 5½″ high. 7 ozs. PP $3.00 . . . . $ 1.00-   2.00

611.   1969 WINDJAMMER COLOGNE, Blue glass bottle, blue label, white sails, blue screw-on lid. 5 ozs. PP $4.00 . . . . $ 4.00-   8.00

612.   1969 WISE CHOICE AFTER SHAVE, Bottle is figural of an owl with a light amber body and a silver head. 4 ozs. PP $4.00 . . . . $ 3.00-   5.00

BITTERS

615   631   632   636

613.	ABBOT'S BITTERS, Round – Amber – 6¼″	$ 2.00-	6.00
614.	ABBOT, C.W. & COMPANY, Round – Amber – 10½″ ...	$ 4.00-	6.00
	8¼	$ 3.00-	7.00
	8½	$ 5.00-	6.00
	2½	$ 4.00-	6.00
615.	ABBOT, C.W. & COMPANY, Round with neck – Brown – 8¼″, & 8″	$ 4.00-	8.00
616.	ACORN BITTERS, Square – Amber – 9x2¾″	$ 60.00-	80.00
617.	AFRICAN STOMACH BITTERS, Round – Amber – 9½″	$ 30.00-	40.00
618.	ALLEN'S CONGRESS BITTERS, Rectangular – Deep emerald green – 10″ high.	$ 75.00-	95.00
619.	AMERICAN CELEBRATED STOMACH BITTERS, Square – Amber – 9½″	$ 40.00-	60.00
620.	AMERICAN LIFE BITTERS, Rectangular – Amber – 9″ .	$135.00-	160.00
621.	AMERICAN STOMACH BITTERS, Square – Amber & Mint with label...................................	$ 40.00-	60.00
622.	AMER PICON, Green – 11¾″	$ 8.00-	20.00
623.	ANGELICA BITTER TONIC, Amber – 9½″	$ 20.00-	40.00
624.	ANGOSTURA BITTERS, on shoulders – Round – Amber 8½″	$ 30.00-	40.00
625.	ANGOSTURA BARK BITTERS, (EAGLE) – Round with neck – Amber – 7″ high...........................	$ 30.00-	60.00
626.	ARABIAN BITTERS, Square – Amber – 9½″	$ 60.00-	100.00
627.	ARP'S STOMACH BITTERS, Round – Aqua – 11½″	$ 20.00-	30.00
628.	ATWOOD'S JAUNDICE BITTERS, 12 sided – Aqua – 6¼″	$ 3.00-	6.00
629.	ATWOOD'S JAUNDICE BITTERS, Clear – 6″	$ 3.00-	6.00
630.	ATWOOD'S (JANNAICA) BITTERS, 12 sided – Aqua – 6″. Note misspelling.............................	$ 10.00-	15.00
631.	ATWOOD'S, L.F. JAUNDICE BITTERS, Clear – 6½″ ...	$ 11.00-	15.00
632.	ATWOOD'S, JAUNDICE BITTERS, MOSES ATWOOD, 12 sided – Aqua – 6″ high.........................	$ 2.00-	4.00
633.	ATWOOD'S QUININE TONIC BITTERS, Rectangular – Aqua – 8½″ high.................................	$ 20.00-	40.00
634.	AUGAUER BITTERS, Rectangular – Light green & emerald green. 8″ high...........................	$ 40.00-	60.00
635.	AUGOSTURA BITTERS, Round – Olive Green – 8¼″ ...	$ 50.00-	70.00
636.	AUNT CHARITY'S BITTERS, Oval – Clear – 8″	$ 10.00-	20.00

654   658   659   660

637.	AYALA MEXICAN BITTERS, Square – Amber – 9½" ...	$ 40.00- 60.00
638.	AYER'S RESTORATIVE BITTERS, Rectangular – 8 7/8". Aqua	$ 50.00- 60.00
639.	BAKER'S ORANGE GROVE BITTERS, Square – Different shades of amber – 9½"	$ 80.00- 90.00
640.	BAKER'S PREMIUM BITTERS, Oval – Aqua – 6½"	$ 50.00- 60.00
641.	DR. BALL'S VEGETABLE STOMACHIC BITTERS, Rectangular – Aqua – 7" high.	$ 60.00- 80.00
642.	BARTLETT'S EXCELSIOR BITTERS, 8 sided – No other information known.	$100.00-200.00
643.	BAXTER'S MANDRAKE BITTERS, 12 sided – Aqua – 6¼"	$ 12.00- 30.00
644.	BAXTER'S MANDRAKE BITTERS, LORD BROS., 12 sided – Aqua – 6½" high.	$ 12.00- 30.00
645.	BEECHAM'S BITTERS, Rectangular – Amber – 8"	$ 10.00- 15.00
646.	BEGG'S DANDELION BITTERS, Square – Amber – 7 7/8" & 9¼"	$ 50.00- 60.00
647.	DR. BELL'S BLOOD PURIFYING BITTERS, Rectangular Amber – 9½" high.	$ 25.00- 60.00
648.	DR. BELL'S COCKTAIL BITTERS, Round – Light Amber 11" high.	$ 50.00- 85.00
649.	BENGAL BITTERS, Square – Amber – 8 5/8".	$ 40.00- 80.00
650.	BENNET'S WILD CHERRY BITTERS, Square – Amber – 9"	$ 40.00-100.00
651.	BENNET'S CELEBRATED STOMACH BITTERS, Square Amber – 9"	$ 40.00- 60.00
652.	BERLINER MAGEN BITTERS, Square – Amber – 9 1/8".	$ 30.00- 60.00
653.	BERRY BITTERS, Rectangular – Aqua & clear – 8"	$ 20.00- 40.00
654.	BERRING BITTERS, Brown – 9½	$ 5.00- 10.00
655.	BEST BITTERS IN AMERICA, Square – Amber – 10" & under.	$ 80.00-110.00
656.	BIG BILL BEST BITTERS, Square – Amber – 12".	$ 60.00-150.00
657.	BISHOP'S WAHOO BITTERS, Rectangular – Amber – 10"	$ 80.00-100.00
658.	BITTERS, Aqua – 8½".	$ 10.00- 20.00
659.	BITTERS, Ladies leg – Emerald Green – 12½".	$ 25.00- 50.00
660.	BITTERS, Dark green – 10½".	$ 20.00- 40.00
661.	BITTERS, PLAIN LABEL, – Amber – 7¾".	$ 6.00- 10.00
662.	BITTERS LABEL, – Amber – Ladies leg – 12".	$ 35.00- 60.00

663   671   692 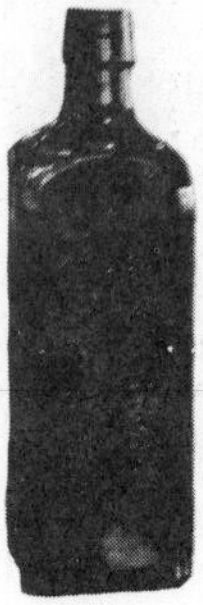   703

663.	B & L INVIGORATIO BITTERS, Clear – 11″	$ 10.00- 20.00
664.	BOERHAVE'S HOLLAND BITTERS, Rectangular – Bluish aqua – 8″.	$ 40.00- 60.00
665.	BOERHAVE'S STOMACH BITTERS, Square – Amber – 8 7/8″.	$ 40.00- 60.00
666.	BONEKAMP BITTERS, Round – Amber – 12¼″.	$ 5.00- 20.00
667.	BONESET BITTERS, Round – Aqua – 9½″	$ 40.00- 50.00
668.	BOTANIC STOMACH BITTERS, Square – Amber – 9″..	$ 40.00- 80.00
669.	BOURBON WHISKEY BITTERS, Barrel shaped – Amber 9¼″	$100.00-200.00
670.	BOUVIER BUCHU BITTERS, Square – Clear – 10½″....	$ 8.00- 20.00
671.	DR. BOYCE'S TONIC BITTERS, Aqua – 7½″.	$ 15.00- 30.00
672.	BRADY'S FAMILY BITTERS, Square – Black glass, 9 7/8″.	$ 40.00- 60.00
673.	BRAZILIAN AROMATIC STOMACH BITTERS, Round – Amber – 11″ to 11½″.	$ 25.00- 50.00
674.	BROWN'S AROMATIC BITTERS, Oval – Aqua – 8″.	$ 40.00- 60.00
675.	BROWN'S CELEBRATED INDIAN HERB BITTERS, Patented 1867 & 1868 – Amber – 12″	$200.00-250.00
676.	BROWN'S IRON BITTERS, Square-paneled – Amber – 8½″.	$ 10.00- 18.00
677.	BROWN'S IRON BITTERS, (on side panel) – Square – Amber – 8½″ high.	$ 10.00- 18.00
678.	BULL'S (JOHN) CEDRON BITTERS, Square – 10″.	$ 55.00-100.00
679.	BULL'S (DR.) STOMACH BITTERS, Square – 9″ – Clear.	$ 10.00- 18.00
680.	BULL'S WILD CHERRY BITTERS, Rectangular – Clear – 8½″.	$ 60.00- 80.00
681.	BURDOCK BLOOD BITTERS, Rectangular – Aqua – 8¼″.	$ 12.00- 18.00
682.	BURDOCK BLOOD BITTERS, Aqua – 7½″.	$ 8.00- 20.00
683.	BURNHAM'S TIMBER BITTERS, Rectangular – Amber With label contents & box.	$ 25.00- 40.00
684.	CALDWELL'S HERB BITTERS, Triangular – Different colors of amber – 12½″.	$100.00-200.00
685.	CALIFORNIA FIG BITTERS, Square – Amber – 9½.	$ 60.00- 70.00
686.	CALIFORNIA WINE BITTERS, Round – Green – 12″.	$ 80.00-120.00
687.	CAMIANA BITTERS, Aqua – 12″.	$ 25.00- 40.00
688.	CAMPBELL'S SCOTCH BITTERS, Amber – 6¼″.	$ 50.00- 60.00
689.	CANTON BITTERS, Round – Amber – 11 7/8″.	$ 75.00-150.00
690.	CARACAS BITTERS, Round – Dark green – 8¼″.	$ 25.00- 30.00
691.	CARMELITER STOMACH BITTERS CO., Square – Amber – 9¼″.	$ 35.00- 50.00
692.	CARONI BITTERS, Round – Black glass – 8″.	$ 12.00- 25.00
693.	CARTER'S LIVER BITTERS, Oval – Dark amber – 8½″..	$ 40.00- 80.00
694.	CASCARA BITTERS, Square – Amber – 9½″.	$ 10.00- 30.00

74

695.	CASSIN'S GRAPE BRANDY BITTERS, Rectangular – Aqua – 8¼"..........................	$ 75.00-100.00
696.	CELEBRATED CROWN BITTERS, Amber............	$ 60.00- 80.00
697.	CELERY TONIC BITTERS, (labeled only), Clear – 9"....	$ 8.00- 15.00
698.	CLARK'S CHERRY WINE BITTERS, Rectangular – Aqua – 8"............................	$ 10.00- 20.00
699.	CLARKE'S VEGETABLE SHERRY WINE BITTERS, Rec. Aqua – 14½"............................	$ 30.00- 40.00
700.	CLIMAX BITTERS, Square – Amber – 9½"............	$ 40.00- 80.00
701.	CLOVER BITTERS, (labeled only), Rectangular – Aqua – 10"...................................	$ 8.00- 20.00
702.	COLLECTION BITTERS, Rectangular – Aqua – 6 5/8"....	$ 10.00- 25.00
703.	COLUMBO PEPTIC BITTERS, Amber – 9½............	$ 25.00- 30.00

710   719   720   727

704.	CONSTITUTION BITTERS, Rectangular – Light amber – 9½".................................	$ 50.00-100.00
705.	CUNDURANGO (MAGUIRE'S) BITTERS, (labeled only) – Round – Amber – 9"........................	$ 8.00- 15.00
706.	CURTIS & PERKINS WILD CHERRY BITTERS, Round – Aqua – 7".............................	$ 50.00- 70.00
707.	DAMIANA BITTERS, Aqua – 11½".................	$ 20.00- 40.00
708.	DEWITT'S STOMACH BITTERS, (labeled only), Square Amber – 8" high........................	$ 10.00- 15.00
709.	DONNELL'S INDIAN ROOT BITTERS, (labeled only), Rectangular – Amber – 9 1/8"................	$ 10.00- 18.00
710.	DOYLES HOP BITTERS, (5 leaf), Amber – 9½".......	$ 40.00- 80.00
711.	DOYLES HOP BITTERS, Amber – 11¼"..............	$ 20.00- 30.00
712.	DOYLES HOP BITTERS, Square paneled – Amber – 9½"...................................	$ 20.00- 40.00
713.	DRAKE'S 1860 PLANTATION BITTERS, Square – Amber & other colors. – 10"...................	$ 50.00-100.00
714.	EAGLE AROMATIC BITTERS, Amber – 7" to 8"........	$ 15.00- 30.00
715.	EASTMAN'S YELLOW DOCK BITTERS, Rectangular – Aqua – 8" and under.....................	$ 40.00- 80.00
716.	EJB (ON BOTTOM), Amber – 9"...................	$ 4.00- 8.00
717.	EJB, Brown – 9 1/8".........................	$ 4.00- 8.00
718.	ELECTRIC BRAND BITTERS, Square – Amber – 9¾"...	$ 10.00- 20.00
719.	ELECTRIC BRAND BITTERS, Ten inches high – Amber.	$ 15.00-23.00
720.	ELECTRIC BRAND BITTERS, H.E. Bucklen & Co. – Amber – 10" high........................	$ 10.00- 20.00
721.	ENGLISH FEMALE BITTERS, Rectangular – Clear & light aqua – 8 1/8" high....................	$ 50.00- 70.00
722.	EXCELSIOR HERB BITTERS, Rectangular – Amber – 10"....................................	$ 80.00-100.00
723.	EXCELSIOR BITTERS, Amber.....................	$ 80.00- 90.00

724.	FENNER'S CAPITOL BITTERS, Rectangular – Aqua – 10 3/8".	$ 25.00-	40.00
725.	FER-KINO GALENO, Brown – 10 1/8".	$ 8.00-	16.00
726.	FERRO-CHINA BISLERI, Round – Green – 9¾".	$ 8.00-	20.00
727.	FERRO-CHINA BISLERI, Round – Amber – 9¾". (labeled).	$ 9.00-	20.00
728.	FERRO QUINA STOMACH BITTERS, Square – Amber – 9".	$ 40.00-	80.00
729.	FISCH'S (DR.) BITTERS, Shaped like fish-11½" Amber.	$125.00-	150.00
730.	FISH BITTERS, Fish shape – Amber – 11½".	$100.00-	150.00
731.	FLINTS (DR.) QUAKER BITTERS, Rectangular – Aqua – 9½" high.	$ 15.00-	35.00
732.	FLANDER'S BITTERS, Square – Amber – 8¾".	$ 30.00-	40.00
733.	FOREST'S (DR.) TONIC BITTERS, Square – Amber.	$ 10.00-	30.00

734    757 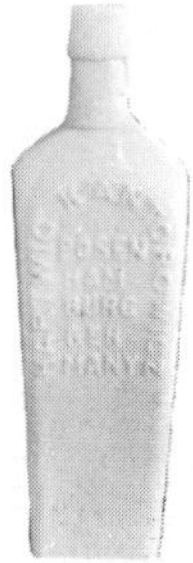   758    762

734.	FRATELLI BARANCA MILANO, Round – Light green – 13½".	$ 10.00-	20.00
735.	FRAZIER'S ROOT BITTERS, Rectangular – Amber – 7".	$ 10.00-	40.00
736.	GARTER'S WILD CHERRY BITTERS, Amber – 7½".	$ 20.00-	30.00
737.	GERMAN TONIC BITTERS, Square – Aqua – 9 5/8".	$ 40.00-	70.00
738.	GLOBE BITTERS, Round – Amber – 11".	$ 40.00-	60.00
739.	GOFF'S HERB BITTERS, Rectangular – Aqua – 5½".	$ 8.00-	15.00
740.	GOLD LION CELERY BITTERS, (Labeled only) – Round Clear ½ pt. size.	$ 8.00-	20.00
741.	GOLF'S BITTERS, Rectangular – Clear – 5½".	$ 8.00-	15.00
742.	GOSTETTER'S STOMACH BITTERS, Square – Green – 9".	$ 10.00-	20.00
743.	GRAND PRIZE BITTERS, Square – Amber – 9".	$ 50.00-	75.00
744.	GRANGER BITTERS, (Labeled only) – Amber – 7 5/8".	$ 10.00-	25.00
745.	GREELEY'S BOURBON BITTERS, Barrel shaped, 10 ribs top and bottom. Various colors of amber & a brownish purple 9" high.	$100.00-	150.00
746.	GREER'S ECLIPSE BITTERS, Square – Amber – 8¾".	$ 50.00-	100.00
747.	HAGAN'S BITTERS, Triangular – Amber – 9½	$ 30.00-	60.00
748.	HALL'S BITTERS, Barrel shaped with 7 ribs top & bottom. Amber – 9¼".	$100.00-	200.00
749.	HALL'S (DR. THOS.) CALIFORNIA PEPSIN WINE BITTERS, Square – Amber – 9".	$ 60.00-	100.00
750.	HAMILTON'S GERMAN BITTERS, (Labeled only) – Rec. Aqua – 6½" high.	$ 8.00-	20.00
751.	HANLAN'S TUNA BITTERS, Round – Clear – 9 1/8".	$ 15.00-	30.00
752.	HARDY'S JAUNDICE BITTERS, Rectangular – Clear – 7".	$ 50.00-	60.00
753.	HARTER'S WILD CHERRY BITTERS, Rectangular – Amber – 7¾" and 4¾" high.	$ 20.00-	40.00
754.	HART'S STAR BITTERS, Oval – Clear – 9".	$ 25.00-	75.00

755.	HART'S VIRGINIA AROMATIC BITTERS, Rectangular 7 5/8" high.	$ 40.00- 80.00
756.	HARTSHORN'S (DR.) JAUNDICE BITTERS, Oval – Aqua 9 5/8" high. With label.	$ 20.00- 40.00
757.	HARTWIG KANTOROWICZ, Nachfolger, Berlin – Rectangular – Bright amber – 10".	$ 40.00- 80.00
758.	HARTWIG KANTOROWICZ, Posen hamburg, Germany Milk glass – 9½" high.	$ 60.00- 85.00
759.	HENLEY'S (DR.) WILD CHERRY ROOT BITTERS, Olive & Aqua – 11½" high.	$ 50.00- 70.00
760.	HENLEY'S (DR.) WILD GRAPE ROOT BITTERS, Aqua – 12¼".	$ 35.00- 60.00
761.	HENTZ CURATIVE BITTERS, Square – ¾ quart.	$ 40.00- 60.00
762.	HERB BITTERS, S.B. Caff's – Aqua – 5½".	$ 10.00- 20.00

780 786 799 807

763.	HERB WILD CHERRY BITTERS, Tall with wild cherry tree on all 4 shoulders – Amber – 8¾".	$ 50.00-110.00
764.	HIBERNIA BITTERS, Square – Amber – 10".	$ 40.00- 60.00
765.	HIERAPICRA BITTERS, Rectangular – Aqua – 9 3/8".	$ 60.00- 80.00
766.	HIGBY TONIC BITTERS, Square – Amber – 9 3/8".	$ 15.00- 30.00
767.	HI HI BITTERS, Three sided – Amber – 9 5/8".	$ 40.00- 75.00
768.	HILL'S MOUNTAIN BITTERS, (Labeled only) – Rectangular – Amber – 8".	$ 8.00- 15.00
769.	HOLTZERMANN'S PATENT STOMACH BITTERS, Cabin rec. – Amber – 9½" high.	$100.00-160.00
770.	HOFFMANN'S CELEBRATED STOMACH BITTERS, Square – Amber – 10" high.	$ 40.00- 80.00
771.	HOME BITTERS, Square – Dark amber – 9".	$ 50.00- 75.00
772.	HOMER'S GINGER BRANDY, (Labeled only) – Round – Amber – ¾ quart.	$ 8.00- 10.00
773.	HOOFLAND'S GERMAN BITTERS, Rectangular – Aqua 8".	$ 30.00- 60.00
774.	HOP & MALT BITTERS, Square – Amber – 9½".	$ 50.00-100.00
775.	HOPKINS UNION STOMACH BITTERS, Square – Amber – 9½".	$ 20.00- 40.00
776.	HOSTETTER'S STOMACH BITTERS, Square – Amber – 8¾".	$ 10.00- 18.00
777.	HOSTETTER'S STOMACH BITTERS, On front panel – 18 fluid oz. on back panel – Square – Amber – 8¾".	$ 9.00- 15.00
778.	HOSTETTER'S STOMACH BITTERS, Square – Amber – 9".	$ 4.00- 8.00
779.	HOSTETTER'S STOMACH BITTERS, On front panel – Amber – 9" high.	$ 9.00- 15.00
780.	HOSTETTER'S STOMACH BITTERS, Amber – 8½".	$ 8.00- 18.00
781.	HUNTIOGTON'S GOLDEN TONIC BITTERS, Square – Amber – 9½".	$ 50.00- 70.00

77

782.	HUTCHING'S DRSPEPSIA BITTERS, Rectangular – Aqua – 8½″.	$ 60.00- 80.00
783.	IMPERIAL KIDNEY LIVER, NERVE, BLOOD & STOMACH BITTERS, Square – Amber – 9¾″.	$ 60.00- 80.00
784.	INDIAN VEGETABLE & SARSAPARILLA BITTERS, Rectangle – Aqua – 8¼″ high.	$ 60.00-100.00
785.	IRON BITTERS, Square – Amber – 8½″.	$ 15.00- 28.00
786.	ITALIAN BITTERS, Olive green – 12″.	$ 15.00- 22.00
787.	JACKSON'S AROMATIC LIFE BITTERS, Rectangular – Green – 9″ high.	$ 50.00- 80.00
788.	JACOB'S CABIN TONIC BITTERS, Rectangular – Cabin Clear – light amethyst, "pinkish" – 7½″.	$100.00-200.00
789.	JEVNE BITTERS, Round – Amber – 1/5th.	$ 30.00- 40.00
790.	JEVNE WINE BITTERS, Round – Clear.	$ 10.00- 20.00
791.	JEWEL BITTERS, Rectangular – Amber – 9¼″.	$ 65.00-100.00
792.	JOCKEY CLUB BITTERS, Square – light green – 10 3/8″.	$ 22.00- 30.00
793.	JOHNSON CALISAYA BITTERS, Square – Amber – 10″.	$ 20.00- 50.00
794.	JOHNSON'S INDIAN DYSEPTIC BITTERS, Rectangular Aqua – 6½″ high.	$ 60.00- 80.00
795.	JONES INDIAN HERB BITTERS, Square – Amber – 9″.	$ 50.00- 60.00
796.	JONES' UNIVERSAL STOMACH BITTERS, Square – Amber – 9″.	$ 70.00- 80.00
797.	KAUFMANN'S SULPHUR BITTERS, Aqua – 8¼″.	$ 10.00- 30.00
798.	KELLY'S OLD CABIN BITTERS, Rectangular cabin – Amber – 9½″.	$200.00-300.00
799.	KENNEDY'S EAST INDIA BITTERS, Clear – 9″.	$ 20.00- 40.00
800.	KEYSTONE BITTERS, Barrel shaped – Clear & amber – 10″.	$ 50.00- 80.00
801.	KIMBALL'S JAUNDICE BITTERS, Rectangular – Amber 7″.	$ 75.00-100.00
802.	KIEL STOMACH BITTERS, Light green – 12½″.	$ 15.00- 30.00
803.	KIMM'S PREMIUM AROMATIC BITTERS, Round – Amber – 7″.	$ 30.00- 40.00
804.	KING SOLOMON BITTERS, Rectangular – Light amber 8½″ and 10½″.	$ 50.00- 80.00
805.	KINKLES BITTER WINE OF IRON, Rectangular – Aqua 7½″.	$ 30.00- 40.00
806.	LACOUR'S BITTERS, Round – Amber & green – 9″.	$ 20.00- 50.00
807.	LADIES LEG BITTERS, Amber – 12″.	$ 20.00- 30.00

808    834    875    882

808.	LADIES LEG BITTERS, SHORT, Amber – 9″.	$ 20.00- 40.00
809.	LAN & FOX STOMACH BITTERS, (Labeled only) – Amber – 8¾″ high.	$ 8.00- 10.00
810.	LANGLEY'S MORNING STAR BITTERS, Three sided – Amber – 12¾″.	$ 75.00-100.00
811.	LANCLEY'S ROOT & HERB BITTERS, Aqua – 6¾″.	$ 20.00- 50.00

812.	LANGLEY'S ROOT & HERB BITTERS, Aqua – 8¾". ...	$ 20.00- 60.00
813.	LASH'S BITTERS, Amber – 11".....................	$ 10.00- 18.00
814.	LASH'S BITTERS, Clear – 11¼ "....................	$ 8.00- 10.00
815.	LASH'S BITTERS, Round – Amethyst – 10 2/3".......	$ 8.00- 10.00
816.	LASH'S BITTERS, Amber – 11½".....................	$ 8.00- 20.00
817.	LASH'S BITTERS, Square – Amber – 9¼"..............	$ 5.00- 15.00
818.	LASH'S BITTERS, Round – Amber – 11¼ "............	$ 9.00- 12.00
819.	LASH'S BITTERS, Oldest bariant – Amber............	$ 20.00- 30.00
820.	LASH'S BITTERS, (SAMPLE) – Square – Amber – 4¼ "..	$ 30.00- 50.00
821.	LASH'S BITTERS, NATURAL STOMACH LAXATIVE – Square – Amber – 9½ " high........................	$ 10.00- 20.00
822.	LASH'S BITTERS, NATURAL TONIC LAXATIVE – Amber – 9½ "..	$ 10.00- 15.00
823.	LASH'S KIDNEY & LIVER BITTERS, Square – Amber – 9"..	$ 6.00- 12.00
824.	LASH'S KIDNEY & LIVER BITTERS, Square – Amber – 8¾ "...	$ 10.00- 15.00
825.	LEDIARD'S CELEBRATED STOMACH BITTERS, Square – Bluish green 10" high....................	$ 40.00- 80.00
826.	LIEB'S BITTERS, with contents – No description.	$ 6.00- 12.00
827.	LIFE OF MAN BITTERS, Rectangular – Aqua – 8"......	$ 30.00- 50.00
828.	LIPPMAN'S GREAT GERMAN BITTERS, Square – Amber – 10"......................................	$100.00-125.00
829.	LOEW'S CELEBRATED STOMACH BITTERS, Square – Green – 9½ "...	$ 50.00-100.00
830.	LORIMER JUNIPER BITTERS, Blue-green – 9½ " & 2¼ "...	$ 30.00- 40.00
831.	LUTZ'S GERMAN STOMACH BITTERS, Rectangular – Amber – 7 7/8"......................................	$ 15.00- 30.00
832.	LYON'S STOMACH BITTERS, Round ladies leg, Amber, 11"..	$ 60.00- 70.00
833.	MARSHALL'S BITTERS, THE BEST LAXATIVE & BLOOD PURIFIER – Square – Amber8½ ".	$ 25.00- 50.00
834.	MAYR'S WONDERFUL STOMACH REMEDY, Purple – 6"..	$ 6.00- 9.00
835.	MCCLINTOCK'S DANDELION BITTERS, Oval – Aqua – Pint...	$ 40.00- 60.00
836.	MACK'S SARSAPARILLA BITTERS, Rectangular – Amber – 9¼ "......................................	$ 25.00- 50.00
837.	MALT BITTERS, Round, Different colors of green, 8¼ ".	$ 30.00- 40.00
838.	MAMPE'S HERB STOMACH BITTERS, Rectangular – Aqua – 7"...	$ 40.00- 80.00
839.	MILE'S TONIC BITTERS, Rectangular – Aqua – 7½"...	$ 10.00- 15.00
840.	MISHLER'S HERB BITTERS, Square – Amber – 8¾ ".,..	$ 40.00- 60.00
841.	MOFFAT'S PHOENIX BITTERS, Rectangular Aqua, Clear & Amber 5 3/8" to 6".......................	$ 30.00- 50.00
842.	MOHICA BITTERS, Square – Amber – 9".............	$ 30.00- 40.00
843.	MOUNTAIN HERB & ROOT BITTERS, Square – Amber, Over 9"...	$ 40.00- 80.00
844.	MOUNTAIN ROOT BITTERS, No description available..	$ 12.00- 20.00
845.	MOWE'S VEGETABLE BITTERS, Rectangular – Aqua – 10"...	$ 50.00- 60.00
846.	NATIONAL BITTERS, Shaped like and ear of corn – Amber – 12¼ " high...............................	$150.00-200.00
847.	NEWTON'S JAUNDICE BITTERS, Rectangular – Aqua – 6 7/8"...	$ 40.00- 50.00
848.	NEW YORK HOP BITTERS, Square – Aqua – 9 3/8"....	$ 40.00- 80.00
849.	NIAGARA STAR BITTERS, Square – Amber – 9 3/8"....	$ 50.00-100.00
850.	NIBOL KIDNEY & LIVER BITTERS, Amber – 9"........	$ 45.00- 60.00
851.	NIGHT CAP BITTERS, Three-sided – Clear – 9¼ ",.....	$ 75.00-100.00
852.	OLD HICKORY BITTERS, Square – Amber – 8¾ "......	$ 75.00-125.00
853.	OLD HOME BITTERS, Tall cabin shaped – Amber – 9¾ " high..	$ 50.00-125.00
854.	OLD HOMESTEAD WILD CHERRY BITTERS, Amber – 9½ "...	$100.00-150.00
855.	OLD SACHEM BITTERS, & WIGWAM TONIC, Barrel-shaped – Amber – 9½ " high.	$ 90.00-150.00
856.	OREGON GRAPE ROOT BITTERS. Round – Clear10". .	$ 40.00- 50.00

857.	ORIZABA BITTERS, Brown – 8½".	$ 40.00- 80.00
858.	ORRURO BITTERS, Green – 10½".	$ 12.00- 20.00
859.	OSWEGO BITTERS, (Labeled only) – Oval – Amber – 7".	$ 10.00- 22.00
860.	OXYGENATED BITTERS, Rectangular – Aqua – 6" & 7½".	$ 50.00- 80.00
861.	PALE ORANGE BITTERS, (Labeled only) – Round – Green – 11" & 12" high.	$ 10.00- 20.00
862.	PARKER'S CELEBRATED STOMACH BITTERS, Square Amber – 9¼" high.	$ 75.00- 85.00
863.	PARMLEE'S HOP IRON & BUCHU BITTERS, Square – Amber – 8".	$ 22.00- 50.00
864.	PEPPER'S LAXATIVE BITTERS, Square – Amber – 11".	$ 11.00- 20.00
865.	PEPSIN BITTERS, (GOLDEN GATE) – Rectangular – 9".	$ 25.00- 50.00
866.	PEPSIN BITTERS, (DAVIS) – Rectangular, light green, 8".	$ 60.00- 90.00
867.	PEPSIN MAGEN BITTERS, (Labeled only) – Round – Clear – 10" high.	$ 10.00- 20.00
868.	PEPSIN CALISAYA BITTERS, Rectangular – Clear & green – 7½" high.	$ 40.00- 60.00
869.	PE-RU-NA BITTERS, Round – Aqua – 9".	$ 20.00- 50.00
870.	PERUVIAN BITTERS, Dark brown – 9".	$ 22.00- 50.00
871.	PERUVIAN BITTERS, Square – Amber – 9".	$ 20.00- 50.00
872.	PERUVIAN KING BITTERS, Triangular – Amber – 10½".	$ 20.00- 50.00
873.	PERUVIAN TONIC BITTERS, Rectangular – Amber – 10¼".	$ 35.00- 75.00
874.	PETZOLD'S GENUINE GERMAN BITTERS, Oval cabin – Dark & light amber – 10¼".	$ 80.00-125.00
875.	PEYCHAUD'S AMERICAN AROMATIC BITTER CORDIAL, Round – Amber – 10 3/8".	$ 20.00- 30.00
876.	PHOENIX BITTERS, Rectangular – Aqua – 6"."	$ 40.00- 50.00
877.	PIERCE'S INDIAN RESTORATIVE BITTERS, Rectangular – Aqua – 7½" high.	$ 30.00- 60.00
878.	PIPIFAX CELEBRATED BITTERS, (Labeled only) – SquareAmber – 9".	$ 10.00- 25.00
879.	PLAIN BITTERS (Labeled only) – Gold – 9½".	$ 15.00- 25.00
880.	PLAIN BITTERS, Amber – 8¾".	$ 3.00- 6.00
881.	PLAIN BITTERS, Amber – 11½".	$ 3.00- 6.00
882.	PLANTATION BITTERS, Amber – 10".	$ 50.00-100.00

890

892

905

932

883.	POCAHONTAS (ORIGINAL) BITTERS, Barrel-shaped – Aqua – 9 3/8" high.	$ 60.00-100.00
884.	POLAND BITTERS, Round – Green – ¾ qt. – (Labeled).	$ 15.00- 40.00
885.	POLAND WINE BITTERS, (Labeled only) – Round – ¾ qt. – Green.	$ 10.00- 30.00
886.	POLP CLUB STOMACH BITTERS, Square – Amber – 9".	$ 65.00-100.00

887.	POND'S BITTERS, Square – Clear – 9¾".	$ 30.00- 50.00
888.	POND'S KIDNEY & LIVER BITTERS, Square – Amber – 9½".	$ 40.00- 50.00
889.	POOR MAN'S FAMILY BITTERS, Faint emblem – Rectangle – Aqua – 9 ¾" high.	$ 25.00- 50.00
890.	POOR MAN'S FAMILY BITTERS, Rectangular – Aqua – 6¼".	$ 18.00- 40.00
891.	PORTER'S MEDICATED STOMACH BITTERS, (Labeled only) – Rectangular – Clear & aqua – 5 5/8".	$ 10.00- 20.00
892.	PRICKLEY ASH BITTERS, Square – Amber – 10".	$ 35.00- 65.00
893.	PRIMLEY'S IRON & WAHOO TONIC BITTERS, Square Amber – 9" high.	$ 10.00- 25.00
894.	PRICKLY ASH BITTERS, Amber – 9½".	$ 20.00- 40.00
895.	PRUNE STOMACH & LIVER BITTERS, Ambers – 9". . . .	$ 20.00- 35.00
896.	PRUSSIAN BITTERS, Square – Amber – 8½".	$ 55.00- 75.00
897.	PULLNA BITTERS – No description.	$ 25.00- 40.00
898.	PURDY'S COTTAGE BITTERS, Rectangular – Amber – 9".	$ 90.00-100.00
899.	QUELLEN BITTERS, (Labeled only) – Olive green.	$ 8.00- 10.00
900.	QUININE BITTERS, Square – Amber.	$ 20.00- 50.00
901.	RADIUM BITTERS, Rectangular – Clear – 10".	$ 10.00- 40.00
902.	RAMSEY'S TRINIDAD BITTERS, Round – Green – 8". . .	$ 50.00- 60.00
903.	RANCHE BITTERS, Square – Light amber – 8 7/8".	$ 20.00- 40.00
904.	RATTINGER'S HERB & ROOT BITTERS, Square – Amber – 9".	$ 85.00-100.00
905.	(RED JACKET BITTERS) – Embossed Bennett & Pieters Co. - Square – Amber – 9½".	$ 50.00- 60.00
906.	RED CROSS LAXATIVE BITTERS, (Labeled only) – Round – flask shaped – Amber – Pt.	$ 8.00- 10.00
907.	RED JACKET BITTERS, (LEWIS) – Round – Amber – 11".	$ 40.00- 60.00
908.	RENZ'S HERB BITTERS, Square – Green & Amber – 10".	$ 75.00-100.00
909.	REED'S BITTERS, Round – Amber – 12½".	$125.00-150.00
910.	REX BITTERS, Round – Amber – 11".	$ 20.00- 30.00
911.	REX KIDNEY & LIVER BITTERS, Square – Amber – 10".	$ 30.00- 40.00
912.	"DRINK REX BITTERS", Round, heavy fluted neck with stopper.	$ 40.00- 60.00
913.	RICHARD'S WINE BITTERS, Square – Amber – 9½". . .	$ 20.00- 30.00
914.	RICHARDSON'S RENOWNED MEDICINAL BITTERS, (Labeled only) – Square – Amber – 9".	$ 8.00- 15.00
915.	RICHARDSON'S, S.O. BITTERS, Rectangular – Aqua – 6¾".	$ 20.00- 40.00
916.	RICHARDSON'S, W.L. BITTERS, Rectangular – Aqua – 7".	$ 40.00- 50.00
917.	RISING SUN BITTERS, Square – Amber – 9½".	$ 40.00- 60.00
918.	RIVAUD'S COCKTAIL BITTERS, Octagonal – Amber – 13".	$ 60.00-100.00
919.	RIVENBURG'S INDIAN VEGETABLE BITTERS, Rectangular – Aqua – 8 5/8".	$ 60.00- 90.00
920.	ROBACK'S STOMACH BITTERS, Barrel-shaped with 6 ribs top & bottom – Amber – 9¼".	$100.00-150.00
921.	ROBACK'S STOMACH BITTERS, Barrel-shaped with 10 ribs top & bottom – Dark brown – 9¾".	$100.00-150.00
922.	ROCKY MOUNTAIN TONIC BITTERS, Square – Amber 9¾".	$ 60.00- 80.00
923.	ROMAINES CRIMEAN BITTERS, Square – Amber – 10".	$ 60.00- 80.00
924.	ROMANY WINE BITTERS, Rectangular – Aqua – 6½". .	$ 50.00- 70.00
925.	ROOT'S (JOHN) BITTERS, Rectangular – Aqua & Amber 10" high.	$ 60.00- 75.00
926.	ROSE'S MAGADOR BITTERS, Square – Amber – 9½". .	$ 50.00- 75.00
927.	ROYAL PEPSIN STOMACH BITTERS, Rectangular – Amber – 9".	$ 60.00-100.00

928.	ROYAL ITALIAN BITTERS, Round – Amber – 13½″. . . .	$ 75.00-100.00
929.	ROYCE'S SHERRYWINE BITTERS, Rectangular – Aqua 8″.	$ 40.00- 55.00
930.	RUSH'S BITTERS, Square – Amber – 9″.	$ 25.00- 50.00
931.	RUSS' ST. DOMINGO BITTERS, Square – Amber – 10″.	$ 40.00- 60.00
932.	RUSSELL MEDICAL CO. PEPSIN CALISAYA BITTERS, Rectangular – Green – 8″.	$ 30.00- 60.00

938   939   940   958   959

933.	RYDER'S CLOVER BITTERS, Rectangular – Amber – 7¼.	$ 30.00- 60.00
934.	ST. DRAKES PLANTATION BITTERS, 5 log cabin – Amber – 9¾″ high.	$ 40.00- 60.00
935.	ST. DRAKES PLANTATION BITTERS, 6 log cabin – Amber – 10″ high.	$ 50.00- 85.00
936.	ST. DRAKES PLANTATION BITTERS, 6 log cabin – Brownish purple – 10″.	$ 50.00- 85.00
937.	ST. DRAKES PLANTATION BITTERS, 4 log cabin – Amber – 10″ high.	$ 60.00- 80.00
938.	ST. JACOB'S BITTERS, Amber – 8½″.	$ 40.00- 60.00
939.	SANLEHNER BITTERS, Emerald green – 9½″.	$ 15.00- 30.00
940.	SARRACENIA LIFE BITTERS, Honey amber & reddish amber – 9½″ high.	$ 50.00- 80.00
941.	SARRACENIA BITTERS, (DR. HUTCHISON'S) – Square blue – 9″ high.	$ 65.00- 90.00
942.	SARASINA STOMACH BITTERS, Square – Amber – 9 1/8″.	$ 50.00- 80.00
943.	SAWENS LIFE INVIGORATING BITTERS, Square – Amber – 10″.	$ 30.00- 50.00
944.	SAZERAC AROMATIC BITTERS, Round lady's leg – Milk white – 12″ high.	$ 75.00-125.00
945.	S.B.H. & CO. (DR.) – Round – Aqua – 9¼″.	$ 4.00- 8.00
946.	S.B.H. & CO. (DR.) – Round – Clear – 9¼″.	$ 6.00- 10.00
947.	S.B.H. & CO. (DR.) – Round – Amethyst – 9¼″.	$ 6.00- 10.00
948.	SCHEETZ'S CELEBRATED BITTERS, CORDIAL, Rectangular – Amber – Pt.	$ 30.00- 60.00
949.	SCHROEDER'S BITTERS, Lady's leg – 9″ 12″.	$100.00-200.00
950.	SCOTT'S NEW YORK ARTILLERY BITTERS, Shaped like a cannon. Amber – 13″.	$300.00-400.00
951.	SEAWORTH BITTERS, Shaped like a lighthouse. Amber – 11½″ high.	$250.00-300.00
952.	SEGUR'S GOLDEN SEAL BITTERS, Rectangular – Aqua – 8″.	$ 55.00- 65.00
953.	SEVERA STOMACH BITTERS, Square – Amber – 9¾″..	$ 25.00- 35.00
954.	SHARP'S MOUNTAIN HERB BITTERS, Square – Amber 9½″.	$ 55.00- 80.00
955.	SHURTLEFF'S BLOOD & DYSPEPSIA BITTERS, Oval – Clear – 9¼″ high.	$ 30.00- 40.00

956.	SIEGERT & HIJOS (DR. J.G.B) – Green – 8 1/8″.	$ 4.00- 10.00
957.	SIEGERT & SONS (DR. J.G.B.) – Round – Green.	$ 4.00- 10.00
958.	SIEGERT & SONS (DR. J.G.B.) – Aqua & amethyst – 9″.	$ 4.00- 10.00
959.	SIEGERT & SONS (DR. J.G.B.) – Emerald green – 8″. ...	$ 6.00- 10.00
960.	SIEGERT & SONS (DR. J.G.B.) – Round – Green – 5″. ...	$ 4.00- 10.00
961.	SIMON'S CENTENNIAL BITTERS, Figural bust – Aqua & clear – 10 1/8″.	$200.00-300.00
962.	SIM'S ANTI-CONSTIPATION BITTERS, Square – Amber Pint	$ 40.00- 50.00
963.	SKINNER'S CELEBRATED BITTERS, Rectangular – Aqua – 9½″.	$ 50.00- 75.00
964.	SKINNER'S SHERRY WINE BITTERS, Rectangular – Aqua – 8½″ high.	$ 60.00- 80.00
965.	SMITH'S TONIC BITTERS, Square – Amber – 8¾″.	$ 40.00- 80.00
966.	SMITH'S OLD STYLE BITTERS, Square – Amber – 7 7/8″.	$ 40.00- 50.00
967.	SOLOMON'S GREAT INDIAN BITTERS, Rectangular – Aqua – 8½″ high.	$ 40.00- 50.00
968.	SOLOMON'S INDIAN WINE BITTERS, Rectangular – Aqua – 8½″ high.	$ 40.00- 60.00
969.	SOLOMON'S STRENGTHENING & INVIGORATING BITTERS, Square – Cobalt blue – 9 7/8″.	$ 85.00-200.00
970.	ST. GOTTHARD HERB BITTERS, Square – Amber – 9″..	$ 50.00- 60.00
971.	STAG BITTERS, (Labeled only) – Square – Amber – 9½″.	$ 4.00- 10.00
972.	STANLEY'S SOUTH AMERICAN INDIAN BITTERS, Square – Amber – 8 7/8″ high.	$ 60.00- 80.00
973.	STAR KIDNEY & LIVER BITTERS, Square – Amber – 9¼″.	$ 45.00- 60.00
974.	STAR ANCHOR BITTERS, Square – Amber – 9″.	$ 50.00- 75.00
975.	STEELE, JOHN W. NIAGARE (STAR) – Square – Amber 9¾″.	$ 40.00- 60.00
976.	STEINFELD'S FRENCH COGNAC BITTERS, Square – Amber – 10½″.	$ 60.00-100.00
977.	STEKETEE'S BLOOD PURIFYING BITTERS, Square – Amber – 6½″ high.	$ 50.00- 60.00
978.	STEWART'S TONIC BITTERS, Rectangular – Amber – 8″.	$ 50.00- 60.00
979.	STOCKTON'S PORT WINE BITTERS, Rectangular – Amber – 9″.	$ 80.00- 90.00
980.	STOEVER'S BITTERS, Square – Amber – 9″.	$ 40.00- 65.00
981.	STOCK'S H. & R. BITTERS, (Labeled only) – Amber – 9½″.	$ 6.00- 10.00
982.	STOUGHTON BITTERS, (Labeled only) – Round – Black.	$ 4.00- 10.00
983.	SUFFOLK BITTERS, Shaped like a pig – Amber – 9¾″..	$185.00-500.00
984.	SUMTER BITTERS, Amber – 9½″.	$ 20.00- 50.00
985.	SUN KIDNEY & LIVER BITTERS, Square – Amber – 9½″.	$ 35.00- 60.00
986.	SUNNY CASTLE STOMACH BITTERS, Square – Amber 9″.	$ 60.00- 75.00
987.	SWAIN'S BOURBON BITTERS, Square – Amber – 9″. ...	$ 60.00-100.00
988.	SWAN BITTERS, Square – Amber – 9½″.	$ 40.00- 80.00
989.	SWEET'S STRENGTHENING BITTERS, Square – Aqua 8½″.	$ 35.00- 50.00
990.	SWISS STOMACH BITTERS, Rectangular – Amber – 9″ & over.	$ 60.00- 70.00
991.	SYMOND'S ZULU BITTERS, Rectangular – Amber – 9″.	$ 40.00- 70.00
992.	TILTON'S COMPOUND DANDELION BITTERS, Round Amber – 10″ high.	$ 40.00- 70.00
993.	TIP TOP BITTERS, Round – Different shades of green – 8½″ high.	$ 20.00- 30.00
994.	TODD'S BITTERS, (Labeled only) – Clear.	$ 4.00- 8.00
995.	TOMPKIN'S VEGETABLE BITTERS, Rectangular – Aqua – 9″.	$ 30.00- 60.00
996.	TONECO STOMACH BITTERS, Square – Clear – 9″. ...	$ 40.00- 55.00
997.	TONECO BITTERS/APPETIZER & TONIC, Square – Aqua – Clear – Amethyst – 9½″.	$ 50.00- 60.00

998.	TONIC BITTERS, Square – Amber – 9¼"..............	$ 15.00- 30.00
999.	TO-NI-TA MUCOUS MEMBRANE BITTERS, Round – Amber – 9½" & 10" high.	$ 20.00- 60.00
1000.	TONOLA BITTERS, Square – Aqua – 8".	$ 30.00- 40.00
1001.	TOWNSEND'S CELEBRATED STOMACH BITTERS, Glass jug – Amber – 9"...........................	$ 60.00- 90.00
1002.	TRAVELER'S BITTERS, Rectangular & oval – Amber – 10½" high.	$100.00-200.00
1003.	TRINER'S AMERICAN ELIXIR OF BITTER WINE, Round	$ 10.00- 20.00
1004.	TRINER'S BITTER WINE, (Labeled only)	$ 2.00- 6.00
1005	TRINER'S ANGELICA BITTER WINE, partially emboss-ed.	$ 4.00- 7.00
1006.	TUFT'S TONIC BITTERS, Round – Aqua – ½ pt........	$ 10.00- 20.00
1007.	TURKISH BITTERS, Square – Amber – 9".............	$ 20.00- 50.00
1008.	TURNER BROTHERS BITTERS, Barrel-shaped – Amber 9".	$100.00-150.00
1009.	TYLER'S STANDARD AMERICAN BITTERS, Square – Amber – 9" high..............................	$ 65.00-100.00
1010.	TYREE'S CHAMOMILE BITTERS, Square – Amber – 9".	$ 40.00- 80.00
1011.	UNDERBERG BITTERS, (Labeled only) – Round lady's leg. Amber – 10" to 10½".....................	$ 35.00- 50.00
1012.	UNCLE TOM'S BITTERS, Square – Amber – 10".	$ 50.00- 70.00
1013.	U.S. GOLD BITTERS, Square – Aqua – 10".	$ 40.00- 80.00
1014.	USQUEBAUGH BITTERS, Square – Clear – 10"........	$ 20.00- 50.00
1015.	VAN DUNCK'S GENEVER COACHMAN, Shaped like a coachman holding a whip – Amber.	$125.00-200.00
1016.	VAN DYKE'S HOLLAND BITTERS, Clear – 7½".	$ 20.00- 30.00
1017.	VAN DYKE'S BITTERS, CO., Rectangular – Clear – 9½".	$ 35.00- 50.00
1018.	VERMO STOMACH BITTERS, Square – Clear – 9½". ..	$ 15.00- 25.00
1019.	VER-MUTH STOMACH BITTERS, Clear – 9¼".	$ 40.00- 60.00
1020.	VON HOPF'S CURACO BITTERS, Square – Amber – 9¼".	$ 40.00- 60.00
1021.	VON HOPF'S CURACOA TONIC BITTERS, Rectangular Amber – 8" high.	$ 40.00- 60.00
1022.	VON HUMBOLDT'S GERMAN BITTERS, Rectangular – Aqua – 6 5/8" high.	$ 60.00- 80.00
1023.	VON HUMBOLDT'S STOMACH BITTERS, Square – Amber – 10".	$ 75.00- 85.00
1024.	W.C. BITTERS, Round – Amber – 10½".	$ 40.00- 80.00
1025.	WAHOO BITTERS, Square – Amber, violet, green, 10".	$ 95.00-110.00
1026.	WAHOO & CALISAYA BITTERS, Square – Amber – 10".	$ 40.00- 70.00
1027.	WA-HOO BITTER WINE, Square – Clear – 8". (Labeled).	$ 8.00- 20.00
1028.	WAIT'S KIDNEY & LIVER BITTERS, Square – Amber – 9".	$ 40.00- 60.00
1029.	WAKEFIELD'S STRENGTHENING BITTERS, Rec-tangular – Aqua – 8 3/8" high.	$ 30.00- 40.00
1030.	WALKENSHAW'S CURATIVE BITTERS, Square – 10". .	$ 50.00- 70.00
1031.	WALKER'S V.B., 8½" high.........................	$ 8.00- 10.00
1032.	WALKER'S VINEGAR BITTERS, Aqua – 8¼".	$ 6.00- 10.00
1033.	WALKER'S WILD CHERRY BITTERS, Square – Clear – ¾ qt.	$ 10.00- 20.00
1034.	WALLACE TONIC BITTERS, Square – Amber – 9".	$ 40.00- 60.00
1035.	WAMPOO BITTERS, Square – Amber – 10".	$ 40.00- 70.00
1036.	WARD'S EUREKA TONIC BITTERS, Square – Clear – 8¾".	$ 20.00- 40.00
1037.	WARNER'S GERMAN HOP BITTERS, Square – Amber – 9½".	$ 50.00- 60.00
1038.	WARNER'S SAFE BITTERS, Oval – Amber – 9 5/8".....	$ 65.00-100.00
1039.	WARNER'S TIPPICANOE BITTERS, Amber – 8¾".	$ 85.00-100.00
1040.	WARREN'S QUAKER BITTERS, Rect. – Aqua – 9 3/8". ..	$ 80.00-100.00
1041.	WEBB IMPROVED STOMACH BITTERS, Square – Amber – 9".................................	$ 50.00- 75.00
1042.	WEBB'S OLD RYE BITTERS, Square – Amber – 9".	$ 40.00- 60.00

1043.	WEST INDIA STOMACH BITTERS, Square – Amber – 10".	$ 40.00- 60.00
1044.	WHEAT BITTERS, Rect. – Amber – 9½".	$ 60.00- 70.00
1045.	WHEELER'S BERLIN BITTERS, Six-sided – Green 9 3/8".	$ 60.00- 80.00
1046.	WHEELER'S SHERRY WINE BITTERS, Round – Clear – 8".	$ 40.00- 60.00
1047.	WHEELER'S GENUINE BITTERS, Oval – Aqua – 9".	$ 40.00- 50.00
1048.	WHITCOMB'S (FAITH) BITTERS, Rect. – Aqua – 9½".	$ 40.00- 50.00
1049.	WHITE'S STOMACH BITTERS, Square – Amber – 9¼".	$ 40.00- 50.00
1050.	WHITWELL'S TEMPERANCE BITTERS, Rect. – Aqua – 7".	$ 25.00- 50.00
1051.	WILDER'S STOMACH BITTERS, Cabin Square – Clear – 10 5/8" high.	$ 90.00-130.00
1052.	WILHELM, KAISER BITTERS, Round – Clear – 10".	$ 50.00- 60.00
1053.	WILLARD'S GOLDEN SEAL BITTERS, Oval – Aqua – 7 5/8".	$ 40.00- 50.00
1054.	WILSON HERBINE BITTERS, Oval – Aqua – 6".	$ 30.00- 40.00
1055.	WINGOLD BRAND STOMACH BITTERS, Round – Clear ¾ qt.	$ 8.00- 20.00
1056.	WONSER'S BITTERS, Square – Aqua – 8½".	$ 20.00- 30.00
1057.	WONSER'S U.S.A. INDIAN ROOT BITTERS, Round – Aqua – 10½" high.	$100.00-150.00
1058.	WOOD'S SARSAPARILLA WILD CHERRY BITTERS, Rect. – Aqua – 8¾" & 9".	$ 50.00- 70.00
1059.	WOODBURY'S BITTERS, Round – Amber – 8".	$ 20.00- 40.00
1060.	WOODCOCK PEPSIN BITTERS, Rect. – Amber – 7 7/8".	$ 30.00- 60.00
1061.	YERBA BUENA BITTERS, Flask shaped – Amber – 8¼".	$ 60.00- 90.00
1062.	YOCHIM BROS. CELEBRATED STOMACH BITTERS, Square – Amber – 8¾" high.	$ 50.00- 60.00
1063.	ZINGARI BITTERS, Round lady's leg – Amber – 11".	$150.00-200.00
1064.	ZOELLER'S STOMACH BITTERS, Rect. – Amber – 9½".	$ 50.00- 85.00
1065.	ZUBROWNICK MEDICINAL BITTER WINE, Round – Amber – 1/5 gal. – (Labeled only).	$ 10.00- 25.00

1066

1067

1068

1066.	HOSTETTERS, DR. J. STOMACH BITTERS, Amber (all shades). Square beveled corners – 9½" – Three sides, plain.	$ 10.00- 18.00
1067.	LASH'S BITTERS, Automatic machine made. LTRC. Amber – 9½ x 2¾".	$ 5.00- 15.00
1068.	LASH'S BITTERS CO., New York, Chicago & San Francisco – Came in clear, amber and aqua – 11½" x 3" – Automatic bottle machine.	$ 10.00- 15.00

| 1069 | 1070 | 1071 | 1072 |

1069. LASH'S PRODUCTS CO., New York, Chicago & San
Francisco – 11″ high – Clear. .... $ 4.00- 10.00
1070. SIEGERT'S BITTERS, 8″ tall – Odd green – Brown in
mold. .... $ 8.00- 10.00
1071. SIEGERT'S BITTERS, Whittle mold – Pontil, Blue. ..... $ 20.00- 30.00
1072. UNEMBOSSED BITTERS, 9″ high – Amber. .... $ 4.00- 6.00

HOUSEHOLD FOODS

1082

1088

1089

1090

1073.	A-1 SAUCE & CO. – Aqua – 7½".	$ 2.00-	5.00
1074.	ADAMS, CHARLES H. SAUCE – Olive Green – 6½".	$ 2.00-	5.00
1075.	AIRLINE TRADE MARK – Clear – 2 5/8".	$ 2.00-	4.00
1076.	ALART & MCGUIRE – Amethyst – 5½.	$ 4.00-	8.00
1077.	ARMOUR'S TOP NOTCH BRAND – Amethyst – 11¼".	$ 4.00-	6.00
1078.	BALDWIN'S CELERY SODA – Amber – 4".	$ 2.00-	4.00
1079.	BORDEAUX DESCAULX – Green – 8".	$ 4.00-	8.00
1080.	BURNETT'S STANDARD FLAVORING EXTRACTS – Aqua – 5½.	$ 2.00-	3.00
1081.	BURNHAM'S CLAM BOUILON – Amethyst – 4".	$ 2.00-	4.00
1082.	BUTTERWORTH'S (MRS.) SYRUP – Brown – 8½".	$ 4.00-	8.00
1083.	BUNTE – Clear – 4 1/8".	$ 2.00-	4.00
1084.	CALIFORNIA OLIVE OIL – Amethyst – 9½".	$ 2.00-	4.00
1085.	CAMPBELL, JOSEPH COMPANY – Amethyst – 8¼".	$ 3.00-	6.00
1086.	CARTER HALES & COMPANY – Light green – 7".	$ 2.00-	4.00
1087.	CARNATION FRESH MILK – Amber – 1 quart.	$ 3.00-	6.00
1088.	CASION BRAND QUEEN OLIVES – Clear – 7½".	$ 6.00-	10.00
1089.	CAT FIGURAL (SYRUP) – Clear – 7".	$ 6.00-	10.00
1090.	CATHEDRAL PICKLE – Light blue – 9½".	$ 15.00-	30.00

1093

1095

1097

1098

1091.	CATSUP, EDDY'S HOMEMADE – Amethyst – 7¾".	$ 3.00-	6.00
1092.	CATSUP, H.J. HEINZ – Amethyst – 9¼".	$ 2.00-	5.00
1093.	CATSUP – 1600 on bottom. Clear or sun colored amethyst. 10" tall.	$ 2.00-	3.00
1094.	CHAMPAGNE CATSUP – Amethyst – 9¾".	$ 3.00-	6.00
1095.	CHUTNEY, Semi-Cathedral, Blue.	$ 8.00-	15.00

87

1096.	CLIMAX SEASONING – Clear – 3¾".	$	3.00-	6.00
1097.	CLOWN (GRAPETTE CO.) – Clear – 7½".	$	4.00-	12.00
1098.	CLOCK (MUSTARD) – Figural – Clear – 4½".	$	4.00-	12.00

1099

1101

1102

1103

1099.	COLUMBIA CATSUP EXTRA QUALITY, (in seal) – 11"	$	2.00-	6.00
1100.	COLUMBIA CATSUP EXTRA QUALITY – Clear – 8".	$	1.00-	2.00
1101.	CREAM BOTTLE – 3½" – SCA.	$	2.00-	4.00
1102.	CURTIS BROS. PRESERVES – Rochester N.Y. embossed in seal. 8" – Ribbed sun colored amethyst – Blown in mold.	$	2.00-	3.00
1103.	CURTIS & PERKINS PROPRIETORS – Mrs. Winslow's Syrup – Green – 5".	$	4.00-	6.00
1104.	D & C MUSTARD – Amethyst – 4¾".	$	2.00-	4.00
1105.	DEDNEY PICKLING CO. – Amethyst – 8¾".	$	2.00-	4.00
1106.	DEPOSE-FRAUN MFG. CO. – Amethyst – 6¾".	$	4.00-	6.00
1107.	DODSON & HILLS – Amethyst – 8½".	$	4.00-	6.00
1108.	DURKEE, E.R. & CO., SALAD DRESSING – Clear – 8".	$	1.00-	2.00

1111

1116

1118

1119

1109.	EDDY & EDDY MFG. CO., – Amethyst – 5¼".	$	2.00-	4.00
1110.	EDDY & EDDY (PICKLES) – Amethyst – 6".	$	4.00-	8.00
1111.	ELEPHANT (GRAPETTE CO.) – Clear – 7½".	$	6.00-	10.00
1112.	ERD & CO. – Green – 8".	$	4.00-	10.00
1113.	EVANGELINE PEPPERSAUCE – Amethyst – 5¼".	$	2.00-	4.00
1114.	FLACCOUS BROS. TABLE DELICACIES – Amethyst – 5".	$	2.00-	4.00
1115.	FOLGER & CO. (FLAVORING EXTRACTS) – Aqua – 3½".	$	2.00-	4.00
1116.	FOLGER'S GOLDEN GATE FLAVORING – 5½" – SCA.	$	2.00-	3.00
1117.	FOX TRADEMARK CLAM TEA – Amethyst – 4".	$	2.00-	4.00
1118.	GRAPE JUICE – Amethyst – 9".	$	4.00-	6.00
1119.	GREEN CAPERS (PEPPER) – Emerald Green – 6½".	$	8.00-	16.00

| 1120 | 1124 | 1126 | 1128 |

1120. GEBHARDT EAGLE CHILI POWDER – Amethyst – 5½". .... $ 3.00- 4.00
1121. GODNEY PICKLING CO. (THE M.A.) – Clear – 8" – Dressing.. $ 2.00- 3.00
1122. GOTHIC, LARGE (1. & B.) – Aqua – 8¾"............... $ 5.00- 10.00
1123. GULDEN, CHARLES MUSTARD – Clear – 3¾"......... $ 1.00- 2.00
1124. HEINZ CO. (H.J.) – Pittsburg, Pa. – 6½" – Aqua........ $ 2.00- 4.00
1125. HEINZ CO. (H.J.) – Gothic horseradish – Aqua – 6".... $ 2.00- 4.00
1126. HIRE'S EXTRACT – For making root beer at home – 2¾". .... $ 2.00- 6.00
1127. HIRE'S HOUSEHOLD EXTRACT – Aqua – 4¾"........ $ 2.00- 3.00
1128. HIRE'S HOUSEHOLD EXRACT – (almost cobalt blue) – For making root beer at home. .... $ 4.00- 8.00

| 1129 | 1132 | 1133 | 1135 |

1129. HIRE'S IMPROVED ROOT BEER MAKER – 5 Gallons – Aqua – 4½" high.................................... $ 3.00- 4.00
1130. HIRSCH'S PEPPER SAUCE – Pink – 7¼". .... $ 2.00- 4.00
1131. HOLBROOKS & CO. – Aqua – 4 5/8". .... $ 1.00- 2.00
1132. HOLBROOKS & CO. – 8" – Aqua. .... $ 2.00- 4.00
1133. HONEY – Clear – 7 1/8"............................ $ 4.00- 8.00
1134. HORLICK'S – Clear – 2¾". .... $ 1.00- 2.00
1135. HOT DOG SAUCE – Clear – 4½"..................... $ 4.00- 10.00
1136. HOWARD, J.F. – Clear – 7¼". .... $ 1.00- 3.00
1137. HUNNEWELL CO. (J.W.) – Aqua – 6¼". .... $ 1.00- 2.00
1138. HUNT'S PICKLES – Clear – 6".................. .... $ 1.00- 2.00

| | 1139 | 1150 | 1152 | 1154 |

1139.	JELLY GLASS – Deep Purple – 6".	$	4.00-	10.00
1140.	JEWELL TEA CO. – Amethyst – 6½".	$	2.00-	4.00
1141.	JAUKAUNA VLUG – Cream – 4".	$	2.00-	4.00
1142.	KEILLER & SONS DUNDE MARMALADE – White pottery – 4¾".	$	6.00-	8.00
1143.	KNIGHT'S EXTRACTS – Clear – 4½".	$	1.00-	2.00
1144.	LEA & PERRINS WORCESTERSHIRE SAUCE – Green 7".	$	2.00-	4.00
1145.	LEWIS & CO. (W.K.) – Aqua – 8".	$	3.00-	6.00
1146.	LUDIN'S CONDENSED JUNIPER-ADE – Aqua – 5".	$	1.00-	2.00
1147.	McCORMICK & CO. – Cobalt – 2 5/8".	$	3.00-	6.00
1148.	McCORMICK & CO. EXTRACTS SPICES & ETC. – Clear 5¼".	$	4.00-	8.00
1149.	McILHENNY & CO. – Amethyst – 8".	$	2.00-	4.00
1150.	McILHENNY CO. – Purple – 8".	$	4.00-	8.00
1151.	MELLIN'S FOOD CO. – Large Size – Aqua – 6 1/8".	$	3.00-	4.00
1152.	MELLIN'S INFANT FOOD – Light green – 4½".	$	3.00-	4.00
1153.	MEYER MFG. CO. – Amethyst – 4".	$	2.00-	4.00
1154.	MILK BOTTLE – Grass green – Qt.	$	2.00-	6.00

| | 1155 | 1157 | 1158 | 1159 |

1155.	MOUTARDE-DIAPHANE – Lovit Freres & Co. – Mustard barrel – 3 rings on shoulder and at base. Ring collar, Graphite Pontil – 5" high – Amethyst.	$	4.00-	6.00
1156.	MOUTARDE-DIAPHANE – Amethyst – 5¼".	$	2.00-	4.00
1157.	MR. & MRS. EXTRACTS – 4½	$	2.00-	4.00
1158.	MUSTARD – 5" – SCA.	$	4.00-	6.00
1159.	MUSTARD – 3½" – SVH – Colored Amethyst.	$	2.00-	4.00

1160   1161   1162   1164

1160.	MUSTARD BARREL – Deep purple – Different varities. .	$	4.00-	8.00
1161.	MUSTARD BARREL – Another variety.	$	4.00-	6.00
1162.	MY WIFE'S SALAD DRESSING – Automatic machine made – 8″ – Sun colored amethyst.	$	4.00-	6.00
1163.	NOSCO THE NATURAL SALT CO. – Amethyst – 3½″. .	$	1.00-	2.00
1164.	OLIVE OIL – Free blown – 12″.	$	4.00-	10.00

1165   1169   1170   1171

1165.	OLIVE OIL – San Juan brand – Wax sealed – 6½″	$	4.00-	8.00
1166.	OLIVE OIL (OLD MISSION) – Amethyst – 8¾″	$	3.00-	6.00
1167.	OLYMPIC – Clear – 6½″	$	1.00-	2.00
1168.	PEPPER SAUCE – Clear – 8¼″.	$	5.00-	15.00
1169.	PEPPER SAUCE – Aqua – 11¾″.	$	10.00-	25.00
1170.	PEPPER SAUCE – Amethyst – 5½″.	$	4.00-	6.00
1171.	PEPPER SAUCE – Amethyst – 6″.	$	4.00-	6.00

1172   1173   1174   1175

1172.	PEPPER SAUCE – Aqua – 8½″.	$	2.00-	4.00
1173.	PEPPER SAUCE – Amethyst – 6½″.	$	4.00-	6.00
1174.	PEPPER SAUCE – Aqua – 7″.	$	2.00-	6.00
1175.	PEPPER SAUCE – Clear – 6½″ – 19 rings.	$	4.00-	6.00

1176   1177   1178   1180

1176.	PEPPER SAUCE – Amethyst – 8½″ – 26 rings.	$	4.00-	8.00
1177.	PEPPER – Amethyst – 7″.	$	3.00-	6.00
1178.	PICKLE – Knadler & Lucas – Amethyst – 8½″ & 10″.	$	3.00-	6.00
1179.	PICKLE BOTTLE – Amethyst – 7½″.	$	3.00-	8.00
1180.	PICKLE – Amethyst – 7½″.	$	3.00-	6.00

1181   1182   1183   1186

1181.	PICKLE – Amethyst – 6″.	$	2.00-	4.00
1182.	PICKLE – Amethyst – 5″.	$	2.00-	4.00
1183.	PICKLES (SWEET) – OK trademark – Clear – 7″.	$	4.00-	6.00
1184.	PRICE-BOOKER MFG. CO. – Aqua – 9″.	$	3.00-	6.00
1185.	PRICE-BOOKER MFG. CO. – Amethyst – 7¾″.	$	3.00-	6.00
1186.	PRICE'S DELICIOUS FLAVORING EXTRACTS – Clear – 4½″-4″.	$	2.00-	3.00

1188   1189   1196

1187.	PRIMROSE REGISTERED BRAND WESTERN MEAT CO. – Clear – 11½" high	$ 2.00-	4.00
1188.	PURE OLIVE OIL – 11" high. SCA.	$ 3.00-	6.00
1189.	PURE OLIVE OIL – Birdsall Olive Co. – Auburn Cal – 11".	$ 3.00-	6.00
1190.	REIF'S SPECIAL CATSUP – Amber – 9¼".	$ 1.00-	2.00
1191.	RED SNAPPER SAUCE – Amethyst – 7¾".	$ 2.00-	3.00
1192.	RE UMBERTO (PEER-AMID BOTTLES) – Clear – 6¾"...	$ 1.00-	2.00
1193.	RE UMBERTO OLIVE OIL – Clear – 6¾".	$ 1.00-	2.00
1194.	ROSE & CO. – Aqua – 8".	$ 3.00-	6.00
1195.	R.T. FRENCH CO., THE – Extract – Philadelphia Pa., 5".	$ 2.00-	6.00
1196.	SAUCE – Clear – 5".	$ 6.00-	12.00

1202 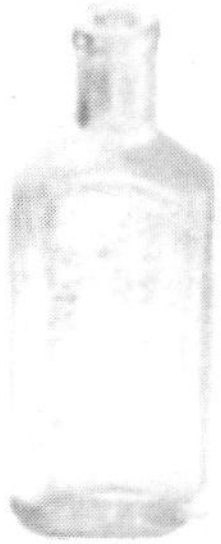   1212   1215   1218

1197.	SAUER'S EXTRACTS – Clear – 4¾".	$ 1.00-	2.00
1198.	SCHILLING & CO. – Amethyst – 3¼".	$ 2.00-	4.00
1199.	SCOTT & GILBERT CO. (CLAM BOUILLON) – Amethyst – 4".	$ 2.00-	4.00
1200.	SOUDER'S FLAVORING EXTRACTS – Amethyst – 6¼".	$ 2.00-	4.00
1201.	SCOWCROFT (JOHN) & SONS CO. – Pure Olive Oil – Amethyst – 7¼" high.	$ 2.00-	4.00
1202.	SMITH'S TRUE FRUIT BRAND LEMON – Prepared by J. Hungerford Smith Co., Rochester N.Y. (on front). Alcohol 84%, 2 fluid ounces (on side). 4½" high.	$ 4.00-	6.00
1203.	SOUTER'S ELEGANT FLAVORING EXTRACTS – Clear – 5".	$ 1.00-	2.00
1204.	SOUVENIR – Pottery in red amber & glazed handle in gold.	$ 4.00-	6.00
1205.	S & P – Green – 8".	$ 4.00-	8.00
1206.	SYLMAR BRAND OLIVE OIL – Clear – 3¼".	$ 1.00-	2.00
1207.	THOMPSON'S – Clear – 5".	$ 2.00-	3.00
1208.	TILLMAN'S EXTRACT – Aqua – 7".	$ 1.00-	2.00

93

1209.	TOMATO KETCHUP – Heinz Co. – Amethyst – 9″......	$	2.00-	4.00
1210.	TOWLE MAPLE SYRUP CO. – Amethyst – 11″.........	$	2.00-	4.00
1211.	VINEGAR BOTTLE – Clear – 11″....................	$	5.00-	8.00
1212.	WAKEFIELD'S BLACKBERRY EXTRACT ROOT COM-POUND – Aqua – 5″ high..........................	$	3.00-	6.00
1213.	WARNER & CO.'S CATSUP – Clear – 8¼″............	$	2.00-	6.00
1214.	WESTERN TEA & SPICE CO. – Amethyst – 6¾″.......	$	4.00-	8.00
1215.	WELCHE'S – Purple – 5″.........................	$	2.00-	3.00
1216.	WHITEHOUSE VINEGAR – Clear – 8″...............	$	6.00-	10.00
1217.	MY WIFE'S SALAD DRESSING – Clear – 8″..........	$	2.00-	4.00
1218.	WITCH BALL BOTTLE – Clear – 6″.................	$	4.00-	8.00

1219   1220   1222   1223

1219.	WORCESTSHIRE SAUCE – Lea & Perrins – Blue – 7 1/8″..	$	2.00-	4.00
1220.	YACHT CLUB SALAD DRESSING – Chicago – 7½″ tall – Sun colored amethyst..........................	$	4.00-	6.00
1221.	YACHT CLUB SALAD DRESSING – Clear – 7½″.......	$	2.00-	4.00
1222.	QUEEN OLIVES – Clear – 5½″....................	$	4.00-	10.00
1223.	SAUER'S EXTRACTS – Clear corker – 5″............	$	2.00-	3.00

HOUSEHOLD COSMETICS

1224

1228

1229

1236

1224.	AMERICAN LILAC (PERFUME) – Clear – 3"..........	$ 8.00- 15.00
1225.	AYER'S HAIR VIGOR – Deep green, blue – 6½".......	$ 10.00- 20.00
1226.	BALDWIN PERFUMER – Amethyst – 6"...............	$ 10.00- 15.00
1227.	BARADENT CO., INC. (THE) – Cream De Camelia For The Comlexion – cobalt – 5".......................	$ 4.00- 8.00
1228.	BARBER BOTTLE – Free blown – Crude Mineral Water (Minah's) 11½" high.	$ 15.00- 30.00
1229.	BARBER'S BAR BOTTLE – Amethyst – 8½"..........	$ 5.00- 12.00
1230.	BACHELOR'S LIQUID HAIR DYE NO. 1 – Aqua – 3"....	$ 2.00- 5.00
1231.	BERLIN COMPANIES BEST GERMAN COLOGNE – Clear – 3½"................................	$ 3.00- 6.00
1232.	CALDER'S DENTINE – Clear – 3"..................	$ 1.00- 2.00
1233.	CARBONA PRODUCTS CO. (HAIR DRESSING) – Aqua 6"...	$ 3.00- 6.00
1234.	CARPENTER-MORTON CO. COLORITE – Amethyst – 4"...	$ 1.00- 2.00
1235.	C. AND C. – Amethyst – 4½".......................	$ 2.00- 4.00
1236.	CHAMBERLAIN'S HAND LOTION – Clear – 2½"......	$ 6.00- 8.00

1240

1241

1242

1243

1237.	CLAIR'S HAIR LOTION – Cobalt – 7¼.	$ 6.00- 10.00
1238.	CLARKE, WOODWARD & CO. – Cobalt – 4¼"........	$ 4.00- 10.00
1239.	COLGATE & CO. PERFUMERS – Amethyst – 3¾"....	$ 3.00- 5.00
1240.	COLGATE PALMOLIVE PETE CO. – SCA – 6½".......	$ 3.00- 6.00
1241.	COSMETICS – Clear – 3".........................	$ 4.00- 6.00
1242.	COSMETICS – Aqua – 2".........................	$ 3.00- 4.00
1243.	COSMETICS – Clear – 2".........................	$ 2.00- 3.00

1244   1245   1246   1247

1244.	COSMETICS – Cobalt – 3″.	$ 4.00-	8.00
1245.	CORN HUSKERS LOTION – Clear – 6″.	$ 4.00-	6.00
1246.	CRANBERRY SWIRL BARBER'S BOTTLE – 8½″ plus cork – I have been told this bottle is very rare and is worth from $200.00 to $250.00. I am not pricing it.		
1247.	CREME DE CAMELIA – for the complexion – The Buradent Co. Inc. San Francisco & New York.	$ 4.00-	8.00
1248.	CREME SIMON – Milk glass – 2¼ ″.	$ 2.00-	4.00

1249   1251   1256   1260

1249.	CREME SIMON – J.S. 80 on bottom. Milk glass – 2½ ″. .	$ 3.00-	4.00
1250.	CREMOLA, DR. WARD'S – Lotion – Clear – 5¼ ″.	$ 2.00-	4.00
1251.	CROWN PERFUME CO. (THE) – Lotion – 3½ ″ – Dark green.	$ 4.00-	12.00
1252.	CROWN PERFUMERY CO. – Green – 2½ ″.	$ 4.00-	10.00
1253.	CUTEX – Frosted – 2½ ″ – Clear – 1½ ″.	$ 2.00-	5.00
1254.	DARBROOK'S DETROIT PERFUMERS – Amethyst – 6″.	$ 2.00-	4.00
1255.	DAGGETT & RAMSDELL'S PERFECT COLD CREAM – Clear – 2 3/8″.	$ 1.00-	2.00
1256.	DAMSCHINSKY LIQUID HAIR DYE – Green – 4 1/8″. . . .	$ 4.00-	8.00
1257.	DEPOSE GUERLAIN PARIS – Clear perfume bottle – 3¼ ″.	$ 4.00-	6.00
1258.	DERWILLO FOR THE COMPLEXION – Clear – 3¾ ″. . . .	$ 1.00-	3.00
1259.	D-DERKOFF PARIS (FOOTED BOTTLE) – Amethyst – 3¼ ″.	$ 2.00-	4.00
1260.	EAV DU COLOGNE – #47n – Bimal – 5″ – Sun amethyst.	$ 4.00-	6.00

| 1261 | 1264 | 1265 | 1269 |

1261.	ESPEY'S FRAGRANT CREAM – Clear – 4½ ".........	$	2.00-	4.00
1262.	ESPEY'S FRAGRANT CREAM LOTION – Clear – 4½ "..	$	2.00-	4.00
1263.	FAHRNEY & SONS CO. (DR. PETER) – Clear – 9" – 7½"			
	– Clear Amethyst – 5 1/8"........................	$	4.00-	6.00
1264.	FITCH, E.W. IDEAL DANDRIFF CURE – 6½" – Sun			
	amethyst.	$	10.00-	15.00
1265.	FLORIDA WATER – Murry & Lanman druggest New			
	York. 6" – Aqua.	$	4.00-	8.00
1266.	FLORIDA WATER – Aqua – 9".......................	$	4.00-	6.00
1267.	FLORIDA WATER REDINGTON & CO. – Aqua – 6".....	$	2.00-	4.00
1268.	FRANCO AMERICAN HYGIENIC CO. – Amethyst – 6"..	$	3.00-	6.00
1269.	FRENCH DRESSING FOR LADIES & CHILDREN –			
	Boots & Shoes (labeled only) – Clear – 4½ "...........	$	1.00-	2.00
1270.	FROSTILLA FRAGRANT LOTION – Clear – 4½ ".......	$	2.00-	6.00

| 1287 | 1273 | 1276 | 1277 |

1271.	FROSTILLA FRAGRANT FOR THE SKIN – Clear – 4½ ".	$	4.00-	6.00
1272.	FROSTILLA COSMETIC – Clear – 4 3/8".............	$	2.00-	4.00
1273.	GLADIATION CO., INC. PERFUMERS – Clear – 12". ...	$	2.00-	4.00
1274.	GOLD MEDAL QUALITY HYDROGEN PEROXIDE –			
	Amber – 8".....................................	$	2.00-	4.00
1275.	GOLDMAN, MARY T. – Amber – 5½ ".	$	3.00-	4.00
1276.	GOURAUD'S ORIENTAL CREAM – New York on one			
	side, London on the other – 4½ " – Clear.	$	2.00-	4.00
1277.	HAIR RESTORER – FCW – 6½ " – Amber.	$	3.00-	8.00
1278.	HALL'S HAIR RENEWER – Blue green – 6 3/8"........	$	10.00-	20.00
1279.	HARMONEY COLD CREAM – Amethyst – 2½"........	$	4.00-	5.00
1280.	HARRIET HUBBARD AYER – Milk glass – 1½" or 2½".	$	4.00-	6.00
1281.	HABER'S MAGIC HAIR COLORING – Cobalt – 6"......	$	6.00-	10.00
1282.	HILL'S HAIR DYE – Aqua – 2¾ ".	$	2.00-	4.00

1283.	HIND'S, A.S. – Amethyst – 5¾".	$	2.00-	4.00
1284.	HIND'S HONEY AND LAMOND CREAM – Clear – 6 3/8".	$	4.00-	8.00
1285.	HINMAN PERFUMER PERFUME – Clear – 2½".	$	1.00-	3.00
1286.	HOLMES FRAGRANTS – PROSTILLA – Clear – 4½".	$	2.00-	4.00

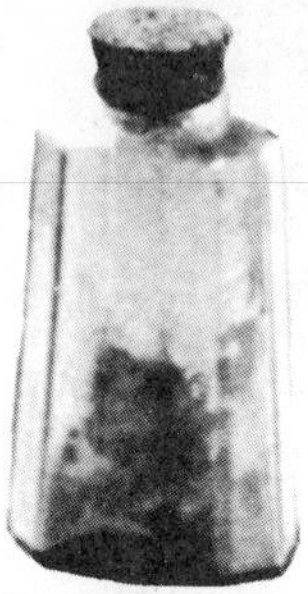

1286    1288 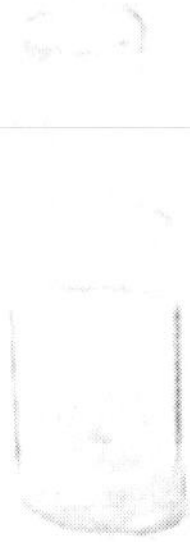   1289    1297

1287.	HONBIGANT TALC POWDER – 5½" – SCA.	$	3.00-	4.00
1288.	HOYLE, E.W. & CO. – 3" & 2½" – Clear – Hoyle Nickel Cologne 2½" high.	$	2.00-	6.00
1289.	HOYT'S GERMAN COLOGNE – E.W. Hoyt & Co. Lowell, Miss. – 3¾" – SCA.	$	2.00-	6.00
1290.	HOYT'S GERMAN COLOGNE – Amethyst – 3½".	$	2.00-	3.00
1291.	HOYT'S 10¢ COLOGNE – Clear – 3¼".	$	1.00-	3.00
1292.	HOYT'S NICKEL COLOGNE – Amethyst – 2 7/8".	$	2.00-	4.00
1293.	HOUBIGANT PARIS FRANCE – Amethyst – 5".	$	2.00-	4.00
1294.	HUBERT'S MALVIAN LOTION – Clear – 5".	$	3.00-	6.00
1295.	HUDNUT, RICHARD PERFUMER – Amethyst – 3".	$	2.00-	4.00
1296.	HUDNET, RICHARD MARVELOUS COLD CREAM – Amethyst – 3".	$	2.00-	4.00
1297.	HUMPHREY'S MARVEL WITCH HAZEL – Amber – 2½" Clear – 3¼".	$	2.00-	4.00

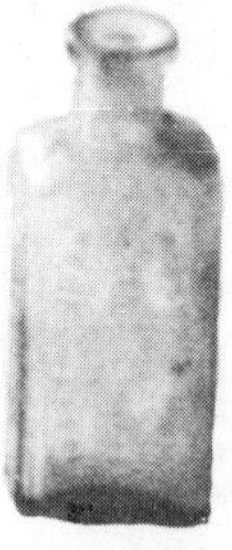

1298 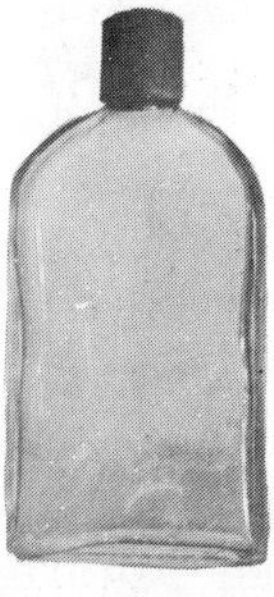   1305 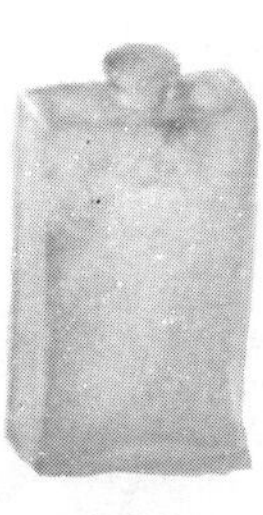   1308    1309

1298.	IMPERIAL HAIR REGINERATOR – Shield with crown in center – Regenerator vertical on front. 4½" – Aqua.	$	3.00-	6.00
1299.	INGRAM'S MILKWEED CREAM – Milk glass – 2¼".	$	2.00-	4.00
1300.	INGRAM'S SHAVING CREAM – Cobalt – 2¼".	$	4.00-	8.00
1301.	KAKEN BARBERS SUPPLY (HAIR TONIC) – Clear – 6¾".	$	2.00-	4.00
1302.	KAKEN – 10 fluid ounces – Clear – 7".	$	1.00-	2.00
1303.	KERKOFF PARIS – Clear – 5".	$	1.00-	2.00
1304.	KRANK'S COLD CREAM – Milk glass – 2¾".	$	4.00-	6.00

1305.	JERGIN'S HAND LOTION – Clear with a black lid. – 5½".	$	2.00-	4.00
1306.	LA CROELE LABORATORIES – Clear – 5¼".	$	1.00-	3.00
1307.	LAIRD, G.W. PERFUMER – Milk glass – 4½".	$	6.00-	8.00
1308.	LALIQUE, R. PERFUMER – 3" high.	$	3.00-	6.00
1309.	LAMP (FIGURAL) – Clear – 2¾".	$	4.00-	6.00
1310.	LA VALLIERE VENUS COLD CREAM – Cobalt – 2½"...	$	4.00-	8.00
1311.	LAZELL PERFUME – Clear – 2½	$	1.00-	3.00

1312   1314   1315   1319

1312.	LUBIN PERFUME, PARIS – Pontil – Clear – 4" and stopper.	$	4.00-	10.00
1313.	LYON'S POWDER – Amber – 4¼".	$	2.00-	4.00
1314.	MEADE & BAKER CARBOLIC MOUTH WASH ANTISEPTIC GARGLE – Amethyst – 5".	$	2.00-	4.00
1315.	McGREGOR SHAVING LOTION – Clear – 4½".	$	4.00-	6.00
1316.	MELBA – Clear – 3½".	$	2.00	4.00
1317.	MILK WEED CREAM – Milk glass – 2½".	$	4.00-	8.00
1318.	MICHELL'S CENTENNIAL COLOGNE – Clear – 2¾"...	$	1.00-	2.00
1319.	MUNGER BROTHERS CO. – Pheonix, Arizona – 7½" – Sun colored amethyst.	$	2.00-	3.00
1320.	NADINOLA CREAM – Milk glass – 2" & 3¼".	$	4.00-	6.00

1321   1323   1324   1326

1321.	NEW BROS. HERPICIDE FOR THE SCALP – Clear – 7".	$	2.00-	4.00
1322.	PALMER'S LOTION – Vegetable Cosmetic – Clear – 4".	$	2.00-	4.00
1323.	PALMER TOILET WATER – Clear – 5¼".	$	4.00-	6.00
1324.	PALMER'S PARFUME (Misspelled) – Peacock green...	$	6.00-	12.00

1325.	PALMER'S PERFUME – Emerald green – 4¾".	$ 6.00- 12.00
1326.	PALMER COSMISTIC – Emerald green – 5".	$ 8.00- 15.00
1327.	PARISIAN SAGE A HAIR TONIS – Buffalo embossed on bottle – Amethyst – 6¾".	$ 2.00- 6.00
1328.	PARKER PRAY – Milk glass.	$ 4.00- 6.00
1329.	PENSLAR – Amethyst – 5".	$ 2.00- 4.00

1330   1331   1332   1333

1330.	PERFUME – Star burst on base – Bottle ground for glass stopper – 3" tall – Sun colored amethyst.	$ 6.00- 8.00
1331.	PERFUME – Clear – 5½".	$ 6.00- 10.00
1332.	PERFUME – Ground throat – 2" – Blue green.	$ 2.00- 6.00
1333.	PERFUME – Clear – 3½".	$ 6.00- 8.00

1334   1335   1336   1341

1334.	PERFUME – Plain bottle – 4" – SCA.	$ 2.00- 4.00
1335.	PERFUME & TOILET WATER – Stretched neck – 6½" – SCA.	$ 6.00- 8.00
1336.	PINAUD, ED, PARIS – with floral embossing – Clear – 5¼".	$ 1.00- 2.00
1337.	PINAUD, ED, PARIS – Clear – 6¾".	$ 2.00- 4.00
1338.	POMPEIAN CREAM – Amethyst – 2 7/8".	$ 1.00- 3.00
1339.	PRICE (DR.) AMERICAN PERFUMES – Clear – 4".	$ 2.00- 4.00
1340.	PUROLA COMPLEXION BEAUTIFIER – Cobalt – 5¼". .	$ 4.00- 8.00
1341.	RESORCIN HAIR TONIC – Goodrich Drug Co., Omaha – 8" high including stopper.	$ 4.00- 8.00

1342   1346   1348   1349

1342.	REVEN GLOSS SHOE DRESSING – Green 5".	$	4.00-	6.00
1343.	RHODE'S HAIR REJUVENATOR – Amber – 6½".	$	3.00-	6.00
1344.	RUBIFOAM FOR THE TEETH – Amethyst – 4".	$	2.00-	6.00
1345.	SANFORD – Amethyst – 2¾".	$	2.00-	3.00
1346.	SCOTT'S FOUR ROSES – Clear – 4½".	$	4.00-	8.00
1347.	SCHEFFLER'S HAIR COLORINE – Clear – 4¼".	$	2.00-	3.00
1348.	SHOE POLISH – Amethyst – 3½" & 4".	$	2.00-	3.00
1349.	SIGN OF PERFUME, THE – Hubbard, Harriet, Ayer (Embossed) – The Genuine – 6½" – SCA.	$	4.00-	8.00

1354   1355   1357   1358

1350.	SOLON PALMER'S FLORIDA WATER – Aqua – 6".	$	4.00-	8.00
1351.	SOZODONT FOR THE TEETH AND BREATH – Clear – 2¼".	$	1.00-	2.00
1352.	STELL & PRICE PERFUMERS – Clear – 5¼".	$	2.00-	4.00
1353.	U-AR-DAS COSMETIC – Cobalt – 2½".	$	4.00-	8.00
1354.	VERITABLE EAU COLOGNE – Clear cut glass – 5½"...	$	2.00-	6.00
1355.	VINAIGRE – J.V. Bonn Bonn of Paris – Clear – 5".	$	3.00-	6.00
1356.	WAKELEE'S COMELLINE LOTION – Amber – 4½". ...	$	2.00-	4.00
1357.	WATKIN'S GARDA CREAM – (on cap).	$	2.00-	5.00
1358.	WILLIAM'S BRILLONTINE – Clear – 3½".	$	2.00-	4.00

POISON BOTTLES

1359   1360   1361   1362

1359.	ACID – Round – Clear or green – 6 3/8"...............	$ 2.00- 4.00
1360.	COBOLT OWL POISON – Small size – Triangular.	$ 10.00- 25.00
1361.	COBOLT OWL POISON – Large size – Triangular.	$ 10.00- 25.00
1362.	DEAD STUCK (INSECTICIDE) – (with label) – The Edward R. Marshall Co. The label gives the uses and directions for use. – Green – 9".....................	$ 10.00- 20.00

1363   1364   1365   1366

1363.	DICK'S ANT DESTROYER – Dick's and Co. Distributors New Orleans, La. – All of this embossed on the bottle. Clear – 6" high....................................	$ 15.00- 30.00
1364.	LRAY (POISON) – (with label) – Embossed ribs on edges – Brown – 3½"..............................	$ 4.00- 8.00
1365.	McCORMICK & CO. – Baltimore Md. embossed on front. A circle with an embossed insect in the center with embossing around it. – Cobalt blue – 3" & 3½". ...	$ 10.00- 15.00
1366.	ODOS – (under bottom) – Milk glass – 5".	$ 8.00- 20.00

1367	1368	1369	1370

1367. POISON TINCT IODINE – embossed on front with an embossed skull and crossbones. – Amber – 2½″...... $ 4.00- 6.00

1368. POISONS – A set of 4 poison bottles with criss-cross embossing – Blue – 4¾″, 5½″, 6½″, & 8½″. ..... Set $ 60.00-150.00

1369. POISON – Rectangular – "Poison" embossed on one side with an embossed skull and crossbones above it. Blue – 3″.. $ 10.00- 25.00

1370. POISON – All three of these bottles are rectangular. All corners have a raised row of marks. "Poison" is embossed vertically on one side – Amber – 3½″ & 4½″ .. $ 4.00- 8.00
2½″. .... $ 8.00- 10.00

1371	1372	1373	1381

1371. POISON – Embossed picture of a rat on the front. – Rectangular – Clear – 6½″......................... $ 4.00- 8.00

1372. POISON – Triangular – "Poison" embossed on sides – Blue – 3¼″ high. .... $ 4.00- 8.00

1373. POISON – Amber – Various sizes from ½ oz. to 1 quart. $ 2.00- 8.00

1374. POISON – Square – Skull and crossbones embossed on one side with "Poison/Liq.?Iodine" embossed below the skull. – Amber – 2¾″, 3¼″................ $ 2.00- 4.00

1375. POISON – Triangular – "Kitchen's" embossed on one side – "Phenyle" emobssed on the other side – Between these two sides "Poisonous/Not To Be Taken" is embossed – Aqua – 9″ high. $ 6.00- 15.00

1376. POISON – 6-sided – 3 oz. – "Carbolid Acid" embossed on one side – "Use with Caution" embossed on the other side – Cobalt blue – 5″. .... $ 4.00- 15.00

1377. POISON – Triangular – "Poison" embossed on 2 sides with embossed symbols around the letters – Cobalt blue – 2½″, 3¼″, & 5″. .... $ 4.00- 10.00

1378. POISON – Square – 2 rings are around the lip – "Poison" is embossed on one side with ribs running down the sides of the embossing. Flat, round stopper – Cobalt blue – 2¾" and 3¼"...................... $ 4.00- 10.00
1379. POISON – Rectangular – Raised ridges – Bright blue – 4".. $ 4.00- 10.00
1380. POISON – Square – Raised ridges – Amber – 2½". .... $ 2.00- 4.00
1381. SHARP & DOHME – Baltimore Md. – Rectangular – Baltimore, Md. embossed on one side, Sharp & Dohme embossed on another side. – Amber – 2½" – 3½"..... $ 4.00- 8.00

1382   1383   1384

1382. SKULL – (figural) – Poison is embossed above the eyes of the skull – Cobalt blue – 4¼". .... $ 85.00-185.00
1383. TRILOIDS – "Poison" embossed on one side – "Triloids" embossed on another side – The third side is plain – Triangular – Blue – 3½"...................... $ 8.00- 10.00
1384. TRI-SEPS ANTISEPTIC – (on label) – Milliken's – Bernay's No. 2 unofficial poison – Picture of an skull and crossbones. – Amber – 3". .... $ 8.00- 10.00

FRUIT JARS

| 1410 | 1411 | 1415 | 1443 |

1385.	A & C, 1885, Glass and lid and wire clip – Quart – Aqua – Round.	$ 50.00- 75.00
1386.	ABC (Large capital letters) – Round lip, glass lid and iron yoke tightened by eccentric, Qt, Aqua.	$ 75.00-150.00
1387.	ACME, 1920's, Glass lid and wire bail, 1 pint, 1 quart and ½ gal. Clear to amber. Rounded square.	$ 3.00- 8.00
1388.	ADLER, 1950's, Glass lid with hinge, Quart, pint, ½ gal., ½ pint. Clear, green, round.	$ 2.00- 6.00
1389.	ADVANCE, 1885, Glass lid with metal clamp. Quart, aqua, round.	$ 30.00- 75.00
1390.	AGEE QUEEN, 1925, Glass lid, quart, clear, rounded square.	$ 5.00- 10.00
1391.	AGNEW, 1876-1892, Wax sealer, quart, aqua, round.	$ 35.00- 65.00
1392.	AGNEW, JOHN & SON, Pittsburgh Pa., Embossed on base, Wax sealer, Aqua.	$ 20.00- 40.00
1393.	A G W L – 1865 – Wax sealer, Aqua, Round.	$ 25.00- 40.00
1394.	AIRTIGHT – 1877 – Wax sealer, Quart, Amber, Barrel-shaped.	$ 30.00- 40.00
1395.	ALLEN'S Pat. June 1871 (on bottom) – Square with glass lip and metal clamp.	$ 40.00- 55.00
1396.	ALL RIGHT – 1868 – Glass lid with wire clamp – Quart – Medium green – Round tapering.	$ 50.00- 70.00
1397.	ALMY – 1877 – Glass cap – Quart – Aqua – Round.	$ 60.00- 70.00
1398.	ALSTON (THE) – 1901 – Metal lid and wire clip – Quart – Pint – Clear – Round.	$ 50.00- 60.00
1399.	AMAZON SWIFT SEAL – 1910-1920 – Glass lid with full wire bail – Quart, pint, ½ gal., Deep blue – Round.	$ 4.00- 6.00
1400.	AMERICAN FRUIT JAR – 1885 - 1895 – Glass lid – ½ gal. – Aqua and olive green – Round.	$ 20.00- 35.00
1401.	AMERICAN PORCELAIN LINED – 1880-1890 – Zinc lid – Quart – Round with tapering sides.	$ 25.00- 40.00
1402.	ANCHOR – 1915 – Glass lid and metal band – Quart – Clear to amethyst – Round.	$ 10.00- 15.00
1403.	ANCHOR HOCKING LIGHTNING – 1937 – Glass lid, wire bail – Clear – Rounded square.	$ 2.00- 6.00
1404.	ANCHOR HOCKING LIGHTNING – 1937 – Lightning beaded neck with glass lid – Pint, ½ gal., Quart – Clear Round.	$ 2.00- 6.00

1405. ANCHOR HOCKING MASON – 1937 – Zinc lid – Clear – Soft square. .... $ 2.00- 3.00
1406. ANCHOR MASON'S PATENT – Zinc lid – Quart – Clear Round – tapering sides............................ $ 4.00- 8.00
1407. ANDERSON PRESERVING CO. – 1920-1930 – Metal lid Quart – Clear to amethyst – Round. .... $ 3.00- 6.00
1408. ATHORHOLT / FISHER & CO. – 1870-1875 – Glass stopper – Quart – Aqua & Clear – Round. .... $ 20.00- 40.00
1409. ATLAS E-Z SEAL No. 1 – 1896 – Glass lid & wire bail – Quart – Aqua, light green – Round. .... $ 15.00- 25.00
1410. ATLAS E-Z SEAL No. 2 – 1896 – Wire bail & glass lid. Quart – Amber, aqua, green, clear to indefinite – Round. .... $ 25.00- 35.00
1411. ATLAS GOOD LUCK, – 1915-1930 – Glass lid full wire bail. ½ pt., 1/3 pt., qt., pt., ½ gal. – Clear – Square. .... $ 3.00- 8.00
1412. ATLAS IMPROVED MASON – 1890's – Glass lid, metal screw band – Aqua, dark green – Round............. $ 5.00- 10.00
1413. ATLAS H-A MASON No. 1 – 1920 – Glass insert metal screw band – Quart, Pint – Clear – Square. .... $ 2.00- 4.00
1414. ATLAS H-A MASON No. 2 – 1920 – Metal band screw band – ½ pint – Clear – Square. .... $ 2.00- 5.00
1415. ATLAS MASON'S PATENT – 1900-1910 – Zinc lid – Quart – Blue, green, Round. .... $ 10.00- 15.00
1416. ATLAS MASON'S PATENT NOV. 30, 1858 – Zinc lid – ½ gal. Blue, green – Round. .... $ 10.00- 15.00
1417. ATLAS SPECIAL – 1910 – Screw top – 2 sizes – Green, blue, clear – squat round. .... $ 2.00- 6.00
1418. ATLAS SPECIAL MASON – 1910-1930 – Zinc lid – Quart Aqua – Round wide mouth........................ $ 2.00- 8.00
1419. ATLAS STRONG SHOULDER MASON – 1915 – Zinc lid Quart, pint – Aqua, green – Round, tapering. .... $ 6.00- 12.00
1420. ATLAS WHOLEFRUIT JAR – 1910 – Glass lid & wire bail Quart, pint, ½ gal. – Clear – Round with wide mouth. .. $ 4.00- 8.00
1421. ATMORE & SON – 1925 – Glass lid & metal screw band Quart – Aqua to green – Round. .... $ 4.00- 10.00
1422. ATTERBURY – Ground lip – 1860 – RARE – Aqua. $150.00-225.00
1423. AUTOMATIC SEALER, THE – 1895 – Glass lid with spring-wire bail – Quart – Aqua to green – Round. ..... $ 25.00- 50.00
1424. BAKER BROS. – 1865 – Wax sealer, groove ring – Pint – Light green to aqua – Round. .... $ 30.00- 40.00
1425. BALL – 1890 – Zinc lid – Quart, pint, ½ gal. – Green – Round... $ 8.00- 15.00
1426. BALL, THE 1890 – Metal lid – Quart – Light green – Round... $ 10.00- 15.00
1427. BALL BROS. GLASS MFG. CO. – Wide zinc screw band with glass insert – Quart – Blue – Round tapering sides. $ 6.00- 10.00
1428. BALL DELUXE JAR – 1930 – Glass lid & half wire bail – Quart – Clear – Round............................ $ 4.00- 8.00
1429. BALL DELUXE JAR – With moldmaker's error. The second L in Ball has been cut as an E and repaired by scraping away the unwanted part of the letter........ $ 10.00- 20.00
1430. BALL ECLIPSE – 1925 – Glass lid, wire bail – Quart, pint, ½ gal. – Clear – Rounded square. .... $ 2.00- 4.00

1431. BALL ECLIPSE WIDE MOUTH – 1920's – Glass lid, wire bail – Quart, pint, ½ gal. – Clear – Square. .... $ 2.00- 4.00

1432. BALL IDEAL, 1915-1920 – Glass lid, wire bail – ½ gal., quart, pint, ½ pint – Aqua – Round. .... $ 1.00- 2.00

1433. BALL IMPROVED – 1910-1922 – Zinc screw band & glass insert – Green – Round & Square. .... $ 3.00- 6.00

1434. BALL IMPROVED MASON'S PATENT – 1900 – Zinc lid – Quart – Green, Blue-green – Round tapering sides. ..... $ 5.00- 10.00

1435. "THE BALL JAR" MASON'S PATENT Nov. 30, 1858 – Zinc screw-on lid – Quart – Aqua – Round. .... $ 3.00- 6.00

1436. BALL MASON – 1895-1910 – Zinc lid – Pint, qt., ½ gal. – Green, blue, clear, amethyst – All round tapering sides except pints which have straight sides. .... $ 6.00- 15.00

1437. BALL MASON (THE) – 1900-1910 – Zinc lid – Quart – Light Aqua – Round tapering. .... $ 4.00- 8.00

1438. BALL MASON'S PATENT – 1900-1920 – Zinc lid – All sizes – Round – Clear. .... $ 4.00- 10.00

1439. BALL MASON'S PATENT – 1900-1920 – Zinc lid – Quart, pint – Green – Round tapering. .... $ 3.00- 6.00

1440. BALL MASON'S PATENT – 1858 – Ground top – Pint, quart, ½ gal. – Green – Round tapering sides. .... $ 4.00- 8.00

1441. BALL JAR MASON'S PATENT 1858 (THE) – 1890 – Zinc lid – Quart – Light green – Round tapering sides. .... $ 5.00- 10.00

1442. BALL PERFECT MASON No. 1 – 1900-1915 – Zinc lid – Amber, aqua, clear, amethyst – Round. .... $ 5.00- 10.00

1443. BALL PERFECT MASON No. 2 – 1900-1910 – Zinc lid – Vertical lines around sides are cup and pint measurements – Amber, olive, blue, clear – Round or square. .... $ 10.00- 30.00

1444　　　　　　1446　　　　　　1488　　　　　　1520

1444. BALL PERFECT MASON No. 3 – 1915 – Zinc lid – Pint, Qt., ½ gal. – Clear to amethyst – Round or square. ..... $ 4.00- 10.00

1445. BALL SANITARY SURE SEAL – 1908-1922 – Glass lid & full wire bail – Quart – Deep blue – Round wide mouth. . $ 3.00- 6.00

1446. BALL SPECIAL – 1910 – Zinc lid – All sizes – Blue, clear, Round or square. .... $ 2.00- 3.00

1447. BALL SPECIAL WIDE MOUTH – 1910-1915 – Zinc lid, later 2 piece metal lids – Clear – Round or square. ...... $ 1.00- 2.00

1448. BALL STANDARD – 1888-1912 – Metal cap lid & glass lid & clamp – All sizes – Blue – Round. .... $ 3.00- 6.00

1449. BALL STANDARD – Wax sealer – Olive green. . . . . $ 20.00- 25.00
1450. BALL SURE SEAL – 1908-1922 – Glass lid – Pint, quart,
½ pint – Green, Deep blue – Round wide mouth. . . . . . . $ 2.00- 4.00
½ pint Blue . . . . $ 7.00- 15.00
1451. BALTIMORE GLASS WORKS – 1865 – Stopper – Quart
Aqua – Round. $100.00-150.00
1452. BANNER WIDEMOUTH – 1915-1935 – Glass lid & half
wire bail – Pint – Deep blue – Round. . . . . $ 6.00- 10.00
1453. BANNER WIDEMOUTH WARRANTED – 1910 – Glass
lid & full wire bail – Quart – Blue – Round wide mouth. . $ 6.00- 10.00
1454. B B G M CO. – 1886-1887 – Glass lid & metal screw
band – Quart – Blue, green, aqua – Round. . . . . $ 30.00- 45.00
1455. B B G M CO. PORCELAIN LINED – 1886-1887 – Glass
lid & metal screw band – Quart – Green – Round. . . . . . $ 50.00- 80.00
1456. BEAVER – 1897 – Glass lid & zinc screw band – Pint,
quart – Amber, green, clear, amethyst – Round. . . . . . . $ 15.00- 30.00
1457. BEAVER (Embossed log over word Beaver) – Amber. . . $ 75.00-150.00
Clear . . . . $ 90.00-150.00
Beaver facing left. RARE Midget, Clear aqua $125.00-160.00
Midget, Amber $200.00-350.00
1458. BECHTEL, GEORGE BREWING CO. (THE) – This bottle
not to be sold back. 9″ – Aqua. $ 6.00- 10.00
1459. BEE HIVE – 1925 – Zinc band & glass insert – 2 sizes –
Light blue – Round. . . . . $ 40.00- 70.00
Midget clear aqua . . . . $ 75.00-100.00
1460. BENNETT'S No. 1 – 1900-1910 – Screw top – Quart –
Aqua – Round. . . . . $ 75.00-100.00
1461. BENNETT'S No. 2 – 1875 – Stopper – Quart – Green –
Round. . . . . $ 75.00-100.00
1462. BERNARDIN MASON – 1930's – Zinc lid – Quart –
Clear – Square. . . . . $ 3.00- 8.00
1463. BEST – 1922 – Zinc screw band & glass insert – Quart –
Green – Round – Wide mouth. . . . . $ 15.00- 20.00
1464. BEST (THE) – 1875 – Glass lid – Quart – Light green –
Round. . . . . $ 10.00- 20.00
1465. BEST (THE) – 1875 – Glass stopper that screws into the
neck. Quart – Light green – Round. . . . . $ 10.00- 18.00
1466. BEST FRUIT KEEPER (THE) – 1896 – Glass lid & wire
clamp. Quart – Green – Round. $ 15.00- 30.00
1467. BEST JAR PAT PEND (THE) – All on glass lid or stop-
per. – Quart – Aqua $125.00-150.00
1468. BEST WIDE MOUTH – 1922 – Zinc band & glass insert –
4 sizes – Aqua, clear – Squat round. . . . . $ 2.00- 4.00
1469. BOLDT MASON – 1905 – Screw top – Quart, pint – Aqua
Round. . . . . $ 15.00- 20.00
1470. BOLDT MASON JAR – 1920's – Zinc lid – 3 sizes – Blue,
green – Round. . . . . $ 8.00- 20.00
1471. BORDEN'S MILK CO. – 1885 – Metal band and glass in-
sert – Pint – Clear – Hexagon. . . . . $ 10.00- 20.00
1472. BOSCO DOUBLE SEAL – 1920 – Glass lid & full bail –
Quart – Clear – Round. . . . . $ 4.00- 8.00
1473. BOYD MASON – 1910-1915 – Zinc lid – Quart, pint –
Pale green, olive green, clear to indefinite – Round. . . . $ 3.00- 6.00

1474.	BOYD'S MASON GENUINE – 1895-1905 – Zinc lid – Quart – Aqua, clear – Round.	$ 4.00- 10.00
1475.	BOYD PERFECT MASON – 1910 – Zinc lid – Quart, pint, ½ pint – Green – Round.	$ 4.00- 6.00
1476.	BRAUN SAFETEE MASON – Zinc lid – 3 sizes – Aqua. .	$ 4.00- 5.00
1477.	BRELLE JAR – 1912-1920 – Glass lid & wire clamp – Quart – Clear – Round, wide mouth.	$ 15.00- 30.00
1478.	BRIGHTON – 1890-1895 – Glass lid, metal wire clamp – Quart – Clear, amber, amethyst – Round.	$ 25.00- 50.00
1480.	BROCKWAY CLEAR – VU MASON – 1925-1936 – Metal screw band & glass insert – Quart, pint – Green, clear- Round.	$ 2.00- 4.00
1481.	C.D. BROOKS BOSTON (on shoulder) – Glass lid and metal clamp.	$ 45.00- 60.00
1482.	BROWN & CO., GEO. D. – 1875 – Glass lid & heavy metal clamp – Quart – Green – Round.	$ 30.00- 60.00
1483.	BUCKEYE 1 – Ground lip with glass lid and iron clamp – Aqua.	$125.00-175.00
1484.	BUFFALO BREWING CO. S.F. AGENCY BB-CO. – Monogrammed on top. 9¼″ high. Amber.	$ 6.00 10.00
1485.	BULACH – Modern – Glass lid & wire clip – Quart – Green – Tall round.	$ 4.00- 10.00
1486.	BURLINGTON, THE – 1880-1890 – Zinc band – Quart – Clear, aqua – Round.	$ 10.00- 20.00
1487.	BURNHAM & CO. – 1865-1870 – Iron lid – Quart – Deep green – Round.	$ 60.00-100.00
1488.	CALCUTT'S PATENT – 1885, Glass lid & wire clip – Pint, Quart – Green – Round.	$ 6.00- 10.00
1489.	CANADIAN JEWEL – 1950's – Glass lid & zinc band – All sizes clear – Round.	$ 2.00- 4.00
1490.	CANADIAN KING – 1920-1940 – Glass lid & full wire bail Pint, quart, ½ pint – Clear – Square.	$ 4.00- 10.00
1491.	CANADIAN MASON JAR – Modern – Zinc lid – Pint, quart, ½ pint – Clear – Square.	$ 2.00- 4.00
1492.	CANADIAN SURE SEAL – 1920-1940 – Metal lid & wide metal screw band – Pint, quart, ½ gal. – Clear – Wide mouth.	$ 2.00- 4.00
1493.	CANTON DOMESTIC FRUIT JAR – 1895 – Glass lid & wire bail – Clear – Quart – Round.	$ 15.00- 40.00
1494.	CARTER'S BUTTER & FRUIT PRESERVING JAR – Pat. Sept. 28, 1897. All lettering is on lid. Aqua.	$ 30.00- 75.00
1495.	CASSIDY – 1885 – Glass lid & wire bail – Clear – Round.	$ 75.00-150.00
1496.	C.C. CO. – 1905 – Glass lid – Aqua – Round.	$ 30.00- 40.00
1497.	C.F.J. CO. – 1871 – Glass lid & metal band – Quart – Green – Round.	$ 10.00- 20.00
1498.	C G CO. – 1890 – Screw lid – Quart – Aqua, clear – Round.	$ 10.00- 20.00
1499.	CHAMPION (THE) Pat. Aug. 31, 1869 – Glass lid & top metal screwband – Quart – Aqua – Round – Straight-sided.	$ 50.00-100.00
1500.	CHEF – July 14, 1908 – Glass lid & wire bail – Quart – Clear – Rounded – Square.	$ 4.00- 8.00
	½ pint – Clear.	$ 9.00- 10.00
1501.	CLARKE FRUIT JAR CO. – 1886-1889 – Glass lid and wire bail with lever-lock clamp – Quart – Aqua – Round.	$ 15.00- 30.00

1502.	CLARK'S PEERLESS – 1882-1898 – Wire bail & glass lid Quart – Green, blue – Round.	$ 10.00- 20.00
1503.	CLEVELAND FRUIT JUICE CO. – 1920-1935 – Glass lid & wire bail – Quart – Clear – Round.	$ 4.00- 6.00
1504.	CLIMAX – 1908 – Full wire bail & glass lid – Pint – Blue Round.	$ 4.00- 8.00
1505.	CLYDE GLASS – 1895 – Glass lid & wire bail – Quart – Clear, aqua – Round.	$ 10.00- 15.00
1506.	CLYDE MASON – 1880's – Screw top – Quart – Green – Round.	$ 10.00- 20.00
1507.	CLYDE (THE) – 1880's – Glass lid – Quart – Green – Round.	$ 10.00- 15.00
1508.	COHANSEY No. 1 – 1870 – Metal cap or glass lid and clamp – Quart – Aqua – Round, barrel-shaped.	$ 10.00- 25.00
1509.	COHANSEY No. 2 – 1870 – Glass lid & wire ring clip – ½ gal. – Light blue – Round.	$ 10.00- 25.00
1510.	COLUMBIA – 1900 – Glass lid with clamp – Quart – Amber, light green – Round.	$ 20.00- 30.00
1511.	COMMONWEALTH FRUIT JAR – 1910 – Glass lid & wire bail – Quart – Green – Round.	$ 30.00- 60.00
1512.	CONSERVE JAR – 1890-1910 – Glass lid & full wire bail Pint, Quart – Clear to amethyst – Round.	$ 4.00- 8.00
1513.	CORONA JAR – 1920-1930 – Zinc screw band & glass lid – Quart – Clear – Round.	$ 2.00- 4.00
1514.	CORONA IMPROVED – 1950's – Glass lid & zinc band – 4 sizes – Clear – Round.	$ 2.00- 4.00
1515.	CORONA JAR – 1925 – Zinc band & glass insert – 4 sizes – Clear – Round.	$ 2.00- 4.00
1516.	CORONA JAR IMPROVED – 1940's – Beaded neck design – 4 sizes – Clear – Round.	$ 2.00- 3.00
1517.	CROWN – 1870-1880 – Glass lid & zinc screw band – Pint, quart, ½ gal. – Aqua – Round.	$ 10.00- 20.00
1518.	CROWN No. 1 – 1870-1880 – Glass lid & zinc screw band – All sizes – Aqua – Round.	$ 5.00- 15.00
1519.	CROWN No. 2 – 1870-1890 – Glass lid & metal screw band – Blue tint – Round.	$ 6.00- 10.00
1520.	CROWN No. 3 – 1870-1890 – Glass lid & zinc screw band – Pint, quart, ½ gal. – Clear – Round.	$ 2.00- 4.00
1521.	CROWN CORDIAL & EXTRACT – 1885 – Glass lid & wire bail – Quart – Light green – Round.	$ 8.00- 16.00
1522.	CROWN IMPERIAL QUART – Glass lid & zinc screw band – Pint, quart – Aqua – Round.	$ 5.00- 10.00
1523.	CROWN IMPROVED – 1910 – Metal band with glass insert – Quart – Clear – Round.	$ 6.00- 10.00
1524.	CROWN (on shoulder, label) – Twisted neck, applied lip, 3 piece mold, deep grooves, iron pontil, Olive	$ 10.00- 20.00
1525.	CROWN MASON – 1910 – Zinc screw band & white opal insert – Pint, quart, ½ gal. – Clear – Round with vertical ribs about the sides.	$ 2.00- 4.00
1526.	CRYSTAL – 1873-1880 – Threaded glass lid – Quart – Green – Round tapering sides.	$ 20.00- 30.00
1527.	CRYSTAL JAR – 1879 – Glass screw-on lid – Quart, pint, ½ gal. – Clear – Round.	$ 20.00- 30.00
1528.	CRYSTAL JAR C.G. – 1878 – Glass screw-on lid – Quart Clear – Round.	$ 20.00- 30.00

1550   1557   1569   1573

1529.	CUNNINGHAM & IHMSEN – 1868-1879 – Wax sealer – Quart, ½ gal – Aqua, cobalt blue – Round.	$ 20.00- 30.00
1530.	CUNNINGHAM'S & CO. PITTSBURGH (on base) – Stopper neck. Base iron pontil. Aqua.	$100.00-150.00
1531.	CUNNINGHAM'S & CO. – 1879 – Wax sealer – Quart – Aqua – Round.	$ 10.00- 20.00
1532.	CURTIS & MOORE – 1900 – Glass lid & wire bail – Quart Clear – Round.	$ 25.00- 35.00
1533.	DAISY, (THE) – 1890 – Glass lid & wire bail – Quart – Aqua – Round.	$ 8.00- 14.00
1534.	DAISY JAR (THE) – 1885-1890 – Heavy iron clamp – Quart – Clear – Round.............................	$ 15.00- 25.00
1535.	DALBEY'S FRUIT JAR – 1866 – Glass lid – Quart – Deep aqua – Round extending wax seal neck.	$ 40.00- 50.00
1536.	DANDY (THE) – 1885 – Glass lid & wire clamp – Quart – Amber, light green – Round & slender.	$ 20.00- 40.00
1537.	DARLING, (THE) – 1885 – Zinc screw band & glass insert – Quart – Aqua – Round tapering sides.	$ 20.00- 40.00
1538.	DECKER DEPENDABLE FOOD – 1910-1920 – Zinc lid – Quart – Clear – Round...........................	$ 2.00- 6.00
1539.	DECKER'S IOWANA – 1935 – Glass lid & wire bail – Quart – Clear – Round............................	$ 3.00- 6.00
1540.	DECKER'S VICTOR – 1935 – Glass lid & wire bail – Quart – Clear – Round............................	$ 3.00- 6.00
1541.	DEXTER – 1865 – Zinc band with glass insert – Quart – Aqua – Round.	$ 30.00- 60.00
1542.	DIAMOND FRUIT JAR – 1915-1920 – Glass lid & full wire bail – Pint, quart, ½ gal. – Clear – Round.	$ 4.00- 10.00
1543.	DICTATIR, THE – 1855-1869 – Wax seal lip & glass or metal cap – Quart – Light blue – Round.	$ 40.00- 65.00
1544.	DILLION – 1890-1895 – Wax sealer – Quart – Aqua – Round..	$ 15.00- 20.00
1545.	DOMINION – 1886-1898 – Zinc band & glass insert – Quart – Clear – Round............................	$ 30.00- 60.00
1546.	DOMINION MASON – 1915-1920 – Zinc lid – Pint, quart, ½ gal. – Clear – Square.	$ 2.00- 4.00
1547.	DOMINION SPECIAL – 1915-1920 – Zinc lid – Quart – Clear – Round wide mouth........................	$ 2.00- 4.00
1548.	DOMINION WIDEMOUTH SPECIAL – 1915-1920 – Zinc lid – Pint, quart, ½ gal. – Clear – Round.	$ 4.00- 6.00

1549.	DOOLITTLE – 1900-1915 – Glass lid – Quart – Clear, aqua – Round, wide mouth.	$ 10.00- 20.00
1550.	DOUBLE SAFETY No. 1 – 1905 – Glass lid & full wire bail – Quart, pint – Clear – Round.	$ 2.00- 4.00
1551.	DOUBLE SAFETY No.2 – 1907 – Glass lid & full wire bail – ½ gal. – Clear – Round.	$ 2.00- 4.00
1552.	DOUBLE SEAL – 1920-1930 – Glass lid & full wire bail – Quart, pint, ½ gal. – Clear to amethyst – Round.	$ 2.00- 6.00
1553.	DREY EVER SEAL – 1910-1920 – Glass lid & full wire bail – Pint, quart, ½ gal. – Clear to amethyst – Round.	$ 2.00- 4.00
1554.	DREY IMPROVED EVER SEAL – 1920-1925 – Glass lid & full wire bail – Pint, quart, ½ gal. – Clear – Round.	$ 2.00- 4.00
1555.	DREY MASON – 1910-1920 – Screw top – 3 sizes – Aqua Round.	$ 2.00- 4.00
1556.	DREY PERFECT MASON – 1910 – Zinc lid – Pint, quart, ½ gal. – Green, clear – Round.	$ 1.00- 2.00
1557.	DREY PERFECT MASON – 1910 – Zinc lid – Pint, quart, ½ gal. – Pale green, Clear – Round.	$ 3.00- 6.00
1558.	DREY SQUARE MASON – 1920-1925 – Zinc lid – Pint, quart, ½ gal. – Clear to amethyst – Square.	$ 1.00- 2.00
1559.	DUNKLEY CELERY CO., THE – Calamazoo (on bottom) Clear, glass lid with fastener.	$ 10.00- 15.00
1560.	DUNKLEY PRESERVING CO., THE – 1898 – Glass lid and metal clamp – Quart – Clear – Round.	$ 10.00- 20.00
1561.	DU PONT – 1910 – Screw-on top – Quart – Aqua to green – Round.	$ 10.00- 20.00
1562.	DURHAM – 1915 – Glass lid & wire bail – Quart – Aqua – Round.	$ 10.00- 15.00
1563.	DYSON'S PURE FOOD – 1920 – Metal band – Quart – Clear – Round.	$ 15.00- 20.00
1564.	EAGLE – 1876 – Glass lid & iron thumbscrew to tighten Quart – Light green – Round.	$ 90.00-103.00
1565.	EASI-PAK MASON – METRO – 1942-1946 – Screw top – Clear – Round.	$ 6.00- 10.00
1566.	EASY VACUUM JAR – 1895 - 1905 – Glass lid – Quart – Clear – Tall & round.	$ 10.00- 15.00
1567.	ECLIPSE (THE) – 1865-1875 – Wax sealer – Quart – Aqua.	$ 65.00- 85.00
1568.	ECLIPSE WAX SEALER – 1865-1875 – Wax sealer – Quart – Green.	$ 50.00- 75.00
	Amber	$100.00-225.00
1569.	ECONOMY – 1905-1915 – Metal lid & spring wire clamp Pint, quart, ½ gal. – Clear to amethyst – Round.	$ 3.00- 6.00
1570.	ECONOMY PAT APPLIED FOR (THE) – Ground lip – Aqua.	$ 75.00- 95.00
1571.	ELECTRIC – 1910 – Glass lid & wire bail – Quart – Aqua Round.	$ 10.00- 20.00
1572.	ELECTRIC FRUIT JAR – 1900-1915 – Glass lid & metal clamp – Quart – Aqua – Round.	$ 25.00- 35.00
1573.	EMPIRE – 1860's – Glass stopper – Quart – Aqua, deep blue – Round.	$ 30.00- 55.00
1574.	EMPIRE (THE) – 1866 – Glass lid with iron lugs to fasten it – Quart – Aqua – Round.	$ 45.00- 65.00
1575.	ERIC (on bottom) – Old Style lightning seal – Clear.	$ 10.00- 15.00
1576.	ERIE FRUIT JAR – 1890's – Screw top – Quart – Clear – Round.	$ 15.00- 35.00

1577. ERMEBLOK – Modern – Hinged glass lid – Quart – Clear – Round. .... $ 8.00- 12.00

1578. EUREKA No. 1 – 1864 – Wax dipped cork or other – Pint Aqua – Round, extending neck. .... $ 10.00- 20.00

1579. EUREKA No. 2 – 1864 – Glass lid & top metal band – Quart – Clear, aqua – Round. .... $ 10.00- 15.00

1580. EVERLASTING JAR – 1904 – Glass lid & double wire hook fastener – Pint, quart, ½ gal. – Green – Round.... $ 10.00- 20.00

1581. EXCELSIOR – 1880-1890 – Zinc screw band & glass insert – Quart – Aqua – Round, tapering. .... $ 15.00- 30.00

1582. EXCELSIOR, (M on bottom) – 9¾" high – Aqua .... $ 10.00- 20.00

1583. F.A. & CO. – 1860-1862 – Glass stopper – Quart – Aqua Round.. $ 25.00- 50.00

1584. F.A. & CO. – (Embossed on base) – Glass stopper – Quart – Aqua – Iron pontil mark on base.............. $ 95.00-120.00

1585. FAHNSTOCK ALBREE & CO. – (Embossed on base) – Wax sealer – Aqua................................. $ 15.00- 30.00

1586. FARLEY – Glass lid & full wire bail – Pint, quart – Clear Square, slender................................. $ 4.00- 10.00

1587. F.C.G. CO. – 1875 – Metal cap – Quart – Round – Amber... $ 40.00- 50.00
Green... $ 20.00- 30.00

1588. FEDERAL FRUIT JAR – 1895 – Glass lid & wire bail – Quart – Olive green – Round. .... $ 15.00- 30.00

1589. FLACCUS BROS. STEERHEAD – 1890 – Glass screw lid Quart – Milk glass amber, green, clear – Round........ $ 75.00-175.00

1590. FLETT W. & J. – 1885 – Glass stopper – Quart – Blue – Round.. $ 40.00- 50.00

1591. FORSTER JAR, THE – 1920-1925 – Zinc band & glass insert – 3 sizes – Clear – Round. .... $ 15.00- 30.00

1592. FOSTER SEALFAST – 1910 – Glass lid & full wire bail – Pint, quart, ½ gal. – Clear, amber, amethyst – Round. ... $ 4.00- 10.00

1593. FRANKLIN FRUIT JAR – 1865-1870 – screw-on lid – Quart – Green – Round.......................... $ 30.00- 50.00
Midget Aqua .... $ 60.00- 75.00

1594. FRANKLIN DEXTER FRUIT JAR – 1865-1875 – Zinc lid – Quart – Aqua – Round tapering sides. .... $ 15.00- 30.00

1595. FRUIT GROWER'S TRADE CO. – 1910 – Wax dipped cork or other. Quart – Green – Oval, extending wax seal neck. .... $ 25.00- 40.00

1596. FRUIT KEEPER – 1895 Glass lid & metal clamp – Quart Deep green – Round straight sided.................. $ 10.00- 20.00

1597. GAYNER, THE – 1915-1925 – Glass lid & wire bail – Quart – Clear – Round........................... $ 9.00- 15.00

1598. GEM, THE No. 1 – 1856 – Zinc band & glass insert – Quart – Amber, aqua, green – Round. .... $ 12.00- 25.00

1599. GEM No. 1 – 1867-1872 – Zinc screw band & glass insert – Pint, ½ gal. – Aqua – Round. .... $ 10.00- 15.00

1600. GEM No. 2 – 1882-1884 – Zinc screw band & glass insert – Quart – Green – Round...................... $ 10.00- 20.00

1601. GEM No. 3 – 1869 – Zinc screw band & glass insert – Pint, quart – Aqua – Round, tapering sides. .... $ 10.00- 15.00

1602. GEM, (THE) – CFJ Monogram – 1882-1884 – Wide zinc screw band & glass insert – Quart – Aqua, green – Round tapering sides......................... $ 10.00- 20.00

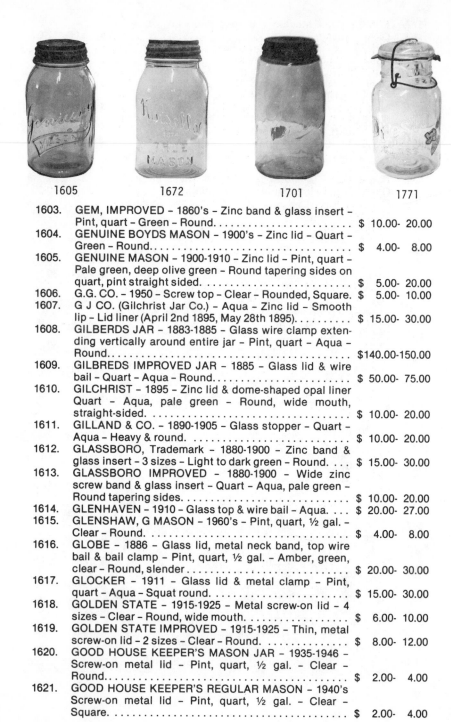

1605   1672   1701   1771

1603. **GEM, IMPROVED** – 1860's – Zinc band & glass insert – Pint, quart – Green – Round. .... $ 10.00- 20.00

1604. **GENUINE BOYDS MASON** – 1900's – Zinc lid – Quart – Green – Round. .... $ 4.00- 8.00

1605. **GENUINE MASON** – 1900-1910 – Zinc lid – Pint, quart – Pale green, deep olive green – Round tapering sides on quart, pint straight sided. .... $ 5.00- 20.00

1606. **G.G. CO.** – 1950 – Screw top – Clear – Rounded, Square. $ 5.00- 10.00

1607. **G J CO.** (Gilchrist Jar Co.) – Aqua – Zinc lid – Smooth lip – Lid liner (April 2nd 1895, May 28th 1895). .... $ 15.00- 30.00

1608. **GILBERDS JAR** – 1883-1885 – Glass wire clamp extending vertically around entire jar – Pint, quart – Aqua – Round. $140.00-150.00

1609. **GILBREDS IMPROVED JAR** – 1885 – Glass lid & wire bail – Quart – Aqua – Round. .... $ 50.00- 75.00

1610. **GILCHRIST** – 1895 – Zinc lid & dome-shaped opal liner Quart – Aqua, pale green – Round, wide mouth, straight-sided. .... $ 10.00- 20.00

1611. **GILLAND & CO.** – 1890-1905 – Glass stopper – Quart – Aqua – Heavy & round. .... $ 10.00- 20.00

1612. **GLASSBORO, Trademark** – 1880-1900 – Zinc band & glass insert – 3 sizes – Light to dark green – Round. .... $ 15.00- 30.00

1613. **GLASSBORO IMPROVED** – 1880-1900 – Wide zinc screw band & glass insert – Quart – Aqua, pale green – Round tapering sides. .... $ 10.00- 20.00

1614. **GLENHAVEN** – 1910 – Glass top & wire bail – Aqua. .... $ 20.00- 27.00

1615. **GLENSHAW, G MASON** – 1960's – Pint, quart, ½ gal. – Clear – Round. .... $ 4.00- 8.00

1616. **GLOBE** – 1886 – Glass lid, metal neck band, top wire bail & bail clamp – Pint, quart, ½ gal. – Amber, green, clear – Round, slender .... $ 20.00- 30.00

1617. **GLOCKER** – 1911 – Glass lid & metal clamp – Pint, quart – Aqua – Squat round. .... $ 15.00- 30.00

1618. **GOLDEN STATE** – 1915-1925 – Metal screw-on lid – 4 sizes – Clear – Round, wide mouth. .... $ 6.00- 10.00

1619. **GOLDEN STATE IMPROVED** – 1915-1925 – Thin, metal screw-on lid – 2 sizes – Clear – Round. .... $ 8.00- 12.00

1620. **GOOD HOUSE KEEPER'S MASON JAR** – 1935-1946 – Screw-on metal lid – Pint, quart, ½ gal. – Clear – Round. .... $ 2.00- 4.00

1621. **GOOD HOUSE KEEPER'S REGULAR MASON** – 1940's Screw-on metal lid – Pint, quart, ½ gal. – Clear – Square. .... $ 2.00- 4.00

114

1622.	GREEN MOUNTAIN – 1900-1915 – Glass lid & wire bail Pint, quart – Aqua – Round	$ 8.00- 10.00
1623.	G SQUARE MASON – 1940's – Metal screw-on lid – Quart – Clear – Rounded square.	$ 4.00- 8.00
1624.	GUTSCH BREWING CO. – 13 on bottom – Red – 8½″ high.	$ 10.00- 20.00
1625.	HAINES – 1880-1885 – Glass lid & iron clamp – Quart – Green – Round.	$ 50.00-100.00
1626.	HAINES' IMPROVED – 1870 – Glass lid & top wire bail – Quart – Aqua, green – Round.	$ 50.00- 75.00
1627.	HAINES' IMPROVED "NE PLUS ULTRA" – Glass lid, lid has three dates. Embossed on base (Putnam Glass Works, Zanesville, Ohio) – Aqua.	$ 75.00-125.00
1628.	HAINES' PATENT MARCH 1, 1870 – Grooved glass lid & top wire bail – Quart – Aqua – Round.	$ 50.00- 75.00
1629.	HARRIS – 1860's – Metal lid – Quart – Deep green – Round.	$ 50.00- 90.00
1630.	HARRIS IMPROVED – 1875-1880 – Glass lid & iron clamp – Quart – Green – Round.	$ 50.00- 75.00
1631.	HASEROT COMPANY – 1915-1925 – Zinc lid – Quart – Green – Round, tapering sides.	$ 10.00- 20.00
1632.	HAZEL – 1895 – Glass lid & wire bail – Pint, quart – Aqua – Round.	$ 10.00- 20.00
1633.	HAZEL-ATLAS LIGHTNING SEAL – 1915 – Full wire bail & glass lid – Pint, quart – Green – Round.	$ 8.00- 12.00
1634.	H & D – 1915 – Metal band & glass insert – Aqua – Round.	$ 6.00- 12.00
1635.	HERO (THE) – 1867 – Wide zinc band & glass insert – Quart, ½ gal. – Green – Round, tapering sides.	$ 15.00- 20.00
1636.	HERO IMPROVED – 1867-1872 – Made by Hero Glass works. Philadelphia, PA – Aqua – Ground lip – Glass lid & screw band top.	$ 8.00- 10.00
1637.	HEROINT, (THE) – 1867 – Wide zinc screw band & glass insert – Quart – Light green – Round.	$ 10.00- 20.00
1638.	HIGH GRADE, (THE) – 1870 – Zinc screw-on top – Clear Round.	$ 15.00- 20.00
1639.	HOLZ, CLARK & TAYLOR – 1875-1885 – Screw-on glass lid – Quart – Aqua – Round.	$100.00-140.00
1640.	HOM-PAK – 1940's – Metal lid – Clear – Round.	$ 3.00- 4.00
1641.	HOM-PAK MASON. – 1940's – Two-piece lid – Pint, quart – Clear – Square.	$ 4.00- 6.00
1642.	HORMEL – 1935-1945 – Glass lid & side wire clips – Pint, quart – Square – Clear – Oval.	$ 3.00- 6.00
1643.	HOSTER CO. – O 665 and mark on bottom – Amber.	$ 6.00- 9.00
1644.	H & R – 1885 – Round wax sealer – Quart – Blue – Round.	$ 10.00- 20.00
1645.	H & S (HALLER & SAMUEL) – Aqua & clear – Ground lip metal stopper fits over outside of neck.	$300.00-400.00
1646.	IDEAL, (THE) – 1885-1900 – Zinc lid – Pint, quart – Clear Round.	$ 10.00- 25.00
1647.	IDEAL WIDE MOUTH JAR – 1930 – Flat metal lid – Quart – Clear – Round or square.	$ 2.00- 4.00
1648.	I.G. CO. – 1900 – Screw top – Quart – Aqua – Round.	$ 15.00- 25.00
1649.	IMPERIAL, (THE) – 1886 – Glass lid & wire clamp – Quart – Pale green – Round.	$ 10.00- 20.00

1650. IMPERIAL IMPROVED QUART – 1920-1925 – Glass lid & wide zinc screw band – Quart – Aqua, light green – Round.. $ 4.00- 8.00

1651. INDEPENDENT – 1885-1890 – Screw-on glass lid – Quart – Clear to amethyst – Round................. $ 15.00- 25.00

1652. INDEPENDENT JAR – 1882 – Glass screw-on lid – Quart – Clear to amethyst – Round................. $ 25.00- 30.00

1653. IVANHOE – 1945-1950 – Glass lid & wire bail – Quart – Clear – Round. .... $ 5.00- 10.00

1654. J & B FRUIT JAR – 1898 – Zinc lid – Pint, quart – Light green – Round................................ $ 20.00- 50.00

1655. JEANNETTE HOME PACKER – 1935 – Zinc screw band & glass insert – Quart – Clear – Round. .... $ 3.00- 6.00

1656. JERSEY – Aqua, clear – Ground lip – Screw band with glass lid. .... $ 60.00-100.00

1657. JEWEL JAR No. 1 – 1915-1920 – Wide zinc screw band & glass lid – Quart – Clear to amethyst – Round. ...... $ 4.00- 8.00

1658. JEWEL JAR No. 2 – 1915-1920 – Wide zinc screw band & glass lid – Quart – Clear – Round. .... $ 6.00- 12.00

1659. J.G. CO. MONOGRAM – 1895 – Zinc lid & domed opal liner – Quart – Green – Round, wide mouth. .... $ 10.00- 24.00

1660. JOHNSON & JOHNSON – 1887-1891 – Metal clamp – Quart – Amber – Square........................ $ 60.00- 90.00

1661. KALAMAZOO, (THE) – 1870-1875 – Wax sealer – Pint, quart – Clear – Round. .... $ 8.00- 12.00

1662. K.C. MASON – 1920 – Zinc lid – Quart – Clear to pink amethyst – Square. .... $ 4.00- 10.00

1663. KEEFFER'S No. 1 – 1870 – Glass screw-on lid – Quart – Aqua – Round. $125.00-150.00

1664. KEEFER'S No. 2 (Same as No. 1) – Clear.

1665. KERR ECONOMY – 1915 – Metal lid & narrow clip band Pint, quart – Clear, amethyst, maize – Round.......... $ 2.00- 3.00

1666. KERR GLASS TOP MASON – 1940's – Flat metal lid – Pint, quart – Clear – Round. .... $ 3.00- 6.00

1667. KERR SELF SEALING MASON – 1920 – Flat metal lid & screw band – Pint, quart, ½ gal. – Clear to amethyst – Round.. $ 2.00- 3.00

1668. KERR SELF SEALING WIDEMOUTH – 1930 – Quart – Aqua, clear – Round. .... $ 3.00- 6.00

1669. K-G – 1920's – Glass lid & wire bail – Quart – Clear – Round.. $ 5.00- 10.00

1670. KILNER JAR, (THE) – 1915 – Zinc screw band & glass insert – Pint, quart – Clear – Round.................. $ 5.00- 10.00

1671. KING – 1910-1920 – Full wire bail & glass lid – Pint, quart, ½ gal. – Clear to amethyst – Oval.............. $ 10.00- 15.00

1672. KINSELLS TRUE MASON – 1874 – Zinc lid – Quart, pint Clear – Round. .... $ 6.00- 12.00

1673. KLINE A.R. – 1863 – Glass fitting lid & clamp – Quart – Aqua – Round. .... $ 10.00- 20.00

1674. KNIGHT PACKING CO. – 1925-1930 – Screw top – Quart Clear – Round. .... $ 3.00- 6.00

1675. KNOWLTON VACUUM FRUIT JAR – 1903 – Zinc lid & glass insert – Quart – Aqua, blue – Round. .... $ 10.00- 25.00

1676. KNOX MASON – 1925-1935 – Zinc lid – Quart, pint, ½ pint – Clear – Square............................. $ 2.00- 4.00

1677.	KOHRS No. 1 - 1908 - Glass lid & half wire bail - Pint, quart, ½ gal. - Clear - Round.	$ 2.00- 6.00
1678.	KOHRS No. 2 - 1930-1940 - Zinc lid - Pint, quart, ½ gal. Clear - Round.	$ 2.00- 6.00
1679.	LAFAYETTE No. 1 - 1864 - Wax dipped cork - Pint, quart - Aqua - Round - Picture.	$175.00-250.00
1680.	LAFAYETTE No. 2 - 1864 - Wax dipped cork - Pint, quart - Aqua, green, clear to amethyst - Round - No picture.	$ 50.00- 90.00
1681.	LAMB MASON - 1940-1950 - Zinc lid - Pint, quart, ½ gal. - Clear to pink - Round.	$ 4.00- 6.00
1682.	LEADER, (THE) - 1892 - Glass lid & wire clamp - Quart Amber - Round - One & two liner.	$ 40.00- 60.00
	Clear - Aqua	$ 20.00- 40.00
1683.	LEE & CO., J. ELWOOD - 1900-1910 - Zinc screw & amber glass insert - Quart - Amber - Square.	$ 8.00- 12.00
1684.	LEOTRIC - 1900 - Glass lid - Pint, quart, ½ gal. - Medium green - Round.	$ 8.00- 14.00
1685.	LIGHTNING - 1882 - Glass lid & full wire bail - Pint, quart - Amber, aqua - Round.	$ 8.00- 20.00
1686.	LINDELL GLASS CO. - 1870 - Wax sealer - Quart - Round - Aqua.	$ 15.00- 20.00
	Amber	$ 35.00- 50.00
1687.	LOCKPORT MASON - 1910 - Zinc lid - Pint, quart, ½ gal. - Aqua - Round.	$ 5.00- 11.00
1688.	LOCKPORT MASON, IMPROVED - 1910 - Zinc screw band - glass insert - Pint, quart, ½ gal. - Aqua, amber Round.	$ 9.00- 20.00
1689.	L & S - 1908 - Glass lid & half wire bail - Quart - Clear - Round.	$ 4.00- 9.00
1690.	LUDLOW'S PATENT JUNE 28, 1859 - Ground lip, glass lid - Aqua.	$ 50.00-100.00
1691.	LUSTRE - 1900 - Glass lid & wire bail - 3 sizes - Aqua - Round.	$ 10.00- 20.00
1692.	L & W - 1860 - Wax sealer - Quart - Green - Round.	$ 25.00- 35.00
1693.	LYMAN, W.W. - 1862 - Glass lid & wire clamp - Quart - Aqua - Round.	$ 35.00- 60.00
1694.	LYON & BOSSARD'S JAR - 1890 - Glass lid & iron clamp - Quart - Aqua - Round.	$125.00-150.00
1695.	LORILLARD & CO. - 1880 - Glass lid & metal clamp - Pint, quart, ½ gal. - Aqua, amber - Round.	$ 9.00- 17.00
1696.	MAGIC FRUIT JAR, (THE) - 1885-1890 - Glass lid & iron clamp - Pint, quart - Aqua, amber - Round.	$ 50.00- 75.00
1697.	MACOMB No. 1 - 1889-1910 - Zinc lid - Pint, quart - White pottery - Round.	$ 5.00- 10.00
1698.	MACOMB No. 2 - 1899 - Zinc lid - Pint, quart - White pottery - Round angled shoulder.	$ 8.00- 12.00
1699.	MALLINGER - 1930's - Zinc lid - Quart - Clear - Round.	$ 8.00- 10.00
1700.	MARION JAR, (THE) - 1858 - Zinc lid - Pint, quart - Aqua, green - Round tapering sides.	$ 8.00- 13.00
1701.	MASON, (THE) - 1930's - Zinc lid - Pint, quart, ½ gal. - Light green - Round tapering sides.	$ 4.00- 6.00
1702.	MASON No. 1 - 1920 - Zinc lid - Pint, quart - Deep green, medium green, yellow green, clear - Round tapering sides.	$ 8.00- 13.00

117

1703. MASON No. 2 – 1910-1920 – Glass lid & zinc screw band – Pint, quart, ½ gal. – Green – Round tapering sides.. $ 8.00- 10.00

1704. MASON FRUIT JAR – 1890-1910 – Zinc lid – Quart – Clear – Round tapering sides....................... $ 4.00- 9.00

1705. MASON FRUIT JAR No. 1 – 1890-1910 – Zinc lid – Pint, quart, ½ gal. – Amber, aqua, light green, clear – Round tapering sides................................... $ 4.00- 12.00
Amber .... $ 25.00- 50.00

1706. MASON FRUIT JAR No. 2 – 1913-1920 – Zinc lid – Pint, quart, ½ gal. – Aqua – Round tapering sides.......... $ 10.00- 17.00

1707. MASON FRUIT JAR PATENT NOV. 30, 1858 – Zinc lid – Pint, quart, ½ gal. – Aqua – Round.................. $ 10.00- 15.00

1708. MASON IMPROVED JAR – 1880-1900 – Zinc lid – Pint, quart, ½ gal. – Green – Round tapering sides........ $ 5.00- 10.00

1709. MASON'S IMPROVED No. 1 – 1867 – Zinc screw band & glass insert – Aqua, light green, olive green – Round tapering sides.................................... $ 3.00- 5.00

1710. MASON'S IMPROVED No. 2 – 1871 – Zinc screw band & glass insert – Pint, quart, ½ gal. – Aqua, green – Round tapering sides.................................... $ 15.00- 30.00

1711. MASON JAR OF 1858 (THE) – Zinc lid – Pint, quart, ½ gal. – Aqua – Round tapering sides.................. $ 8.00- 15.00

1712. MASON JAR OF 1872 (THE) – Zinc screw band & glass insert – Quart – Light green – Round. .... $ 20.00- 30.00

1713. MASON PATENT NOV. 30, 1880 – Zinc lid – Pint, quart, ½ gal. – Clear – Round tapering sides. .... $ 10.00- 20.00

1714. MASON'S PATENT 1858 – Zinc lid – Pint, quart – Amber, green – Round tapering sides................ $ 20.00- 28.00

1715. MASON'S PATENT 1858 – Zinc lid – Pint, quart, ½ gal. Aqua – Round tapering sides........................ $ 5.00- 7.00

1716. MASON'S PATENT NOV. 30, 1858 – Zinc lid – Pint, quart, ½ gal. – Amber, yellow, green – Round......... $ 6.00- 10.00

1717. MASON'S PATENT NOV. 30, 1858 – Zinc lid – Pint – Aqua, green – Round, straight sided................. $ 50.00- 75.00

1718. MASON'S PATENT NOV. 30, 1858 – Zinc lid – Pint, quart, ½ gal. – Clear – Round tapering sides.......... $ 10.00- 30.00

1719. MASON'S CFJ PATENT NOV. 30, 1858 – Zinc lid – Pint, quart, ½ gal. – Amber, aqua, green – Round tapering sides... $ 10.00- 20.00

1720. MASON'S CG PATENT NOV. 30, 1858 – Zinc lid – Pint, quart, ½ gal. – Dark green – Round.................. $ 8.00- 12.00

1721. MASON'S PATENT – 1900 – Zinc lid – Pint, quart, ½ gal. – Aqua, deep green – Clear – Round tapering sides. $ 3.00- 6.00

1722. MASON'S KEYSTONE – 1869 – Zinc screw band & glass insert – Quart – Deep aqua – Round tapering sides... $ 8.00- 10.00

1723. MASON STAR-DESIGN JAR – 1960's – Zinc lid – Pint, quart, ½ gal. – Clear – Square. .... $ 5.00- 10.00

1724. MATTHIA'S & HENDERSON – 1905 – Glass lid & heavy wire clamp – Quart – Clear – Round. .... $ 10.00- 20.00

1725. McDONALD NEW PERFECT SEAL – 1908 – Wire bail & glass lid – Quart – Blue – Round. .... $ 7.00- 10.00

1726. METRO EASI-PAK MASON – 1942-1946 – Threaded neck – Pint, quart – Clear – Round................... $ 1.00- 2.00

1727. M F A – 1941-1945 – Metal screw-on lid – Quart – Clear – Rounded square. .... $ 8.00- 15.00

1728.	MICHIGAN MASON – 1911-1916 – Zinc lid – Quart – Clear – Round tapering sides.	$ 5.00- 10.00
1729.	MID WEST – 1930's – Wide zinc screw band & glass lid Pint, quart, ½ gal. – Clear, amethyst – Round.	$ 2.00- 4.00
1730.	MILLVILLE IMPROVED – 1885 – Zinc lid & glass insert Quart – Aqua – Round.	$ 10.00- 20.00
1731.	MISSION MASON JAR – 1925 – Zinc lid – Pint, quart, ½ gal. – Light green, clear, amethyst – Round.	$ 6.00- 9.00
1732.	MODEL MASON – 1910 – Zinc lid – Quart – Green – Round tapering sides.	$ 8.00- 14.00
1733.	MOORE, JOHN M. – 1865-1875 – Glass lid & heavy iron clamp – Quart – Aqua – Round.	$ 75.00-125.00
1734.	MOORE'S PATENT DEC. 3, 1861 – Glass lid with cast iron clamp & screw – Quart – Aqua, green – Round.	$ 40.00- 70.00
1735.	MY CHOICE – Aqua – Ground lip and glass lid.	$ 75.00-150.00
	Amber	$300.00-475.00
1736.	NATIONAL – 1885 – Metal lid – Quart – Aqua – Round.	$ 35.00- 60.00
1737.	NATIONAL SUPER MASON – 1870 – Glass lid & iron clamp – Quart – Clear – Round.	$ 10.00- 16.00
1738.	NEWARK – 1910 – Zinc lid – Clear.	$ 10.00- 15.00
1739.	NEW GEM – Wide zinc screw band & glass lid – Pint, quart, ½ gal. – Clear to amethyst – Round.	$ 2.00- 4.00
1740.	NEWMARK – 1925-1938 – Zinc lid – Quart – Clear – Round.	$ 5.00- 11.00
1741.	N STAR – Metal lid & wax seal – Quart – Blue – Round.	$ 10.00- 20.00
1742.	N W ELECTROGLASS WIDE MOUTH MASON – 1950-1955 – Zinc lid – Pint, quart – Clear to amethyst – Round.	$ 4.00- 6.00
1743.	O. G. – 1900 – Glass lid & wire bail – Quart – Clear – Round.	$ 15.00- 20.00
1744.	OHIO QUALITY MASON – 1924-1926 – Zinc screw-on lid – 2 sizes – Clear – Round.	$ 10.00- 16.00
1745.	OPLER BROTHERS – 1909 – Glass lid & wide wire clamp – Quart – Clear – Square.	$ 6.00- 12.00
1746.	OSBURN, N. ROCHESTER, NEW YORK – Aqua – Possibly cork stopper.	$200.00-250.00
1747.	PACIFIC GLASS WORKS – 1870-1880 – Zinc band & glass insert – Quart – Green – Round.	$ 25.00- 50.00
1748.	PACIFIC MASON – 1930 – Zinc lid – Quart – Clear to indefinite – Round.	$ 5.00- 10.00
1749.	PARAGON, NEW – 1875 – Glass lid & iron clamp – Quart – Green – Round.	$ 50.00-100.00
1750.	PATENT APPLIED FOR – 1865 – Metal lid & wax seal – Quart – Green – Round, extending wax seal neck.	$100.00-175.00
1751.	P C G CO. – 1875 – Wax sealer – Quart – Aqua – Round.	$ 17.00- 23.00
1752.	PEARL, (THE) – 1860's screw band & glass insert – Quart – Light green – Round.	$ 10.00- 20.00
1753.	PEERLESS – 1860's – Wax dipped cork – Quart – Light green – Round extending ridge neck.	$ 60.00-100.00
1754.	PENN, (THE) – 1870-1875 – Metal cap & wax seal – Quart – Aqua, green – Round.	$ 40.00- 75.00
1755.	PEORIA POTTERY – Metal lid & wax seal – Pint, quart – Glazed brown stoneware – Round.	$ 10.00- 20.00
1756.	PERFECTION – 1887 – Double wire bail & glass lid – Quart – Clear – Round, tall, slender.	$ 20.00- 40.00

1757.	PERFECT SEAL – 1925 – Full wire bail & glass lid – Pint, quart, ½ gal. – Aqua, clear – Round or square.	$	4.00- 8.00
1758.	PET – 1870-1875 – Glass stopper – Quart – Green – Round.	$	50.00- 75.00
1759.	PET – 1885-1895 – Glass lid & wire bail – Quart – Aqua – Round.	$	25.00- 50.00
1760.	PETTIT H.W. – 1905-1910 – Glass lid & wide metal clamp – Quart – Green – Round, narrow, straight-sided.	$	6.00- 10.00
1761.	PINE DELUXE JAR – 1927-1929 – Full wire bail & glass lid – Pint, quart – Clear – Square.	$	4.00- 8.00
1762.	PINE MASON – 1927-1929 – Zinc lid – Pint, quart, ½ gal. – Clear – Round.	$	4.00- 8.00
1763.	PORCELAIN LINED No. 1 – 1880 – Zinc lid – Quart – Aqua – Round tapering sides.	$	10.00- 25.00
1764.	PORCELAIN LINED No. 2 – 1880's – Zinc lid – Quart, ½ gal. – Green – Round tapering sides.	$	10.00- 20.00
1765.	PORTER, ROBERT BREWING CO. – Amber – 7¼″ high.	$	10.00- 20.00
1766.	POTTER & BODINE – 1865-1870 – Glass lid & clamp – Quart – Aqua – Round.	$	35.00- 75.00
1767.	PREMIUM COFFEE – 1910-1920 – Wire ring & glass lid Quart – Clear to amethyst – Round.	$	10.00- 20.00
1768.	PREMIUM IMPROVED – 1925 – Glass lid & side wire clips – Quart – Clear to amethyst – Round, straight-sided.	$	10.00- 14.00
1769.	PRESTO – 1930's – Screw-on lid – 3 sizes – Clear – Round.	$	2.00- 6.00
1770.	PRESTO FRUIT JAR – 1925 – Screw top – Clear – Round.	$	5.00- 10.00
1771.	PRESTO GLASS TOP – 1935 – Half wire bail & glass lid Pint, quart, ½ gal. – Clear to amethyst – Round.	$	2.00- 4.00

1779

1806

1834

1772.	PRESTO SUPREME MASON – 1930's – Threaded neck Pint, quart, ½ gal. – Clear to amethyst – Round.	$	1.00- 2.00
1773.	PRESTO WIDEMOUTH GLASS TOP – 1930's – Threaded neck – Pint, quart, ½ gal. – Clear – Round.	$	1.00- 2.00
1774.	PRINCESS – 1920 – Glass lid & wire bail – Pint, quart – Clear – Round.	$	6.00- 12.00
1775.	PROTECTOR – 1887 – Flat zinc cap & welded wire clamp – Pint, quart – Aqua – Round.	$	20.00- 40.00
1776.	PURITAN, (THE) – 1875 – Glass lid & wire clamp – Pint – Aqua – Round.	$	20.00- 25.00
1777.	PUTNAM GLASS WORKS – 1865 – Wax sealer – Quart – Green – Round.	$	15.00- 25.00
1778.	QUEEN – 1909-1920 – Glass lid & wire bail – 3 sizes – Clear – Rounded square.	$	8.00- 13.00

1779.	QUEEN IMPROVED SHIELD DESIGN – 1909 – Glass lid and wire clamps – Pint, quart – Clear – Square.	$ 10.00- 20.00
1780.	QUEEN, (THE) – 1875 – Zinc band – Quart – Aqua, green Round.	$ 22.00- 30.00
1781.	QUICK SEAL – 1908 – Glass lid & wire bail – Pint, quart Green, blue, clear – Round.	$ 2.00- 6.00
1782.	QUONG HOP & CO. – 1925 – Glass lid & wire bail – Pint Clear – Round.	$ 2.00- 4.00
1783.	QUONG YEUN SING & CO. – Half wire bail & glass lid – Pint – Clear to maize – Round.	$ 2.00- 6.00
1784.	RAMSEY JAR – Glass lid – Quart – Aqua – 12 sided jar. Base Pat. 4-1866611-67	$400.00-600.00
1785.	RAU'S IMPROVED GROOVE RING JAR – 1910 – Wax sealer – Pint, quart – Pink – Round.	$ 10.00- 25.00
1786.	RED KEY MASON – 1915 – Zinc lid – 3 sizes – Green – Round tapering sides.	$ 10.00- 16.00
1787.	RED KEY MASON'S PATENT NOV. 30, 1858 – Zinc lid – Pint – Aqua, green – Round tapering sides.	$ 5.00- 10.00
1788.	REID, MURDOCK & CO. – 1920 – Zinc lid – Quart – Clear Round.	$ 8.00- 10.00
1789.	RELIABLE MASON – 1940's – Zinc screw band & glass insert – Quart – Clear – Round.	$ 1.00- 2.00
1790.	RELIANCE BRAND – 1920's – Screw-on lid – 3 sizes – Clear – Rounded square.	$ 2.00- 4.00
1791.	ROSE, (THE) – 1920 – Screw-on lid – 3 sizes – Clear – Round.	$ 10.00- 30.00
1792.	ROYAL – 1900 – Glass lid & full wire bail – Pint, quart, ½ gal. – Light green, clear – Square.	$ 10.00- 25.00
1793.	SAFE SEAL – 1935 – Glass lid & wire bail – Pint, quart – Aqua, clear – Round.	$ 3.00- 4.00
1794.	SAFETY – 1900 – Full wire bail & glass lid – Pint, quart, ½ gal. – Amber – Round.	$ 25.00- 50.00
1795.	SAFETY SEAL – 1920-1930 – Half wire bail & glass lid – Pint, quart – Clear – Round.	$ 2.00- 4.00
1796.	SAFETY VALVE – 1895 – Metal lid & clamp – Quart, ½ gal. – Green, clear – Round straight-sided.	$ 10.00- 20.00
1797.	SAFETY WIDE MOUTH MASON – 1910-1915 – Zinc lid – Quart, ½ gal. – Aqua, pale green – Round.	$ 8.00- 14.00
1798.	SAMCO GENUINE MASON – 1925 – Zinc screw band & opal insert – All sizes – Clear – Square.	$ 2.00- 4.00
1799.	SAMCO SUPER MASON – 1920 – Zinc screw band & opal insert – All sizes – Clear – Round.	$ 2.00- 4.00
1800.	SAMPSON IMPROVED BATTERY – 1895 – Screw-on lid Quart – Aqua – Square.	$ 5.00- 10.00
1801.	SANETY WIDE MOUTH MASON – 1920 – Zinc lid – Quart – Aqua, pale green – Round, wide mouth.	$ 8.00- 12.00
1802.	SANFORD – 1900 – Metal screw band & glass insert – Quart – Clear – Round.	$ 10.00- 15.00
1803.	SANITARY – 1900 – Glass lid & wire bail – Quart – Aqua Round.	$ 10.00- 17.00
1804.	SAN YUEN CO. – 1925 – Glass lid & half wire bail – Quart – Clear – Round.	$ 6.00- 10.00
1805.	SCHAFFER JAR, (THE) – 1885-1895 – Glass lid & bail type clamp – Quart – Light aqua – Round, tall, slender.	$100.00-150.00

1806.	SCHRAM AUTOMATIC SEALER – 1909 – Flat metal lid & wire clamp – All sizes – Clear – Round, straight-sided.	$ 6.00- 12.00
1807.	SCRANTON JAR, (THE) – 1870-1880 – Glass stopper & wire bail – Quart – Aqua – Round.	$125.00-150.00
1808.	SEALFAST – 1915 – Full wire bail & glass lid – All sizes Clear to amethyst – Round.	$ 2.00- 6.00
1809.	SEASON'S MASON – Metal band & glass insert – 3 sizes – Clear – Round.	$ 8.00- 15.00
1810.	SEALTITE WIDE MOUTH MASON – 1925 – Flat metal lid and screw band – Quart – Green – Round.	$ 6.00- 10.00
1811.	SECURITY – 1900 – Glass lid & wire bail – Quart – Clear Round.	$ 10.00- 14.00
1812.	SECURITY SEAL – 1900 – Full wire bail & glass lid – Pint, quart – Clear to amethyst – Round.	$ 3.00- 5.00
1813.	SELCO SURETY SEAL – 1908 – Half wire bail & glass lid Pint, quart – Green, blue – Round.	$ 6.00- 10.00
1814.	SILICON GLASS COMPANY – 1925 – Wire bail & glass lid – Quart – Clear, aqua – Round.	$ 6.00- 10.00
1815.	SIMPLEX – 1900-1920 – Glass screw lid – Pint, quart – Clear – Round.	$ 10.00- 20.00
1816.	SIRRA MASON JAR – Zinc lid – Pint, quart – Clear – Round.	$ 10.00- 18.00
1817.	SMALLEY No. 1 – 1896-1907 – Zinc screw band & milk glass insert – Quart – Amber – Round.	$ 20.00- 40.00
1818.	SMALLEY No. 2 – 1892-1896 – Zinc lid – Quart – Clear – Square.	$ 4.00- 7.00
1819.	SMALLEY ROYAL – 1910-1920 – Zinc screw band – Pint, quart – Clear – Rounded square.	$ 8.00- 10.00
1820.	SMALLEY SELF-SEALER WIDE MOUTH – 1900 – Full wire bail & glass lid – Pint, quart – Clear – Round.	$ 5.00- 9.00
1821.	SMALLEY'S NU-SEAL – 1904 – Full wire bail & glass lid Pint, quart – Clear to amethyst – Round.	$ 4.00- 6.00
1822.	SPENCER – 1865 – Glass lid & iron clamp – Quart – Aqua – Round.	$ 30.00- 60.00
1823.	SPENCER'S PATENT – 1868 – Wax dipped cork – Quart Aqua – Round.	$ 25.00- 50.00
1824.	STANDARD – 1870 – Wax sealer – Quart – Aqua – Round.	$ 10.00- 15.00
1825.	STANDARD MASON – 1920 – Zinc lid – Pint, quart – Light aqua, light green – Round tapering sides.	$ 4.00- 9.00
1826.	STAR – 1895 – Zinc band & glass insert – Quart – Clear Round.	$ 50.00-100.00
1827.	STERLING MASON – 1940's – Zinc lid – Pint, quart – Clear – Round.	$ 2.00- 4.00
1828.	STEVEN'S – 1875 – Wax sealer – Quart – Green – Round.	$ 75.00- 85.00
1829.	STONE MASON FRUIT JAR – 1900 – Zinc lid – Pint, quart – White pottery – Round angle shoulder.	$ 25.00- 50.00
1830.	SUN – 1895-1925 – Glass lid & metal clamp – Quart – Light green – Round.	$ 25.00- 50.00
1831.	SUREME MASON – 1920 – Screw top – Pint, quart – Clear – Round.	$ 4.00- 7.00
1832.	SURE SEAL – 1920 – Full wire bail & glass lid – Pint, quart, ½ gal. – Deep blue – Round.	$ 3.00- 4.00
1833.	SWAYZEE'S FRUIT JAR – 1895 – Zinc lid – Pint, quart – Aqua – Square-shouldered round.	$ 8.00- 13.00

1834.	SWAYZEE'S IMPROVED MASON – 1905 – Zinc lid – Pint, quart – Aqua, green – Round tapering sides.	$ 4.00- 8.00
1835.	TAYLOR J.E. & CO. – 1910 – Wire bail & glass lid – Quart – Aqua – Round.	$ 8.00- 10.00
1836.	TELEPHONE JAR – 1910-1915 – Full wire bail & glass lid – Quart – Medium green – Round.	$ 8.00- 15.00
1837.	TEXAS MASON – 1949-1950 – Screw-on lid – Pint, quart Clear – Round.	$ 8.00- 15.00
1838.	THOMPSON'S FLAVORS NEW YORK PRODUCE JAR – Wire bail and glass lid – Amber.	$ 60.00- 75.00
1839.	TIGHT SEAL – 1908 – Half wire bail & glass lid – All sizes – Green, blue – Round.	$ 2.00- 4.00
1840.	TORINO, S.A. – Gray snake around bottle – 12¼" – Clear.	$ 8.00- 14.00
1841.	TROPICAL CANNERS – 1940 – Metal lid – Quart – Clear Round.	$ 2.00- 6.00
1842.	TRUE FRUIT – 1900-1910 – Glass lid & metal clamp – Clear – Quart – Round.	$ 5.00- 10.00
1843.	TRUE SEAL – 1920's – Glass lid & wire bail – Clear – Round.	$ 10.00- 15.00
1844.	UNION FRUIT JAR – 1865-1870 – Wax sealer & metal lid Quart – Aqua – Round.	$ 10.00- 20.00
1845.	UNION No. 1 – 1860-1870 – Wax sealer & metal lid – Quart – Deep aqua – Round, extending neck.	$ 10.00- 25.00
1846.	UNIVERSAL – 1910 – Screw top – Quart – Clear – Round.	$ 5.00- 10.00
1847.	VACUUM SEAL (THE) FRUIT JAR PAT. NOV. 1st 1904 – Glass lid – Quart – Clear – Round, slender extending neck.	$ 40.00- 60.00
1848.	VALVE JAR (THE) – 1868 – Glass or tin lid – Quart – Aqua – Round. On base, 3-10-1886, Co. Phila.	$ 75.00-125.00
	1½ pint	$100.00-150.00
1849.	VAN VLIET (THE) – 1881 – Glass lid & iron band with screw – Quart – Aqua, green – Round.	$200.00-275.00
1850.	VICTOR (THE) – 1899 – Flat metal lid & clamp – Quart – Light green – Round.	$ 25.00- 40.00
1851.	VICTOR (THE) – 1900 – Same as 1899.	
1852.	VICTORY – 1875 – Flat glass lid & side wire clips – Pint, quart – Clear – Round.	$ 6.00- 15.00
1853.	"W" – 1875-1885 – Wax sealer – Quart – Green – Round.	$ 10.00- 25.00
1854.	WALES, GEO. E. – 1900-1905 – Glass lid & metal clamp Quart – Clear – Round.	$ 10.00- 20.00
1855.	WALLACEBURG GEM – Glass insert & zinc screw band Pint, quart – Clear to amethyst – Round.	$ 5.00- 10.00
1856.	WAN-ETA COCA BOSTON – 1925-1935 – Zinc lid – Quart – Amber, blue – Round.	$ 8.00- 16.00
1857.	WEARS JAR – 1915-1920 – Glass lid & wire clamp – Pint, quart – Clear – Oval.	$ 8.00- 15.00
1858.	WEIR (THE) – 1892 – Wire bail – Quart – Pottery – Round.	$ 10.00- 15.00
1859.	WEIR SEAL – 1892 – White stoneware lid & wire bail – Quart – White stoneware – Round.	$ 6.00- 10.00
1860.	WESTERN PRIDE – Patented June 22, 1877 – Metal clamp – Aqua – Quart – N within star on base.	$ 50.00- 75.00
1861.	WHEELER – 1885-1890 – Glass lid & wire bail – Aqua, green – Round.	$ 10.00- 30.00
1862.	WHITALL'S – 1861 – Glass lid & clip with screw tightener – Quart – Pale green – Round.	$ 20.00- 26.00

1863.	WHITE BEAR – 1920 – Full wire bail & glass lid – Pint, quart – Clear – Round.	$ 9.00- 14.00
1864.	WHITE CROWN MASON – 1910 – Zinc lid – Pint, quart – Aqua – Round.	$ 4.00- 6.00
1865.	WHITNEY MASON – 1858 – Zinc lid – Quart – Aqua, light green – Round tapering sides.	$ 6.00- 10.00
1866.	WILCOX – 1867 – Flat metal lid & clamp – Quart – Green – Round.	$ 20.00- 30.00
1867.	WILLS & CO. – 1880-1885 – Glass stopper & metal clamp – Green, blue – Round.	$ 35.00- 44.00
1868.	WINSLOW JAR –1870-1873 – Glass lild & wire clamp – Quart – Green – Round – Ground lid.	$ 80.00-125.00
1869.	WOODBURY – 1884-1885 – Glass lid & metal band clamp – Quart – Aqua – Round.	$ 18.00- 26.00
1870.	WOODBURY IMPROVED – 1885 – Zinc cap – 3 sizes – Aqua – Round.	$ 15.00- 30.00
1871.	X Y Z – 1858 – Zinc screw-on lid – Aqua – Round.	$ 25.00- 32.00
1872.	YEOMAN'S FRUIT BOTTLE – 1855-1870 – Wax sealer – Aqua – Small mouth, round.	$ 30.00- 50.00
1873.	YELONE JAR – 1895-1900 – Glass lid & wire bail – Clear	$ 10.00- 14.00
1874.	YOUNG, GEO. CALIFORNIA TAP BEER – Reserve Pat. 1872 – 10½" high – Amber.	$ 30.00- 60.00

MISCELLANEOUS HOUSEHOLD BOTTLES

1877   1881   1882   1890

1875.	ABSORBINE M.F.G. – Amber – 7½″.	$	2.00-	6.00
1876.	A.F. COMPANY – Printed in a diamond on the front – Amber – 8″ high.	$	3.00-	5.00
1877.	AIRPLANE (Figural) – Candy – Clear – 4″ long.	$	6.00-	18.00
1878.	ALLEN'S SPERM SEWING MACHINE OIL – No measurements.	$	1.00-	2.00
1879.	AMMONIA – Manufactured by S.F. Gaslight Co. – Aqua 8″ high.	$	2.00-	3.00
1880.	BABCOK HAND GRENADE ON ROUND PANEL – S. Des Plaines St. Chicago non-freezing – Manufactured by Fire Extinguisher Manf'd Co. – Aqua – Ball shaped – 15 rings around ball – 7½″ high.	$	20.00-	60.00
1881.	BABY BOTTLE – Embossed on side – "The ovale nurser non-rolling" – 6½″ tall – Sun colored amethyst.	$	3.00-	7.00
1882.	BABY BOTTLE – (flat side) – Teddy's pet – (front side) for your baby – 8-10 Testimony: 10-15 Ceremony: 15-20 Matrimony: 20-30 Alimony: 30-40 Easy money: Nothing doing. 4½″.	$	8.00-	15.00
1883.	BATTERY OIL – Thomas A. Edison – Aqua – 4½″.	$	2.00-	4.00
1884.	BARRON CO. – Clear – 4¾″ – Shoe Polish.	$	2.00-	4.00
1885.	BATTERY JAR – Aqua – 6″.	$	2.00-	4.00
1886.	BEACH & CLARRIDGE CO. – Amethyst – 9¼″.	$	2.00-	3.00
1887.	BEARD, L. – Blobmouth – Cream & blue pottery – 10½″.	$	6.00-	15.00
1888.	BENTON HOLLADAY & CO. – Aqua – 4 7/8″ – Shoe polish.	$	2.00-	6.00
1889.	BIXBY – Aqua – 3½″.	$	3.00-	8.00
1890.	BLUING – 7″ – Aqua.	$	2.00-	6.00

1891   1892   1896   1897

1891.	BOOT FIGURAL – Clear – 2½".	$	6.00-	18.00
1892.	"BOTSON" (Misspelled) – Whittemore – 5½" – SCA.	$	6.00-	12.00
1893.	BOYE NEEDLE CO. – Clear – 6¼".	$	3.00-	5.00
1894.	BUCKINGHAM WHISKER DYE – Amber – 4¾".	$	2.00-	4.00
1895.	CAMPBELL, V.V. – The genuine always bears this signature – Clear – 5 1/8".	$	3.00-	5.00
1896.	CANDY – Clear – 3".	$	8.00-	12.00
1897.	CANDY – Clear – 4½".	$	6.00-	10.00

| 1898 | | 1899 | 1902 | 1903 |

1898.	CANDY – Clear – 4" long.	$	8.00-	12.00
1899.	CAR (candy, figural) – Clear – 4½".	$	8.00-	14.00
1900.	CARBONA PRODUCTS CO. – Aqua – 6".	$	10.00-	17.00
1901.	CENTAUR LINIMENT – Aqua – 5".	$	2.00-	4.00
1902.	CERTO Reg. U.S. PAT. OFFICE – Natures Tiffany – 7½".	$	1.00-	2.00
1903.	COMBAULT'S J.E. CAUSTIC BALM – Aqua – 6½".	$	8.00-	10.00
1904.	CAULK'S PETROID CEMENT – Clear – 2¼".	$	1.00-	2.00
1905.	CAULK, L.D. CO. – 20th Century Alloy Cement – Clear – 2" high.	$	1.00-	2.00
1906.	CURTIS, GEORGE M. PURE OLIVE OIL – Clear – 7".	$	1.00-	2.00

| 1907 | 1908 | 1909 | 1910 |

1907.	DIABLO SALSA – Clear – 6".	$	1.00-	2.00
1908.	DOG (Figural) – Clear – 3½".	$	4.00-	12.00
1909.	DOG (Figural) – Clear – 10".	$	10.00-	15.00
1910.	DOG (Figural) – Candy – Clear – 3".	$	5.00-	12.00

| 1911 | 1912 | 1915 | 1916 | 1917 |

1911. EVANGELINE PEPPER SAUCE – 12 sided. . . . . $ 4.00- 6.00
1912. FRANK MILLER DRESSING – Aqua – 5". . . . . $ 1.00- 2.00
1913. FRENCH GLOSS – Aqua – 4¾". $ 1.00- 2.00
1914. FRENCH GLOSS SHOE POLISH – Blue – 4 5/8". . . . . . . $ 1.00- 2.00
1915. FURST-McNESS CO. – Clear – Rect. . . . . $ 2.00- 3.00
1916. GILT EDGE DRESSING – Pat. 1880 on base – Aqua. . . . $ 10.00- 15.00
1917. GILT EDGE SHOE POLISH – Green – 4". . . . . $ 8.00- 12.00

| 1919 | 1920 | 1925 | 1926 |

1918. GOLD METAL QUALITY (Hydrogen Peroxide) – Amber
8". . . . . $ 2.00- 6.00
1919. GRADUATED NURSING BOTTLE, THE – 7" tall. . . . . . . $ 8.00- 12.00
1920. GREAT SEAL – STYRON BEGGS & CO. – Clear – 5". . . . $ 1.00- 4.00
1921. HAMMER DRY PLATE CO. – Amethyst – 6¼". . . . . $ 2.00- 3.00
1922. HAND MFG CO. – Clear – 5¼". $ 1.00- 3.00
1923. HARKNESS FIRE DESTROYER – Ball shaped with 5
rings on the neck & 10 horizontal rings on the body –
Blue – 6". . . . . $ 30.00- 50.00
1924. HOLTON'S ELECTRIC OIL – Amethyst – 3¼". . . . . $ 2.00- 4.00
1925. HORTON-CATO CO. – Clear. . . . . $ 1.00- 2.00
1926. HOUSEHOLD-MISC. – Clear – 5½". . . . . $ 1.00- 2.00

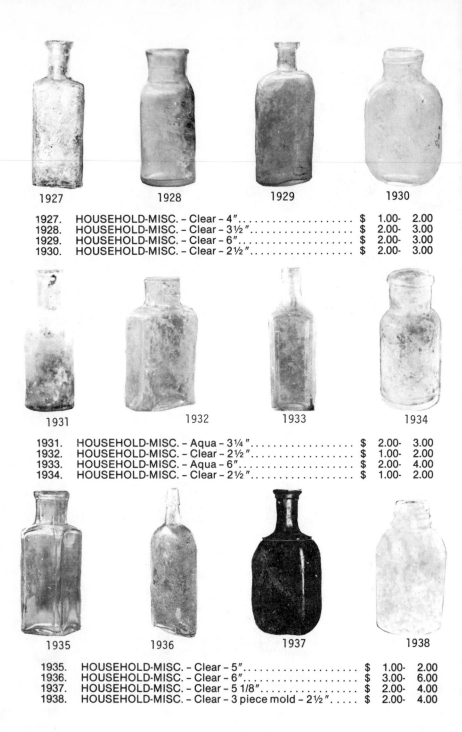

1927.   1928.   1929.   1930.

1927.   HOUSEHOLD-MISC. – Clear – 4".................... $ 1.00-   2.00
1928.   HOUSEHOLD-MISC. – Clear – 3½".................. $ 2.00-   3.00
1929.   HOUSEHOLD-MISC. – Clear – 6".................... $ 2.00-   3.00
1930.   HOUSEHOLD-MISC. – Clear – 2½".................. $ 2.00-   3.00

1931.   1932.   1933.   1934.

1931.   HOUSEHOLD-MISC. – Aqua – 3¼".................. $ 2.00-   3.00
1932.   HOUSEHOLD-MISC. – Clear – 2½".................. $ 1.00-   2.00
1933.   HOUSEHOLD-MISC. – Aqua – 6".................... $ 2.00-   4.00
1934.   HOUSEHOLD-MISC. – Clear – 2½".................. $ 1.00-   2.00

1935.   1936.   1937.   1938.

1935.   HOUSEHOLD-MISC. – Clear – 5".................... $ 1.00-   2.00
1936.   HOUSEHOLD-MISC. – Clear – 6".................... $ 3.00-   6.00
1937.   HOUSEHOLD-MISC. – Clear – 5 1/8".................. $ 2.00-   4.00
1938.   HOUSEHOLD-MISC. – Clear – 3 piece mold – 2½"..... $ 2.00-   4.00

1939.   HOUSEHOLD-MISC. – Aqua – 7 7/8"................. $ 8.00- 10.00

1939   1940   1944   1946

1940.   HOUSEHOLD-MISC. – Zinone oil – Aqua – 3½ ", 5½ " –
        Sample zinone oil Emerald green – SET .... $ 8.00- 15.00
1941.   IMPORTERS – Amber – 10"....................... $ 3.00-   5.00
1942.   IMPERIAL CEMENT – Clear – 3"................. $ 1.00-   2.00
1943.   JOHNSON, S.C. & SON – Aqua – 4 5/8". .... $ 2.00-   5.00
1944.   J.A.F. & CO. – Clear – 4½ "...................... $ 3.00-   6.00
1945.   KEEN KUTTER – Simmons Hardware Co. – Clear – 4". . $ 3.00-   5.00
1946.   LARKIN CO. – Amethyst – 8"..................... $ 2.00-   4.00
1947.   LILLY'S LIQUID SOAP – Wet the hands before using –
        Satin glass – 5½ "................................ $ 4.00-   8.00

1947   1948   1949   1950

1948.   LINCOLN PENNY BAND – Figural Lincoln – Clear –
        3¼ "... $ 6.00- 18.00
1949.   McALLISTER'S MOCKINGBIRD FOOD – Aqua – 7". ... $ 2.00-   4.00
1950.   McCORMIC & CO. SPICE GRINDERS – Clear frosty –
        5½ ". .... $ 2.00-   4.00

1951   1953   1954   1956

1951.	MODJISHA DERMA-BALM – Clear – 5".	$	1.00-	2.00
1952.	OLIVE OIL – Clear – 8¼	$	1.00-	2.00
1953.	OLIVE OIL – Amethyst – 8".	$	4.00-	8.00
1954.	OLIVE OIL – Amethyst – 10".	$	4.00-	8.00
1955.	PURE SPERM SEWING MACHINE OIL – Amethyst – 5¼".	$	1.00-	2.00
1956.	PA-POOSE – Clear – 6 ozs.	$	1.00-	2.00

1957   1958   1959   1960

1957.	PEER-AMID BOTTLES – Clear – 7".	$	8.00-	10.00
1958.	PIG (Figural) – Clear – 5½".	$	4.00-	10.00
1959.	PRICES DELICIOUS FLAVORING EXTRACTS – Amethyst – 5½".	$	1.00-	3.00
1960.	PRICE-BOOKER MFG. CO. – Aqua – 9".	$	2.00-	3.00
1961.	PUROLA TOILER PREPARATION – Amethyst – 7½"...	$	2.00-	3.00

1962   1963   1964   1967

1962.	PUTNAM DRY CLEANER (embossed on shoulder) – Sun colored amethyst – 5¾".	$	2.00-	4.00
1963.	REM-OIL REMINGTON UMC POWDER SOLVENT LUBRICANT RUST PREVENTIVE – Aqua, Light green – 5".	$	3.00-	6.00
1964.	SANITOL – For the teeth (on back side) – Ridged front – 4¾" – Clear.	$	2.00-	6.00
1965.	SAPO ELIXIR DRY CLEANER – Clear – 6".	$	2.00-	3.00
1966.	SILMERINE PARKER BELMONT & CO. – Clear – 5".	$	2.00-	3.00
1967.	SINGER MACHINE CO. – Clear – 5".	$	2.00-	4.00

| 1968 | 1969 | 1970 | 1974 |

1968. SPARK'S HORSERADISH – Aqua – 7″. . . . . $ 2.00- 4.00
1969. SPOTINE TRADE MARK – Brown – 5½″. . . . . $ 2.00- 4.00
1970. STAR DYE COLORS – (5 point star embossed) – C.F.
Fuelling – New York – 5″ – Aqua. . . . . $ 4.00- 6.00
1971. STAR HARDEN HAND GRENADE FIRE EXTIN-
GUISHER – Ball shaped – Blue – 8″. . . . . $ 40.00- 65.00
1972. STEWART'S (MRS.) BLUING – Aqua – 5½″. . . . . $ 1.00- 3.00
1973. SYMON'S PENZANCE – Aqua – 6 3/8″. . . . . $ 1.00- 2.00
1974. TANK (Candy) – Clear – 4″ long. . . . . $ 8.00- 12.00

| 1975 | 1976 | 1977 | 1978 |

1975. TELEPHONE (Candy) – Clear – 4″. . . . . $ 8.00- 12.00
1976. TELEPHONE (Candy) – Clear – 1½″. . . . . $ 8.00- 10.00
1977. THOMAS EDISON SPECIAL BATTERY OIL – Orange
New Jersey – 4¾″ high. . . . . $ 2.00- 4.00
1978. WAKELEE'S CARMALLINE – Amber – 4¾″. . . . . $ 2.00- 4.00

131

1979   1981

1979. WIDE MOUTH HORSERADISH – Aqua – 5½″. . . . . $ 3.00- 6.00
1980. WINONA MINN. – Once a week shine shoe polish –
      Aqua – 4 7/8″ high. . . . . $ 2.00- 4.00
1981. WHITTEMORE – Green – 5¼″ – Shoe polish. . . . . $ 4.00- 6.00

MEDICINE BOTTLES

| 1986 | 1998 | 2007 | 2008 |

1982. ABELL'S WHITE PINE BALSAM – Rectangular – Clear
4 7/8" high. .... $ 2.00- 4.00
1983. ABERNATHY'S GINGER BRANDY – Round – Amber –
10½". .... $ 4.00 6.00
1984. ABBOTT ALKALOIDAL COMPANY – Rectangular –
Amber – 2½". .... $ 1.00- 2.00
1985. ABILENA NATURAL CATHARTIC WATER – Round –
Amber – 9¾". .... $ 2.00- 3.00
1986. ABSORBINE JR. – 4 ozs. – 5" – Sun colored amethyst. . $ 1.00- 3.00
1987. ACEITE MEXICANO – Rectangular – Clear – 5½"...... $ 2.00- 4.00
1988. AGNEW'S CURE FOR THE HEART – Rectangular –
Clear – 8¼". .... $ 10.00- 20.00
1989. AKER'S ENGLISH REMEDY – Rectangular – Cobalt – 5
5/8". .... $ 4.00- 10.00
1990. ALDRICH & DUTTON – Rectangular – Clear – 5"....... $ 1.00- 2.00
1991. ALEMBERTE, DRUGGIST & APOTHECARY – Flat-oval
Clear – 6½" high. .... $ 2.00- 3.00
1992. ALLEN'S DYSPEPTIC MEDICINE – Rectangular – Aqua
6". .... $ 7.00- 10.00
1993. ALLEN'S LUNG BALSM – Rectangular – Deep aqua – 7
7/8". .... $ 6.00- 10.00
1994. ALEXANDER'S SURE CURE FOR MALARIA – Rec-
tangular – Amber – 8" high. .... $ 8.00- 15.00
1995. ANCHOR WEAKNESS CURE – Square – Amber – 8¼" . $ 8.00- 15.00
1996. ANDERSON'S COUGH DROPS – Round – Aqua – 3½". $ 3.00- 4.00
1997. ANDERSON'S DERMADOR – Oval – Aqua – 4" & 6".... $ 2.00- 3.00
1998. ANDERSON, TAZ. L., DRUGGIST – Clear – 6¼". ...... $ 3.00- 6.00
1999. ANGIER'S EMULSION – Oval – Aqua – 8¾". .... $ 4.00- 6.00
2000. ANGIER'S PETROLEUM EMULSION – Oval – Aqua –
7". .... $ 2.00- 3.00
2001. ANTEDILUVIAN LUYTIER BROTHERS – Round –
Amber .... $ 3.00- 4.00
2002. ARNICA & OIL LINIMENT – Aqua – 6½". .... $ 2.00- 3.00
2003. ARNICATED EUREKA CREAM – Amethyst – 4". .... $ 2.00- 3.00
2004. ASEPTIC – Oval – Aqua – 9¼". .... $ 3.00- 4.00
2005. ASHLEY'S RED SEA BALSAM – Aqua & clear – 4¼". ... $ 4.00- 6.00
2006. ATHLOPHORAS – Rectangular – 6". .... $ 1.00- 2.00
2007. ATIS CLAPP & SONS – Malt & cod liver oil – Rectangular – Mint & amber – 7¾". .... $ 4.00- 8.00
2008. AYER – (embossed in bottle) – Potil mark – Aqua – Very
old – 7½". .... $ 8.00- 15.00
2009. AYER – Flask shaped – Aqua – 7½". .... $ 2.00- 3.00
2010. AYER'S – AGUE CURE LOWELL – Rectangular – Aqua
7". .... $ 8.00- 15.00
2011. AYER'S CHERRY PECTORAL LOWELL – Rectangular –
Aqua – 7" & 7½"..... .... $ 2.00- 3.00

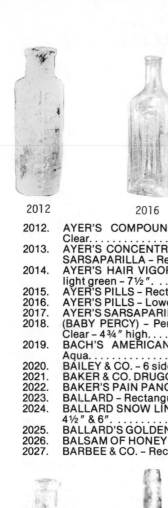

| 2012 | 2016 | 2017 | 2026 |

2012. AYER'S COMPOUND EXTRACT SARSAPARILLA –
Clear.. $ 4.00- 10.00
2013. AYER'S CONCENTRATED COMPOUND EXTRACT OF
SARSAPARILLA – Rectangular – Aqua – 7¾"........ $ 20.00- 25.00
2014. AYER'S HAIR VIGOR – Crown shaped – Blue, green,
light green – 7½"................................. $ 10.00- 20.00
2015. AYER'S PILLS – Rectangular – Aqua – 2"............ $ 1.00- 2.00
2016. AYER'S PILLS – Lowell, Mass. – Aqua – 2"x¾"x1". ... $ 2.00- 4.00
2017. AYER'S SARSAPARILLA – Blue – 8½". .... $ 8.00- 10.00
2018. (BABY PERCY) – Percy Medicine Co. – Rectangular –
Clear – 4¾" high.................................. $ 2.00- 3.00
2019. BACH'S AMERICAN COMPOUND – Rectangular –
Aqua... $ 30.00- 35.00
2020. BAILEY & CO. – 6 sides – Cobalt – 5"............... $ 4.00- 10.00
2021. BAKER & CO. DRUGGISTS – Oval – Clear – 5". .... $ 2.00- 3.00
2022. BAKER'S PAIN PANCEA – Rectangular – Aqua – 5¾".. $ 4.00- 6.00
2023. BALLARD – Rectangular – Clear – 3½". .... $ 4.00- 8.00
2024. BALLARD SNOW LINIMENT CO. – Rectangle – Clear –
4½" & 6".. $ 1.00- 2.00
2025. BALLARD'S GOLDEN OIL – Round – Clear – 3½". ..... $ 1.00- 2.00
2026. BALSAM OF HONEY – Round – Aqua – 3¾".......... $ 2.00- 6.00
2027. BARBEE & CO. – Rectangular – Clear – 6"............ $ 3.00- 6.00

| 2028 | 2029 | 2032 | 2035 |

2028. BARIE, M.A. DRUGGIST – Clear – 4 1/8".............. $ 2.00- 3.00
2029. BARIE, M.A. DRUGGIST – Blue – 5¾". .... $ 2.00- 6.00
2030. BARKER, MOORE & MEIN MEDICINE COMPANY –
Rectangular – Aqua, blue – 6"...................... $ 3.00- 6.00
2031. BARNES' ESS. OF JAMAICA GINGER – Round – Aqua
6"... $ 3.00- 4.00

134

2032.	BARRETT, MARK D. PH. CO – Prescription pharmacist Newcastle Col. – Sun colored amethyst – 5½"........	$ 2.00-	4.00
2033.	BARRY'S PEARL CREAM – Milk white – 4"...........	$ 8.00-	10.00
2034.	BARRY'S TRICOPHEROUS FOR THE SKIN AND HAIR 6½"..	$ 4.00-	6.00
2035.	BASON MEDICINE CO. – Blue – 2½"................	$ 4.00-	10.00
2036.	BAUER & BLACK ASEPTIC GAUZE-MOIST – Square – Amber – 4"..	$ 3.00-	4.00
2037.	BAUER'S INSTANT COUGH CURE – Rectangular – Aqua – 7"..	$ 8.00-	15.00
2038.	BAUER'S ANTIDIABETICUM – Label only.	$ 2.00-	4.00
2039.	BAZIN (X) – Round – Clear – 3"....................	$ 1.00-	2.00
2040.	BAZIN & SARGENT – Aqua – 6"....................	$ 2.00-	3.00
2041.	BEAR'S OIL – Rectangular – Aqua – 3"...............	$ 3.00-	8.00
2042.	BELL & CO. INC. PA-PAY-ANS – Rectangular – Amber – 3¾" high......................................	$ 2.00-	6.00
2043.	BELL-AND, BELL & CO.............................	$ 1.00-	2.00
2044.	BELL'S PINE TAR HONEY FOR COUGHS AND COLDS Rectangular – Aqua – 5 5/8".......................	$ 2.00-	4.00
2045.	BESS'S SARSAPARILLA – Rectangular – Aqua – 9½"..	$ 10.00-	15.00
2046.	BELT & SON – Rectangular – Clear – 5½"...........	$ 1.00-	2.00

2047   2067   2071   2091

2047.	BETTES PHARMACY – Clear – 4½"................	$ 1.00-	2.00
2048.	B.F.B. CO. – Round – Aqua – 7 5/8"................	$ 2.00-	3.00
2049.	BIENVILLE PHARMACY – Rectangular – Clear – 4½"..	$ 1.00-	3.00
2050.	BILLINGS & CO. – Round – Aqua – 7½"..............	$ 3.00-	4.00
2051.	BILLINGS & CLAPP & CO. – Aqua – 10"..............	$ 2.00-	3.00
2052.	BINNINGERS OLD DOMINION WHEAT TONIC – Square – Amber – 10" high........................	$ 8.00-	10.00
2053.	BINZ BRONCHI-LYPTUS – Rectangular – Amber – 5½".	$ 1.00-	2.00
2054.	BIRD COMPANY – 3-sided – Clear – 4¾"............	$ 1.00-	2.00
2055.	BIRD (JOHN) COMPANY – Rectangular – Clear – 5¾"..	$ 1.00-	2.00
2056.	BIRNEY'S CATARRAL POWDER – Round – Clear – 2½".	$ 2.00-	4.00
2057.	BISHOP'S GRANULAR CITRATE OF MAGNESIA – Light cobalt – 6¼" high.	$ 2.00-	6.00
2058.	BLACK DRAUGHT SYRUP – Rectangular – Clear – 5½".	$ 1.00-	2.00
2059.	BLACK & WHITE – Green – 3½".....................	$ 2.00-	4.00
2060.	BLAIKIE CO. DRUGGISTS – Clear – 5½".............	$ 1.00-	2.00
2061.	BLISS LIVER & KIDNEY CURE – Rectangular – Clear – 9½".	$ 8.00-	20.00
2062.	BLOCK'S GERMAN BITTERS – Square – Amber – 10"..	$ 25.00-	50.00
2063.	BLOCKSON BROS. – Rectangular – Aqua – 5".	$ 4.00-	8.00
2064.	BLOOD & LIVER SYRUP – Aqua – 10".	$ 2.00-	3.00

2065.	BLUD-LIFE THE GREAT ANTI-TOXIC – Rectangular – Clear – 8 3/8" high.	$	2.00-	5.00
2066.	BOERICKE & RUNYON CO. – Square – Clear – 7 ¾".	$	1.00-	2.00
2067.	BOERICKE & TAFEL – Sun colored amethyst – 2 ¾".	$	1.00-	2.00
2068.	BOGLE'S HYPERION FLUID FOR THE HAIR – Aqua – 7".	$	4.00-	8.00
2069.	BON-OPTO FOR THE EYES – Square – Clear – 3".	$	1.00-	2.00
2070.	BONNINGTON'S IRISH MOSS – Rectangular – Aqua – 5¼".	$	3.00-	4.00
2071.	BOOKER MANUFACTURING CO. – Green – 7½".	$	4.00-	10.00
2072.	BOSANKO'S COUGH & LUNG SYRUP – Rectangular – Aqua – 6".	$	2.00-	3.00
2073.	BOSCHEE'S GERMAN SYRUP – Rectangular – Aqua – 6¾".	$	2.00-	3.00
2074.	BOTICA AMERICANA – Rectangular – Aqua – 2¾", 3 1/3", 4¼" & 6¼".	$	3.00-	4.00
2075.	BOTICA CENTRAL – Rectangular – Aqua – 2¾".	$	1.00-	2.00
2076.	BOTICA MEXICANO – Aqua – 3¼".	$	1.00-	2.00
2077.	BOUVIER BROS. – Rectangular – Clear – 4".	$	2.00-	3.00
2078.	BOVRIE – Round, flat – Amber – 1 & 2 ozs.	$	2.00-	3.00
2079.	BOWER HAIR RENEWER – Rectangular – Amber – 7".	$	1.00-	2.00
2080.	B.P. CO. – Round – Cobalt – 3".	$	4.00-	8.00
2081.	BRADFIELD'S FEMALE REGULATOR – Rectangular – Aqua – 8½".	$	3.00-	6.00
2082.	BRAGDON APOTHECARY – Rectangular – Clear – 4 1/8".	$	1.00-	2.00
2083.	BRANT'S INDIAN PULMONARY BALSAM – 8-sided – 7" – Pontil.	$	20.00-	35.00
2084.	BRANT'S INDIAN PURIFYING EXTRACT	$	10.00-	15.00
2085.	BRAZILIAN BALM – Rectangular – Amethyst – 6".	$	3.00-	6.00
2086.	BRIGG'S THROAT REMEDY – No description.	$	4.00-	8.00
2087.	BRIGG'S TONIC PILLS – Aqua – 2½".	$	3.00-	4.00
2088.	BRISTOL'S GENUINE SARSAPARILLA – Rectangular – Aqua – 10½" high.	$	8.00-	15.00
2089.	BRITTON'S DRUG STORE – Clear – 4".	$	1.00-	2.00
2090.	BRODENTINE – Rectangular – Clear – 7".	$	1.00-	2.00
2091.	BROEMMELS PHARMACY – San Francisco – Sun colored amethyst – 5¾" high.	$	2.00-	4.00
2092.	BROMO-CARREINE – Round – Cobalt blue – 3".	$	2.00-	4.00
2093.	BROMO-NERVINE – Oval – Cobalt – 4¾".	$	2.00-	6.00

2094   2095   2098

2094.	BROMO-SULTZER – Emerson Drug Co. Baltimore Md. – 4".	$	1.00-	3.00
2095.	BROMO-SELTZER – Blue – 4".	$	2.00-	4.00
2096.	BROWN – Label "Herbal Ointment" – Square – Aqua – 2 5/8" high.	$	1.00-	2.00
2097.	BROWN'S ACACIAN BALSAM – Carried "Dr. O. Phelps Brown's" name.	$	10.00-	20.00

2098.	BROWN'S ESSENCE OF JAMAICA GINGER – Oval – Aqua – 5¾"x1¾"x2 3/8"...........................	$	4.00-	8.00
2099.	BROWN'S ESSENCE OF JAMAICA GINGER – Oval – Aqua – 5½" & 6" high.............................	$	4.00-	8.00
2100.	BROWN'S INSTANT RELIEF – Mint..................	$	1.00-	2.00
2101.	BROWN'S INSTANT RELIEF FOR PAIN – Rectangular Clear – 5¼" high................................	$	1.00-	2.00
2102.	BROWN'S IRON TONIC – Rectangular – Aqua – 10"....	$	8.00-	12.00
2103.	BURNETT – Clear – 4 1/8".........................	$	2.00-	3.00

2103   2104   2106   2119

2104.	BRUNS & LITTLE – Clear – 3½".....................	$	1.00-	2.00
2105.	BRUSKE & CO. – Oval – Clear – 6".................	$	3.00-	4.00
2106.	BURWELL-DUNN – Clear – 4½".....................	$	2.00-	3.00
2107.	BRYAN PHARMACH INC. – Clear – 10".............	$	2.00-	3.00
2108.	BULL EXTRACT OF SARSAPARILLA – Rect. – Aqua – 7"...	$	10.00-	20.00
2109.	BULL'S (DR. J.W.) COUGH SYRUP – Rect. – Aqua – 6"..	$	2.00-	4.00
2110.	BULL'S (W.H.) HERBS & IRON – Oval – Amber – 9".....	$	6.00-	16.00
2111.	BURNETT, BOSTON – 6½" flask – 7½" round.	$	1.00-	2.00
2112.	BURNETT, BOSTON – 8-sided – Aqua – 5½"..........	$	1.00-	2.00
2113.	BURNETT'S COCAINE – Rectangular – Aqua.	$	2.00-	4.00
2114.	BURNET'S CORDIAL EXTRACT – Rect. – Aqua – 5½"..	$	2.00-	4.00
2115.	BURRINGTON'S VEGETABLE CROUP SYRUP – Round Clear – 5½"...................................	$	2.00-	3.00
2116.	BUTLER'S WHITE PINE EXPECTORANT (COUGH CURE) – Clear – 5" high..........................	$	8.00-	15.00
2117.	BUXTON'S RHEUMATIC CURE – Rect. – Aqua – 8½"..	$	10.00-	15.00
2118.	CADLER'S DENTINE – Round – Clear – 3"............	$	1.00-	2.00
2119.	CALDWELL'S SYRUP PEPSIN – Aqua – 3".	$	2.00-	6.00

2122   2137   2138   2141

2120.	CALDWELL'S (DR. W.B.) – Rectangular – Aqua – 7"....	$	1.00-	2.00
2121.	CALDWELL'S LAXATIVE – Rectangular – Aqua – 6 7/8".	$	1.00-	2.00
2122.	CALIFORNIA FIG SYRUP – Rectangular – Clear – 7"...	$	1.00-	2.00
2123.	CALOMEL AROMATIC PILLS – Rectangular – Clear....	$	1.00-	3.00
2124.	CAMELLINE – Oval – Amber – 4 fl. ozs.	$	1.00-	2.00
2125.	CAMPBELL – Rectangular – Clear – 4"...............	$	1.00-	2.00
2126.	CANANEA STORES – Rectangular – Clear – 5 5/8".....	$	2.00-	3.00
2127.	CAPUDINE – Rectangular – Amber – 6¼"..............	$	2.00-	3.00
2128.	CARBONA – 12-sided – Clear, aqua – 5"...............	$	1.00-	4.00
2129.	CARDIU, THE WOMAN'S TONIC – Rectangular – Clear, aqua – 8½" high.	$	1.00-	2.00
2130.	CARLO ERBA – Square – Green, aqua – 7½".	$	4.00-	8.00
2131.	CARLSBAD LS (on base) – Round – Green – 10½".	$	6.00-	8.00
2132.	CARMELITER BITTERS FOR ALL KIDNEY & LIVER COMPLAINTS – Square – Amber – 10½"..............	$	40.00-	60.00
2133.	CARPANO – Round – Clear – 4¾".	$	1.00-	4.00
2134.	CARPENTER, WALLINGTON & CO. – Round – Cobalt – 2½".	$	2.00-	4.00
2135.	CARTER'S (DR.) COMPOUND – Rectangular – Aqua. ..	$	4.00-	6.00
2136.	CASTORIA: CHARLES H. FLETCHER'S – Rectangular Aqua, blue, clear – 5 5/8", 5 7/8" & 5¾".	$	1.00-	2.00
2137.	CASTOR OIL – Aqua – 4½"..........................	$	2.00-	3.00
2138.	CASTOR OIL – Aqua – 5".	$	2.00-	4.00
2139.	CASWELL, MACK & CO. – Flared tip – Cobalt blue – 8".	$	8.00-	15.00
2140.	CAUVIN'S SYRUP FOR BABIES – Round – Aqua – 4 5/8".	$	2.00-	3.00
2141.	CELERY CAFFEEN – Blue – 4 1/8".	$	8.00-	12.00

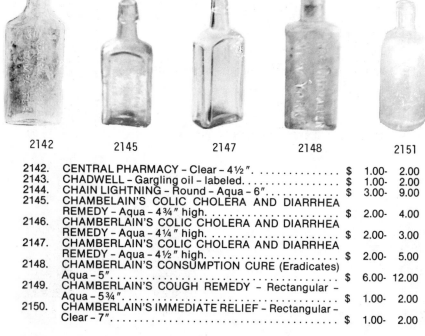

| | 2142 | 2145 | 2147 | 2148 | 2151 |

2142.	CENTRAL PHARMACY – Clear – 4½".	$	1.00-	2.00
2143.	CHADWELL – Gargling oil – labeled.	$	1.00-	2.00
2144.	CHAIN LIGHTNING – Round – Aqua – 6"..............	$	3.00-	9.00
2145.	CHAMBELAIN'S COLIC CHOLERA AND DIARRHEA REMEDY – Aqua – 4¾" high.	$	2.00-	4.00
2146.	CHAMBERLAIN'S COLIC CHOLERA AND DIARRHEA REMEDY – Aqua – 4¼" high.	$	2.00-	3.00
2147.	CHAMBERLAIN'S COLIC CHOLERA AND DIARRHEA REMEDY – Aqua – 4½" high.	$	2.00-	5.00
2148.	CHAMBERLAIN'S CONSUMPTION CURE (Eradicates) Aqua – 5".	$	6.00-	12.00
2149.	CHAMBERLAIN'S COUGH REMEDY – Rectangular – Aqua – 5¾".	$	1.00-	2.00
2150.	CHAMBERLAIN'S IMMEDIATE RELIEF – Rectangular – Clear – 7".	$	1.00-	2.00

2151.	CHAMBERLAINS SUMMER FEVER CURE	$ 8.00-	16.00
2152.	CHENEY'S (DR. F.M.) EXPECTORANT – Rectangular – Clear – 5″ high.	$ 1.00-	2.00
2153.	CHESEBROUGH MFG. CO. VASELINE – 2½ ″ – Amber.	$ 2.00-	4.00
2154.	CHEVALIER, PROF. – Clear – 4 1/8″.	$ 2.00-	4.00
2155.	CITRATE OF MAGNESIA – Rectangular – Clear & mint 6½ ″.	$ 2.00-	4.00
2156.	CITRATE OF MAGNESIA – Round – Clear – 8″.	$ 1.00-	3.00

2157	2164	2165	2166

2157.	CITRATE OF MAGNESIA – Blown in mold – Magnesia embossed in shield – Amethyst – 8″.	$ 2.00-	3.00
2158.	CITY DRUG STORE – Rectangular – Clear – 6″.	$ 1.00-	2.00
2159.	CLAPP & SON, MALT & COD LIVER OIL – Rect. – Amber – 7½ ″ high.	$ 2.00-	3.00
2160.	CLEMENT'S TONIC – Rect. – Bright amber – 6 5/8″. . . .	$ 3.00-	4.00
2161.	CLYSONIC – Bowling pin shape – Green – 9½ ″.	$ 6.00-	8.00
2162.	COBLENTZ CURE – Round – Cobalt – 7½ ″.	$ 8.00-	12.00
2163.	COBURN PHARMACIST – Rect. – Clear – var. sizes. . . .	$ 1.00-	2.00
2164.	COD LIVER OIL – Brown – 7 3/8″.	$ 4.00-	12.00
2165.	CODY'S PHARMACY – Merced, Cal. – Sun colored amethyst – 3¾″ high.	$ 2.00-	4.00
2166.	COLSSONS APOTHECARIES – Clear – 6½ ″.	$ 1.00-	2.00
2167.	COLT'S FOOT EXPECTORANT – Rect. – Clear, aqua – 6½ ″.	$ 1.00-	3.00
2168.	COMPOUND OXYGEN STARKEY & PALEY – Round – Cobalt – 7½ ″.	$ 5.00-	8.00
2169.	CONSTITUTIONAL CATARRAH REMEDY – Rect. – Aqua – 7½ ″ high.	$ 3.00-	4.00
2170.	CONWAY – Round – Clear – 3¼ ″.	$ 4.00-	6.00
2171.	CRAB APPLE CREAM – Rectangular – Clear – 5″.	$ 1.00-	2.00
2172.	CRAB ORCHARD WATER COMPANY – Oval – Amber – 5¾″.	$ 1.00-	2.00
2173.	CRANE'S EXTRACT COMPANY – Round – Clear – 6″ & 7″.	$ 4.00-	9.00
2174.	CREOMULSION FOR COUGHS DUE TO COLDS – Rectangular – Clear – 8¼ . . . . Bottle with cork	$ 2.00-	3.00
	Screw top	$ 1.00-	4.00
2175.	CRESCENT DRUG CO. – Clear – 7″.	$ 2.00-	3.00
2176.	CROOK & COMPANY – Square – Amber – 8 oz.	$ 4.00-	6.00
2177.	CROSSMAN MIXTURE – Round – Aqua – 4″.	$ 2.00-	4.00
2178.	CULLEN'S-ROWNAD & WALTON – Rect. – Aqua – 5¾″.	$ 2.00-	4.00
2179.	CUMMING'S BEGETINE – Oval – Aqua – 9 5/8″.	$ 3.00-	4.00
2180.	CUTICURA SYSTEM FOR BLOOD AND SKIN PURIFICATION – Square – Aqua – 9 1/8″.	$ 2.00-	3.00
2181.	CUTICURA TREATMENT FOR AFFECTIONS OF THE SKIN – Square – Light aqua – 6½ oz. bottle.	$ 4.00-	6.00

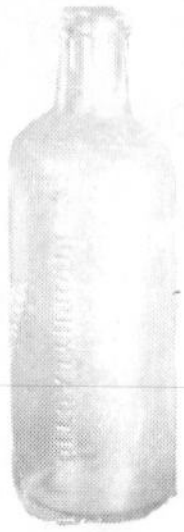

| 2182 | 2190 |  2211 | 2219 |

2182.	DALBY'S CARMINATIV – (No e) – Round – Aqua – 3¾".	$	6.00- 10.00
2183.	DALLIMOND & CO. – Amber – 3".	$	2.00- 6.00
2184.	DALTON'S SARSAPARILLA AND NERVE TONIC – Rect. – Aqua – 9".	$	8.00- 15.00
2185.	DANA'S SARSAPARILLA – Rect. – Aqua – 9".	$	3.00- 6.00
2186.	DANIEL'S COUGH COLD AND FEVER DROPS – Rect. – Clear – 4½".	$	2.00- 4.00
2187.	DANIEL'S COLIC CURE – Square – Clear – 3½".	$	4.00- 10.00
2188.	DANIEL'S VETERINARY COLIC DROPS – Square – Pinkish & Clear – 3½".	$	1.00- 2.00
2189.	DANIEL'S WONDER WORKER LOTION – Rect. – Clear 6½".	$	2.00- 6.00
2190.	DARBY'S PROPYLACTIC FLUID – Aqua – 7¼".	$	2.00- 3.00
2191.	DARBY'S PROPYLACTIC FLUID – Round – Aqua – 4".	$	1.00- 2.00
2192.	DAVILA BOTICA MEXICANA – Rect. – Aqua – 4¼".	$	2.00- 3.00
2193.	DAVIS & LAWRENCE CO. – Rectangular – Clear – 4¾".	$	2.00- 6.00
2194.	DAVIS BOTTLE STORE – Aqua – 4¼" & 6".	$	4.00- 6.00
2195.	DAVIS VEGETABLE PAIN KILLER – Round – Aqua – 4¼".	$	4.00- 6.00
	Rectangular – Aqua – 5 7/8"	$	2.00- 5.00
	Rectangular – Aqua – 6 5/8"	$	3.00- 6.00
	Rectangular – Aqua – 8½"	$	4.00- 6.00
2196.	D.D.D. – Square – Clear – 3½".	$	1.00- 2.00
2197.	D.D.D. – Rectangular – Clear – 5½".	$	1.00- 2.00
2198.	DEGRATH'S ELECTRIC OIL – Aqua – 4½" – 5 5/8".	$	2.00- 4.00
2199.	DEGUILLIE ELIXIR – Round – Green – 7".	$	4.00- 11.00
2200.	DEKONING TILLY – Vial – Aqua – 3¼".	$	5.00- 9.00
2201.	DELAVAN'S REMEDY WHOOPING COUGH CROUP – Aqua – 6".	$	3.00- 4.00
2202.	DEMING & COMPANY – Round – Clear – 5".	$	4.00- 8.00
2203.	DENNIS SYSTEM RENOVATOR & BLOOD PURIFYING SYRUP – Square – Clear – 5¼".	$	2.00- 4.00
2204.	DEWITT'S COLIC & COLERA CURE – Rect. – Aqua – 4 7/8".	$	4.00- 10.00
2205.	DEWITT & CO. ONE MINUTE COUGH CURE – Rect. – Aqua – 5½".	$	4.00- 10.00
2206.	DEXTER'S INDIAN SALVE – Round – Aqua – 2¾".	$	6.00- 10.00
2207.	DICKEY'S OLD RELIABLE EYE WATER – Round – Clear – 3¾".	$	1.00- 2.00
2208.	DILL'S BALM OF LIFE – Clear – 6".	$	3.00- 6.00
2209.	DINNEFORD'S MAGNESIA – Oval – Clear, aqua – 7".	$	2.00- 3.00
2210.	DINSMORE'S COUGH & CROUP BALSAM – Rect. – Aqua – 6 1/8".	$	4.00- 6.00
2211.	DISBROW'S ANISETT – Clear – 4½".	$	5.00- 11.00
2212.	DODGE – Square – Clear – 8".	$	2.00- 4.00
2213.	DODSON – Rectangular – Clear – 6¾".	$	1.00- 2.00
2214.	DODSON'S LIVER TONE – Rectangular – Clear – 7".	$	2.00- 3.00
2215.	DOWN'S VEGETABLE BALSAMIC ELIXIR – Cylinder – Aqua – 7½" -4½".	$	4.00- 10.00

2216.	DRAKE'S COUGH REMEDY – Rect. – Aqua – 6¼".	$	2.00-	4.00
2217.	DUBOIS – Rectangular – Aqua – 6".	$	1.00-	2.00
2218.	DUNBAR – 10-sided cylinder – Aqua – 4".	$	5.00-	10.00
2219.	EAST INDIAN CORN PAINT – Rectangular – Clear – 2".	$	2.00-	3.00
2220.	EBLING'S HERB MEDICINE – Rectangular – Aqua.	$	5.00-	15.00
2221.	EDDY & EDDY – Clear – 5".	$	2.00-	4.00

2221   2222   2227   2237

2222.	EDWARDS & SON – For whooping cough – Clear – 5". .	$	6.00-	12.00
2223.	ELABBUSSEMENTS CHATELAIN – Flat – Amber – 5¾".	$	1.00-	2.00
2224.	ELIXIR ALIMENTAIRE – Rectangular – Aqua – 8 1/8". . .	$	3.00-	4.00
2225.	ELKAY'S WIRE-CUT LINIMENT – Rect. – Aqua – 8". . . .	$	3.00-	4.00
2226.	ELY'S CREAM BALM – Rectangular – Amber – 2½". . . .	$	2.00-	6.00
2227.	ELY'S CREAM BALM – Owego, New York – 2½"x1"x1 3/8" – Amber.	$	2.00-	6.00
2228.	ENO'S FRUIT SALT – Rectangular – Clear.	$	2.00-	4.00
2229.	ESSENCE OF PEPPERMINT – Clear – 2¾".	$	4.00-	8.00
2230.	EVANS CHEMICAL COMPANY – Oval – Clear – 5¼". . .	$	2.00-	3.00
2231.	FAHRENSTOCK'S VERMIFUGE – Round – Aqua – 3¾" & 4"	$	5.00-	10.00
2232.	FAHRNEY, THE RELIABLE OLD-TIME PREPARATION FOR HOME USE – Square & oval – Clear – 8 7/8".	$	2.00-	4.00
2233.	FAIRBANKS & BEARD – Round – Blue-green – ½ pint. .	$	8.00-	15.00
2234.	FAIRCHILD BROS. & FOSTER ESSENCE OF PAPSINE Oval – Clear – 7¾".	$	4.00-	6.00
2235.	FARMACIA CENTRAL DE SONORA – Square – Aqua – 2½".	$	1.00-	2.00
	4"	$	2.00-	3.00
2236.	FATHER JOHN'S MEDICINE – Rect. – Amber – 7½". . . .	$	3.00-	6.00
2237.	FEDERAL DRUG CO. – Oakland Cal. – Sun colored amethyst.	$	2.00-	6.00

2239   2240   2245   2246

2238.	FELLOWS & CO CHEMISTS – Square, oval – Aqua – 8".	$	1.00-	3.00
2239.	FELLOWS SYRUP OF HYPOPHOSPHITES – Clear – 8".	$	2.00-	4.00
2240.	FELLOWS SYRUP OF HYPOPHOSPHITES – Oval, square – Aqua – 7¾" high.	$	4.00-	10.00
2241.	FENNER'S KIDNEY AND BACKACHE CURE – Oval – Amber – 10¼".	$	20.00-	40.00
2242.	FERROL, THE IRON OIL FOOD – Rect. – Aqua – 9½.	$	2.00-	3.00
2243.	FIELD'S PRUNE SYRUP AND SENNA – Clear – 7¾".	$	6.00-	10.00
2244.	FINK'S MAGIC OIL – Rectangular – Aqua – 4".	$	1.00-	2.00
2245.	FINEST CASTOR OIL – Blue – 6½".	$	10.00-	12.00
2246.	FITCH CO. (THIS BOTTLE IS LOANED BY) – Clear – 8".	$	4.00-	8.00
2247.	FITCH'S DANDRUFF CURE – Rect. – Clear – 6½".	$	4.00-	6.00
2248.	FIVE DROPS – Rectangular – Aqua – 5½".	$	1.00-	2.00
2249.	F-K – Round – Aqua – 1½".	$	2.00-	4.00
2250.	FLAGG – Rectangular – Aqua – 6¼".	$	1.00-	2.00
2251.	FLAZY'S – Aqua – 5".	$	5.00-	10.00

2252    2262 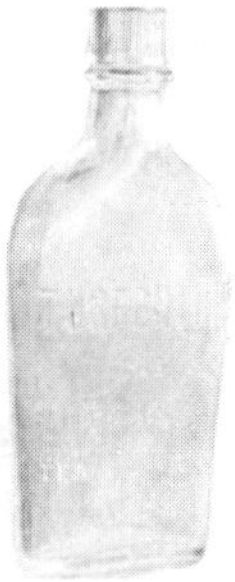   2263    2271

2252.	FLETCHER'S CASTORIA LAXATIVE – Clear – 7".	$	1.00-	2.00
2253.	FLORIDA WATER – Round – Aqua – 5 7/8".	$	2.00-	4.00
2254.	FLUID BEEF CORDIAL – Round – Amber – 8".	$	2.00-	4.00
2255.	FOLEY & CO. – Rectangular – Clear – 5½" & 6½".	$	2.00-	4.00
2256.	FOLEY'S HONEY & TAR – Rectangular – Aqua – 5¼".	$	1.00-	2.00
2257.	FOLEY'S KIDNEY & BLADDER CURE – Amber & clear – 7¼".	$	8.00-	15.00
2258.	FOLEY'S KIDNEY & BLADDER CURE – Rect. – Amber – 7½".	$	6.00-	15.00
2259.	FOLEY'S SAFE DIARRHEA & COLIC CURE – Rect. – Aqua – 5 1/8" high.	$	4.00-	8.00
2260.	(FOUR EIGHTS) 8888 KIDNEY & BLADDER REMEDY – Square – Amber – 8½".	$	2.00-	4.00
2261.	FRAGA'S CUBAN VERMIFUGE – 8-sided – Aqua – 3¾".	$	2.00-	6.00
2262.	FRANK TEA & SPICE CO. – CASTOR OIL – Clear – 5½".	$	3.00-	4.00
2263.	FRANK TEA & SPICE CO. – TURPENTINE – Clear – 5½".	$	3.00-	4.00
2264.	FRANKS TURKEY FEBRIFUGE FOR THE CURE OF FEVER & AGUE – Rectangular – Aqua.	$	10.00-	20.00
2265.	FREEZONE – for corns – 8-sided – Clear – 2¼".	$	1.00-	2.00
2266.	FRIENDRICHSHALL COPPELL & CO. – Green – 8½".	$	3.00-	6.00
2267.	FRONTIER ASTHMA CO. – Round – Amber – 6".	$	1.00-	2.00
2268.	FRUITOLA, PINUS MEDICINE CO. – Rect. – Clear, amber – 6¼".	$	1.00-	.00
2269.	FRY PRESCRIPTION DRUGGISTS – Rect. – oval – Aqua – 5½".	$	1.00-	2.00
2270.	FRYE – Rectangular – Clear – 3¼".	$	1.00-	2.00
2271.	FURST CO. – Clear – 3½".	$	2.00-	3.00
2272.	FURST McNESS CO. – Rectangular – Aqua – 8½".	$	3.00-	4.00

| 2276 | 2294 | 2295 | 2296 |

2273.	GALLATIN DRUG CO. – Rectangular – Clear – 3½". . . .	$ 1.00-	2.00
2274.	GALLOGHY & CO. – Rectangular – Aqua – 5½".	$ 1.00-	3.00
2275.	GARGLING OIL – Rectangular – Cobalt, green – 5", 5¼", 5¾" & 7¼".	$ 10.00-	30.00
2276.	GARRETT & CO. – Clear – 5¼".	$ 2.00-	3.00
2277.	GAUSS ELIXIR – Rectangular – Amber – 8".	$ 2.00-	6.00
2278.	GAYFER, JOHN DRUGGIST – Oval – Clear – 4".	$ 2.00-	4.00
2279.	GENARO R. LIMA, FARMACEUTICA ISLA DE CUBA – Rectangular – Aqua – 9¼".	$ 6.00-	12.00
2280.	GEROLAMO PAGLIANO – Rectangular – Aqua – 4¼". .	$ 6.00-	12.00
2281.	GETS IT – Square – 2".	$ 2.00-	4.00
2282.	GIBB'S, L.E. BONE LINIMENT – 6-sided – Aqua – 4¼".	$ 8.00-	15.00
2283.	GIBSON'S TABLETS – Round – Aqua – 12".	$ 5.00-	10.00
2284.	GILMAN'S PHARMACY – Rectangular – Clear – 3".	$ 1.00-	2.00
2285.	GLOBE FLOWER COUGH SYRUP – Rectangular – Aqua – 7".	$ 1.00-	2.00
2286.	GLOVER'S, H. CLAY – Rectangular – Amber – 5".	$ 1.00-	2.00
2287.	GLOVER'S IMPERIAL MANGE MEDICINE – Rectangular – Amber – 6½" high.	$ 4.00-	6.00
2288.	GLOVER'S IMPERIAL DISTEMPER REMEDY – Rectangular – Amber – 5" high.	$ 2.00-	3.00
2289.	GLYCO-HEROIN – Round – Amber – 7½".	$ 1.00-	2.00
2290.	GLYCO-THYMOLINE – Amethyst – 4¼".	$ 2.00-	3.00
2291.	GLYCO-THYMOLINE – Square – Clear – 6".	$ 1.00-	3.00
2292.	GLYCO-THYMOLINE – Square – Clear – 2".	$ 1.00-	4.00
2293.	GOFF'S OIL LINIMENT – Rectangular – Aqua – 6".	$ 1.00-	2.00
2294.	GOLDMAN, MARY T – St. Paul Minn. (on front panel) – 5½".	$ 2.00-	4.00
2295.	GOLDMAN, MARY T – Brown – 5 1/8".	$ 2.00-	3.00
2296.	GOLDMAN, MARY T – St. Paul Minn. – Amber – 6".	$ 4.00-	6.00
2297.	GOMBOULT'S CAUSTIC BALSAM – 8-sided – Aqua – 6½".	$ 4.00-	10.00
2298.	(GORDAK) JELLY OF POMEGRANATE – Flat with a large neck – Aqua – 7" high.	$ 1.00-	2.00
2299.	GORDAK'S DROPS – Round – Aqua – 5".	$ 3.00-	4.00
2300.	GOURAUD'S ORIENTAL CREAM – Green – 8¼".	$ 4.00-	10.00
2301.	GRAHAM'S DYSPEPSIA CURE – Rectangular – Clear – 8¼".	$ 8.00-	12.00

2302   2311   2319   2320

2302.	GRAVES PECTORAL COMPOUND – Blue – 7¼".	$	8.00- 20.00
2303.	GRAY'S SYRUP OF RED SPRUCE – Rect. – Aqua – 5½".	$	2.00- 4.00
2304.	GREGORY'S INSTANT CURE – Square – Aqua – 5". RARE	$	10.00- 25.00
2305.	GREAT SEAL – Oval – Clear – 5".	$	1.00- 2.00
2306.	GREEN, L.M. – Rectangular – Aqua – 7".	$	1.00- 4.00
2307.	GREENE'S NERVURA – Aqua – 9".	$	3.00- 6.00
2308.	GREENE'S SARSAPARILLA – Square – Amber.	$	8.00- 15.00
2309.	GRODER'S BOTANIC DYSPEPSIA SYRUP – Rect. – Aqua – 9".	$	5.00- 10.00
2310.	GROSSMAN'S SPECIFIC MIXTURE – Rect. – Aqua – 4".	$	1.00- 2.00
2311.	GROVE'S TASTELESS CHILL TONIC – Green – 5¼".	$	2.00- 4.00
2312.	GUINN'S ANTISEPTIC – Rectangular – Amber – 8".	$	5.00- 8.00
2313.	GUINN'S PIONEER BLOOD RENEWER – Rect. – Amber – 9" high.	$	8.00- 15.00
2314.	GUNN'S ANTISEPTIC – Rectangular – Amethyst – 8".	$	4.00- 9.00
2315.	HAAN'S BALSAM TAR COMPOUND & HONEY – Rect. – Clear – 7" high.	$	1.00- 2.00
2316.	HAAS, BARACK & CO. – 12-sided – 7" & 9".	$	6.00- 10.00
2317.	HAGAN'S MAGNOLIA BALM – Rect. – Milk glass – 5".	$	10.00- 15.00
2318.	HAGEE'S CORDIAL OF THE EXTRACT OF COD LIVER OIL – Rect. – Clear – 8".	$	3.00- 6.00
2319.	HALL'S CATARRH CURE – Aqua – 4½".	$	4.00- 8.00
2320.	HAMLIN'S WIZARD OIL – Aqua – 6 1/8".	$	1.00- 3.00
2321.	HAMILTON'S OLD ENGLISH BLACK OIL – 8-sided – Aqua – 4½".	$	8.00- 10.00
2322.	HAND (DR. D.B.) – Oval – Aqua – 5½".	$	1.00- 4.00

2329   2323   2326   2327

2323.	HARARD & HARARD CHEMISTS – Clear – 2¼ ".	$	3.00-	6.00
2324.	HARRISON – Rectangular – Aqua – 9½ ".	$	4.00-	8.00
2325.	HARTER'S IRON TONIC – Rectangular – Amber – 9".	$	6.00-	10.00
2326.	HARTMANN, M.H. – Amethyst – 4".	$	2.00-	3.00
2327.	HAWK'S UNIVERSAL STIMULANT – Round – Aqua – 3½ ".	$	2.00-	3.00
2328.	HAYDEN'S VIBURNUM COMPOUND – Rectangular – Aqua – 5".	$	2.00-	4.00
2329.	HAYNES ARABIAN BALSAM – 12-sided – Green – 4".	$	8.00-	10.00
2330.	HAYS HAIR HEALTH – Rectangular – Amber – 6¾"...	$	4.00-	8.00
2331.	HAYS HAIR HEALTH – Same as above but 7½ ".	$	4.00-	8.00

2332   2334   2335   2339

2332.	HAZELTINE & CO. – Blue – 5".	$	4.00-	6.00
2333.	HEIMSTREET & CO. – 8-sided – Cobalt – 6 7/8".	$	15.00-	20.00
2334.	HEINITSH, W.E. – Clear – 4 1/8".	$	1.00-	2.00
2335.	HEINITSH, W.E. – Clear – 6".	$	2.00-	3.00
2336.	HELEY'S CELERY BEEF & IRON – Amber – 9½ ".	$	6.00-	10.00
2337.	HEMACOLOIDS – Rectangular – Amber – 7½ ".	$	2.00-	6.00
2338.	HENLEY'S ROYAL BALSAM – Rectangular – Clear or amethyst – 6¾ " high.	$	4.00-	8.00
2339.	HERBINE – Rectangular – Aqua – 6¾ ".	$	1.00-	2.00
2340.	H.H.H. THE CELEBRATED HORSE MEDICINE – Rec. – Aqua – 7".	$	4.00-	8.00

2341   2342   2344   2346

2341.	H.H.H. THE CELEBRATED HORSE MEDICINE – 6½".	$	4.00-	8.00
2342.	HICK'S CAPUDINE FOR HEADACHES – Rectangular – Amber – 5¾" & 6½".	$	2.00-	4.00
2343.	HIMALAYA, NATURE'S CURE FOR ASTHMA – Square Amber	$	5.00-	15.00
2344.	HINDS, A.S. – Clear – 5½ ".	$	1.00-	2.00

2345.	HINKLEY'S BONE LINIMENT – Rectangular – Clear – 5¼".	$	1.00-	2.00
2346.	HOBO MEDICINE – Clear – 8".	$	3.00-	4.00
2347.	HOLDEN'S COUGH SYRUP – Rectangular – Aqua – 5".	$	1.00-	2.00

2348   2350   2358   2359

2348.	HOOD'S COMPOUND EXTRACT – Clear – 9".	$	8.00-	10.00
2349.	HOOD'S PILLS CURE LIVER ILLS – Oval – Clear – 2".	$	3.00-	6.00
2350.	HOOKER & CO. – Blue – 4 7/8".	$	4.00-	10.00
2351.	HOSTETTERS ESSENCE OF JAMAICA GINGER – Oval Aqua – 6".	$	4.00-	9.00
2352.	HOUCK'S PATENT PANACEA – Round – Aqua – 6½".	$	8.00-	10.00
2353.	HOWARD'S VEGETABLE CANCER & CANKER SYRUP Rectangular – Amber – 8½".	$	10.00-	12.00
2354.	HUBBARD'S VEGETABLE GERMICIDE DISENFEC-TANT & DEODORIZER – Round – Clear – 4¾".	$	2.00-	3.00
2355.	HUNT'S LINIMENT – Aqua – 4½".	$	3.00-	6.00
2356.	HUSBAND'S CALCINED MAGNESIA – Square – Aqua – 4½".	$	4.00-	8.00
2357.	HYDROZONE – Round, heavy metal – Amber – 7".	$	2.00-	3.00
2358.	HYGIENIC CO. – Clear – 2½".	$	2.00-	3.00
2359.	IMPERIAL HAIR REGINERATOR – 4½".	$	2.00-	6.00

2362   2364   2366   2367

2360.	INDIAN ROOT BEER EXTRACT – Square, Rectangular Aqua – 4½" high.	$	1.00-	2.00
2361.	INGRAM'S NERVINE PAIN EXTRACT – Rect. – Aqua – 4 7/8".	$	1.00-	2.00
2362.	IODINE – Cobalt – 3½", 3¾" & 2 ¾".	$	4.00-	6.00
2363.	IRON NUXATED – Round – Clear – 3¼".	$	1.00-	4.00
2364.	JACOBS PHARMACY – Clear – 3".	$	1.00-	2.00
2365.	JADWIN'S SUBDUING LINIMENT – Aqua – 4".	$	1.00-	2.00
2366.	JARABE DE LEONARDI – Green – 5½".	$	2.00-	4.00

2367.	JAYNE'S & CO. – Clear – 3½".	$	2.00-	3.00
2368.	JAYNE'S ALTERNATIVE – Aqua – 5 1/8".	$	2.00-	3.00
2369.	JAYNE'S CAMINATIVE BALSAM – Aqua – 5 1/8".	$	4.00-	6.00
2370.	JAYNE'S EXPECTORANT – Light green – 5¼" & 6¼"..	$	4.00-	6.00
2371.	JAYNE'S TONIC VERMIFUGE – Rectangular – Aqua – 5¼".	$	3.00-	4.00
2372.	JEWELL TEA CO. – Rectangular – Clear – 6½".	$	15.00-	20.00
2373.	J & J – Round – Cobalt – 2½".	$	2.00-	4.00
2374.	JOHNSON DRUGGIST – Rectangular – Clear – 2 7/8"...	$	1.00-	2.00
2375.	JOHNSON & SON – Round – 6¼" – Clear.	$	1.00-	2.00

2376   2378   2380   2382

2376.	JOHNSON, W.M. DRUGGIST – Clear – 4½".	$	2.00-	3.00
2377.	JOHNSON'S AMERICAN ANODYNE LINIMENT – Round – Aqua – 4½" & 6½" high.	$	1.00-	2.00
2378.	JOHNSON'S CHILL AND FEVER TONIC – Rectangular Clear – 5½" & 6".	$	2.00-	4.00
2379.	JONES BROS. – Rectangular – Amethyst – 7".	$	3.00-	4.00
2380.	JONES' LINIMENT – Rectangular – Aqua – 5".	$	1.00-	2.00
2381.	JOY'S SARSAPARILLA – Rectangular – Aqua – 8 7/8"..	$	10.00-	15.00
2382.	KALO-COMPOUND FOR PYSPEPSIA – Rectangular – Clear & mint – 7½" high.	$	2.00-	3.00

2384   2395   2397   2403

2383.	KAYTON'S OIL OF LIFE – Rectangular – Aqua – 6". ...	$	1.00-	2.00
2384.	KEASBEY, MATTISON C. – Blue – 3½".	$	3.00-	6.00
2385.	KEATING'S HOREHOUND – Rectangular – Aqua – 5"..	$	1.00-	2.00
2386.	KELLOGG BROS. – Rectangular – Clear – 6".	$	5.00-	8.00
2387.	KEMP'S BALSAM – Oval, rectangular – Aqua, clear – 2¾" high.	$	4.00-	8.00
2388.	KENDALL'S SPAVIN CURE – 12-sided – Amber – 5½"..	$	8.00-	10.00

2389.	KENNEDY'S RHEUMATIC LINIMENT – Aqua – 6 5/8"...	$	3.00- 4.00
2390.	K`⌐⌐LER – Square, oval, rectangular – Amber – 6½" & 7½".	$	2.00- 6.00
2391.	KESSLER MALT EXTRACT – Round – Amber – 8½". ..	$	2.00- 6.00
2392.	KICKAPOO COUGH CURE – Round – Aqua – 6".	$	6.00- 15.00
2393.	KICKAPOO INDIAN COUGH CURE – Round – Aqua – 5½".	$	8.00- 15.00
2394.	KIDDE DYSENTARY CORDIAL – Round – Aqua – 7½"..	$	8.00- 10.00
2395.	KILMER'S SWAMP ROOT – Blue – 8 3/8".	$	8.00- 12.00
2396.	KILMER'S (THE GREAT DR.) SWAMP-ROOT KIDNEY LIVER AND BLADDER CURE – Rectangular – Aqua – 8½".	$	8.00- 10.00
	Blue – 8¼"	$	6.00- 10.00
	Aqua – 8½"	$	6.00- 10.00
	Aqua – 7"	$	4.00- 6.00
2397.	KILMER'S SWAMP-ROOT KIDNEY CURE – (Sample bottle) – Aqua – Birmingham N.Y. – 3½".	$	6.00- 10.00
2398.	KILMER'S SWAMP-ROOT KIDNEY REMEDY – Round – Aqua – 4¼".	$	3.00- 6.00
2399.	KILMER'S U & W OINTMENT – Round – Aqua – 1¾". ..	$	3.00- 5.00
2400.	KIMBALL – Octagonal – Amber – 6".	$	4.00- 8.00
2401.	KING'S NEW DISCOVER FOR COUGHS AND COLDS – Rectangular – Clear – Aqua – 6¾".	$	4.00- 6.00
2402.	KINGS MEN DISCOVERY FOR CONSUMPTION – Rectangular – Aqua – 6½" and 4¼".	$	3.00- 6.00
2403.	KING'S NEW DISCOVERY FOR COUGHS AND COLDS Embossed as above on front. On right H.E. Bucklin Co. On left Chicago Ill. – Aqua – 6¾"x1 1/8"x2¼".	$	4.00- 8.00

2404    2409    2419    2420

2404.	KING'S MEN DISCOVER FOR COUGHS AND COLDS – Blue – 6½".	$	6.00- 10.00
2405.	KING'S MEN LIFE PILLS – Square – Clear – 2½".	$	3.00- 4.00
2406.	KING'S NEW DISCOVERY RHEUMATIC LINIMENT – Blue, 4 1/8".	$	3.00- 5.00
2407.	KINSMAN DRUGGIST – Oval – Bright aqua – 4½".	$	1.00- 2.00
2408.	KLINE'S GREAT NERVE RESTORER – Rectangular – Aqua – 8½".	$	2.00- 3.00
2409.	KNABE & BROS. PHARMACISTS – Clear – 6".	$	2.00- 3.00
2410.	KNAPP'S ROOT BEER EXTRACT – Aqua – 4".	$	3.00- 4.00
2411.	KODAL DYSPEPSIA CURE – Rectangular – Aqua – 9". .	$	5.00- 10.00
2412.	KODAL NERVE TONIC – 3½".	$	3.00- 4.00
2413.	KOLA MONAVON LYON – Round – Aqua – 11".	$	3.00- 4.00
2414.	KOLMSTOCK'S VERMIFUGE – Round – Aqua – 3½"...	$	4.00- 10.00
2415.	KUHN REMEDY CO. – Round – Clear – 7".	$	1.00- 2.00
2416.	KURNITSKI'S AROMATIC WIRE GRASS TONIC – Square – Amber – 9½" high.	$	15.00- 30.00

2417.	KURRASCH DRUGGIST – Oval – Clear – 6″.	$	1.00-	2.00
2418.	KUTNOW'S POWDER – Rectangular – Aqua – 4½″.	$	1.00-	2.00
2419.	LA AMERICA DRUG STORE – Clear – 4½″.	$	2.00-	3.00
2420.	LACTOPEPTINE – Clear – 3½″.	$	2.00-	4.00
2421.	LADSTONE'S CELERY & PEPSIN COMPOUND – Rectangular – Amber – 7″ high.	$	3.00-	6.00
2422.	LANE'S MEDICINES ARE GOOD – Oval – Aqua – 5″.	$	2.00-	4.00

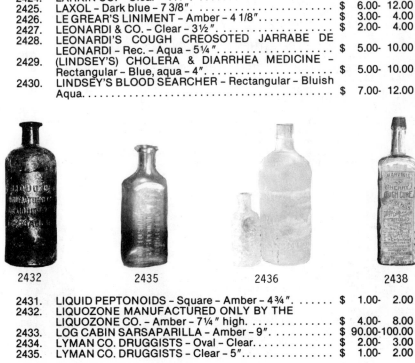

2423   2424   2425   2427

2423.	LANMAN & KEMP – Aqua – 8″.	$	2.00-	4.00
2424.	LARKIN CO. – Clear – 4¼″.	$	2.00-	4.00
2425.	LAXOL – Dark blue – 7 3/8″.	$	6.00-	12.00
2426.	LE GREAR'S LINIMENT – Amber – 4 1/8″.	$	3.00-	4.00
2427.	LEONARDI & CO. – Clear – 3½″.	$	2.00-	4.00
2428.	LEONARDI'S COUGH CREOSOTED JARRABE DE LEONARDI – Rec. – Aqua – 5¼″.	$	5.00-	10.00
2429.	(LINDSEY'S) CHOLERA & DIARRHEA MEDICINE – Rectangular – Blue, aqua – 4″.	$	5.00-	10.00
2430.	LINDSEY'S BLOOD SEARCHER – Rectangular – Bluish Aqua.	$	7.00-	12.00

2432   2435   2436   2438

2431.	LIQUID PEPTONOIDS – Square – Amber – 4¾″.	$	1.00-	2.00
2432.	LIQUOZONE MANUFACTURED ONLY BY THE LIQUOZONE CO. – Amber – 7¼″ high.	$	4.00-	8.00
2433.	LOG CABIN SARSAPARILLA – Amber – 9″.	$	90.00-	100.00
2434.	LYMAN CO. DRUGGISTS – Oval – Clear.	$	2.00-	3.00
2435.	LYMAN CO. DRUGGISTS – Clear – 5″.	$	1.00-	2.00

2436.	LYON MANUFACTURING CO. – MEXICAN MUSTANG LINIMENT – Green – 3¼".	$	2.00-	6.00
	Aqua – 5¼"	$	2.00-	5.00
2437.	LYSOL – Round – Amber.	$	2.00-	4.00
2438.	MARVINIS CHERRY COUGH CURE – Brown – 9 7/8". (labeled)	$	4.00-	8.00
2439.	McBRADY & CO. – Rectangular – Clear – 6".	$	1.00-	2.00
2440.	McCANNONS – Rectangular – Clear – 7".	$	1.00-	2.00
2441.	McCORMICK & CO. – Rectangular – Clear – 5".	$	1.00-	2.00

2442   2445   2447   2451

2442.	McELREES WINE FOR CARDUI – Aqua – 8½"	$	4.00-	6.00
2443.	McLANE'S AMERICAN WORM SPECIFIC – Round – Aqua – 3½".	$	4.00-	8.00
2444.	McLEAN'S LIVER & KIDNEY BALM – Clear, aqua – 6¼" & 9".	$	8.00-	12.00
2445.	McLEAN'S STRENGTHENING CORDIAL & BLOOD PURIFIER – Green – 8" high.	$	4.00-	10.00
2446.	McLEAN'S TAR WINE BALM – Light green – 7".	$	4.00-	8.00
2447.	McLEAN'S VOLCANIC OIL – Square – Blue, aqua – 9", 4" and 4¼" high.	$	3.00-	6.00
2448.	McMILLAN & KEATER'S ESSENCE OF JAMAICA GINGER – Round – Aqua – 5½".	$	5.00-	7.00
2449.	McMUNN'S ELIXIR OF OPIUM – Round – Aqua – 4½".	$	4.00-	8.00
2450.	MEADE & BAKER CARBOLIC MOUTH WASH – Rectangular – Amethyst – 4¾" high.	$	2.00-	3.00
2451.	MEDICAL SALTS – Heavy rough pontilled – Cobalt – Blown in mold – Amber.	$	8.00-	10.00

2455   2456   2457   2458

2452.	MELVIN & BADGER APOTHECARIES – 6-sided – Cobalt – 6¾" high	$	10.00-	12.00
2453.	MELLEN'S MEDIUM DROPS – Round – Aqua – 3¾".	$	3.00-	6.00
2454.	MENTHOLATUM – White – 2¾".	$	2.00-	3.00
2455.	MERRELL'S MILK OF MAGNESIA – Blue – 8".	$	5.00-	10.00
2456.	MEXICAN MUSTANG LINIMENT – Green – 4".	$	3.00-	6.00
2457.	MEYERS & CO. – Blue – 6".	$	2.00-	4.00
2458.	MILES MEDICAL CO. – Blue – 8¼"."	$	2.00-	4.00
2459.	MILES NERVINE – Rectangular – Aqua – 8¼".	$	3.00-	5.00
2460.	MILES RESTORATIVE – Rectangular – Aqua – 8¼".	$	4.00-	8.00
2461.	MILKS EMULSION – Round – Amber – 6¼".	$	1.00-	2.00
2462.	MILLER'S HAIR INVIGORATOR – Oval – 5½".	$	6.00-	10.00
2463.	MINARDS LINIMENT – Round – Clear – 5".	$	2.00-	3.00
2464.	MISTOL – Rectangular – Clear – 2".	$	2.00-	3.00

2465

2466

2469

2470

2465.	MOHR & SON PHARMACISTS – Clear – 4".	$	2.00-	3.00
2466.	MOONE'S EMERALD OIL – Emerald green – 5".	$	2.00-	6.00
2467.	MOORE'S ESSENCE LIFE – Round – Aqua – 3¾".	$	6.00-	10.00
2468.	MOREAU'S SOOTHING CORDIAL – Round – Aqua – 5".	$	2.00-	4.00
2469.	MOROLINE – Clear – 4".	$	3.00-	4.00
2470.	MORTON & CO. – Clear – 5½".	$	2.00-	3.00

2471

2472

2476

2480

2471.	MORTON & CO. – Clear – 7".	$	1.00-	2.00
2472.	MOTHERS FRIEND – Aqua – 7".	$	3.00-	5.00
2473.	MOUNTAIN MINT TONIC – Aqua – 10".	$	3.00-	6.00
2474.	MULFORD & CO. – Rectangular – Amber – 4".	$	1.00-	2.00
2475.	MULL'S GRAPE TONIC – Amber – 7½".	$	4.00-	8.00

No.	Description		
2476.	MULLRYNE & CO. – Clear – 4 3/8"...................	$ 2.00-	4.00
2477.	MUNYON'S GERMICIDE SOLUTION – Rectangular – Green – 3½"................................	$ 2.00-	4.00
2478.	MUNYON REMEDY CO. – Round – Clear – 7¼"......	$ 2.00-	3.00
2479.	MURINE EYE REMEDY – Clear – 2½".............	$ 2.00-	3.00
2480.	MYERS ANGELO – Purple – 6"....................	$ 6.00-	12.00

| 2481 | 2482 | 2487 | 2492 |

2481.	MYERS ANGELO – Clear – 6 7/8".................	$ 6.00-	10.00
2482.	NATIONAL REMEDY COMPANY – Rec. – Aqua – 5 7/8".	$ 2.00-	3.00
2483.	NATCHEZ DRUG CO., ASEPTOL – Oval – Amber – 6½".	$ 2.00-	4.00
2484.	NATURELLE, THE DUPREE CHEMICAL CO. – Square – Amethyst – 6¾" high........................	$ 3.00-	6.00
2485.	NEWBRO'S HERPICIDE KILLS THE DANDRUFF GERM Round – Clear – 6" & 7"........................	$ 6.00-	9.00
2486.	NEW YORK PHARMACAL ASSN. – Square – Cobalt – 12"..	$ 10.00-	20.00
2487.	NICHOLS, J.R. & CO. – Aqua – 10"...............	$ 2.00-	3.00
2488.	NICOLAI – Rectangular – Clear – 3 3/8"...........	$ 2.00-	4.00
2489.	NUNN'S BLACK OIL – Round – Clear – 5½".........	$ 3.00-	5.00
2490.	NYAL'S EMULSION OF COD LIVER OIL – Rectangular Amber – 9" high............................	$ 3.00-	6.00
2491.	NYAL'S LINIMENT – Rectangular – Amber – 7"......	$ 2.00-	4.00
2492.	N.Y. DRUG CONCERN – New York – 4½" – Aqua......	$ 2.00-	4.00

| 2493 | 2497 | 2498 | 2501 |

2493.	OAK CITY DRUG CO. – Clear – 3½"................	$ 2.00-	4.00
2494.	OCULUM – Rectangular – Clear – 5 5/8".............	$ 1.00-	4.00
2495.	OD CHEMICAL CO. – Square – Amber – 5"..........	$ 1.00-	2.00
2496.	OLD CORNER DRUG STORE – Rectangular – Clear – 3 7/8"..	$ 1.00-	2.00

2497.	OLD RELIABLE EYE WATER – Blue – 3¼".	$	3.00-	6.00
2498.	OMEGA OIL – Green – The Omega Chemical Co. – Clear – Round – 4½".	$	3.00-	6.00
2499.	ONE MINUTE COUGH CURE – Rectangular – Aqua – 4¼".	$	4.00-	8.00
2500.	OPODELDOC LIQUID – Round – Aqua – 4½".	$	2.00-	4.00
2501.	OPPENHEIMER – Clear – 3½".	$	1.00-	2.00
2502.	ORDWAY'S CELEBRATED PAIN DESTROYER – 12-sided – Clear – 4¼" high.	$	3.00-	6.00

2507   2515   2516   2521

2503.	OTTO'S CURE FOR THE THROAT & LUNGS – Rectangular – Aqua – 6".	$	4.00-	8.00
2504.	OWL DRUG CO. – Rectangular – Clear – 3 7/8".	$	4.00-	6.00
2505.	OXEDINE – Oval – Clear – 6".	$	1.00-	2.00
2506.	OZOMULSION – Rectangular – Amber – 6 7/8".	$	2.00-	4.00
2507.	PATRICK'S COURT SQUARE PHARMACY – Clear – 5¼".	$	2.00-	3.00
2508.	PAIN KILLING MAGIC OIL – Rectangular – Aqua – 6".	$	2.00-	4.00
2509.	PAIN'S CELERY COMPOUND – Square – Amber – 9¾".	$	4.00-	8.00
2510.	PARKER'S GINGER TONIC – Rectangular – Amber – 6½".	$	1.00-	2.00
2511.	PENDLETON'S PANACEA – 12-sided – Clear – 4¼".	$	2.00-	3.00
2512.	PENERLEUM – Rectangular – Clear – 3½".	$	1.00-	4.00
2513.	PEPTENZYME – Square – Cobalt – 7".	$	4.00-	8.00
2514.	PEPTOGENIC MILK POWDER – Round – Amber – 8".	$	2.00-	3.00
2515.	PEPTO-MANGAN – Green – 6¼".	$	3.00-	5.00
2516.	PEPTO-MANGAN – "Gude" – Embossed – 6-sided – Aqua – 7".	$	4.00-	8.00
2517.	PERRINE'S (apple) GINGER – Amber – 10".	$	5.00-	10.00
2518.	PERRY'S DEAD SHOT VERMIFUGE – Oval – Aqua – 4".	$	8.00-	12.00
2519.	PETER'S KURIKO – no description	$	4.00-	8.00
2520.	PHILLIPS CHEMICAL CO. – Square – Clear – 4½".	$	1.00-	4.00
2521.	PHILLIPS MILK OF MAGNESIA – Blue – 5½".	$	2.00-	4.00
2522.	PHILLIPS PALATABLE COD LIVER OIL – Rectangular – Amber – 7½" high.	$	2.00-	4.00
2523.	PHYTOLINE POWERFUL ANTI-FAT – Round – Amber – 4".	$	2.00-	4.00

| 2524 | 2530 | 2532 | 2534 |

2524. PIERCE'S ANURIC TABLETS FOR KIDNEYS AND
   BACKACHE – Aqua – 3½"x1¼"..................... $ 2.00- 6.00
2525. PIERCE'S FAVORITE PRESCRIPTION – Rectangular –
   Aqua – 8¼".................................... $ 3.00- 7.00
   8½" $ 2.00- 3.00
2526. PIERCE'S TABLETS FOR KIDNEYS & BACKACHE –
   Green – 3½"................................... $ 2.00- 6.00
2527. PIERCE (R.V.) EXTRACT OF SMART-WEED – Rectangular – Clear – 5"........................... $ 4.00- 6.00
2528. PIK-RON – Rectangular – Aqua – 5"............. $ 2.00- 5.00
2529. PINEX TRADE MARK – Rectangular – Clear – 5 5/8".... $ 1.00- 2.00
2530. PINKHAM'S HERB MEDICINE – Clear – 8¼"......... $ 4.00- 6.00
2531. PINKHAM'S MEDICINE – Oval – 14½ ozs. – Clear – 8",
   8¼".. $ 1.00- 2.00
2532. PINKHAM'S VEGETABLE COMPOUND – Aqua – 8¼".. $ 2.00- 4.00
2533. PIPIFAX – Square – Amber – 9".................... $ 10.00- 20.00
2534. PISO COMPANY – Green & brown – 5¼" & 5½"....... $ 3.00- 6.00

| 2535 | 2536 | 2537 | 2542 |

2535. PISO COMPANY – Green – 5"..................... $ 2.00- 4.00
2536. PISO'S CURE FOR CONSUMPTION – Green – 5"...... $ 4.00- 8.00
2537. PITCHER'S CASTORIA – Blue – 6"................. $ 2.00- 4.00
2538. PLANK'S CHILL TONIC CO. – Oval – 6½"........... $ 1.00- 2.00
2439. PLANTER'S OLD TIME REMEDIES – Rectangular –
   Aqua – 6".................................... $ 2.00- 3.00
2540. PLAZA PHARMACY – Rectangular – Clear – 3½"...... $ 2.00- 3.00
2541. PoDoLax – Rectangular – Aqua – 7".............. $ 1.00- 2.00
2542. POND'S EXTRACT – Blue – 7 7/8"................. $ 4.00- 8.00

2543	2544	2546	2548

2543. POND'S EXTRACT – Aqua – Bim. 1846 on base – 5 3/8". $ 4.00- 6.00
2544. PORTER'S (MRS.) – Higgins Supply Co. – Cincinnati
Ohio – No. 2 – Amber – 4"............................ $ 2.00- 4.00
2545. PORTER'S CURE OF PAIN – Rectangular – Pinkish or
clear – 6¾" high. .... $ 4.00- 10.00
2546. PORTER'S PAIN KILLER – Rectangular – Clear – 6½".. $ 4.00- 10.00
2547. POST OFFICE DRUG STORE – Rectangular – Clear –
3¼". .... $ 1.00- 4.00
2548. POTTER'S HYGIENIC SUPPLY CO. – Brown – 4". ...... $ 2.00- 3.00

2549	2551	2556	2558

2549. POWERS & CO. – Clear – 5 1/8".................... $ 2.00- 3.00
2550. PRAIRIE WEED BALSAM – Aqua. .... $ 5.00- 10.00
2551. PRICE'S DELICIOUS FLAVORING EXTRACTS – Clear –
5 5/8". .... $ 1.00- 5.00
2552. PRIMLEY'S IRON & WAHOO TONIC – Square – Amber
9". .... $ 9.00- 10.00
2553. PROTONUCLEIN – Rectangular – Amber – 3"......... $ 1.00- 2.00
2554. PSYCHINE – Oval & rectangular – Brown, aqua – 5¼".. $ 2.00- 3.00
2555. PSYCHINE FOR CONSUMPTION AND LUNG
TROUBLES – Rectangular – Aqua – 9½". .... $ 6.00- 12.00
2556. PURITANA – Blue – 7". .... $ 4.00- 9.00
2557. PUROXIA – Oval – Aqua – 8". .... $ 4.00- 8.00
2558. QUALITY PURITY – Clear – 5¼". .... $ 1.00- 2.00
2559. RABELL EMULSION – Rectangular – 9½"............ $ 3.00- 6.00
2560. RADWAY & CO. – Rectangular – Clear – 5¾". .... $ 2.00- 3.00
2561. REDWAY'S RENOVATING RESOLVANT – Rectangular
Aqua – 7½". .... $ 8.00- 10.00

2564   2569   2571   2573

2562.	RAMON'S NERVE & BONE OIL – Rectangular – Aqua – 5¾".	$	2.00- 4.00
2563.	RAMON'S RELIEF – Rectangular – Clear – 5¾".	$	2.00- 3.00
2564.	RAYMON'S PEPSIN CHILL TONIC – Amber & mint – 7".	$	4.00- 8.00
2565.	REB PEELER – Rectangular – Clear.	$	1.00- 2.00
2566.	RED HAVEN – Round – Amber – 8".	$	3.00- 6.00
2567.	REED & CUTTER – Aqua – 7½".	$	4.00- 8.00
2568.	REEDER'S HEALING OIL – Blue – 4½".	$	2.00- 4.00
2569.	REID & CO. – Clear – 5½".	$	2.00- 4.00
2570.	REMINGTON – Rectangular – Aqua – 5½".	$	2.00- 4.00
2571.	RENNES MAGIC OIL PAIN KILLING – Aqua – 6".	$	2.00- 4.00
2572.	RESINOL CHEMICAL CO. – Round – Milk white – 2".	$	2.00- 4.00
2573.	REXALL STORE DUCKON'S – Rectangular – 8".	$	1.00- 2.00
2574.	RHODES' FEVER & AGUE CURE – Rectangular – Aqua 8¼".	$	6.00- 12.00
2575.	RIDENOUR-BAKER GROCERY CO. – Rectangular – Clear.	$	2.00- 4.00
2576.	RIO CHEMICAL CO. – Round – Amber – 5½.	$	1.00- 2.00
2577.	RIPANS TABULES – Square – Light green – 4½".	$	1.00- 4.00
2578.	ROCHESTER GERMICIDE CO. – Square – Clear – 5" & 8".	$	1.00- 2.00
2579.	RODERIC WILD CHERRY COUGH BALSAM – Rectangular – Clear – 5¼" high.	$	4.00- 10.00
2580.	RODGER'S VEGETABLE WORM SYRUP – Rectangular Aqua – 4¼".	$	2.00- 4.00
2581.	ROGER & GALLET – Rectangular – Clear – 5¾".	$	1.00- 2.00
2582.	ROSE – Square – Aqua – 5".	$	5.00- 11.00
2583.	ROSE & CO. – Lime water – Aqua – 11" & 14".	$	5.00- 10.00
2584.	ROSS' JAMAICA LIME JUICE – Cylinder – Aqua – 12".	$	2.00- 4.00
2585.	ROY'S & CO. – Rectangular – Clear – 4¼".	$	1.00- 2.00

2589   2590   2598   2600

2586.	ROYAL DIGESTO – Rectangular – Amber – 7¼ ″.......	$	2.00-	3.00
2587.	ROYALINE OIL – Rectangular – Aqua – 6″...........	$	2.00-	4.00
2588.	RUBIFOAM FOR THE TEETH – Flat-oval – Clear – 4″...	$	2.00-	4.00
2589.	RUMFORD CHEMICAL WORKS – Emerald green – 5½″..	$	4.00-	8.00
2590.	RUMFORD CHEMICAL WORKS – Aqua – 5½ ″ & 7½ ″..	$	5.00-	9.00
2591.	RUSH'S SARSAPARILLA 7 IRON – Rectangular – Aqua 9″...	$	6.00-	10.00
2592.	RU-TO-NA – Rectangular – Amber – 9″..............	$	2.00-	3.00
2593.	SAGWA – Rectangular – Amber – 8½″..............	$	2.00-	3.00
2594.	SALLADE AND CO. – Magic Mosquito Bite Cure – Oval Aqua – 7 5/8″ high...............................	$	10.00-	15.00
2595.	SALTER'S EYE LOTION – Rectangular – Aqua – 4½ ″. .	$	3.00-	4.00
2596.	SAMUELS – Shiny amethyst – Rectangular – 3½ ″.....	$	1.00-	2.00
2597.	SANFORD'S LIVER INVIGORATOR – Clear – 7½ ″.....	$	2.00-	3.00
2598.	SANGSTER & RIGGS CITY DRUG STORE – Clear – 5″..	$	3.00-	6.00
2599.	SANITOL FOR THE TEETH – Clear – 4½ ″............	$	6.00-	10.00
2600.	SAW PALMETTO GENUINE VERNAL BERRY WINE – Square – Clear – 10″ high........................	$	4.00-	8.00
2601.	SAYMAN PRODUCTS ARE SUPREME – Rectangular – Clear – 6½ ″....................................	$	2.00-	3.00

2602

2608

2611

2613

2602.	S.B. – Amethyst – 4½ ″...........................	$	3.00-	4.00
2603.	SCHENCK'S SEAWEED TONIC – Square – Aqua – 6¾ ″.	$	5.00-	10.00
2604.	SCHLIEPER & CO. – Oval – Clear – 4 5/8″...........	$	2.00-	3.00
2605.	SCHOLL'S LIGTONE – Rectangular – Clear – 5 7/8″....	$	1.00-	2.00
2606.	SCHOTT & CO. – Rectangular – Clear – 4½ ″.........	$	2.00-	3.00
2607.	SCOTT & BROWNE PREVENTINA – Oval – Green – 4″..	$	5.00-	11.0C
2608.	SCOTT'S EMULSION WITH LIME & SODA COD LIVER OIL – Aqua – Rectangular – 9″.....................	$	6.00-	8.00
2609.	SCOVILL BLOOD & LIVER SYRUP – Rectangular – Aqua – 9½ ″......................................	$	4.00-	5.00
2610.	S & D – Rectangular – Amber – 3″...................	$	1.00-	4.00
2611.	SEABURY PHARMACAL LABORATORIES – Dark blue 3″..	$	4.00-	8.00
2612.	SHAKER SYRUP NO. 1 – Aqua – 7½ ″................	$	10.00-	15.00
2613.	SHARP & DOHME – Amber – 2¾ ″.	$	4.00-	8.00

| 2614 | 2618 | 2624 | 2625 |

2614. SHARP & DOHME – Amber – 2½". . . . . $ 2.00- 3.00
2615. SHELDON'S MAGNETIC LINIMENT – Rectangular – Green – 5 7/8" high. . . . . $ 4.00- 8.00
2616. SHERMAN – Square – Clear – 2 5/8". . . . . $ 1.00- 2.00
2617. SHILOH'S CATARRH REMEDY – Aqua – 2¼". . . . . $ 2.00- 3.00
2618. SHILOH'S CONSUMPTION CURE – Sample – Aqua – 4½". . . . . $ 3.00- 8.00
2619. SHOOP'S FAMILY MEDICINES – Aqua – 6¾". . . . . $ 2.00- 3.00
2620. SHOOP'S FOR CURE OF RHEUMATISM – Aqua – 6¾". $ 4.00- 10.00
2621. SIEGERT & HIJOS – Round – 8½". . . . . $ 4.00- 6.00
2622. SIEGERT & HIJOS – Green – 8½". . . . . $ 4.00- 6.00
2623. SKODA'S CONCENTRATED EXTRACT SAR-SAPARILLA – Rectangular – Amber – 9". . . . . $ 15.00- 25.00
2624. SLOAN'S LINIMENT – Clear – 5". . . . . $ 1.00- 2.00
2625. SLOAN'S N & B LINIMENT – Blue – 5". . . . . $ 2.00- 3.00
2626. SLOAN'S SURE COLIC CURE – Square – Aqua – 3¼". . $ 4.00- 10.00
2627. SLOCUM'S COLTSFOOTE EXPECTORANT – Oval – Aqua – 2¼". . . . . $ 1.00- 4.00

| 2628 | 2631 | 2632 | 2636 |

2628. SMITH & CO. – Clear – 4½". . . . . $ 2.00- 4.00
2629. SMITH'S GREEN MOUNTAIN RENOVATOR – Rect. – Amber – 8½". . . . . $ 5.00- 9.00
2630. SNOW & MASON CROUP & COUGH SYRUP – Round – Aqua – 5½". . . . . $ 2.00- 3.00
2631. SOLOMONS CO. – Clear – 5½". . . . . $ 2.00- 4.00
2632. SOLOMONS CO. – Clear – 6¼". . . . . $ 5.00- 10.00
2633. SOURCE PERRIER – Green – 7" & 8½". . . . . $ 4.00- 8.00
2634. SPENCER & CO. FOR THE HAIR – Rectangular – Clear. $ 4.00- 9.00
2635. SRACA'S CUBAN VERMIFUGE – Aqua – ¾". . . . . $ 2.00- 3.00
2636. ST. JACOBS OIL – (OEL) – Blue – 6". . . . . $ 3.00- 6.00

2637

2638

2643

2644

2637.	ST. JOSEPHS ASSURES PURITY – Clear – 5½".	$	2.00- 4.00
2638.	ST. JOSEPH'S, THE NAME, ASSURES PURITY – Clear 8".	$	3.00- 6.00
2639.	ST. LUKE'S HOSPITAL – Rectangular – Clear – 4 1/8".	$	2.00- 3.00
2640.	ST. LAWRENCE PHARMACY – Oval – Clear – 4½".	$	1.00- 2.00
2641.	STABLER & CO. – Rectangular – Aqua – 6½".	$	6.00- 14.00
2642.	STELLA-VITAE (STAR OF LIVE) – Rectangular – Amethyst – 8" high.	$	3.00- 6.00
2643.	STEPHENS & SPEER DISPENSING CHEMISTS – Clear 4 1/8".	$	1.00- 2.00
2644.	STEPHENS & SPEER DISPENSING CHEMISTS – Clear 4½".	$	2.00- 3.00
2645.	STODDARD (G.S.) & CO. – Clear – 5¼".	$	3.00- 4.00
2646.	STOWE'S AMBROSIAL NECTAR – Round – Light green.	$	7.00- 14.00
2647.	SULTAN DRUG CO, – Rectangular – Clear.	$	1.00- 2.00
2648.	SULTAN DRUG CO. – Amber – 7½".	$	3.00- 4.00

2649

2651

2659

2668

2649.	SUTHERLAND, E.E. – Aqua – 5½".	$	2.00- 4.00
2650.	SWEET BYE & BYE – Clear – 3¼"	$	2.00- 4.00
2651.	SWEET OIL – Aqua – 5½".	$	4.00- 8.00
2652.	SWEET'S LINIMENT INFALLIBLE – Aqua – 5¼".	$	2.00- 3.00
2653.	SYKES SPECIFIC BLOOD MEDICINE – Clear – 6½". . .	$	2.00- 4.00
2654.	SYLMAR BRAND OLIVE OIL – Round – Clear – 3½". . .	$	1.00- 4.00
2655.	TAFT'S ASTHMALENE – Rectangular – Aqua.	$	3.00- 5.00
2656.	TARRANT & CO. DRUGGIST – Clear – 5 1/8".	$	1.00- 2.00
2657.	TARRANT CO. CHEMISTS – Rectangular – Clear – 5". .	$	1.00- 3.00
2658.	TATEM DRUGGIST – Oval – Clear – 4".	$	3.00- 6.00
2659.	TEMPLE PHARMACY – Clear – 5".	$	1.00- 2.00
2660.	THACHER'S DIARRHEA REMEDY – Square – Amethyst 3 3/8".	$	4.00- 8.00

2661.	THACHER'S LIVER & BLOOD SYRUP – Amber – 3½ ". .	$	4.00-	6.00
2662.	THACHER'S LIVER & BLOOD SYRUP – Rectangular – Amber – 8¼ " high........................	$	6.00-	10.00
2663.	THACHER'S LIVER & BLOOD SYRUP – Aqua – 8".	$	2.00-	4.00
2664.	THACHER'S VEGETABLE SYRUP – Rectangular – Amethyst – 7" high..............................	$	2.00-	4.00
2665.	THACHER'S WORM SYRUP – Square – Aqua – 7".	$	6.00-	8.00
2666.	THOMAS' ELECTRIC OIL – Rectangular – Clear – 4¼ ".	$	2.00-	4.00
2667.	THOMPSON'S COMPOUND SYRUP OF TAR FOR CONSUMPTION – Aqua – Rectangular – 5½ ".............	$	8.00-	10.00
2668.	THOMPSON'S EYE WATER – New London, Connt. – 4"..	$	4.00-	8.00
2669.	THOMPSON'S EYE WATER – Round – Aqua – 3¾ ". . . .	$	2.00-	4.00

| 2670 | 2671 | 2673 | 2674 |

2670.	THOMPSON'S EYE WATER – New London, CT – Aqua 4"..	$	3.00-	6.00
2671.	THUPTRINE DRUGGIST – Green – 5 1/8".............	$	3.00-	6.00
2672.	TICHENOR'S ANTISEPTIC – Rectangular – Aqua 5 7/8 ".	$	2.00-	4.00
2673.	TIKHELL – Blue – 6½"............................	$	4.00-	6.00
2674.	TIMERHOF, W.H. – Prescott, Arizona – Sun colored amethyst – 5" high.	$	3.00-	5.00
2675.	TOBIAS BENETIAN LINIMENT – 8-sided – Aqua – 6½ ".	$	4.00-	10.00

| 2676 | 2681 | 2682 | 2684 |

2676.	TONSILINE – Green – 6¾ ".	$	4.00-	7.00
2677.	TOWNSEND'S LINIMENT – Oval – Clear – 4".	$	1.00-	2.00
2678.	TOWNSEND'S SARSAPARILLA – Olive green – 9".	$	8.00-	10.00
2679.	TRAFTON'S BUCKTHORN SYRUP FOR SCROFULA – 8-sided – 7" – Aqua.	$	8.00-	15.00
2680.	TRUE'S ELIXIR – Clear or aqua – 6" & 6½ ".	$	2.00-	3.00

160

2681.	TUCKER, MOSLEY F. DRUGGIST – Clear – 3½".......	$	1.00-	2.00
2682.	TUCKER PHARMACAL CO. – Clear – 6½"............	$	2.00-	3.00
2683.	TULLEY'S 1180 PRESCRIPTION – Rectangular – Aqua 6¼"...	$	2.00-	3.00
2684.	TUTTLE'S ELIXIR CO. – Aqua – 6"..................	$	4.00-	6.00
2685.	UNITED STATES MEDICINE COMPANY – Rectangular Aqua – 6"...	$	2.00-	4.00
2686.	USBORNE'S READY OIL LINIMENT – Clear – 5½".....	$	1.00-	4.00
2687.	VALENTINE MEAT JUICE – Amber – 3¼"...........	$	4.00-	6.00
2688.	VANDERWAL – Round – Aqua – 4".................	$	1.00-	4.00
2689.	VAPO-CRESOLENE CO. – Square – Aqua – 3 7/8"......	$	2.00-	4.00

2690   2691   2692   2693

2690.	VARN'S PHARMACY – Clear – 5½".................	$	1.00-	2.00
2691.	"VASELINE" – Amethyst – 2¼"....................	$	2.00-	4.00
2692.	"VASELINE" – Amethyst – 2½" & 3".................	$	2.00-	3.00
2693.	"VASELINE" – Chesebrough Mfg. Co. – Amber – 2¾"..	$	1.00-	2.00

2694   2697   2699   2701

2694.	VICK'S VA-TRA-NOL – Round – Cobalt – 3"...........	$	2.00-	3.00
2695.	WAIT'S WILD CHERRY TONIC – Square – Amber – 8¾"...	$	10.00-	12.00
2696.	WALNUT LEAF HAIR RESTORER – Amber.	$	4.00-	5.00
2697.	WALPOLE & CO. – Clear – 8½".....................	$	2.00-	4.00
2698.	WALPOLE'S PREPARATION – Rectangular – Clear – 8¼"...	$	3.00-	4.00
2699.	WARNER & CO. – Clear – 2½".	$	2.00-	4.00
2700.	WARNER'S SAFE CURE – Oval – Amber – 5½".	$	8.00-	18.00
2701.	WARNER'S SAFE KIDNEY AND LIVER CURE – Oval – Amber – 9¾"x1 5/8"x3½".........................	$	8.00-	18.00
2702.	WARNER'S SAFE NERVINE – Brown – 7 3/8".	$	10.00-	20.00

| 2704 | 2705 | 2707 | 2710 |

2703. WARNER'S SAFE REMEDIES – 16 ozs. – Amber & aqua. .... $ 8.00- 20.00
2704. WARNER, W.R. & CO. – Philadelphia & St. Louis – Clear 4" high. .... $ 2.00- 4.00
2705. WARNER, W.R. & CO. – Philadelphia Pa. – 2¾". ...... $ 2.00- 4.00
2706. WATFORD DRUG CO. – Clear – 3½". .... $ 1.00- 4.00
2707. WATKIN'S – Purple – 6". .... $ 2.00- 4.00
2708. WATKIN'S MEDICAL CO. – Square – Clear. .... $ 2.00- 5.00
2709. WEAVER'S CANKER & SALT SYRUP – Oval – Aqua – 9". .... $ 8.00- 15.00
2710. WEEDON DRUG CO. – Clear – 5". .... $ 1.00- 2.00

| 2711 | 2717 | 2721 | 2723 |

2711. WEEDON DRUG CO. – Clear – 4". .... $ 2.00- 4.00
2712. WELL'S ELECTRIC FLUID – Rectangular – Clear – 5¼". .... $ 2.00- 4.00
2713. WELL'S NEURALGIA CURE – Clear – Rectangular – 6¾". .... $ 6.00- 10.00
2714. WHEELER & CO. – Round – 9". .... $ 4.00- 8.00
2715. WHITHURST – Oval – Pale gray – 3½". .... $ 1.00- 2.00
2716. WILLIAMS' PINK PILLS FOR PALE PEOPLE – Amethyst – 2¼". .... $ 5.00- 10.00
2717. WILSON, N.E. CO. INC. PHARMACISTS – 5¾"........ $ 3.00- 6.00
2718. WINANS BROS. INDIAN CURE FOR BLOOD – Rectangular – Aqua – 9" high. .... $ 6.00- 10.00
2719. WINCHELL'S TEETHING SYRUP – Round – Aqua – 5 1/8". .... $ 3.00- 4.00
2720. WINSLOW'S SOOTHING SYRUP – Round – Aqua – 5".. $ 4.00- 8.00
2721. WINSTEAD'S LAX-FOS – Rectangular – Amber – 7½".. $ 2.00- 4.00
2722. WINTERSMITH – Amber – 8½" & 9"................. $ 3.00- 4.00
2723. WISTAR'S BALSAM OF WILD CHERRY – Blue – 5". .... $ 6.00- 10.00

| 2724 | 2725 | 2728 | 2729 |

2724.	WINGFIELD DRUGGIST – Clear – 5½".	$	2.00-	4.00
2725.	WINSTHROP – Clear – 3".	$	4.00-	6.00
2726.	WOOD'S GREAT CURE FOR COUGHS & COLDS – Rect. – Aqua – 7".	$	6.00-	15.00
2727.	WOODWARD'S VEGETABLE TINCTURE – Aqua – 5½".	$	5.00-	10.00
2728.	WYETH & BROS. – Clear – 4½".	$	2.00-	3.00
2729.	WYETH, JOHN & BROS. – Clear – 3".	$	2.00-	4.00
2730.	YAGER'S SARSAPARILLA – Rectangular – Amber – 8 3/8".	$	10.00-	20.00
2731.	ZEMO FOR PIMPLES & DISEASES OF THE SKIN & SCALP – Clear – Rectangular – 6".	$	2.00-	4.00
2732.	ZMO FOR PAIN – Rectangular – Aqua – 4".	$	2.00-	4.00

| 2733 | 2734 | 2735 | 2736 |

2733.	DOG FIGURAL RING IN HAND – Blue – 8".	$	10.00-	20.00
2734.	POTTER FRUG & CHEMICAL – Aqua – 9½".	$	8.00-	15.00
2735.	MEDICAL – Aqua – 5½".	$	2.00-	3.00
2736.	MEDICAL – Clear – 5".	$	2.00-	3.00

	2737	2738	2739		2740	

2737. MEDICAL – Aqua – 3½ ". . . . . $ 2.00- 3.00
2738. MEDICAL – Amber. . . . . $ 2.00- 3.00
2739. MEDICAL – Clear – 6½ ". . . . . $ 2.00- 3.00
2740. MEDICAL – Clear – 5½ ". . . . . $ 2.00- 3.00

2741	2742	2743	2744

2741. MEDICAL – Amber – 4". . . . . $ 1.00- 2.00
2742. MEDICAL – Amber – 4". . . . . $ 2.00- 3.00
2743. MEDICAL – Clear – 5". . . . . $ 2.00- 3.00
2744. MEDICAL – Clear & aqua – 1½ " to 3½ ". . . . . $ 2.00- 3.00

2745	2746	2747	2748

2745.	MEDICAL – Amber – 3″.	$	2.00-	3.00
2746.	MEDICAL – Nature Tiffany – 8″.	$	6.00-	12.00
2747.	MEDICAL – Clear.	$	1.00-	3.00
2748.	MEDICAL – Quinine, Cobalt – 2½″ & 3″	$	3.00-	8.00

2749   2750   2751   2752

2749.	MEDICAL – Clear – 3″	$	2.00-	3.00
2750.	MEDICAL – Honey amber – 3½″	$	2.00-	3.00
2751.	MEDICAL – Amber – 7″.	$	2.00-	3.00
2752.	MEDICAL – Amber – 7½″.	$	2.00-	3.00

2753   2754   2755   2756

2753.	MEDICAL – Aqua – 8″	$	2.00-	3.00
2754.	MEDICAL – Clear – 5½″	$	1.00-	2.00
2755.	MEDICAL – Aqua – 4″	$	1.00-	2.00
2756.	MEDICAL – Clear – 5″	$	4.00-	8.00

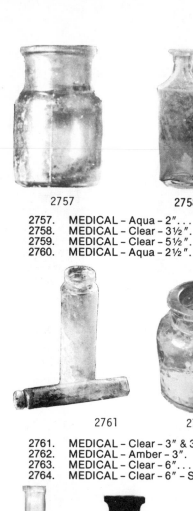

| 2757 | 2758 | 2759 | 2760 |

2757. MEDICAL – Aqua – 2″............................ $ 1.00- 2.00
2758. MEDICAL – Clear – 3½″........................... $ 1.00- 2.00
2759. MEDICAL – Clear – 5½″........................... $ 1.00- 2.00
2760. MEDICAL – Aqua – 2½″............................ $ 1.00- 2.00

| 2761 | 2762 | 2763 | 2764 |

2761. MEDICAL – Clear – 3″ & 3½″........................ $ 1.00- 2.00
2762. MEDICAL – Amber – 3″. .... $ 1.00- 2.00
2763. MEDICAL – Clear – 6″............................ $ 1.00- 2.00
2764. MEDICAL – Clear – 6″ – Sheered lip. .... $ 4.00- 6.00

| 2765 | 2766 | 2767 | 2768 | 2769 |

2765. MEDICAL – Aqua – 5½″............................ $ 3.00- 6.00
2766. MEDICAL – Amber – 3″. .... $ 1.00- 2.00
2767. MEDICAL – Nature's Tiffany – 3½″. .... $ 4.00- 6.00
2768. MEDICAL – Amber – 4″. .... $ 3.00- 4.00
2769. MEDICAL – Amber – 6″. .... $ 3.00- 4.00

DAIRY PRODUCT BOTTLES

| 2770 | 2771 | 2773 | 2774 |

2770. BABBLIN-BROOK – One pint – Clear – 7¼ ". . . . . $ 4.00- 6.00
2771. BIRELEYS – Trade Mark Registered, Hollywood, California – 6¾ ozs. – 5¼ " – Clear. . . . . $ 2.00- 4.00
2773. BLUE BONNET PASTURIZED DAIRY PRODUCTS – Half pint liquid – Sealed Lg. S. – Clear – Red lettering – 5½ ". . . . . $ 2.00- 4.00
2774. CARNESS BROS. DAIRY – Phone W-227 Ring 2 – One pint liquid – Clear – 7¼ ". . . . . $ 4.00- 8.00

| 2775 | 2776 | 2777 | 2778 |

2775. C.D. CO. PROPERTY OF, TRADE MARK REGISTERED One pint – Light amethyst – 8". $ 4.00- 6.00
2776. CITY CREAMERY MILK (USE) – Phone 382-(?) – On back: "We guarantee every bottle of City Creamery Pasturized Milk." One quart liquid – Registered – Sealed S2 Lg. – Pat No. 2076124 – Clear – 9½ ". . . . . $ 4.00- 8.00
2777. COTTAGE CHEESE – Amethyst – 10-sided – 4½ ". . . . . $ 2.00- 6.00
2778. COTTAGE CHEESE – Dark amethyst – 6¼ ". . . . . $ 3.00- 8.00

2779

2780

2781

2782

2779.	DAIRYLAND MILK, FRESH, PURE, RICH, SAFE – Half pint liquid – Clear – Red lettering – By Duraglass – 4¼".	$ 2.00- 4.00
2780.	DAIRYLAND PRODUCT (A) – (on bottom) CLEVELAND Clear – 7" high.	$ 2.00- 6.00
2781.	DAZEY CHURN NO. 80 – Patented Feb. 14, 1922 by Dazey Churn & Mfg. Co. St. Louis, Mo. – Made in U.S.A. Clear – Metal top – Wooden pedals – 15½".	$ 12.00- 20.00
2782.	EARLY MILK BOTTLE – Light amethyst – 8".	$ 6.00- 15.00

2783

2784

2785

2786

2783.	FOREMOST-FOREMOST – Trademark painted on front "Your family gets the most from Formost" slogan painted on back. Amber – 1 qt. – Square – 8½".	$ 4.00- 10.00
2784.	GANDY'S FINE DAIRY PRODUCTS – 1 Gal. liquid – Registered – Sealed Lg. C739-6 – Clear – Red lettering – Metal handle – 10¾" high.	$ 4.00- 10.00
2785.	GANDY'S INC. – One pint liquid – Registered – Sealed S2.	$ 4.00- 8.00
2786.	HALF PINT – Amethyst – 5½".	$ 2.00- 4.00

2787	2788	2789	2790

2787. HALF PINT LIQUID – Registered – Sealed – Clear – 5¼". . . . . $ 3.00- 6.00

2788. HALF PINT LIQUID – Reg., Sealed Lg. S. – Clear – 5½". $ 2.00- 6.00

2789. HIGHLAND DAIRY FARMS CO. – Property of – One pint – Registered – Highland, Ill. – Clear – 7¼". . . . . $ 3.00- 6.00

2790. HOEIER DAIRY, SPRINGFIELD, ILL. – (on back) – "Hey Mom, I want my glass of milk." – Lettering painted in red – Embossed near base: "One quart liquid, Reg., Sealed No. 1394. . . . . $ 4.00- 8.00

2791	2792	2793	2794

2791. J.C. HOOD BROWNWOOD, TEXAS – One pint – Clear – 7¼". . . . . $ 4.00- 8.00

2792. McILHANEY'S GRADE A PASTEURIZED MILK – Back – "Can't sleep? Drink warm milk before retiring." Embossed around base: Sealed BB48 – Registered – One quart liquid – On bottom – Duraglass – Clear with red lettering – Cream top – 9½". . . . . $ 3.00- 8.00

2793. METZGER'S MILK – Baby face embossed on front – Clear – 5½" high. . . . . $ 2.00- 6.00

2794. MINUTE MAID ORANGE JUICE – Maid embossed on both sides – Screw-on lid – Clear – 7¼". . . . . $ 2.00- 4.00

2795   2796   2797   2798

2795.	OLD MILK BOTTLE – Amethyst – 10½"..............	$ 3.00-	6.00
2796.	¼ PINT CREAM BOTTLE – Clear – 4"...............	$ 1.00-	2.00
2797.	PRICE'S DAIRY CO. – One half pint – Phone Maine 2050 – El Paso, Texas – Wash and return – "P" on bottom – Duraglass – Clear – 5 3/8"....................	$ 4.00-	8.00
2798.	PRICE'S DAIRY CO., – One quart – (on back) Phone Maine 2050 El Paso, Texas – Wash and return – "P" embossed on bottom – Clear – 9½"....................	$ 4.00-	8.00

2799   2800   2801   2802   2803

2799.	PRIMROSE JERSEY FARM – Primrose Jersey Products, Abilene, Texas – Half pint liquid – Reg. sealed – Clear with red lettering – 5 3/8"...................	$ 3.00-	6.00
2800.	SAN ANGELO DAIRY PRODUCTS CO., GRADE A – Half pint liquid – Clear – 5¼"...........................	$ 4.00-	8.00
2801.	SEALED 51 – One pint liquid, U.C.P.51 – Wheat clear – 7¼" high..	$ 2.00-	6.00
2802.	SHELTON BROS. DAIRY – One pint liquid – Clear – 7¼"..	$ 3.00-	5.00
2803.	TROPICANA GRAPEFRUIT JUICE – Net 32 fl. oz. (1 qt.) Good Housekeeping Approved – Clear with red lettering – Screw-on lid – 8¼"........................	$ 3.00-	6.00

APOTHECARY

| 2804 | 2805 | 2806 | 2807 |

2804. APOTHECARY BOTTLE – Clear glass – Solid glass bottom – 6″ high. .... $ 10.00- 20.00
2805. APOTHECARY BOTTLE – Clear graphite pontil – Ground glass stopper – 6½″. .... $ 10.00- 25.00
2806. APOTHECARY BOTTLE – Clear – graphite pontil – Ground glass stopper – 8″. .... $ 10.00- 25.00
2807. DR. SIMMONS COMPOUND ASPIRIN LAXATIVE TABLETS FOR PAIN – C.F. Simmons Medicine Co. – J.H. Zeilin & Co. St. Louis, Mo. – Clear – Paper label shielded by glass cover. .... $ 10.00- 20.00

SODA & MINERAL BOTTLES

| 2808 | 2817 | 2825 | 2831 |

2808. ABILENA NATURAL CATHARTIC WATER – Amber – 10″. .... $ 2.00- 6.00
2809. ABILENA, THE IDEAL CATHARTIC WATER – Amber – Applied top – Paper label – 10″. .... $ 2.00- 4.00
2810. ADAM'S SPRINGS MINERAL WATER – Blob top cylinder – Aqua – 11½″ high. .... $ 6.00- 10.00
2811. AETNA MINERAL WATER – Light green bottle with dark lettering that reads, "Aetna Mineral Water" – 7½″. .... $ 2.00- 4.00
2812. AETNA MINERAL WATER – Round – Aqua – 11½″. .... $ 3.00- 6.00

171

2813. AETNA MINERAL WATER, NATURAL MINERAL WATER – Aqua – Applied top – 6½" – One side reads, "Natural Mineral Water" the other reads, "Aetna Mineral Water". .... $ 6.00- 15.00

2814. ALHAMBRA NATURAL MINERAL WATER CO. – Maritnez California – Aqua – Applied top – 11¼". ...... $ 5.00- 15.00

2815. ALLEN MINERAL WATER – Amber – Applied top – 12" Vertical lettering on the front reads, "Allen Mineral Water". .... $ 4.00- 10.00

2816. ALLEN SPRINGS MINERAL WATER – Aqua – Applied top – 11½" – Paper label. .... $ 2.00- 6.00

2817. A.M. & B. CO., THE WACO, TEXAS – Registered Monterrey – We Pay for Evidence Convicting Thieves for Refilling our bottles. – Aqua – Applied lip – 8½".... $ 8.00- 10.00

2818. A.N.M.W. CO. MARTINEZ CAL. – Aqua – 8" – "A.N.M.W. CO." on the front of this bottle. .... $ 4.00- 8.00

2819. A.P. NEW ALMADEN VICHY WATER, CALIFORNIA – Olive amber – Applied lip – Lettering on the front gives the name and place plus a trademark above the name. . $ 6.00- 15.00

2820. APOLLINARIS MINERAL WATER – Green – 12" – Crown top bottle with paper label that gives the name and other information. .... $ 2.00- 4.00

2821. APOLLINARIS NATURAL MINERAL WATER, LONDON S.W. – 12" – Blop top bottle is olive green with a paper label that gives the name & place & other information. . $ 6.00- 12.00

2822. ARIZONA BOTTLING WORKS, PHOENIZ ARIZONA – This bottle must be returned – Aqua – Applied top – 8". $ 4.00- 10.00

2823. ARTER & WILSON MANUF. BOSTON – Light green – 7" Applied top – Lettering on the front of this bottle runs vertically and gives the same as listed above. .... $ 10.00- 20.00

2824. ARTINGANA---LOUROES – Light green – Applied top – 11¼" – Lettering on the front gives the name with a star between the two words. .... $ 6.00- 10.00

2825. ASHTON MINERAL WATER CO. LTD., THE, PORTLAND ST. ASHTON-U-LYNE – Inner rubber screw stopper – No. 1287. .... $ 8.00- 12.00

2826. ASTROG SPRINGS MINERAL WATER S.F. CAL. – Light green – Blob top – 7" – Lettering on the front gives the name and place as listed above. .... $ 6.00- 15.00

2827. AUBURN BOTTLING WORKS A.W. KENISON CO. AUBURN CAL. – Dark aqua – Applied top – 11¾" – Comes with either lettering or a paper label. .... $ 4.00- 8.00

2828. A.W.K. CO. AUBURN CALIFORNIA – Light green – 8" – The name of this bottle is found on the bottom. .... $ 4.00- 8.00

2829. "B" – Light green – Crown cap – 8¼" – A large "B" is on the front. .... $ 1.00- 3.00

2830. "B" – Dark aqua – Applied top – Round bottle with a large "B" on the front – 7½". .... $ 4.00- 8.00

2831. BABRICA DE BEBIDAS CASEOSAS GARCIA GON-CHNOS REYES SEN C. EXCELSIOR – Aqua – Blob top with Hutchinson closure – 7" high. .... $ 8.00- 15.00

2832. BACON'S SODA WORKS SONORA CAL. – Light green 7" – Blob top – Lettering on the front gives the name and place as listed above. .... $ 6.00- 10.00

2833. B & C SAN FRANCISCO – Cobalt blue – Applied top – Round bottle with lettering on the front that reads "B & C San Francisco". .... $ 20.00- 40.00

172

2855   2838   2849   2872

2834. BAKER, JOHN S. SODA WORKS – Aqua – Applied top –
       7" – Six-sided bottle with vertical lettering that gives
       the name of the bottle as listed above. . . . . $ 8.00- 10.00
2835. BARCLAY STREET 41 NEW YORK – Light green – Ap-
       plied top – 7¼" – Round bottle with small lettering that
       reads, "Barclay Street New York" and in the center is
       "41". . . . . $ 8.00- 15.00
2836. BARTLETT SPARKLING WATER – Clear – 8" – Round
       bottle with a paper label that reads "Bartlett's Sparkl-
       ing Water-The Body Conditioner." . . . . $ 2.00- 4.00
2837. BARTLETT SPRING MINERAL WATER CALIFORNIA –
       Aqua – Blob top – 12" – Round bottle with a round label
       reading "Bartlett Spring Mineral Water, California." . . . $ 3.00- 6.00
2838. BEE CANDY MFG. CO., THE SAN ANTONIO, TX –
       Amethyst – Applied top – 8". . . . . $ 6.00- 8.00
2839. BELFAST GINGER ALE CO. S.F. – Light green – Ap-
       plied top – 7" – Round bottle with the name and place
       of the bottle as listed above in 2 lines with an emblem
       between them. . . . . $ 6.00- 8.00
2840. BETHESDA WATER – Light green – 12" – Round bottle
       with a pear-shaped paper label. $ 2.00- 4.00
2841. BILLINGS, E.L., SACRAMENTO CAL. GEYSER SODA –
       Aqua – 7½". . . . . $ 4.00- 10.00
2842. BLOUNT SPRINGS NATURAL SULPHUR WATER –
       Round – Cobalt. . . . . $ 30.00- 55.00
2843. BOLEY & CO. SAC CITY CAL. – Cobalt blue – Applied
       top – 7½" – Round bottle with lettering on the front
       that reads "Boley Co. Sac City Cal.". . . . . $ 15.00- 30.00
2844. BORELLO & ALLARIA MERCED CALIF. – Light green –
       7½" – Round bottle with lettering on the bottom of the
       bottle that gives the name as listed above. . . . . $ 4.00- 10.00
2845. BORELLO BROS. SAN RAFAEL CALIF. – Light green –
       8" – Round bottle with lettering on the front that gives
       the name, as listed above, in 2 lines with a large "BB"
       between the two lines of writing. $ 10.00- 15.00
2846. BOTTLE SEAL CO. PAT. 85 BALTO MD. – Light green –
       Applied top – 7½" – Round bottle with the name as
       listed above, in a circle on the front of the bottle. . . . . . $ 6.00- 10.00
2847. BOWLING PIN BOTTLES – These are round bottles in
       the shape of a bowling pin. Light aqua, 8¾" – Dark
       green, 9¼" – Light green, 8¼". . . . . $ 8.00- 10.00
2848. BREMENKAMPF & REGLI EUREKA NEV. – Aqua – Ap-
       plied top – 7" high. . . . . $ 6.00- 10.00
2849. BRYANT'S ROOT BEER, THIS BOTTLE MAKES FIVE
       GALLONS – Amber – Applied top – 4½". . . . . $ 2.00- 3.00

173

2850.	BUFFALO LICK SPRINGS COMPANY - Crown top - Clear.	$ 4.00-	12.00
2851.	BUFFALO LITHIA WATER - Round - Aqua or clear - 10", 11".	$ 6.00-	10.00
2852.	BUFFALO MINERAL SPRINGS WATER - Aqua - 10". . .	$ 8.00-	20.00
2853.	BUFFALO N.Y. - Dark aqua - Applied top - 7" - 8-sided with vertical lettering that reads, "Buffalo, N.Y.".	$ 8.00-	15.00
2854.	BURGIN & SONS PHILADA GLASS WORKS - Medium green - Applied top - 7½".	$ 20.00-	25.00
2855.	BURKE, CAT - Embossed on bottom of this bottle - Amber - Crown top - 7¾".	$ 2.00-	4.00
2856.	BURT, W.H., SAN FRANCISCO - Dark green - Applied top - Round bottle with lettering on the front that gives the name as listed above - 7½".	$ 10.00-	15.00
2857.	BYTHINIA WATER - Amber - 10" - Round bottle with lettering just below the neck.	$ 2.00-	4.00
2858.	CODE, WM & CO. LIVERPOOL - Medium green - Applied top - 9½" high.	$ 3.00-	8.00
2859.	CALIFORNIA BOTTLING CO. S.F. - Light aqua - Applied top - 11½" - Round bottle with vertical writing on the front that gives the name as listed above.	$ 4.00-	8.00
2860.	CALIFORNIA BOTTLING WORKS T BLAUTH 407 K STREET SACRAMENTO - Aqua - 8" - Applied top - Round - Name as listed above.	$ 4.00-	6.00
2861.	CALIFORNIA BOTTLING WORKS THEO BLAUTH SONS CO. SAN FRANCISCO - Light green - 8½" - Round - Name as above.	$ 4.00-	8.00
2862.	CALIFORNIA BOTTLE WORKS, T. BLAUTH 407 K STREET SACRAMENTO - Light green - Applied top - 7" - Round - Name as above.	$ 4.00-	8.00
2863.	CALIFORNIA GAZOSA WORKS MADE IN ITALY - Light green - 8" - Applied top - Round - Lettering on front that gives the name as listed above.	$ 10.00-	15.00
2864.	CAPE ARCO SODA WORKS, MARSHFIELD ORE. - Light green - 7" - Applied top - Round - Name as listed above on front.	$ 6.00-	10.00
2865.	CARNE & SONS BURFORD OXON - Olive green - 10". .	$ 3.00-	5.00
2866.	CASCADE GINGER ALE - Light green - 8" - Round bottle with a paper label that gives the name as listed above.	$ 3.00-	6.00
2867.	CHAMPAGNE MEAD - Dark aqua - Applied top - 7½" 6-sided bottle with vertical lettering that reads, "Champagne Mead".	$ 20.00-	30.00
2868.	CHAMPION SPOUTING SPRING - Round - Aqua - 7½".	$ 15.00-	20.00
2869.	CHATTOLANEE WATER - Round - Aqua - 11½".	$ 8.00-	20.00
2870.	CHICO SODA WORKS - Clear - Applied top - 6¼". . . .	$ 4.00-	6.00
2871.	CHIEF - Clear - Round bottle with carvings around the middle and an Indian's head with "Chief" spelled out just below the neck of the bottle - 9" & 9½".	$ 6.00-	8.00
2872.	CITY ICE & BOTTLING WORKS GEORGETOWN, TEXAS - Aqua - 7½" - Applied lip.	$ 2.00-	4.00
2873.	C & K EAGLE WORKS SAC. CITY - Cobalt blue - Applied top - 7" - Round bottle with large lettering that reads, "C & K" with smaller "Eagle Works Sac. City". . .	$ 25.00-	55.00
2874.	CLARKE & CO. NEW YORK - Blue - 8" - Round bottle with the name embossed on the front.	$ 20.00-	40.00
	Dark green	$ 15.00-	13.00
2875.	CLARKE, JOHN NEW YORK - Olive green - Applied top - 7½".	$ 15.00-	30.00
2876.	CLARKE, JOHN N.Y. SPRING WATER - Round - Green 7".	$ 50.00-	65.00

174

2880   2883   2884   2885

2877.   CLARKE & WHITE NEW YORK – Olive green – Applied top – 7½" high. .... $ 20.00- 35.00
2878.   CLARKE & WHITE N.T. SPRING WATER – Round – Green – 9". .... $ 15.00- 20.00
2879.   CLASSEN & CO. SAN FRANCISCO – Medium green – Applied top – 7" – Round bottle with a blob top with lettering on the front that gives the name as listed above. $ 10.00- 20.00
2880.   CLIQUIST CLUB, TRADE MARK REGISTERED – Bright green – 9½" – Crown top – Bail and rubber stopper. .... $ 4.00- 6.00
2881.   CLYSMIC NATURAL MINERAL WATER JOHN L. LOCKWOOD – Olive green – 12" – Round bottle with a slender neck with a paper label that gives the name and other information. .... $ 6.00- 10.00
2882.   COCO-COLA – Clear – 8" – 6½ fl. oz. – Older than light green ones used today – Embossed lettering. .... $ 3.00- 5.00
2883.   COCA-COLA – Light green – 8" – 6½ fl. oz. – Embossed lettering. .... $ 2.00- 4.00
        White painted lettering $ .10- .20
2884.   COCA-COLA – Light green – 10" – 10 fl. ozs. – Embossed lettering. .... $ 2.00- 4.00
        Painted lettering $ .10- .15
        Painted lettering and Coke on the neck $ 1.00- 2.00
2885.   COCA-COLA – Light green – One pint – 11½"......... $ 1.00- 2.00

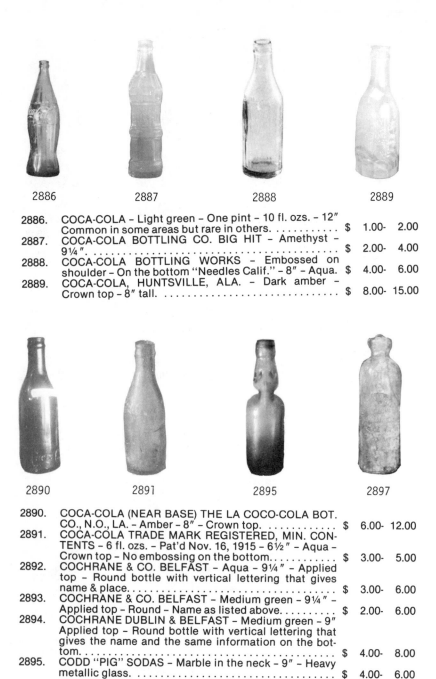

2886	2887	2888	2889

2886. COCA-COLA – Light green – One pint – 10 fl. ozs. – 12″
Common in some areas but rare in others. . . . . $ 1.00- 2.00
2887. COCA-COLA BOTTLING CO. BIG HIT – Amethyst –
9¼″. . . . . $ 2.00- 4.00
2888. COCA-COLA BOTTLING WORKS – Embossed on
shoulder – On the bottom "Needles Calif." – 8″ – Aqua. $ 4.00- 6.00
2889. COCA-COLA, HUNTSVILLE, ALA. – Dark amber –
Crown top – 8″ tall. . . . . $ 8.00- 15.00

2890	2891	2895	2897

2890. COCA-COLA (NEAR BASE) THE LA COCO-COLA BOT.
CO., N.O., LA. – Amber – 8″ – Crown top. . . . . $ 6.00- 12.00
2891. COCA-COLA TRADE MARK REGISTERED, MIN. CON-
TENTS – 6 fl. ozs. – Pat'd Nov. 16, 1915 – 6½″ – Aqua –
Crown top – No embossing on the bottom. . . . . $ 3.00- 5.00
2892. COCHRANE & CO. BELFAST – Aqua – 9¼″ – Applied
top – Round bottle with vertical lettering that gives
name & place. . . . . $ 3.00- 6.00
2893. COCHRANE & CO. BELFAST – Medium green – 9¼″ –
Applied top – Round – Name as listed above. . . . . $ 2.00- 6.00
2894. COCHRANE DUBLIN & BELFAST – Medium green – 9″
Applied top – Round bottle with vertical lettering that
gives the name and the same information on the bot-
tom. . . . . $ 4.00- 8.00
2895. CODD "PIG" SODAS – Marble in the neck – 9″ – Heavy
metallic glass. . . . . $ 4.00- 6.00

2896. COLUMBIA SODA WORKS S.F., C.C. DALL – Dark aqua
Applied top – 7″. . . . . $ 8.00- 10.00
2897. CONCHO BOTTLING WORKS, SAN ANGELO, TEXAS –
Aqua – 7½″ – Spring stopper. . . . . $ 8.00- 15.00

2898   2899   2900   2904

2898. CONCHO BOTTLING WORKS – Blob top – Aqua – 8¾″
Torpedo shaped. . . . . $ 6.00- 10.00
2899. CONGRESS & EMPIRE SPRING, CO., SARATOGA, N.Y.
"C" embossed in center – "Congress Water" emboss-
ed on back – 8″ – Green – Applied top. . . . . $ 18.00- 30.00
2900. CONGRESS SPRING CO. S.S. N.Y. – Green – Blob top –
9½″. . . . . $ 8.00- 20.00
2901. CONNOLLY BROS., S.F. – Medium green – Applied top
7½″ – Round – Name on front as listed above. . . . . $ 8.00- 10.00
2902. CONSTITUTION WATER – Rectangular – Amber – 6½″. $ 4.00- 8.00
2903. CONSUMERS BOTTLING CO. KEY WEST FLA. – Clear
Blob top – 7″ – Round bottle with embossing on the
front in a circle that gives the name and place as listed
above. . . . . $ 3.00- 6.00
2904. CONSUMER'S S & MW MFG., LTD. N.O., LA. – This Bot-
tle Not To Be Sold – Aqua – Crown top – 7″. . . . . $ 2.00- 4.00

2905   2915   2924   2925

2905. CONSUMERS, S & M.W. MFG. CO., LTD. N.O., LA. –
This Bottle Not To Be Sold – Aqua – Crown top – 7″. . . . $ 3.00- 5.00
2906. COTTON & MA---BOSTON MASS. – Aqua – Applied top
9″ – Round bottle with lettering that reads, "Cotton &
Ma Boston Mass. Registered" and in the center a large
intertwined "C & M". . . . . $ 3.00- 8.00

177

2907. CRAZY MINERAL WATER – Round – Clear – ½ gal. ... $ 3.00- 8.00
2908. CRIPPLE CREEK BOTTLING WORKS, CRIPPLE CREEK COLORADO – Aqua – Applied top – 7″ – Round bottle with embossing in a circle in the middle with the name as above. .... $ 4.00- 8.00
2909. CROCKERR, DAVY LIQUOR CO. ANGELS – Aqua – Applied top – 8″ – Round – Name as listed above. .... $ 3.00- 6.00
2910. CRYSTAL BOTTLING COMPANY – Los Angeles – Aqua 9″ – Applied top – Round bottle with lettering around a diamond on the front and an intertwined "CB" in the diamond. .... $ 4.00- 8.00
2911. CRYSTAL SODA PATENTED NOV. 12, 1872 U.S.P. – Aqua – 7½″ – Applied top – Round, blob top bottle with lettering on the back that reads, "Patented Nov. 12, 1872 U.S.P." .... $ 4.00- 8.00
2912. CRYSTAL SODA WATER CO. – Blue – Applied top – 7¾″ – Round – "Crystal Soda Water" embossed on the front. .... $ 4.00- 8.00
2913. CRYSTAL S.W. CO. S.F. – Aqua – Applied top – 7″ – Round – Lettering on front reads "Crystal S.W. Co. S.F." .... $ 3.00- 8.00
2914. CUDWORTH, A.W. SAN FRANCISCO – Light green – 7¼″ – Applied top – Round, blob top bottle. .... $ 6.00- 10.00
2915. DAVID CITY BOTTLING WORKS DAVID CITY NEBR. – Clear – 8″. .... $ 4.00- 6.00
2916. DEAMER GRASS VALLEY – Aqua – 7¼″ – Applied top Round, blob top bottle. Name as listed above. .... $ 3.00- 6.00
2917. DEARBORN, J & A N.Y. Back side – UNION GLASSWORKS, D NEW YORK – Dark blue – Applied top – Front side lettering reads "J. & A. DEARBORN N.Y." .... $ 6.00- 10.00
2918. DENISON, A.W. CO. AUBURN CAL. – Dark aqua – Applied top – 11¾″ – Round. .... $ 3.00- 6.00
2919. DELAWARE PUNCH – Clear – 7½″ – Round bottle with crown top – Lettering on the front with name as listed above. .... $ 2.00- 3.00
2920. DEMOTTS, C.V. – Light green – Applied top – 7½″. ..... $ 3.00- 6.00
2921. DENNALTER BOTTLER, THE SALT LAKE UTAH – Clear Applied top – 7″. .... $ 3.00- 6.00
2922. DENNALTER, JOHN H. SODA WATER CO. PROVO. UTAH – Light green – 11½″. .... $ 2.00- 6.00
2923. DISTILLED WATER CO., CUYAMACA SAN DIEGO – Aqua – 12½″ – One gallon bottle with lettering in a circle on front. .... $ 4.00- 8.00
2924. DEUTCHER BRUNNEN LIEHPLASCHE – Bright green 9¾″ – Inside rubber screw stopper. .... $ 4.00- 8.00
2925. DEVIL MONO (on base) – 8″ – Aqua – Blob top. .... $ 2.00- 3.00
2926. DOR-S, I.A., NATURAL MINERAL WATER – Amber – Round – Crown top – 7¾″ high. .... $ 2.00- 6.00

| 2927 | 2928 | 2929 | 2932 |

2927. DRAGON BOTTLING CO., SAN ANGELO, TEXAS – Clear – Crown top – 10″ high. .... $ 2.00- 4.00
2928. DR. PEPPER – Light green – 12″ – 26 fl. ozs. – L-G 723-3 64 embossed on the bottom – Common in some areas but rare in others. .... $ 4.00- 8.00
2929. DR. PEPPER, GOOD FOR LIFE! – (back) 6½ ozs. – 10-2-4 o'clock – Clear – Crown top – 8″. .... $ 2.00- 4.00
2930. D.S. & CO. SAN FRANCISCO – Cobalt blue – Applied top – 7½″ – Round. .... $ 10.00- 20.00
2931. D.S. & CO. SAN FRANCISCO – Green – Applied top – 7″ – Round – Blob top. .... $ 10.00- 20.00
2932. DUBLIN & BELFAST – See that each cork is branded Cochrane Cantrell – Aqua – 9½″. .... $ 4.00- 8.00

| 2938 | 2939 | 2941 | 2951 |

2933. DYOTTVILLE GLASS WORKS PHILAD. – Light green – Applied top – 7½″ – Round, blob top bottle. .... $ 10.00- 20.00
2934. DUERLERM F. CO., SAN ANTONIO, TEXAS, MINE SLYDRIDE – A pure double distilled table water L.A. – Clear – 14″. .... $ 4.00- 8.00
2935. EAGLE – Embossed soda – Green – Applied top – 7″ – Round – Eagle embossed on the front. .... $ 4.00- 10.00
2936. EAST BAY GAZZOSA – Light green – Applied top – 8″ – Round – Indentures on the neck. Lettering on the front gives the name, contents, and place. .... $ 4.00- 8.00
2937. EASTERN CIDER CO. – Light amber – Applied top – 7″ Round. .... $ 8.00- 10.00

179

2938.	EASTMAN – Amethyst – 5".	$ 2.00- 4.00

2938. EASTMAN – Amethyst – 5"........................ $ 2.00- 4.00
2939. EBBERWEIN, G. SAVANNAH GA. – Amber – Blob top –
8".. $ 15.00- 30.00
2940. EBBERWEIN MINERAL WATER – Round – 7¾" –
Cobalt.. $ 20.00- 35.00
Amber .... $ 10.00- 15.00
Ice blue .... $ 10.00- 15.00
2941. E.B. CO., EVARRSVILLE, IND. – Aqua – Blob top – 7"... $ 2.00- 8.00
2942. EL DORADO – Aqua – Applied top – 7½" – Round –
Blob top....................................... $ 3.00- 6.00
2943. ELIAS BARTH BURLINGTON N.J. – Aqua – Applied top
7" – Round, blob top............................. $ 3.00- 5.00
2944. ENGLISH SODA – Light green – Applied top – Round –
8".. $ 2.00- 4.00
2945. ENTERPRISE – Light green – 8" – Round, crown cap
bottle with"Enterprise" printed near the base......... $ 2.00- 4.00
2946. E.T.R. POWELL NEVADA CITY SODA WORKS – Clear –
8" – Round – Crown cap.......................... $ 2.00- 4.00
2947. EUREKA CALIFORNIA SODA WATER CO. S.F. – Light
green – Applied top – 7" – Round bottle with lettering
that gives the name as above and an eagle between the
lines... $ 4.00- 8.00
2948. EXCELSIOR SPRING SARATOGA N.Y. – Green – 7¾"
& 9¾" high...................................... $ 8.00- 15.00
2949. FARREL & COMPANY MINERAL WATER – Cylinder –
Blue – 7½"...................................... $ 25.00- 35.00
2950. FARREL, J.A. GRASS VALLEY – Aqua – Blob top – 7
3/8" – A large "F" on the back side of the bottle. .... $ 3.00- 6.00
2951. FIZZ, SOUTHERN STATE SIPNON BOTTLING CO. –
Golden amber – 11" high.......................... $ 6.00- 15.00

2953   2959   2974   2983

2952. FLEMING'S EXPORT PURE RYE – Bottled expressively
for family & medicinal uses – Square – Clear –
8½"x3¼".. $ 4.00- 8.00
2953. FOASTER POUGHKEEPSIE N.Y. – Blob top – 7"....... $ 4.00- 6.00
2954. FOREST HILL ELECTRIC CO. FOREST HILL CALIF. –
Light green – 8" – Round – Crown cap. .... $ 4.00- 6.00
2955. FREIDMAN, WM. CHAMPION SODA FACTORY KEY
WEST FLA. – Clear – 6½" high. .... $ 2.00- 6.00
2956. FRIEDRICHSHALL BITTER WATER – Light green –
8½" – Round – Paper label gives the name and other
information. .... $ 3.00- 4.00
2957. FULLER, M.O. 1861 BROOKLYN N.Y. – Dark aqua – Applied top – 7½" high............................. $ 6.00- 8.00
2958. GARDEN CITY EXTRACT CO. SAN JOSE – Aqua – Applied top – 8" – Round, crown cap bottle with lettering
that gives the name as listed above plus a large "C"
with an "X" in the middle of it. .... $ 2.00- 3.00

2959.	GEMUNDEN, G.C.A. SAVANNAH GEO. – Aqua – Blob top – 7½"...	$ 10.00-	20.00
2960.	GETTYSBURG KATALYSING WATER – Olive green.	$ 8.00-	15.00
2961.	GETTYSBURG KATALYSINE WATER – Olive green – 9½" – Round bottle with name embossed around a circle on the front.	$ 6.00-	10.00
2962.	GEYSER SODA – Light green – 7½" – Round, blob top with letters reading "Geyser Soda".	$ 3.00-	5.00
2963.	GEYSER SODA SPRINGS – Dark aqua – Applied top – 7" – Round – Blob top.............................	$ 4.00-	8.00
2964.	GEYSER SODA SPRING NATURAL MINERAL WATER Light green – Applied top – 7½" – Round.	$ 6.00-	10.00
2965.	GINGER ALE CO. S.F. CAL. – Light green – Applied top 9½" high.	$ 4.00-	6.00
2966.	GLENDALE SPRING CO. – This bottle not to be sold – Cylinder – Aqua – 7".............................	$ 4.00-	6.00
2967.	GLENN SPRINGS MINERAL WATER – Round – Aqua – Qt.	$ 6.00-	10.00
2968.	GOLDEN STATE SACRAMENTO CALIF. – Clear – 9½" Round with ribs around the middle and letters reading "Property Golden State" – "Sacramento" near the bottom.	$ 10.00-	20.00
2969.	GOLDEN WEST SODA WORKS BRUNS & NASH MOUNTAIN VIEW CAL. – Light green – 7" – Round, short-neck bottle with lettering that gives the name as listed above.	$ 6.00-	12.00
2970.	GRAF, JOHN MILWAUKEE WIS. – Dark amber – Applied top – 8" – 6-sided bottle with lightning closure – Lettering on the front sections reads, "John Graf Milwaukee Wis. This Bottle is Never Sold".	$ 10.00-	20.00
2971.	GREAT BEAR SPRINGS, FULTON N.Y. – Aqua – Applied top – 12" – Round.	$ 4.00-	10.00
2972.	GROSJEAN & HOLDAWAY, SACRAMENTO CAL. – Light green – 8" – Round – Crown cap – Lettering and emblem on front.	$ 4.00-	8.00
2973.	GUILFORD MINERAL SPRING WATER – Quart – Round – Green....................................	$ 10.00-	15.00
2974.	HANICHEN, C.F.A. PARKERSBURG, W. VA. – Aqua – Blob top – 7½" tall.	$ 8.00-	12.00
2975.	HANSSEN BROS. C.W.B. GRASS VALLEY CAL. – Aqua Applied top – 7" – Round bottle with "Hanssen Bros. Grass Valley Cal", around a circle on the front and a "C.W.B." in the center of the circle..................	$ 4.00-	8.00
2976.	HAWTHORN SPRING MINERAL WATER – Olive green Amber, black – 9½" high.	$ 20.00-	60.00
2977.	HAWTHORN SPRINGS SARATOGA N.Y. – Olive green Applied top – 7½" – Letters spelling "Saratoga" is written across the base with "Hawthorn Springs" arched above it.	$ 20.00-	40.00
2978.	HAWAIIAN SODA WORKS, HONOLULU T.H. – Aqua – Applied top – 7½" – Name and place embossed on the front.	$ 6.00-	10.00
2979.	HELIDON SPA WATER CO., BRISBANE – Light green – Applied top – 9½" – Bowling pin-shaped bottle with lettering vertically down the front..................	$ 8.00-	12.00
2980.	HENRY BECKER, TERRE HAUTE IND. – Aqua – Applied top – 6½" – "Henry Becker" arched over an intertwined "HB" and "Terre Haute, Ind."	$ 3.00-	5.00
2981.	HENRY DONNELLY, NEW MELFORD CONN. – Clear – Applied top – 9½" – Lettering on this round bottle is: "Registered" near the top with "Henry Donnelly New Melford Conn." in a circle near the middle............	$ 4.00-	6.00

2982.	HIGGINS, W.J. & CO. COR. 1st AND BROADWAY SOUTH BOSTON – Clear or amethyst – Applied top – 9½" – Round bottle with lettering in a circle near the middle.	$ 3.00-	5.00
2983.	HIPPO SIZE SODA WATER – The Big Bottle Drink, Alamo Bottle Works, San Antonio, Bottle Patented Nov. 2, 1926 – Clear – 10" – Crown top.	$ 4.00-	6.00
2984.	HIRES – Light green – Applied top – 8".	$ 2.00-	4.00
2985.	HIRES CARBONATED BEVERAGES – Light green – 10" – Applied top – "Hires" in large letters, "Carbonated beverages" in smaller letters.	$ 2.00-	6.00
2986.	HIRES REGISTERED – Amber – 8".	$ 2.00-	4.00
2987.	HIRES "TRADE MARK AROUND SHOULDER" – Light green – 8½" – Round – Paper label – Trademark embossed below neck.	$ 2.00-	4.00

2988   3006   3010   3011

2988.	HOYLE, S. LIMITED KEIGHTLEY – Aqua – Inside thread rubber stopper – 8½".	$ 6.00-	10.00
2989.	HONESDALE GLASS WORKS PA. – Dark green – Applied top – 7" – "Pa" near the center with "Glassworks" ached over it and "Honesdale" arched over that.	$ 8.00-	10.00
2990.	HOLDEN'S GA. – Blue – Applied top – 8" – Round – "G.A." near the middle with "Holden's" above it.	$ 8.00-	15.00
2991.	"H" SAC. – Dark aqua – Applied top – 7½".	$ 2.00-	4.00
2992.	HUGH CASEY EAGLE SODA WORKS – Light green – Applied top – 7" high.	$ 3.00-	6.00
2993.	HUMBOLDT ARTESIAN MINERAL WATER – Aqua – Applied top – 7½" high.	$ 3.00-	6.00
2994.	HUMBOLDT ARTESIAN MINERAL WATER, EUREKA CAL. – Aqua – Applied top – 7".	$ 8.00-	12.00
2995.	I-ADORA NATURAL MINERAL WATER – Round – Amber – 9½".	$ 8.00-	10.00
2996.	IMPROVED TRADE MARK MINERAL WATER – Dark aqua – Applied top – 7".	$ 6.00-	10.00
2997.	ISHAM'S CALIFORNIA WATERS OF LIFE – Clear – Applied top – 10½" – Round.	$ 8.00-	10.00
2998.	ITALIAN SODA WATER MANUFACTURING, SAN FRANCISCO – Dark green – Applied top – 7½" – Round.	$ 10.00-	25.00
2999.	JACKSON BOTTLING WORKS – Aqua – Applied top – 8" – Round – Crown cap. Lettering reads "Jackson Bottling Works" and an intertwined "CP" in the center.	$ 2.00-	4.00
3000.	JACKSON'S NAPA SODA – Light green – Applied lip – 7¼" & 7" – Round – Crown cap.	$ 2.00-	4.00

3001.	JACKSON'S NAPA SODA SPRINGS - 7½" - Round, slender bottle with the name and place as listed above, in the middle.	$ 6.00-	8.00
3002.	JOHNSTON, MATTHEW NEW YORK - Aqua - Applied top - 7½" - Round.	$ 4.00-	6.00
3003.	JONES, R.D. MINERAL WATER OSWESTR. - Light green - Applied top - 7½".	$ 4.00-	8.00
3004.	KALAK WATER - Green - 12" - Round, crown cap bottle with checked label with the name on it.	$ 2.00-	4.00
3005.	KAPAA ICE & SODA WORKS - Clear - 8" - Round - Crown cap.	$ 2.00-	4.00
3006.	KARSCH, JOHN & SONS, EVANSVILLE IND. - Aqua - Blob top - 6½" high.	$ 4.00-	8.00
3007.	KEARNEY, R. PHILADA. - Dark green - Applied top - 7" - Round.	$ 8.00-	10.00
3008.	KISSINGER MINERAL WASSER - Light green - 12" - Tall, slender bottle with paper label.	$ 2.00-	4.00
3009.	KNOWLTON, D.A. SARATOGA N.Y. - Olive green - 10" Applied lip - Round.	$ 10.00-	20.00
3010.	KOLSHORN, CHAS. & BRO., SAVANNAH, GA. - Aqua - Blob top - 8" high.	$ 10.00-	20.00
3011.	KUCK, HENRY SAVANNAH GA. - Aqua - Blob top - 7½".	$ 8.00-	15.00

3012   3013   3016   3019

3012.	KUCK, HENRY SAVANNAH GA. - Green, Blob top - Iron Pontil - 7¼" high.	$ 12.00-	20.00
3013.	LAND, WM. C. & CO. LIMITED SOUTH ST. SCARBOROUGH - Inside threads with rubber stopper.	$ 8.00-	10.00
3014.	L & B - Light green - Applied top - 7½" - Round, blob top bottle with a large "L & D" on the front.	$ 8.00-	10.00
3015.	LEWIS SODA BOTTLES SACRAMENTO - Clear - 8½" Tall, slender bottle with letters that read "This Bottle Is The Property of Lewis Soda Bottles Sacramento" on the front.	$ 6.00-	8.00
3016.	LIQUID, THE xx (base) - Clear, aqua - 7½".	$ 1.00-	2.00
3017.	LODI SODA WORKS - Light green - 7" - Round.	$ 4.00-	6.00
3018.	LOS ANGELES SODA WORKS - Aqua - 8" - Round, slender bottle with the name of the bottle printed in a circle around a star in the center.	$ 2.00-	4.00
3019.	LUBS, HENRY & CO. 1885, SAVANNAH, GA. - Aqua - Blob top - 7½" high.	$ 8.00-	16.00

| 3020 | 3022 | 3033 | 3034 |

3020. LUBS, HENRY & CO. 1885, SAVANNAH GA. – Emerald
green – Blob top – 7¼ ". .... $ 15.00- 24.00
3021. LYNDE & PUTNAM MINERAL WATER, SAN FRAN-
CISCO CALIF. – 7½ " – Cobalt blue – Applied top –
Round, blob top bottle with the name & place printed
near the center of the front. .... $ 20.00- 30.00
3022. MAHER, THOS. – Emerald green – Blob top – Iron pontil – Slug plate. .... $ 10.00- 25.00
3023. M CRONAR 230 K STREET SACRAMENTO – Aqua –
Applied top – 7" – Round. .... $ 3.00- 6.00
3024. McBRIDE EARL & POLLAND REGISTERED, DETROIT
MICHIGAN – 7½ " – Light green – Applied top. .... $ 3.00- 6.00
3025. McKINNLEY, F. PHILAD. – Aqua – Applied top – 7" –
Large "F" in the middle of the front of the bottle. ..... $ 4.00- 6.00
3026. MEINCKE & EBBERWEIN (Mineral water) – Round –
Cobalt – 7¾ " high................................ $ 10.00- 30.00
3027. MENDOCIN BOTTLING WORKS, A.L. REYNOLDS –
Light green – 7" high. .... $ 6.00- 8.00
3028. MEREDITH, JAMES E. TOWANDA PA. – Aqua – Applied top – 12" high............................... $ 3.00- 6.00
3029. MIDDLETOWN HEALING SPRINGS – Quart – Round –
Amber – Grays & Clark. .... $ 15.00- 20.00
3030. MILL'S SELTZER SPRINGS – Aqua – 7" high.......... $ 6.00- 12.00
3031. MILLVILLE GLASS WORKS – Dark green – Applied top
7" – Round – Blob top............................. $ 15.00- 30.00
3032. MILTON AERATED WATER WORKS QUEENS CO., N.S.
Light green – Applied top – 8½ " – "Milton Aerated
Queen's Co. N.S." written in a circle with "Water
Works" written through the circle.................... $ 4.00- 6.00
3033. MINC SLYDRIDE A PURE DOUBLE DISTILLED TABLE
WATER LA. DUERLERM F. CO. SAN ANTONIO, TEXAS
Clear porcelain – 14" high. .... $ 4.00- 8.00
3034. MINERAL WATER – Green – 9½ "................... $ 3.00- 6.00
3035. MINERAL WATER – Medium green – Applied top – 7" –
Round, blob top bottle with "Mineral Water" below
neck. .... $ 10.00- 20.00

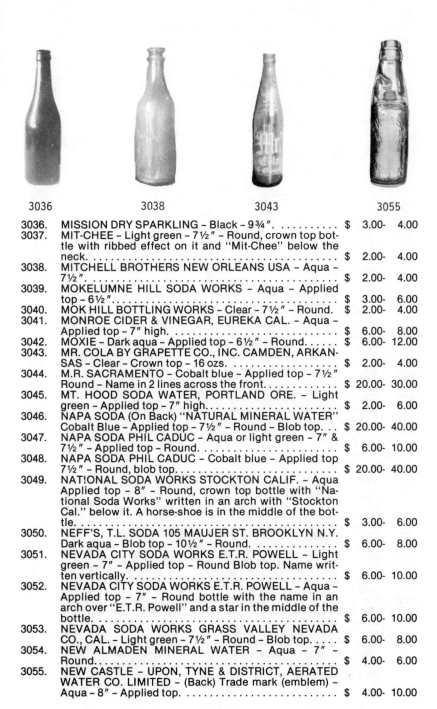

3036   3038   3043   3055

3036.	MISSION DRY SPARKLING – Black – 9¾".	$ 3.00-	4.00
3037.	MIT-CHEE – Light green – 7½" – Round, crown top bottle with ribbed effect on it and "Mit-Chee" below the neck.	$ 2.00-	4.00
3038.	MITCHELL BROTHERS NEW ORLEANS USA – Aqua – 7½".	$ 2.00-	4.00
3039.	MOKELUMNE HILL SODA WORKS – Aqua – Applied top – 6½".	$ 3.00-	6.00
3040.	MOK HILL BOTTLING WORKS – Clear – 7½" – Round.	$ 2.00-	4.00
3041.	MONROE CIDER & VINEGAR, EUREKA CAL. – Aqua – Applied top – 7" high.	$ 6.00-	8.00
3042.	MOXIE – Dark aqua – Applied top – 6½" – Round.	$ 6.00-	12.00
3043.	MR. COLA BY GRAPETTE CO., INC. CAMDEN, ARKANSAS – Clear – Crown top – 16 ozs.	$ 2.00-	4.00
3044.	M.R. SACRAMENTO – Cobalt blue – Applied top – 7½" Round – Name in 2 lines across the front.	$ 20.00-	30.00
3045.	MT. HOOD SODA WATER, PORTLAND ORE. – Light green – Applied top – 7" high.	$ 2.00-	6.00
3046.	NAPA SODA (On Back) "NATURAL MINERAL WATER" Cobalt Blue – Applied top – 7½" – Round – Blob top. . .	$ 20.00-	40.00
3047.	NAPA SODA PHIL CADUC – Aqua or light green – 7" & 7½" – Applied top – Round.	$ 6.00-	10.00
3048.	NAPA SODA PHIL CADUC – Cobalt blue – Applied top 7½" – Round, blob top.	$ 20.00-	40.00
3049.	NATIONAL SODA WORKS STOCKTON CALIF. – Aqua Applied top – 8" – Round, crown top bottle with "National Soda Works" written in an arch with "Stockton Cal." below it. A horse-shoe is in the middle of the bottle.	$ 3.00-	6.00
3050.	NEFF'S, T.L. SODA 105 MAUJER ST. BROOKLYN N.Y. Dark aqua – Blob top – 10½" – Round.	$ 6.00-	8.00
3051.	NEVADA CITY SODA WORKS E.T.R. POWELL – Light green – 7" – Applied top – Round Blob top. Name written vertically.	$ 6.00-	10.00
3052.	NEVADA CITY SODA WORKS E.T.R. POWELL – Aqua – Applied top – 7" – Round bottle with the name in an arch over "E.T.R. Powell" and a star in the middle of the bottle.	$ 6.00-	10.00
3053.	NEVADA SODA WORKS GRASS VALLEY NEVADA CO., CAL. – Light green – 7½" – Round – Blob top.	$ 6.00-	8.00
3054.	NEW ALMADEN MINERAL WATER – Aqua – 7" – Round.	$ 4.00-	6.00
3055.	NEW CASTLE – UPON, TYNE & DISTRICT, AERATED WATER CO. LIMITED – (Back) Trade mark (emblem) – Aqua – 8" – Applied top.	$ 4.00-	10.00

185

3056.	NEW LIBERTY S.W. CO. S.F. – Light green – Applied top – 7" high.	$ 3.00-	6.00
3057.	NICHOLL, S. 648 66 LEONARD N.Y. – Dark green – Applied top – 7½" – Round.	$ 4.00-	8.00
3058.	NORRIS, C. & CO. CITY BOTTLING WORKS, DETROIT MICHIGAN – Cobalt blue – Applied top – 7½" – Round.	$ 20.00-	40.00
3059.	NU GRAPE – Light green – 8".	$ 2.00-	4.00
3060.	OAKLAND BOTTLING CO. – Light green – 7¼" – "Oakland Bottling Co." is on the front of the bottle in an arch with the patent date near the bottom.	$ 3.00-	6.00
3061.	OAK ORCHARD ACID SPRINGS – Amber – Applied top 10".	$ 6.00-	8.00
3062.	OAKLAND PIONEER SODA WATER CO. OAKLAND CAL. – Clear – 7½" high.	$ 2.00-	4.00
3063.	OCALA BOTTLING WORKS OCALA FLA. – Aqua – Blob top – 8" – The name is in a circle in the center of the bottle and "Registered" is near the bottom.	$ 2.00-	4.00
3064.	OCEANO WATER REG. AQUAMARINE CO. SAN FRANCISCO – Clear or amethyst – Applied top – 9½" – Round – Crown cap.	$ 2.00-	4.00
3065.	OCEANVIEW BOTTLING WORKS N & B PROPS MENDOCINO CAL. – 7" – Aqua – Round.	$ 4.00-	10.00
3066.	OHIO BOTTLING WORKS SANDUSKY OHIO – Light green – Applied top – 5½" – The name is on the front of the bottle with a large intertwined "O & Z" in the middle.	$ 4.00-	8.00
3067.	O.P.S.W. CO. OAKLAND CAL. – Aqua – 7" – The name is on the front of the bottle with a large "O" with a bottle through the middle of it.	$ 4.00-	8.00
3068.	OTIS S. NEALE, HOWARD ST. BOSTON MASS. – Aqua Applied top – 9" – The name is on the front in 5 lines, and a larger entertwined "O S & N" is in the center of the name.	$ 4.00-	8.00
3069.	ORANGE CRUSH CO. PAT'D JULY 20, 1926 – Light green – 9".	$ 2.00-	3.00
3070.	OWEN CASEY EAGLE SODA WORKS – Cobalt blue – Applied top – 7½" – The name is 3 lines on the front of this round, blob top bottle.	$ 20.00-	50.00
3071.	PACHANGA MINERAL WATER – Clear – 10" – Screw top & paper label that gives the name & other information.	$ 2.00-	3.00
3072.	PACIFIC CONGRESS WATER – Aqua – Applied top – 7½.	$ 4.00-	8.00
3073.	PACIFIC CONGRESS WATER – Medium blue – Applied top – 7" – Round, blob top bottle with "Pacific Congress" in an arch over "Water".	$ 8.00-	10.00
3074.	PARKER, J.C. & SON NEW YORK – Cobalt blue – Applied top – 7½" – Round.	$ 15.00-	40.00
3075.	PATTERSONS, T. 140 CHURCH ST. NEW YORK – Dark blue – 8" – Applied top.	$ 10.00-	25.00
3076.	PEARSON BROS., PLACERVILLE – Aqua – Blob top – 7".	$ 3.00-	5.00
3077.	PERRIER – Clear – 8½" – Bowling pin shaped bottle with a paper label.	$ 2.00-	4.00
3078.	P.H. CRYSTAL SPRING WATER – ½ pint – Aqua.	$ 4.00-	8.00
3079.	PHENIS NERVE BEVERAGE CO. BOSTON U.S.A. – Clear – Applied top – 9½" – Round, crown cap bottle with the name on the front in 4 rows.	$ 3.00-	4.00
3080.	PHILLIPS NAPA MINERAL WATER – Dark aqua – Applied top – 7½" – Round bottle with "Phillip's MIneral Water" written in a circle on the front with "Napa" through the center of the circle.	$ 8.00-	10.00

186

3081. PIONEER BEVERAGE LTD. – Clear or light green – 8½" – The name is on the front with large leaves above and below the name. . . . . $ 2.00- 3.00
3082. PIONEER SODA WORKS SAN FRANCISCO – Medium green – Applied top – 7" – Round – Blob top. . . . . $ 8.00- 10.00

3086

3092

3093

3096

3083. PIONEER SODA WATER CO. S.F. – Light green – Applied top – 7½" – The name is arched above and below a picture of a buffalo in grass on the center front of the bottle. . . . . $ 8.00- 10.00
3084. POLAND WATER – Medium green – 9½" – Round, crown cap bottle with a paper label. . . . . $ 2.00- 4.00
3085. POLAND SPRINGS WATER – Round. . . . . $ 10.00- 20.00
3086. PORT CLINTON BOTTLING WORKS, OHIO – Aqua – 7½ fl. ozs. . . . . $ 2.00- 4.00
3087. PORTERVILLE SODA WORKS PORTERVILLE CALIF. – Light green – 8" – The name is in a circle with "Soda Works" in the center of the circle. . . . . $ 2.00- 6.00
3088. POSTENS, J. PHILA. – Clear – Applied top – 7" – Round, blob top bottle with "Trade" written above the seal that has the name written around it & "Mark" written below this seal. . . . . $ 4.00- 8.00
3089. POSTOL, HENRY J. SACRAMENTO CAL. – Aqua – 7" – Round. . . . . $ 6.00- 8.00
3090. PRIEST NATURAL SODA – Light green – 7½" – Round bottle with the name in large letters on the front. . . . . . $ 6.00- 10.00
3091. PURE SOFT SPRING WATER ENGLIS SPRING WATER 177 COLFAX AVENUE MINNEAPOLIS – Aqua – Applied top – 12½" – Large, round bottle with the name in 5 lines on the front. . . . . $ 6.00- 15.00
3092. QUALITY BRAND SODA WATER PROPERTY OF COCA-COLA BOTTLING CO. ASHVILLE N.C. – Clear – 7½". . . . . $ 2.00- 4.00
3093. QUINAN, M.T. 1884 SAVANNAH, GEO. (on front) – (on back) MINERAL "M" WATER – Cobalt blue – Blop top – 8". . . . . $ 20.00- 40.00
3094. QUINAN MINERAL WATER – Round – Cobalt – 7¾". . . . $ 20.00- 40.00
3095. RAPID CITY BOTTLING WORKS – Light green – Applied top – 8" – Round – Crown cap – 8 fl. ozs. . . . . $ 2.00- 4.00
3096. RAY, JAMES 1878 SAVANNAH GA. – Clear – Blob top – 7½". . . . . $ 8.00- 15.00

3097	3098	3099	3108

3097. RAY, JAMES "HAS RAY SAVANNAH GA." – Green – Blob top – 7½" high. .... $ 10.00- 25.00

3098. RAY, JAMES SAVANNAH, GA. – Aqua – Blob top – 7¼". .... $ 8.00- 12.00

3099. RAY, JAMES SAVANNAH, GEO. – Aqua – Blob top – 7½". .... $ 8.00- 12.00

3100. RICHARD J. LLOYD 302 E. 96th ST. NEW YORK – Aqua Applied top – 9". .... $ 4.00- 6.00

3101. RICHARDSON'S MINERAL WATER, RICHARDSON SPRINGS – Amber – 12" – Tall, round bottle with paper label. .... $ 4.00- 8.00

3102. RICHMOND – Clear – 8" – Round, crown cap bottle with "Richmond" in large letters with a head embossed on the front of the bottle. .... $ 2.00- 4.00

3103. ROBINSON, A.B. BANGOR ME. – Aqua – Applied top – 7½" – Round, blob top bottle. .... $ 4.00- 6.00

3104. ROSE CITY SODA WORKS MATHEWS & ROBERTS, SANTA ROSA CALIF. – Aqua – Applied top – 8½" – Round – Crown cap. .... $ 6.00- 8.00

3105. ROSS'S ROYAL BELFAST GINER ALE IRELAND – Medium green – Applied top – 10" – Round bottle with diamond shaped paper label that gives the name and other information. .... $ 2.00- 4.00

3106. RYAN, JOHN – 1866 – Cobalt blue – Blob top – 7½" – Without iron pontil. .... $ 20.00- 40.00

3107. RYAN, JOHN – 1866 – Cobalt blue – Blob top – 7½" – With iron pontil. .... $ 25.00- 60.00

3108. RYAN, JOHN – 1866 – (on front) – EXCELSIOR SODA WORKS, SAVANNAH, GEO. (on back) – Cobalt blue – Blob top – 7½" – Iron pontil. .... $ 20.00- 50.00

3109	3110	3111	3112

3109. RYAN, JOHN EXCELSIOR MINERAL WATER, SAVAN-
NAH, GA. – 7½ " – No date – Cobalt blue – Blob top –
Iron pontil. . . . . $ 30.00- 60.00
3110. RYAN, JOHN EXCELSIOR MINERAL WATER, SAVAN-
NAH, GA,1859 – Cobalt blue – Blob top – 7" – Iron pon-
til. . . . . $ 25.00- 50.00
3111. RYAN, JOHN EXCELSIOR MINERAL WATER, SAVAN-
NAH GA., 1859 – Cobalt blue – Natures Tiffany – Blob
top – 7¼ " – Pontil. . . . . $ 30.00- 60.00
3112. RYAN, JOHN EXCELSIOR MINERAL WATER, SAVAN-
NAH, GA. – UNION GLASSWORKS PHILA., THIS BOT-
TLE NEVER SOLD (on back) – Blob top – Cobalt blue –
7½ " – Iron pontil. . . . . $ 40.00- 80.00
3113. SAMUEL SODA BOTTLING WORKS ST. HELENA
CALIF. – Aqua – Applied top – 9". . . . . $ 2.00- 4.00

3114   3120   3128   3133

3114. SANDAHL BEVERAGES AUSTIN, TEX. – Clear – 8". . . . $ 3.00- 4.00
3115. SANFORD SODA WORKS J.S. – Light green – Applied
top – 8" high. . . . . $ 3.00- 4.00
3116. SAN FRANCISCO SODA WORKS – Aqua – Dark – Ap-
plied top – 7". . . . . $ 4.00- 8.00
3117. SAN FRANCISCO SODA WORKS – Aqua – Applied top
7". . . . . $ 4.00- 8.00
3118. SAN JOSE SODA WORKS JOHN BALZHOUSE PROP.
SAN JOSE CAL. – Light green – 7". . . . . $ 4.00- 8.00
3119. SARATOGA RED SPRINGS WATER – Round – Pint –
Emerald green. . . . . $ 30.00- 60.00
3120. S-A-W (SAVANNAH AERATED WATER) – Amber – 10". $ 4.00- 6.00
3121. S.A.W. – Amber – 10". . . . . $ 3.00- 6.00
3122. SAXLEHNERS, HUNYADI JANOS BITTER QUELLE –
Olive green – Applied top – 9" – Round. . . . . $ 2.00- 8.00
3123. "SCHNERS" – Light green – 9" – Round. . . . . $ 3.00- 4.00
3124. S. C. O. N. M. W. ASS'N SACRAMENTO – Aqua – Ap-
plied top – 8" – Round – Crown cap. . . . . $ 2.00- 4.00
3125. SCOTT & GILBERT & CO. SAN FRANCISCO U.S.A. –
Brown – 10" – Round, crown cap bottle. . . . . $ 2.00- 4.00
3126. SELTERS – Olive green – 9½ " – Round, bottle with a
long slender neck with "Selters" written just below the
neck. . . . . $ 6.00- 9.00
3127. SEQUOIA SODA WORKS, ANGELS CALIF. – Aqua –
7½ ". . . . . $ 2.00- 6.00
3128. 7-UP – Brown – Squat type – Crown top – 6". . . . . $ 8.00- 12.00
3129. SHARON SPRING SULPHUR WATER – Round – Blue-
green – Pint. . . . . $ 30.00- 40.00
3130. SHASTA CREAM SODA – Light green – 8" – Round,
crown cap bottle with a diamond-shaped paper label. . . $ 2.00- 4.00
3131. SILVER STATE RENO NEVADA – Clear – 9½ " – Name
is written on the front with a figural picture of a miner. . $ 4.00- 8.00

189

3132.	S.J.E. – Green – Applied top – 7½".................	$	3.00-	5.00
3133.	SODA WATER-PROPERTY COCA-COLA BOTTLING CO., – Aqua – 6½" – Crown top – 6 fl. ozs.	$	2.00-	4.00
3134.	SOLANO SODA & ICE WORKS VACAVILLE – Clear – 8" Net contents 7 fl. ozs.	$	2.00-	4.00
3135.	SOLANO SODA WORKS VACAVILLE CAL. – Aqua – Applied top – 8" high.	$	2.00-	4.00
3136.	STANDARD BOTTLING CO., FORT BRAGG – Light green – Applied top – 6½"........................	$	3.00-	6.00
3137.	STAR SODA WORKS SONOMA CALIFORNIA – Light green – 8½" – The name is written in a circle with a large star in the center of the circle.	$	2.00-	4.00
3138.	STEPHAN, P.G. – Dark aqua – Applied top – 7" – 6-sided bottle with name written vertically down the front...	$	8.00-	10.00
3139.	STILL SHASTA – Amber – 11½" – Round, crown cap bottle – "Still Shasta" embossed above a paper label. .	$	2.00-	4.00
3140.	STOCKTON SODA WORKS STOCKTON CAL. – Aqua – 8"..	$	2.00-	4.00
3141.	SUMMIT MINERAL WATER J.H. – Medium green – Applied top – 8" high................................	$	4.00-	10.00
3142.	SUN-RISE SODA WORKS, SACRAMENTO CAL. – Aqua 7½"...	$	2.00-	4.00

3146   3151   3153   3154

3143.	TAHOE SODA SPRINGS NATURAL MINERAL WATER Light green – 7½" high.	$	6.00-	10.00
3144.	TALL ONE – Clear & light green – Round, crown cap bottle with a figural man with a tall hat...............	$	2.00-	4.00
3145.	THE LOWER SODA SPRINGS SHASTA CO. CALIF. – Aqua – Applied top – 8".	$	2.00-	4.00
3146.	THIS BOTTLE NOT TO BE SOLD – Clear – Blob top – Metal head – 11½" high............................	$	3.00-	6.00
3147.	TOLENAS SODA SPRINGS – Aqua – 7½" – "Tolenas Springs" is written through the center with "Soda" through the center of the circle....................	$	6.00-	8.00
3148.	T & W 141 FRANKLIN N.Y. – Aqua – Applied top – 7½" Blob top – Round.	$	6.00-	8.00
3149.	UNION GLASS WORKS PHILA. – Dark green – Applied top – 7½" high.....................................	$	15.00-	30.00
3150.	UNION GLASS WORKS PHILAD. – Dark blue – Applied top – 7½" – The name is on the reverse side – Blob top.	$	15.00-	21.00

190

3151. UVALDE BOTTLING WORKS, UVALDE, TEXAS – Aqua
Blob top – 7″ high. .... $ 8.00- 10.00
3152. VICHY SPRINGS NAPA CALIF. – Dark aqua – Applied
top – 7″ high – Round. .... $ 6.00- 10.00
3153. VERONICA MEDICINAL SPRING WATER – Amber –
10½″. .... $ 6.00- 10.00
3154. WEBB & RELEY, JOLEET, ILL. TRADEMARK – Aqua –
7″. .... $ 4.00- 8.00
3155. WEDDLE, J.T. JR. CELEBRATED SODA OR MINERAL
WATERS – Light green – Applied top – 7½″. .... $ 8.00- 10.00
3156. WESTON & CO. SARATOGA N.Y. (C.W. WESTON) –
Olive green – Applied top – 8″ – The name is in 3 lines
on the front of this bottle. .... $ 10.00- 20.00
3157. WHISTLE – Clear – 8½″ – Round – Paper label. .... $ 2.00- 4.00
3158. WHISTLE – Clear – 11½″ – Round bottle with a paper
label that reads, "Whistle A Liquid Food" plus other
information .... $ 2.00- 4.00
3159. WILLIAMS & SEVERANCE, SAN FRANCISCO CAL. –
Dark green – Applied top – 8″. .... $ 10.00- 15.00
3160. WILSON'S SODA WORKS, EUREKA CALIF. – Aqua –
8″. .... $ 2.00- 4.00

3161   3164   3166

3161. WINTLE, A.J. & SONS BILL MILLS NR. ROSS – Aqua –
Bowling pin shape – Blob top – 7″. .... $ 4.00- 6.00
3162. WITTER SPRINGS WATER – Clear – 10″ – Round bottle
with a paper label. .... $ 2.00- 4.00
3163. XLCR SODA WORKS MARTINEZ – Light green – Applied top – 7¼″ – "XLCR" is written above a shield that
contains a star with "Soda Works" written vertically on
each side of the shield and "Martinez" written below
the shield. .... $ 3.00- 6.00
3164. YOUNG'S BOTANIC BREWERY LD. HANLEY – Olive
green – Inside rubber screw – 6½″. .... $ 10.00- 15.00
3165. YUBA BOTTLING WORKS – Aqua – 8″ – Round. ...... $ 2.00- 4.00
3166. TYPES OF TOPS ON SODA & MINERAL BOTTLES –
Left – Hutchison; Center – Applied top; Right – Crown
top. .... $ 4.00- 8.00

BEER

| 3167 | 3179 | 3180 | 3181 |

3167.	A.B. CO. (on base) – Amber – Fat squat – Corker – 7½" Circa 1890's.	$	2.00- 4.00
3168.	ABERDEEN BR'W'G. CO. – Aberdeen, Wash. – Amber – Blob top – 9½" high.	$	3.00- 6.00
3169.	A.B.C.M. CO. – Amber opalescent – Crown top – 9½".	$	2.00- 6.00
3170.	A.B.G.M. CO. – Cobalt blue – Applied top – 9½".	$	20.00- 50.00
3171.	A.B.G.M. CO. – Aqua – Crown top – 11¼".	$	2.00- 4.00
3172.	ACME BREWING CO. – Aqua – 9½".	$	3.00- 6.00
3173.	AMERICAN BREWING & C.I. CO. BAKER CITY, ORE. – Dark amber – Crown top – 11¼".	$	2.00- 4.00
3174.	A.M.G. CO. – Amber – Applied top – 11½".	$	4.00- 6.00
3175.	ANHEUSER BUSCH INC. – Amber – 9½".	$	1.00- 2.00
3176.	ANHEUSER BUSCH – AB on base – Aqua – Crown top – 9½".	$	2.00- 4.00
3177.	ARNAS – (Embossed on bottom) – Amber – Applied top 8".	$	2.00- 4.00
3178.	AROMA – Amber – F on the bottom.	$	3.00- 6.00
3179.	BEER – No Deposit, No Return, Not to be refilled – Amber – Crown top – 9".	$	.25- 1.00
3180.	BEER – Amber – Blob top – 9½".	$	4.00- 6.00
3181.	BEER – Light golden amber – Crown top.	$	2.00- 4.00

| 3185 | 3186 | 3191 | 3192 |

3182.	BEER – Amber opalescent – Applied top – 11½".	$	4.00- 10.00
3183.	BEER – Amber opalescent – Blob top – 11¾".	$	4.00- 10.00
3184.	BERRY, C. & CO., 84 Leverett St., Boston, – Registered Emerald green – Applied crown top – 9 3/8".	$	4.00- 8.00

3185.	BISCOMBE'S – Brown and tan pottery – Inside threads – 8½" high.	$ 4.00-	8.00
3186.	BOHEMIA ALE – Brewed and bottled by Cerveceria Cuauhtemoc, S.A. Monterrey, Mexico, Contents 6.5 fl. oz. – Imported by: Carta Blanca Imp. and Dist. Co. Laredo, Texas – Amber – Crown top – 7".	$ .50-	1.00
3187.	BOHEMIAN LAGER BEER, BODIE BOTTLING WORK, BODIE CAL. – Aqua – Crown top.	$ 3.00-	6.00
3188.	BORN & CO., COLUMBUS, OHIO – Name is in a diamond shape – Blob top – Amber – Qt.	$ 5.00-	7.00
3189.	BURKHARDT, G.G. Boston Mass. – Amber – Blob top – 9¼".	$ 6.00-	12.00
3190.	C & CO. LIM. – Honey amber – Blob top – 9 3/8".	$ 4.00-	8.00
3191.	C.S. & CO. LO. – Dark amber – Crown top – 8½".	$ 2.00-	4.00
3192.	C.V. CO. #2 MILU – Golden amber – Vienna type – 11½".	$ 2.00-	4.00

3193   3197   3205   3209

3193.	CHINESE (1917) – with characters.	$ 4.00-	6.00
3194.	CLAUSSEN BREW'G ASS'N – Seattle, Wash. – Amber – 3 piece mold – Crown top.	$ 2.00-	4.00
3195.	CLAUSSEN-SWEENEY BREWING CO., Seattle, Wash. Green – Blob top. – 12".	$ 4.00-	8.00
3196.	CLAUSSEN & SWEENEY BREWING CO. – Aqua – Blob top – 10½".	$ 4.00-	8.00
3197.	COCK'N BULL GINGER BEER – Contents 12 fl. ozs. – Brown and tan painted glass – Crown top – 7".	$ 3.00-	5.00
3198.	COOK BOOK BEER – Amber – 9¼" – Labeled.	$ 1.00-	3.00
3199.	COOKS 500 ALE – Labeled – Aqua – 9½".	$ 2.00-	5.00
3200.	CONNECTICUT BREWERIED CO., THE – Bridgeport, Conn. – 9½" – Registered – Light green – Lightning bottle closure.	$ 2.00-	4.00
3201.	DIAMOND JIMS BEER – Labeled – Aqua – 9¼".	$ 3.00-	7.00
3202.	DU BOIS – Amber – Blob top – 8".	$ 2.00-	5.00
3203.	EL PASO BREWERY – Amber – 8".	$ 4.00-	8.00
3204.	ETNA BREWERY, Etna Mills – Amber – Blob top – 7¾".	$ 2.00-	4.00
3205.	F.H.G.W.S. – Amber – Lady's leg neck – Blob top – 12".	$ 4.00-	12.00
3206.	FLORIDA BREWING CO., THE TAMPA,FLA. – Aqua – "F.B. CO." on the bottom – 6¾".	$ 3.00-	5.00
3207.	GALLITZIN BOTTLING CO. – Clear – 326 on bottom – 10".	$ 4.00-	6.00
3208.	GALLITZIN BOTTLING CO. – Aqua – 9½".	$ 3.00-	4.00
3209.	GRAND PRIZE BEER – GULF BREWING COMPANY – Houston, Texas – Clear – Paper label – Crown top – 9".	$ 4.00-	6.00

3211	3212	3213	3215

3210. GUTSCH BREW. CO. – Amber – Red – 13 on bottom –
8½ ". . . . . $ 4.00- 8.00
3211. HAMM'S – Amber – Ceramic cap & bail – 10¼ ". . . . . . . $ 4.00- 8.00
3212. HAMM'S – St. Paul – Bottle not to Be Sold – Aqua –
Crown top – 9". . . . . $ 2.00- 4.00
3213. HAWK'S & CO. GINGER BEER THAMES DITTON – Pot-
tery – Inside threads – 7". . . . . $ 4.00- 12.00
3214. HENNINGER – Machine made – Amber – 11½ ". . . . . . . $ 2.00- 4.00
3215. H.G. CO. (on base) – Amber – Blob top – 9¾ ". . . . . $ 4.00- 8.00

3216	3221	3226	3227

3216. HOFF, JOHANN – Olive green – Blob top – 8". . . . . $ 4.00- 8.00
3217. HOHMAN & BARTLETT SCHLITZ – Manchester, N.H. –
Registered – Amber – Crown top – 9¼ ". . . . . $ 4.00- 6.00
3218. INDIANAPOLIS BREWING CO. – R.C. Co. on bottom –
Amber – 7¼ " high. . . . . $ 3.00- 7.00
3219. KAHNY & BURGBACHER BOTTLERS, Redding, Cal. –
Amber – Blob top – 8". . . . . $ 4.00- 8.00
3220. KANSAS CITY BREWERIES CO., THE – Amber – Crown
top – 9". . . . . $ 3.00- 5.00
3221. KESSLER MALT EXTRACT – Amber – Squat typer – Ap-
plied top – 8½ " high. . . . . $ 4.00- 8.00
3222. LEMP – AB CO. on bottom – Aqua – 9½ ". . . . . $ 2.00- 4.00
3223. LIMP, ST. LOUIS – (in a shield) – Amber – Blob top –
8¾ " high. . . . . $ 4.00- 8.00
3224. LION BREWERY LTD. – Registered – Embossed figure
of a lion-Auckland Lion Ale & Stout, This bottle is the
Property of the Lion Brewery LTD. – Amber – Crown top
11¾ ". . . . . $ 4.00- 6.00

194

3225.	MARYLAND BREWING CO., THE – Amber – 9"........	$	4.00-	8.00
3226.	MILLER BREWING CO. - Milwaukee, Property of – Aqua – Blob top – 9¼".............................	$	1.00-	2.00
3227.	MINIATURE BEER (on bottom) Bills Milwaukee – 4½".	$	3.00-	6.00
3228.	MINERAL SPRING BEER – Labeled – Aqua – 9".......	$	2.00-	4.00
3229.	MOBILE BREWERY, MOBILE ALA. – Aqua – 10".......	$	4.00-	8.00

3230	3231	3239	3242

3230.	MULLIGAN, Wm. 2804 Jackson St., Philada. – Aqua – Blob top – 9½"...................................	$	4.00-	6.00
3231.	NATIONAL BREWING CO. - Chicago, This Bottle Property of – This Bottle Registered Not to be Sold – Aqua Blob top – 9" high.	$	6.00-	10.00
3232.	NEBRASKA BREWING CO. - Omaha, Neb. – Red amber – Blob top – 9" high.........................	$	8.00-	10.00
3233.	T.L. NEFF'S SONS – Aqua – Case bottle trade mark on back – 11" high.	$	6.00-	8.00
3234.	NORTH WESTERN BREWERY, Chicago – United Breweries Co. - This bottle not to be sold – Aqua – Lightning bottle stopper – 9¼"....................	$	4.00-	8.00
3235.	OAKLAND BOTTLING CO., OAKLAND, CAL. - (embossed on the shoulder) – Blob top – Amber – 9"......	$	4.00-	8.00
3236.	O.B. CO. - On bottom – Labeled – Amber – 9¾".....	$	3.00-	5.00
3237.	OCONTO BREWING CO. - Amber – Blob top.	$	4.00-	8.00
3238.	PABST BLUE RIBBON BEER, SOUVENIR SPECIAL – "Bottled at the Brewery." - Amber – Metal lid – Crown top – Paper label – About 25 years old – 4¼"..........	$	4.00-	8.00
3239.	PABST BREWING CO. - This bottle not to be sold – Aqua – Blob top – Bail and rubber closure – 9".	$	4.00-	6.00
3240.	PABST BREWING CO. OF MILWAUKEE – Amber – 12".	$	4.00-	8.00
3241.	PIEL BROS. - This bottle not to be sold, on back – Clear – 9" high...............................	$	3.00-	8.00
3242.	PITTSBURG BREWING CO. - Amber – Crown top – 12".	$	2.00-	4.00
3243.	PORTNER, ROBERT BREWING CO. - Amber – 7¼". ..	$	4.00-	8.00
3244.	PUTNAM, W.O. - Clear – 9½".....................	$	3.00-	5.00
3245.	RAHR'S BEER – Amber – Labeled – 9¼"..............	$	3.00-	5.00
3246.	R & CO-D – Aqua – Blob top – 9 1/8".	$	4.00-	6.00
3247.	R.C. & A. - New York on the back – Cobalt blue – Tapered top – 9".	$	15.00-	30.00
3248.	RENO BREWING CO., Reno, Nev. - Dark amber – Blob top – 11" high.	$	4.00-	6.00
3249.	ROSEBURG BREWING CO., R.B. CO., Roseburg, Or. – Amber – Crown top – 11¾"..........................	$	4.00-	6.00
3250.	ROSE NECK BREWING CO., RICHMOND VA. - Crown top – Aqua – Round – Embossed star – 9¾"..........	$	2.00-	4.00

3251

3256

3260

3251. SAVANNAH BREWING COMPANY, CHAMPAGNE CABINET & WURTZBURGER BEERS – This bottle not to be sold – Aqua – Blob top – 9″ high. . . . . $ 6.00- 8.00
3252. SCHLITZ, JOS BREWING CO. – 7½″. . . . . $ 2.00- 4.00
3253. SCHLITZ, MILWAUKEE – (on bottom) – Tapered top – Amber – 5½″ high. . . . . $ 8.00- 15.00
3254. SOUTHERN BREWING CO. – Machine made – Green – 9½″. . . . . $ 2.00- 4.00
3255. STROHM, JOHN JACKSON, CAL. – J.S. embossed on front – Four piece mold – Light amber – 7¾″. . . . . $ 2.00- 6.00
3256. TEXAS BREWING CO., Property of, TBC Fort Worth, Texas – Frosted – Crown top – 9¼″. . . . . $ 3.00- 5.00
3257. TOLEDO BREWING & MALTING CO. – Amber – 9½″. . . $ 4.00- 7.00
3258. TROMMER'S EVERGREEN BR'Y – Aqua – 9¼″. . . . . . $ 3.00- 6.00
3259. VA. BREWING CO. – Aqua – 9¾″. . . . . $ 4.00- 8.00
3260. WAGNER, SIDNEY O. – Amber – Crown top – 11½″. . . . $ 2.00- 4.00
3261. WEINHARD, H. Portland, Or. – Light green – Porcelain top stopper – 7½″. . . . . $ 6.00- 8.00
3262. WIELAND'S, JOHN EXPORT BEER S.F. – Amber – Blob top – 7½″ high. . . . . $ 6.00- 10.00
3263. WISCONSIN SELECT BEER – Aqua – 9¼″. . . . . $ 3.00- 5.00
3264. YOERG BREWING CO., ST. PAUL, MINN. – Aqua – 9½″. . . . . $ 3.00- 6.00

WINE AND GINS

3272

3273

3284

3285

3265.	A.V.H. – Dark olive – Square base case gin – 2 piece mold – Applied top – 11¼ ".	$ 20.00-	36.00
3266.	AMELIORATED SCHIEDAM HOLLAND GIN – Amber – 9½ "	$ 13.00-	22.00
3267.	ASPARAGUS GIN, THE ROTHENBURG CO. – Aqua – Corker – 10".	$ 6.00-	12.00
3268.	AVAN HOBOKEN & CO., Rotterdam – Olive green – Blob top – 11¼ " high.	$ 15.00-	30.00
3269.	BAIRD DANIELS CO. DRY GIN – Aqua – Tapered & ring top – 9" high.	$ 7.00-	11.00
3270.	BART, E.L. DRY GIN – Light green – Corker – 8¾ ".	$ 2.00-	4.00
3271.	BERGOMASTER, GENEVA FIN – Cobb Hersey Co., Boston – Olive green – Blob top – Paper label – 10½ ".	$ 4.00-	6.00
3272.	BIANCO DELLA COSTA TOSCANA, ANTINORI 1965 – White Tuscany Wine for fish – Prodotto in Italia – Green – 13".	$ 10.00-	20.00
3273.	BIG 6 GIN – Original – 8 ozs. – Amethyst – Corker – 6½ ".	$ 4.00-	9.00
3274.	BOUVIER'S, DR. C. BUCHU GIN – Clear – Corker – 11¾ ".	$ 3.00-	5.00
3275.	BUNGALOW – Amber – Gin label – Tapered top – 10½ ".	$ 10.00-	20.00
3276.	CASE GIN – Olive green – Applied top – 6½ ".	$ 10.00-	20.00
3277.	CASE GIN – Olive green – Square base – Machine made 7½ " high.	$ 2.00-	6.00
3278.	CASE GIN – Olive green – Applied top – 9¼ ".	$ 4.00-	6.00
3279.	CASE GIN – Four stars on bottom – Olive green – Square bottom – Applied top – 9½ ".	$ 5.00-	8.00
3280.	CASE GIN – Amber – 8¾ " – 2 piece mold – Applied top Square base.	$ 8.00-	12.00
3281.	CASE GIN – Amber – Square base – 2 piece mold – Applied top – "E" on base – 9¼ ".	$ 8.00-	12.00
3282.	CASE GIN – Olive green – Square base – 2 piece mold – Applied top – 10 1/8".	$ 8.00-	12.00
3283.	CASE GIN – Olive green – Applied top – 10¼ ".	$ 8.00-	12.00
3284.	CHIANTI WINE – Emerald green – Wicker – About 3 feet tall.	$ 8.00-	15.00
3285.	CHILE, M.R. FRANCISCO UNDURRABA, Est. Sta. Ana. Emerald green – Corker – Wine – 7".	$ 5.00-	10.00
3286.	DE KUYPER GIN – Labeled – Dark amber – 10½ ".	$ 8.00-	15.00

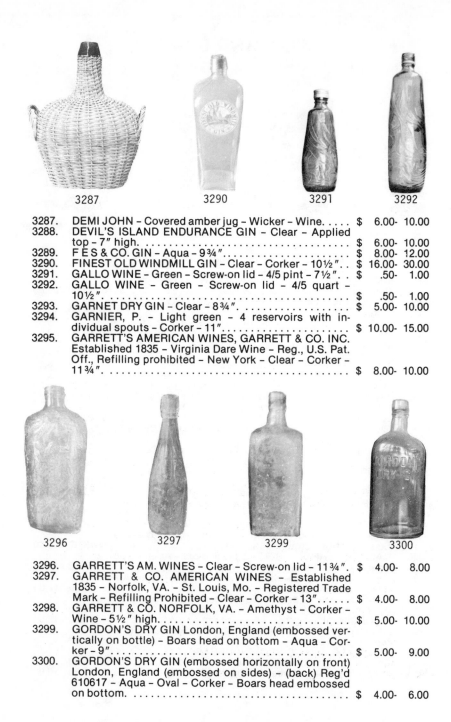

3287

3290

3291

3292

3287. DEMI JOHN – Covered amber jug – Wicker – Wine. . . . . . $ 6.00- 10.00
3288. DEVIL'S ISLAND ENDURANCE GIN – Clear – Applied top – 7″ high. . . . . $ 6.00- 10.00
3289. F E S & CO. GIN – Aqua – 9¾″. . . . . $ 8.00- 12.00
3290. FINEST OLD WINDMILL GIN – Clear – Corker – 10½″. . $ 16.00- 30.00
3291. GALLO WINE – Green – Screw-on lid – 4/5 pint – 7½″. . $ .50- 1.00
3292. GALLO WINE – Green – Screw-on lid – 4/5 quart – 10½″. . . . . $ .50- 1.00
3293. GARNET DRY GIN – Clear – 8¾″. . . . . $ 5.00- 10.00
3294. GARNIER, P. – Light green – 4 reservoirs with individual spouts – Corker – 11″. . . . . $ 10.00- 15.00
3295. GARRETT'S AMERICAN WINES, GARRETT & CO. INC. Established 1835 – Virginia Dare Wine – Reg., U.S. Pat. Off., Refilling prohibited – New York – Clear – Corker – 11¾″. . . . . $ 8.00- 10.00

3296

3297

3299

3300

3296. GARRETT'S AM. WINES – Clear – Screw-on lid – 11¾″. $ 4.00- 8.00
3297. GARRETT & CO. AMERICAN WINES – Established 1835 – Norfolk, VA. – St. Louis, Mo. – Registered Trade Mark – Refilling Prohibited – Clear – Corker – 13″. . . . . . $ 4.00- 8.00
3298. GARRETT & CO. NORFOLK, VA. – Amethyst – Corker – Wine – 5½″ high. . . . . $ 5.00- 10.00
3299. GORDON'S DRY GIN London, England (embossed vertically on bottle) – Boars head on bottom – Aqua – Corker – 9″. . . . . $ 5.00- 9.00
3300. GORDON'S DRY GIN (embossed horizontally on front) London, England (embossed on sides) – (back) Reg'd 610617 – Aqua – Oval – Corker – Boars head embossed on bottom. . . . . $ 4.00- 6.00

| 3302 | 3303 | 3304 | 3305 |

3301.	GRAVES GIN – Labeled – Clear – 6".	$	3.00-	5.00
3302.	GUMPS GIN, G. Gump & Sons Baltimore – Clear – Applied top – 6" high.	$	6.00-	10.00
3303.	HARMONY MEDIUM SHERRY – Produced and bottled by Ed. Delange Terez De La Frontera, Spain – Imported by American Wine Importing Co. Dallas, Texas – Amber guitar figural – 16".	$	6.00-	12.00
3304.	HOCK WINE – Amber – 9½".	$	4.00-	6.00
3305.	HOCK WINE – Red and teal blue – 12".	$	4.00-	6.00

| 3306 | 3307 | 3309 | 3313 |

3306.	HOCK WINE – Red and teal blue – 14" & 3" in diameter.	$	4.00-	8.00
3307.	ITALIAN WINE – Green – Rifle figural – 16".	$	6.00-	10.00
3308.	JUNIPER LEAF GIN – Amber – Case type – 10½".	$	15.00-	30.00
3309.	KENNET, RON DESTILERIA LaESCOCESA, S.A. – Hicho en Mexico – Amber – Screw-on lid – Paper label on front & back – Wine – 3½".	$	2.00-	3.00
3310.	L. & T. GIN – Anchor on the front – Olive – 9".	$	50.00-	75.00
3311.	LUHFELD, HY. H. CO., PREMIUM LONDON GIN – Amethyst – Corker – 8".	$	8.00-	12.00
3312.	MELCHER GIN – Labeled – Dark olive – 10¾".	$	4.00-	8.00
3313.	ONION BOTTLES – Free blown with pontils – Circa 1670-1710 – Dutch made, exported to U.S.	$	50.00-	125.00

3314	3317	3318	3321

3314.	RARE DOURO PORT – Emerald green – Paper label wine – 8½".	$ 3.00-	9.00
3315.	ROSS'S IRISH GIN – Labeled – 3 part mold – Aqua – Quart.	$ 4.00-	7.00
3316.	RUCKER DRY GIN – 1 on bottom – Aqua – 9".	$ 6.00-	9.00
3317.	SCHLESINGER & BENDER INC., SAN FRANCISCO CAL. – Pure California Wines and Brandies – Amber – Lady's leg neck – 12" high.	$ 4.00-	8.00
3318.	SEAGRAM'S EXTRA DRY GIN – Clear – Screw-on lid – 10½".	$ 1.00-	3.00
3319.	SEAHORSE HOLLANDS GIN – Tapered top.	$ 50.00-	65.00
3320.	VAN EMDEN, H. POSTHOORN GIN – "M" in a ring on the bottom – Clear – Amethyst – 10 5/8".	$ 8.00-	12.00
3321.	WINE – Clear – Screw-on lid – 7".	$ .25-	1.00

3322	3323

3322.	WINE – Emerald green – Screw-on lid – By Duraglass – 10½".	$ 1.00-	3.00
3323.	WINE – Drinking spout – Honey amber – Pontil mark.	$ 15.00-	20.00
3324.	WINE – Figural of a bunch of grapes – Clear – Screw-on lid – 5" high.	$ 4.00-	6.00

WHISKEY BOTTLES

3329 3331 3332 3338

3325.	AMERICAN SUPPLY CO. – Amethyst corker – 12" – Quart.	$ 4.00-	8.00
3326.	AMIDONS UNION GINGER BRANDY – Clear – 11¾"...	$ 8.00-	12.00
3327.	AVAN HOBOKEN & CO. – Amber corker – 10¾"......	$ 8.00-	15.00
3328.	AVAN HOBOKEN & CO. – Olive green – 11¼".	$ 15.00-	20.00
3329.	BAR BOTTLE – Son colored amethyst – 12".	$ 6.00-	10.00
3330.	B.B. EXTRA SUPERIOR – Amber – 10½".	$ 10.00-	15.00
3331.	BEAM, JIM – 1966 – 10" – Quart.	$ 2.00-	4.00
3332.	BELLOWS & COMPANY – New York & Chicago – Clear 11" high – Round bottle with a blob seal.	$ 8.00-	15.00
3333.	BENEDICTINE – Green corker – 8½" – Round.	$ 2.00-	4.00
3334.	BENEDICTINE – Green – Round – 10½".	$ 3.00-	6.00
3335.	BININGER, A.M. & CO. – Green – 8" – Round........	$ 50.00-	75.00
3336.	BINSWANGER, SIMON & BROS. – Clear – 6¾".	$ 5.00-	8.00
3337.	BLANKENHEYM & MOLET – Green – 9¼".	$ 10.00-	15.00
3338.	BONNIE BROS. – Amethyst – 11½" – "Bonnie Bros." embossed above circle which has "Bonnie" embossed across center....	$ 8.00-	15.00
3339.	BOOZ, E.G. – Old Cabin Whiskey – 8½" – Amber – Shaped like an old log cabin. Reproductions can be identified by a period missing after "Whiskey" which appears on original. .... Original	$100.00-	up
	Early Reproductions	$ 15.00-	50.00
	Recent Reproductions	$ 5.00-	15.00

3340 3347 3360 3361

3340. BOSTON, MR. PINE WHISKEY. – Amber – 8½" – Screw-on lid – Boston man embossed on front with buildings and mountains in the background. .... $ 5.00- 10.00
3341. BOWER'S, O.C. – Best Quality – Clear – 7¼". .... $ 2.00- 4.00
3342. BROWN FORMAN CO. – Amethyst – 11¼". .... $ 5.00- 11.00
3343. BUCHANAN, JAMES & CO. – LTD DISTILLERS – Olive green – 7" high. .... $ 5.00- 10.00
3344. CATTO'S WHISKEY – Olive green – 9". .... $ 7.00- 9.00
3345. CHAPIN & GORE SOUR MASH – Amber – 8½". .... $ 5.00- 10.00
3346. CHEVALIER, (THE F.) CO. – Whiskey Merchants – Amber – 7¾" high. .... $ 16.00- 22.00
3347. "COFFIN FLASK" or "SHOO-FLY FLASK." – Amethyst 7½". .... $ 2.00- 5.00
3348. COBLENTZ & LEVY – Amethyst – 11½". .... $ 6.00- 10.00
3349. COBWEB DESIGN – Clear – 8". .... $ 2.00- 4.00
3350. COCA MARIANI – PARIS – Bright green – 8¾". ...... $ 3.00- 5.00
3351. COMMODORES ROYAL O.K. OLD BOURBON – Clear – 11¾". .... $ 6.00- 10.00
3352. COURAGE – Amethyst – 8½". .... $ 2.00- 4.00
3353. CRESENT BRANDY – Green – 11½". Amethyst – 11 5/8". Amethyst – 12". .... $ 3.00- 5.00
3354. CREME DE MENTHE – In the shape of a bird's let with toes and claws – Amber – 11". .... $ 10.00- 20.00
3355. CROWN DISTILLERIES – Whiskey (sample) – Amethyst 3½" high. .... $ 15.00- 25.00
3356. CROWN DISTILLERIES COMPANY – Round – Amber – 4½". .... $ 4.00- 8.00
3357. CROWN DISTILLERIES COMPANY – Whiskey – Amber 10" – 11". .... $ 9.00- 16.00
3358. CUTTER, J.H. – Old Bourbon – Amber – 11¾" – Round. $ 12.00- 20.00
3359. CUTTER, J.H. – Old Bourbon – Amber – 7¾" – Flask corker. .... $ 12.00- 20.00
3360. CUTTY SARK, BLENDED SCOT'S WHISKEY – Green glass – Black & yellow label – 11 7/8". .... $ 2.00- 4.00
3361. CYLINDER WHISKEY BOTTLE – Red amber with lady's leg neck. .... $ 5.00- 10.00

3364   3365   3369   3372

3362. DALLEMAND & CO. – Creme Rye – (sample) – Amber – 2¾". .... $ 5.00- 10.00
3363. DALLEMAND & CO. INC. – Brandy – Amber – 11½". .... $ 5.00- 10.00
3364. DANIEL'S, JACK OLD NO. 7 – Clear – 10½" – Black and white paper label and black plastic screw-on lid. ...... $ 2.00- 4.00
3365. DEACON'S FLASK – Clear – 6½". .... $ 10.00- 20.00
3366. DEEP SPRING (Tennessee Whiskey) – (sample) – Amber – 4 3/8" high. .... $ 16.00- 30.00

202

3367.	DE FREMERY, JAMES & CO. – Amber – 11″ – Round...	$	2.00-	4.00
3368.	DEWAR-OWNED BY JOHN DEWAR & SONS – Amber – Round – 12″.	$	2.00-	4.00
3369.	DUFFY MALT WHISKEY CO. – Dark amber corker – Embossing on the front in a circle.	$	4.00-	6.00
3370.	DUFFY MALT WHISKEY CO. – Whiskey (sample) – Amber corker – 3 7/8″ high.	$	10.00-	25.00
3371.	EAGLE SPRINGS DISTILLERY CO. – Amethyst – 7″....	$	3.00-	5.00
3372.	EVAION*H*EVAIA – Flint glass – 10½″ – Rectangular.	$	10.00-	20.00

3373   3374   3375   3378

3373.	FANCY BACK-BAR SALOON DECANTER – Sun colored amethyst.	$	3.00-	9.00
3374.	FLASK – Amber – 6¾″ – Bulbous neck.	$	4.00-	6.00
3375.	FLASK – Aqua – 7½″ – Sure seal closure.	$	2.00-	4.00
3376.	FLECKENSTEIN, HENRY & CO. – Clear – 11″.	$	5.00-	10.00
3377.	FORMAN, BROWN CO. – Clear – 11½″.	$	4.00-	6.00
3378.	FOUR ROSES SPIRITUS FRUMENTI – Amber – 8½″ – Heavy embossing of four roses and a large number of leaves on the front. Screw-on lid.	$	10.00-	15.00
3379.	FRIENDSHIP – It has a shield with a form of clasped hands in it.	$	2.00-	4.00
3380.	GAELIC OLD SMUGGLER SCOTCH WHISKEY – (label) Aqua corker – 8¾″ high.	$	5.00-	9.00

3381   3382   3383   3385

3381.	GAHN, BELT & CO. – Amethyst with applied lip – 6½".	$ 5.00- 10.00
3382.	GIBSON'S EIGHT YEARS OLD – DISTILLED IN KENTUCKY – Amber – 9½" high.	$ 3.00- 5.00
3383.	GILKA, J.A. – Amber – 9".	$ 30.00- 60.00
3384.	GILKA, J.A. – Amber – 9¼".	$ 30.00- 60.00
3385.	GOLDEN ERA WHISKEY – Clear corker with paper label – 8½" high.	$ 3.00- 6.00

3386

3389

3398

3399

3386.	GOLDEN WEDDING – Bell embossed on front – "Federal Law Forbids Resale of this Bottle" – "Since 1896, Has had no peers for 50 years" – Carnival glass – 6½".	$ 10.00- 15.00
3387.	GOOD OLD O C B WHISKEY – Jug shaped – White or amber – 4¼" high.	$ 6.00- 10.00
3388.	GUGENHEIMER, H. & BROS. – Clear corker – 10".	$ 5.00- 10.00
3389.	HABANERO PIZA S.A. MEXICO D.F. – Amber – 8½".	$ 6.00- 10.00
3390.	HAND MADE SOUR MACH – Clear corker – 4½".	$ 3.00- 6.00
3391.	HANLEY MERCANTILE CO. – Amber – 10¼".	$ 5.00- 10.00
3392.	HANNIS DISTILLING CO. – Re-Use prohibited – Amber corker – 4 7/8" high.	$ 7.00- 9.00
3393.	HARPER, I.W. – Amber corker – 10".	$ 9.00- 14.00
3394.	HARPER, I.W. – Amber corker – 9½".	$ 15.00- 20.00
3395.	HARPER, I.W., OLD – Clear corker – 7".	$ 8.00- 10.00
3396.	HARPER I.W. WHISKEY – Letters in white paint – Clear corker – 2¾" high.	$ 4.00- 8.00
3397.	HARRIS, ADOLPH & CO. – Amber corker – 7½".	$ 3.00- 5.00
3398.	HARVEST KING DISTILLING CO. – Corker bottle with heavy embossing on the front. – Aqua – 12".	$ 25.00- 35.00
3399.	HARVARD RYE – Clear with "Harvary Rye" embossed on the front – 4" high.	$ 16.00- 21.00

| 3401 | 3406 | 3409 | 3410 |

3400. HAWLEY GLASS CO. – Amber – 8¼".................. $ 5.00- 16.00
3401. HAYNER WHISKEY – DISTILLER TROY, OHIO – Light amethyst – 11½" high. .... $ 8.00- 16.00
3402. HERE'S TO YOU. LONG LIFE & PROSPERITY – Clear corker – 6½" high.................................... $ 6.00- 15.00
3403. HIGH GRADE – Amethyst – 12¾". .... $ 9.00- 13.00
3404. HOMER'S CALIFORNIA – Ginger Brandy – Amber corker – 11¼"... $ 7.00- 11.00
3405. HORN OF PLENTY – Light amber corker – 8½". ...... $ 10.00- 20.00
3406. JAPANESE (1878) WHISKEY....................... $ 4.00- 8.00
3407. JOHANN HOFF – Berlin – Olive green – 8". .... $ 6.00- 15.00
3408. JOHNSON – Liverpool – Green corker – Round – 11¾". $ 9.00- 12.00
3409. JOHNSTON, W. SALOON – Amethyst – 6¾". .... $ 5.00- 10.00
3410. "JO-JO FLASKS" – Light amethyst – 5 7/8" & 7½"..... $ 10.00- 20.00

| 3411 | 3412 | 3413 | 3414 |

3411. JONES, PAUL WHISKEY – Amber – Flask – 7". .... $ 6.00- 15.00
3412. JONES, PAUL – Amber – Blob seal – 9½". Original condition with wicker work. .... $ 12.00- 16.00
3413. JONES, PAUL FOUR ROSES – Amber with heavy embossing – 9½" high. .... $ 9.00- 16.00
3414. JUG AND PITCHER – Brown and white – 6" & 6½" – These are the pitcher and jug that Dr.'s carried on their saddles when traveling the country to see their patients. The jug was for whiskey and the pitcher was for heating water.................................. $ 5.00- 7.00
3415. KELLERSTRASS DISTILLING CO. – Amethyst – 12". .. $ 10.00- 15.00
3416. KELLY, P.J. PURE WHISKIES – Amber corker – 5½". .. $ 7.00- 12.00
3417. KEYSTONE WHISKEY, 1854 (MALT) – Amber corker – 10½". .... $ 5.00- 15.00

3420 3422 3424 3425

3418.	KIDERLEN, E. – Amber corker – 9¼".	$ 12.00- 15.00
3419.	KILMARNOCK WHISKEY (WALKER'S) – Aqua corker – 10¼".	$ 10.00- 15.00
3420.	KING'S RANSOM SCOTCH WHISKEY – Clear – 7½"...	$ 3.00- 5.00
3421.	KING GEORGE IV WHISKEY PROPRIETORS – Green – 10¾".	$ 4.00- 9.00
3422.	LAURS 66 – Applied lip – 6¼".	$ 4.00- 8.00
3423.	LIBERTY (EAGLE) – Bright green corker – 8½".	$ 2.00- 4.00
3424.	LIND, JENNY – Amber – 9½" – Reproduction.	$ 8.00- 15.00
3425.	LIQUOR BOTTLE – Clear – 8½" – Metal screw-on lid...	$ 2.00- 4.00
3426.	"LITTLE BROWN JUG" – Brown pottery – 2¾".	$ 15.00- 30.00

3431 3435 3436 3437

3427.	LITTLEMORE – Amethyst flask – "Registered" is embossed across the upper portion of the flask – "Littlemore" is embossed vertically on the front side. – 5" high.	$ 5.00- 10.00
3428.	LOWEIRSTEIN & CO. OLD HARVEST CORN WHISKEY Amethyst – 6" high.	$ 3.00- 5.00
3429.	HENRY LUTHER WINES & LIQUORS – Amber corker – 7½".	$ 3.00- 5.00
3430.	LYONS, E.G. CO. – Clear corker – 11¼".	$ 6.00- 10.00
3431.	MARKS, J.C. LIQUOR CO. – (back) – Our sign 3 red barrels, purity, (three barrels stacked on top of each other), J.G.M.L. CO. embossed on bottom barrel – This bottle prohibited by law for refilling – Light amethyst – 9".	$ 10.00- 20.00
3432.	McDONALD, SANDY – Amber corker – 10".	$ 5.00- 10.00
3433.	McGLINN, JOHN DISTILLING CO. – Amber corker – 9½".	$ 5.00- 10.00
3434.	MEDLEY DISTILLING COMPANY – Clear corker – 10¾".	$ 7.00- 12.00
3435.	M & M T CO. – Clear flask – 4½".	$ 5.00- 10.00
3436.	MINIATURE BAR BOTTLE – Amethyst.	$ 5.00- 10.00
3437.	MINIATURE FLASK – Aqua – 4".	$ 2.00- 4.00

| 3438 | 3439 | 3443 | 3446 |

3438. MITCHELL BROS. LIMITED – Heather Dew Blended Scotch Whiskey Gray pottery with paper label. . . . . . . $ 8.00- 20.00

3439. MYERS & COMPANY DISTILLERS – Pure Fulton Straight Whiskey – Dark amethyst – 10 3/8″ – One gal. jug. . . . . $ 15.00- 20.00

3440. NORTH POLE, THE ANDERSON BROS. – Clear corker 7″. . . . . $ 6.00- 12.00

3441. NYE, H.L. BOURBON – Amber – Round – 11″. . . . . $ 3.00- 5.00

3442. OAK RUM WHISKEY (B.T.&P.) – Amber corker – 4¼″. . . $ 3.00- 6.00

3443. OBERMANN, J.B. CO. – Amber – 12″. . . . . $ 15.00- 30.00

3444. "OLD BUSHMILLS" DISTILLERY CO., THE – Aqua corker – 10″ high. . . . . $ 6.00- 11.00

3445. OLD CAMP RYE – Amber corker – 11¼″. . . . . $ 2.00- 4.00

3446. OLD CHARTER STRAIGHT BOURBON – Amber corker 11½″. . . . . $ 2.00- 4.00

3447. OLD CONTINENTAL WHISKEY – Amber corker with white – Shaped like a jug – 3″. $ 2.00- 5.00

| 3448 | 3449 | 3453 | 3454 |

3448. OLD CROW DISPLAY BOTTLE – Clear – Paper label – Metal frame rigged to bend for pouring. . . . . $ 10.00- 20.00

3449. OLD GRAND DAD DISPLAY BOTTLE – Oil derrick metal frame bends for pouring – Bottle is 20″ tall – Bottle with frame is 23″ tall – Clear – Paper label. . . . . $ 10.00- 20.00

3450. OLD KENTUCKY BOURBON – Distilled in 1848 – Amber 8″. . . . . $ 8.00- 15.00

3451. OLD KENTUCKY BOURBON – Distilled in 1848 – Amber 7¾″ high. . . . . $ 15.00- 20.00

3452. OLD KENTUCKY BOURBON – Distilled in 1848 – Amber 9¼″. . . . . $ 10.00- 20.00

3453. OLD QUAKER MINIATURE WHISKEY – 3½″. . . . . $ 2.00- 6.00

3454. OLD QUAKER – Clear flask – Screw-on lid – 6½″. . . . . . $ 2.00- 3.00

207

3459   3463   3464   3465

3455. OLD PIONEER – Clear corker – 6".................. $ 6.00- 12.00
3456. OLD THIMBLE SCOTCH WHISKEY – Amber corker –
8"..................................... $ 7.00- 11.00
3457. OLD TAYLOR – Clear corker – 8".................... $ 4.00- 6.00
3458. OREGON IMPORTING CO. – Amber corker – 11½".... $ 9.00- 14.00
3459. O.T. (embossed) – Refilling by others is illegal – New
Drinks Ltd. San Francisco – Distributors for O.T.
Limited England, Canada, Australia. .... $ 6.00- 10.00
3460. PAP'S PICNIC'S S.C. CO. – Amber corker – 4"......... $ 8.00- 11.00
3461. PERRINE'S PURE BARLEY MALT WHISKEY TRADE
MARK – Amber corker – 10"........................ $ 5.00- 11.00
3462. PHOENIX OLD BOURBON – Amber corker – 11¾".... $ 5.00- 10.00
3463. PUMPKIN SEED ROOT SNORT – Small – Aqua........ $ 6.00- 10.00
3464. PUMPKIN SEED FLASK – Embossed owl. .... $ 5.00- 15.00
3465. "PUNKIN-SEED" or "PICNIC FLASK" – Clear – 5½".... $ 3.00- 5.00

3466   3467   3469   3470

3466. RANUZZI, "THE HEAD HUNTER" – Black over aqua
glass – 10½" high................................ $ 4.00- 6.00
3467. RECTANGULAR FLASK – Amber – 8". .... $ 6.00- 13.00
3468. RED RAVEN SPLITS – Amber – 8". .... $ 1.00- 2.00
3469. RED TOP WHISKEY – Aqua flask – 6½".............. $ 6.00- 10.00
Aqua corker – 11½". .... $ 8.00- 14.00
3470. RED TOP RYE – Ferdinand Westheimer and Sons – Red
amber – 12" high................................. $ 7.00- 15.00

| 3471 | 3478 | 3479 | 3480 |

3471. REGISTERED-FULL ½ PINT – Clear flask – 7". . . . . $ 2.00- 3.00
3472. REMINGTON COMMERCIAL CO. – Distilled Just Right
Clear corker – 12". . . . . $ 6.00- 11.00
3473. ROSEDALE O K WHISKEY – San Francisco – Siebe
Bros. & Plagermann – Clear, amber – Quart – 11½". . . . $ 4.00- 12.00
3474. ROTH & COMPANY – Amber corker – 7½". . . . . $ 8.00- 12.00
3475. ROTH & CO. – San Francisco – Guaranteed full quart –
SCG Rect. – Corker – 10". . . . . $ 12.00- 20.00
3476. RUTHERFORD & KAY – 3 piece mold – Olive – Corker –
10½". . . . . $ 6.00- 8.00
3477. SCOTT PURE MALT WHISKEY – Amber corker – 11". . . $ 3.00- 4.00
3478. SEAGRAM'S SEVEN CROWN BLENDED WHISKEY –
Amber – 28½" – Display bottle. . . . . $ 20.00- 40.00
3479. "SHOO-FLY FLASK" – "COFFIN FLASK" – Clear – 6". . $ 2.00- 4.00
3480. SILVER TIP WHISKEY – Insured Good Quality – Big
Spring Distilling Co., Louisville, Ky. – Full ½ pint –
Clear – Corker – Approximately 6" – Flask. . . . . $ 10.00- 20.00

| 3481 | 3486 | 3487 | 3488 |

3481. STAMPEDE (SEARS) WHISKEY – A 6-inch amber flask
covered with embossing. . . . . $ 6.00- 12.00
3482. STRUNSKY WINE & LIQUOR CO. – Amber corker –
11½". . . . . $ 2.00- 4.00
3483. SUNNY BROOK, THE PURE FOOD WHISKEY – Clear
corker – 11½" high. . . . . $ 9.00- 13.00
3484. TAYLOR AND WILLIAMS INCORPORATED WHISKEY
Clear corker – 4¼" high. . . . . $ 6.00- 9.00
3485. TAYLOR AND WILLIAMS INCORPORATED WHISKEY
Amethyst – Corker – 12". . . . . $ 9.00- 13.00

3486.	T & S – Clear flask – 6½".	$	3.00-	5.00
3487.	TRAGER, I. CO., THE – Amber – Lady's leg neck – 11½".	$	5.00-	15.00
3488.	TURN MOLD WHISKEY BOTTLE – Amber – 12".	$	4.00-	6.00
3489.	TURNER BROTHERS – Green corker – 10".	$	6.00-	10.00
3490.	VAN DUNK'S GENEVER TRADE MARK & SCHMITZ – Amber corker – 8¾" high.	$	25.00-	50.00

3491   3492   3493   3494

3491.	WAKELEE'S MAGNOLIA SPIRIT – Cobalt.	$	4.00-	10.00
3492.	WARRANTED FLASK – Amethyst – 7½".	$	5.00-	8.00
3493.	WHISKEY – 12" tall – Sun colored amethyst.	$	3.00-	6.00
3494.	WHISKEY – Dark amber – 10½".	$	1.00-	2.00
3495.	WHISKEY JUG – White and brown crock – 7¼".	$	6.00-	9.00

3496   3497   3498   3499

3496.	WHISKEY – Federal Law Forbids . . . – Amber – Screw-on lid – 8¾" high.	$	2.00-	4.00
3497.	WHISKEY – One pint – Federal Law Forbids – Amber – Screw-on lid – 7¾".	$	2.00-	3.00
3498.	WHISKEY BOTTLE – Amber – White horse painted on back and a small horse embossed on the front just below the neck. (On back) Federal Law Forbids Sale or Re-Use of this Bottle. – (On bottom) Exporters White Horse Distillers Ltd. Glascow, Scotland – Clamp closure – 10¾" high – 3¾" wide.	$	15.00-	30.00
3499.	WHISKEY – Amber – 1".	$	3.00-	5.00
3500.	WHITE HORSE WHISKEY – Olive green corker – 10¾".	$	3.00-	5.00
3501.	WILD CHERRY JUICE – (label) – Clear – 11".	$	8.00-	10.00

3502   3503   3507

3502.	WILKEN FAMILY BLENDED WHISKEY – Clear – Paper label – 8″ high.	$ 4.00-	6.00
3503.	WOOD CYLINDER BOTTLE – Wooden corker – 12″. . . .	$ 5.00-	10.00
3504.	WOOLLACOTT, H.J. – Los Angeles – (HJW) – Corker – 12″.	$ 8.00-	12.00
3505.	WRIGHT & TAYLOR DISTILLERS – Louisville, KY. – Registered – Amber – Corker – 9¾″.	$ 6.00-	10.00
3506.	YE OLD MOSSROOF BOURBON – Amber corker – 9¾″.	$ 4.00-	8.00
3507.	ZIMMERMAN, F. & CO. – Red amber corker – 12¼″. . . .	$ 10.00-	20.00

These bottles belong to Mr. George H. Ohmar of Dayton, Ohio and have never been opened. Mash dates 1918 and bottled in 1927, 100 proof. Various bars pay handsome prices for prohibition bottle of whiskey for display purposes, generally about $100.00 to $150.00 per pint.

SNUFF BOTTLES

3508   3509   3510

3508.	GARRETT SNUFF CO. – The one on the left has a blown mouth.	$ 2.00-	3.00
3509.	LOAILLARD, P. CO. – (On base) – Black amber.	$ 8.00-	15.00
3510.	LEVI GARRETT & SONS – Dark amber – 4".	$ .50-	1.00
3511.	MARSHALL'S (DOCT) CATARRH SNUFF – 3¼" – Aqua.	$ 2.00-	4.00

3512   3513

3512.	RAILROAD MILLS SNUFF (label) – Maccoby snuff – Amber.	$ 4.00-	8.00
3513.	¼ SNUFF – Natures Tiffany – 2½".	$ 3.00-	4.00
3514.	SNUFF BOTTLE – Bubbles in the glass – Applied lip – Amber - Square – 4".	$ 1.00-	3.00
3515.	SNUFF BOTTLE – Gold Glass non embossed. A very beautiful glass piece.	$ 4.00-	10.00
3516.	SNUFF BOTTLE – Yellow – 4".	$ 15.00-	30.00
3517.	SNUFF BOTTLE – Green – 4 1/8".	$ 10.00-	25.00
3518.	SNUFF BOTTLE – Amber – 4".	$ 5.00-	20.00
3519.	SNUFF BOTTLE – Olive-amber – 4 1/8".	$ 10.00-	20.00
3520.	SNUFF BOTTLE – Amber – 2¾".	$ 5.00-	7.00
3521.	SNUFF BOTTLE – Aqua – 3¼".	$ 6.00-	8.00
3522.	SNUFF BOTTLE – Amber – 5¾".	$ 8.00-	12.00
3523.	SNUFF BOTTLE – Ceramic – Brown – 8".	$ 10.00-	20.00
3524.	SNUFF BOTTLE – Dark amber – 7½".	$ 12.00-	16.00
3525.	SNUFF BOTTLE – Amber – 4¾".	$ 10.00-	15.00
3526.	SNUFF BOTTLE – Olive-amber – 4¾".	$ 15.00-	30.00
3527.	SNUFF BOTTLE – Amber – 5¼".	$ 15.00-	35.00
3528.	SNUFF BOTTLE – Amber – 4½".	$ 14.00-	18.00
3529.	SNUFF BOTTLE – Green – 4 1/8".	$ 10.00-	25.00

INK BOTTLES

3533

3542

3543

3544

3530.	ALLING'S – Sheared top & teapot spout – Blue-green – 1 7/8"x1¼"x2¼".	$ 8.00- 12.00
3531.	ANTOINE ET FILS – Straight collar with pouring lip – Glazed brown pottery – 8 3/8"x3".	$ 6.00- 12.00
3532.	ARNOLD, P & J – Collared with pouring lip – Brown – 9¼"x3½".	$ 10.00- 15.00
3533.	ARNOLD'S – 2½" – Amethyst – Round.	$ 3.00- 5.00
3534.	BANKER'S WRITING INK, BILLING & CO. – B embossed in center bottom – Light aqua – 2"x1 7/8".	$ 5.00- 10.00
3535.	BELL – Sheared top – Amethyst – 3"x2½".	$ 3.00- 4.00
3536.	BERTINGUIOT – Sheared top – Amber – 2"x2¼".	$ 20.00- 30.00
3537.	BILLINGS, J.T. & SON – Sheared top – Aqua – 1 7/8"x 2".	$ 4.00- 9.00
3538.	BIXBY S.M. & CO. – Aqua – 2 1/8"x2¼".	$ 6.00- 12.00
3539.	BLACKMAN, C. – Green – 2½"x2½".	$ 16.00- 20.00
3540.	BONNEY, W.E. – Aqua – 2½"x3"x1½".	$ 13.00- 16.00
3541.	BROOKS, D.B. & CO. – Amber – 2"x2½".	$ 10.00- 20.00
3542.	CARTER'S (on lid) – Clear – Screw-on lid – "13" embossed on bottom – 1 1/8".	$ 1.00- 2.00
3543.	CARTER'S INK – Blown in mold – Applied lip – Sun colored amethyst – 2"x1½".	$ 3.00- 6.00
3544.	CARTER'S NO. 8 – (on base) – Sun colored amethyst – 3 ozs. – 2¾" high.	$ 2.00- 5.00

3545

3546

3552

3556

3545.	CARTER'S – Made in USA (on base) – 2½" tall – Sun colored – amethyst.	$ 2.00-	6.00
3546.	CARTER'S RYTO PERMANENT – Blue-black Ink for fountain pen and general use – The Carter's Ink Co. – Carter embossed near base – "The Cathedral" – Paper label – 9¾".	$ 30.00-	40.00
3547.	CARTER'S INK CO. – Two bottles, one in the shape of a man and one in the shape of a woman – Black shoes & yellow hair – Rolling pin in her left hand – Man has tan trouser, blue jacket & red tie. 3 5/8"x2".	$ 40.00-	80.00
3548.	CARTER'S PENCRAFT COMBINED OFFICE & FOUNTAIN PEN FLUID – Clear – 7½".	$ 6.00-	10.00
3549.	CAW'S INK CO. – Aqua – 2¼".	$ 3.00-	5.00
3550.	CHALLENGE – Light green – 2¾".	$ 5.00-	10.00
3551.	CLIMAX – Clear – 2 1/8".	$ 5.00-	10.00
3552.	CONE – Honey amber – 2½".	$ 5.00-	8.00
3553.	CONE – Aqua – 2½".	$ 3.00-	5.00
3554.	CONE – Cobalt blue – 2½".	$ 5.00-	8.00
3555.	CONE – Amber – 2 5/8".	$ 5.00-	8.00
3556.	CONE – Light blue – 2¾".	$ 5.00-	8.00

3557

3562

3576

3577

3557.	CONE – Amethyst – 3".	$ 4.00-	7.00
3558.	CONTINENTAL INK – Long tapered collar & pouring lip Aqua – 7¾".	$ 5.00-	10.00
3559.	CROSS PEN COMPANY – Aqua – 2¾".	$ 5.00-	10.00
3560.	DAVID'S THADDEUS CO. – Pinched pouring lip – Clear 6 3/8" high.	$ 10.00-	15.00
3561.	DAVIS, W.A. – Clear – 2¼".	$ 3.00-	5.00
3562.	DIAMOND INK CO. – Clear – 1½".	$ 3.00-	5.00
3563.	DIAMOND & ONYX – Aqua – 3".	$ 3.00-	5.00
3564.	DOULTON, LAMBETH – Pouring lip – Brown pottery – 4½".	$ 8.00-	15.00
3565.	DUNBAR, S.O. – Stopper or cork – Aqua – 2½".	$ 6.00-	10.00
3566.	EARLE'S INK CO. – Pouring lip – Tan – 6 1/8".	$ 5.00-	10.00
3567.	E.B. – Amethyst – Inside threads – Cone shape – 2 1/8".	$ 3.00-	4.00
3568.	EDISON INK CO. – Clear – 2 7/8".	$ 6.00-	10.00
3569.	FARLEY, L.P. CO. – Sheared top – Dark green – 2".	$ 15.00-	35.00
3570.	FORSTER, H.B. – Aqua – 7¾".	$ 5.00-	11.00
3571.	GATES – Clear – 6".	$ 2.00-	3.00
3572.	GLENN & CO. – Clear – 1 5/8".	$ 3.00-	7.00
3573.	GREENWOOD'S – Sheared top – Clear – 1½".	$ 5.00-	10.00
3574.	HALEY INK CO. – Clear – 2 5/8".	$ 6.00-	10.00

3575.	HARRISON'S COLUMBIAN INK – Sheared top – Aqua – 1½".	$ 25.00- 35.00
3576.	HIGGINS DRAWING-INK – Clear – Round – 2".	$ 1.00- 2.00
3577.	HIGGINS DRAWING-INK – (embossed on bottom) – Clear – 3" – Paper label – Plastic stopper – Round.	$ .50- 1.00

3578   3579   3580   3584

3578.	HIGGINS DRAWING INK – (embossed on bottom) – Clear – 3" – Paper label – Rubber stopper – Round.	$ .50- 1.00
3579.	HIGGINS ETERNAL INK – 1¼ oz. – 2½" – Square – Screw-on lid – Paper label.	$ .25- .50
3580.	HIGGINS PEN REMOVER – 2½ ozs. – 2½ – Clear – Round – Screw-on lid.	$ .25- .50
3581.	HIGGINS INKS, BROOKLYN, N.Y. – 2" – Amethyst – Round.	$ 2.00- 4.00
3582.	HOOKER'S – Sheared top – Aqua – 2".	$ 11.00- 16.00
3583.	HOVER – Aqua – 2".	$ 17.00- 24.00
3584.	HUNT PEN CO. SPEEDBALL, U.S.A., CAMDEN, N.J. (embossed on bottom) – 2¾" – Clear -- Round – Screw-on lid – Paper label.	$ .50- 1.00

3585   3587   3593

3585.	HUNT MFG. CO., SPEEDBALL, U.S.A., STAIESVILLE, N.C. (embossed on bottom) – 2¾" – Clear – Wide-mouth cone – Screw-on lid – Paper label.	$ .25- .50
3586.	IMPROVED PROCESS GLUE CO. – Aqua – 2 3/8".	$ 3.00- 5.00
3587.	INK – Sun colored amethyst – Plain bottle – 2½".	$ 3.00- 6.00
3588.	IRVING – Aqua – 2½".	$ 20.00- 25.00
3589.	JOHNSON INK CO. – Sheared top – Dark green – 5 7/8".	$ 21.00- 26.00
3590.	KIDDER, F. – Thin lip with red sealing wax – Light green 2½" high.	$ 21.00- 26.00

3591.	KIRKLAND'S WRITING FLUID – Aqua – 2¼ ".	$	2.00-	5.00
3592.	KELLER – 2½ " – Amethyst – Round.	$	3.00-	4.00
3593.	KELLER INK, DETROIT – 2" – Amethyst – Square – Screw-on lid.	$	7.00-	10.00
3594.	LAKE'S – Aqua – 2½".	$	15.00-	20.00
3595.	LOMBARD'S LILAC INK – Clear – 2 3/8".	$	5.00-	10.00

3596	3607	3614	3619

3596.	MAJOR'S CEMENT, NEW YORK – 2½" – Aqua – Round.	$	3.00-	5.00
3597.	MAGNUS – Tan pottery – 4 5/8".	$	6.00-	10.00
3598.	MANCHESTER NOVELTY CO. – Aqua – 2 5/8".	$	3.00-	11.00
3599.	MAYNARD'S WRITING INK – Sheared top – Dark green Amber case – 2".	$	15.00-	30.00
3600.	MOORE & SON – Sheared top – Aqua – 1 7/8".	$	6.00-	12.00
3601.	MOORE, J. & I.E. – Aqua – 1½".	$	6.00-	11.00
3602.	MORGAN – Sheared lip – Aqua – 2".	$	10.00-	15.00
3603.	MOSES BRICKETT – Olive green – 4½".	$	10.00-	22.00
3604.	NATIONAL SURETY INK – Clear – 9".	$	5.00-	10.00
3605.	NEWMAN & CO. – Olive green – 1¾".	$	15.00-	30.00
3606.	NICHOLS & HALL – Clear – 2 7/8".	$	6.00-	10.00
3607.	OLIVE TYPEWRITER (THE) – Clear – Round – 2".	$	6.00-	10.00
3608.	OLIVER – Clear – 1¾".	$	6.00-	10.00
3609.	OPHYKE – Barrel shaped with 4 rings around barrel – Clear – 2" high.	$	10.00-	20.00
3610.	PALMER – Golden amber – 4¼".	$	50.00-	75.00
3611.	PARKER – Clear – 2½".	$	25.00-	30.00
3612.	PAUL'S – Aqua – 5½".	$	10.00-	15.00
3613.	PEERLESS – Sheared top – Amethyst – 3".	$	10.00-	15.00
3614.	PELIKAN, GUNTHER WAGNER – Made in Germany, Drawing Ink – 2½" – Clear – Screw-on lid – Paper label Label in four languages.	$	.25-	1.00
3615.	PENNELL, J.W. – Aqua – 2".	$	15.00-	20.00
3616.	POMEROY INK – Aqua – 2½".	$	6.00-	10.00
3617.	READ'S – Aqua-blue – 2".	$	10.00-	20.00
3618.	ROUND – 2 3/8" – Light blue.	$	2.00-	4.00
3619.	ROUND – 2½" – Clear.	$	.50-	1.00

3620   3622   3623   3624

3620.	ROUND – 2½″ – Cobalt blue.	$	3.00-	5.00
3621.	ROUND – 2 5/8″ – Clear.	$	2.00-	4.00
3622.	ROUND – 3″ – Cobalt blue.	$	3.00-	5.00
3623.	ROUND – 9″ – Blue pouring spout.	$	10.00-	15.00
3624.	ROUND – 9 5/8″ – Cobalt blue – Pouring spout.	$	10.00-	15.00
3625.	RUSSIA CEMENT CO., SIGNET INK AND LEPACE'S GLUE – 8¼″ – Round – Screw-on lid.	$	8.00-	10.00

3626   3628   3629   3630

3626.	SANFORD – Sun colored amethyst – 2½″	$	2.00-	4.00
3627.	SANFORDS – 2½ – Clear – Round – Crown top.	$	2.00-	3.00
3628.	SANFORD'S (IN BASE) – Aqua – 2½″x2¼″.	$	3.00-	8.00
3629.	SANFORD'S BELLWOOD, ILL. – Made in U.S.A. 44CC. (embossed on bottom) – Sanfords – 1½″ – Red plastic Metal screw-on lid.	$	.10-	.25
3630.	SANFORD'S FOUNTAIN PEN INK. – Automatic machine made – Clear – 2″ square base – Chimney 1½″ tall – Base ½″ thick.	$	4.00-	8.00
3631.	SANFORD'S INKS – 2¾″ – Aqua – Round.	$	2.00-	4.00
3632.	SANFORD'S INKS AND LIBRARY PASTE – One pint 7 3/8″ – Amber – Oval base – Crown top.	$	2.00-	5.00

3633

3634

3636

3637

3633. SANFORD'S PENIT GREEN, FOUNTAIN PEN INK (on lid) – 1 7/8″ – Embossed diamond pattern – Clear – Square – Screw-on lid............................... $ 1.00- 2.00
3634. SCHOOL HOUSE – Aqua – 3″ tall – 1 ¾″ square. ...... $ 2.00- 5.00
3635. SCHLESINGER'S HYDRAULIC INK – White and black crock – Copper top – 6″ high. .... $ 22.00- 28.00
3636. SKRIP – Tighten cap. Tip Bottle to Fill The Well (on metal lid) – Pat'd 1759866 (embossed on bottom) 2¾″ – Clear – Ink well – Screw-on lid. .... $ 5.00- 10.00
3637. SIGNET INK – Threaded for screw top – Cobalt blue – 7¾″ high. .... $ 16.00- 22.00

3638

3642

3643

3638. SIGNET INK – Russia Cement Co. – Cobalt blue – 7¾″x2¾″ – Mouth threaded for screw cap. .... $ 4.00- 10.00
3639. SISSON & CO. – Sheared top – Pale green-aqua 1 5/8″. .... $ 5.00- 10.00
3640. SONNEBORN & ROBBINS – Flared lip, corks stopper topped with brass – Tan or cream pottery – 5½″....... $ 5.00- 10.00
3641. SQUARE – 2 3/8″ – Cobalt blue – Squat. .... $ 4.00- 6.00
3642. SQUARE – 2½″ – Amethyst...................... $ 2.00- 4.00
3643. SQUARE – 2½″ – Aqua. .... $ 3.00- 5.00
3644. SSS FOUNTAIN PEN INK – Bottle – Aqua. .... $ 2.00- 4.00
3645. STAFFORD'S INKS – Made in U.S.A. – 6″ – Cobalt blue Pouring spout. .... $ 10.00- 20.00
3646. STEPHENS, HENRY C. LTD. – Pouring spout – Dark brown pottery – 9″ high. .... $ 5.00- 10.00

3650   3652   3660

3647.	SUPERIOR INK – Tan & brown pottery – 2".	$ 5.00-	10.00
3648.	SWIFT & PEARSON – Lip & neck drawn out & shaped by hand – Bulbous neck – Dark green – 7 5/8".	$ 35.00-	50.00
3649.	THOMAS, L.H. & CO. – Aqua – 2¼ ".	$ 2.00-	4.00
3650.	3 1/8 fl. oz. Net – 3" – Clear – Round.	$ 1.00-	2.00
3651.	TODD, W.B. – Green – 2 7/8".	$ 5.00-	10.00
3652.	UMBRELLA – 2½ " – Aqua.	$ 8.00-	12.00
3653.	UNDERWOOD, JOHN & CO. – Cobalt blue – 9½.	$ 25.00-	40.00
3654.	UNION INK CO. – Aqua – 2¼ ".	$ 10.00-	15.00
3655.	VOLGER'S – Clear – 2".	$ 5.00-	10.00
3656.	WARD, SAMUEL & CO. – Sheared top – Clear – 3".	$ 10.00-	15.00
3657.	WARD'S INK – 4¾ " – Olive green – Pouring spout.	$ 10.00-	15.00
3658.	WATERMAN, L.E. CO. – Clear – 2 5/8".	$ 2.00-	3.00
3659.	WATERMAN, L.E. CO. – Clear – Round – Srew-on lid – 3 1/8" high.	$ 2.00-	4.00
3660.	WATERMAN'S IDEAL INK. New York – Mold mark ends at ridge on base of neck made for metal screw-on top – 3" – Sun colored amethyst.	$ 3.00-	8.00
3661.	WATERS, E. – Aqua – 6½ ".	$ 6.00-	11.00
3662.	WHEELER'S BLACK INK – Bottle – Aqua.	$ 9.00-	15.00
3663.	WHITALL, J.M. – Green – 11¾ ".	$ 6.00-	10.00
3664.	WHITTEMORE BROS & CO. – Dark green – 9¼ ".	$ 5.00-	11.00
3665.	WILLIAMS – Light green – 5½ "	$ 5.00-	8.00
3666.	WOOD'S – Aqua – 2½ ".	$ 15.00-	30.00
3667.	WORDEN'S INK – Threaded mouth & metal screw cap – Aqua – 1½ ".	$ 10.00-	20.00

GLASS AND FIGURAL DECANTERS

3669   3678   3685   3686

3668.	BARSOTTINI ALPINE PIPE (1968) – Ceramic figural with Alpine lake scene on bowl – 10″ – Can be used as ash tray.	$ 6.00- 10.00
3669.	BARSOTTINI ALPINE PIPE (1968) – Ceramic figural of Florence, Italy – Bowl of pape used as ash tray – 10″.	$ 6.00- 10.00
3670.	BARSOTTINI APOLLO (1969) – Ceramic figural of Apollo space ship – 12″.	$ 10.00- 16.00
3671.	BARSOTTINI ARCH DE TRIUMPH (1968) – Ceramic figural of the "Paris Arc Triomphe" – Top serves as ash tray – 7½″.	$ 10.00- 18.00
3672.	BARSOTTINI EIFFEL TOWER (1968) – Ceramic figural in grey and white – 15″.	$ 8.00- 10.00
3673.	BARSOTTINI ELK (1969) – Ceramic, B.P.O.E. 1869-1969 inscribed on the base – 17″.	$ 20.00- 25.00
3674.	BARSOTTINI GIOTTO-FLORENTINE STEEPLE (1967) – Ceramic figural in grey & white – 15″."	$ 8.00- 15.00
3675.	BARSOTTINI LOVE BIRDS (1969) – Ceramic figural of two black and gray birds flying past a tree – 12″.	$ 15.00- 20.00
3676.	BARSOTTINI ROMAN TRIBUNE (1969) – Ceramic blue and grey figural of Roman warrior head – 11″.	$ 14.00- 20.00
3677.	BARSOTTINI ROOSTER (1966) – Ceramic figural of a multicolored rooster – 15″.	$ 14.00- 20.00
3678.	BELL'S SCOTCH WHICKEY – Perth-Scotland – Royal Doulton, Made in England – Brown china with gold trimmings – 9 7/8″ high.	$ 16.00- 22.00
3679.	BISCHOFF GRECIAN VASE (1969) – White porcelain Greek figures against off-white rock wall – 12″.	$ 11.00- 13.00
3680.	BISCHOFF EGYPTIAN – Two compartments (1966) – Ancient Egyptian chariot scene on side – Dark and light brown stoneware – 9″.	$ 15.00- 30.00
3681.	BISCHOFF JUNGLE SCENE TOPAZ (1952) – Jungle scene on body of decanter in yellow and clear (Also came in ruby) – Glass – 15¼″ high.	$ 30.00- 35.00
3682.	BISCHOFF MASK (1963) – Stonware in varying shades of grey-brown – 11″.	$ 16.00- 21.00
3683.	BISCHOFF SPANISH BOY (1961) – Porcelain bull fighter figure with red, blue, and black clothing – 14½″.	$ 20.00- 42.00
3684.	BISCHOFF SPANISH GIRL (1961) – Porcelain Spanish senorita in purple dress, black and white blouse, red shoes, white and gold fan – 14½″.	$ 20.00- 42.00
3685.	EZRA BROOKS AMERICAN ORIGINALS – Firearms Series #1 – Over and Under Flintlock (1969) – Glass with a purple background – 10″.	$ 6.00- 10.00
3686.	EZRA BROOKS AMERICAN ORIGINALS – Firearms Series #1 – 1859 Pepperbox (1969) – Glass with red background – 10″.	$ 5.00- 10.00

3687. EZRA BROOKS AMERICAN ORIGINALS – Firearms Series #1 1865 Derringer (1969) – Glass with green background – 10". .... $ 6.00- 8.00
3688. EZRA BROOKS AMERICAN ORIGINALS – Firearms Series #1 1873 Colt .45 Peacemaker (1969) – Glass with blue background – 10" high. .... $ 6.00- 8.00

3687   3688   3707   3708

3689. EZRA BROOKS CIGAR STORE INDIAN (1968) – Heritage China – Figural in golden brown color. ...... $ 8.00- 10.00
3690. EZRA BROOKS GOLDEN GRIZZLY BEAR (1968) – Ceramic figural – 13½" high. .... $ 8.00- 10.00
3691. EZRA BROOKS SAN FRANCISCO CABLE CAR – China figural of cable car on slope – 3 colors: grey, brown & green – 7¼" high. .... $ 6.00- 10.00
3692. EZRA BROOKS POT BELLIED STOVE (1968) – Ceramic figural of a pot bellied stove – 10". .... $ 9.00- 12.00
3693. EZRA BROOKS IRON HORSE (1969) – Ceramic figural of an old train engine – 8"tall & 10" long. .... $ 9.00- 12.00
3694. EZRA BROOKS OIL GUSHER (1969) – Ceramic figural of an oil derrick with oil gushing out of the top – 16½". $ 10.00- 15.00
3695. EZRA BROOKS CHICAGO WATER TOWER (1969) – Ceramic figural of an old Chicago tower – 12"........ $ 10.00- 14.00
3696. EZRA BROOKS ANTIQUE CANNON (1970) – Ceramic figural of antique cannon trimmed in gold – 6¾" tall – 12" long. .... $ 8.00- 10.00
3697. EZRA BROOKS JAWHAWK (1969) – Ceramic figural of a comical bird with red head, blue body and yellow hat, beak and eyes. He is perched on a log – 8½" tall & 10¼" wide. .... $ 10.00- 15.00
3698. EZRA BROOKS GOLDEN ROOSTER (1969) – Ceramic figural of a solid gold rooster – Limited issue of 6,000 decanters – 10¼" high............................ $100.00-150.00
3699. EZRA BROOKS ARKANSAS RAZORBACK (1970) – Ceramic figuralof a red Arkansas University "Hog" – 8½" wide &8½" tall .... $ 14.00- 20.00
3700. EZRA BROOKS CALIFORNIA QUAIL (1970) – Ceramic figural of a quail in lifelike colors – 11½"............. $ 10.00- 20.00
3701. EZRA BROOKS NEW HAMPSHIRE STATE HOUSE (1970) – Ceramic figural of New Hampshire State House with gold eagle and dome on stopper – 11¾"... $ 15.00- 28.00
3702. EZRA BROOKS DISTILLERY CLUB BOTTLE (1970) – Ceramic figural of Ezra Brooks Distillery – Very limited edition – 7¼" tall and 8½" wide. $100.00-125.00
3703. EZRA BROOKS BUCKET OF BLOOD (1970) – Ceramic figural of a bucket with blood pouring over the top – 6". $ 21.00- 30.00
3704. EZRA BROOKS TROUT & FLY (1970) – Heritage china figural of a rainbow trout leaping out of the water to catch a fly – 12" high. .... $ 10.00- 16.00

221

3705.	EZRA BROOKS INDIAN CEREMONIAL (1970) – Ceramic figural of an Indian dancer in costume – 12½"….	$ 20.00- 30.00
3706.	EZRA BROOKS GOLDEN HORSESHOE (1970) – Ceramic figural of a horseshoe coated with 22-karat gold. Made for the Horseshoe Club, Reno – 10½"……….	$ 45.00- 60.00
3707.	CABIN STILL SPORTSMAN'S SERIES 1965 BIRD DOG Clear decanter with painted scene – Amber corked glass stopper………………………….	$ 11.00- 20.00
3708.	CABIN STILL SPORTSMAN'S SERIES 1964 PHEASANT – Clear decanter with painted scene – Amber corked glass stopper. ………………………….	$ 16.00- 20.00
3709.	CABIN STILL SPORTSMAN'S SERIES 1968 QUAIL – Clear decanter with painted scene – Amber corked glass stopper………………………….	$ 5.00- 10.00
3710.	CABIN STILL SPORTSMAN'S SERIES 1969 TROUT – Seventh in series – Clear decanter with painted scene – Amber corked glass stopper. ………………….	$ 4.00- 6.00

| 3709 | 3710 | 3711 | 3712 |

3709. CABIN STILL SPORTSMAN'S SERIES 1968 QUAIL – Clear decanter

3711.	CUT GLASS DECANTER – Clear – 8"……………….	$ 10.00- 20.00
3712.	DANT, J.W. AMERICANA SERIES – "BOSTON TEA PARTY" On the back is embossed an eagle – Matching glass stopper………………………….	$ 8.00- 12.00
3713.	DECANTER – Machine pressed design – Clear – 9½". .	$ 2.00- 4.00
3714.	DECANTER – Machine pressed design – Clear – 12". . .	$ 2.00- 4.00
3715.	DECANTER – Machine pressed design – Clear – 14". . .	$ 2.00- 4.00

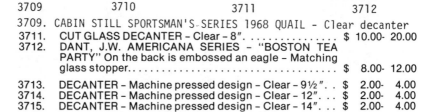

| 3713 | 3714 | 3715 | 3724 |

3716.	GARNIER APOLLO (1969) – Quarter moon figural with silver Apollo near top – Blue cloud forms base – China 13½".	$ 22.00- 30.00
3717.	GARNIER CARDINAL (1969) – Bright red Cardinal perched on a tree – China – 11½".	$ 11.00- 15.00
3718.	GARNIER DRUNK ON LAMPPOST (1956) – Colorful drunk hanging onto a bent lamp post – China – 13".	$ 20.00- 25.00
3719.	GARNIER JOCKEY (1961) – Figural of a jockey and horse leaping over a hurdle – Black and gold majolica pottery – 12¼" high.	$ 18.00- 20.00
3720.	GARNIER LOCOMOTIVE (1969) – Figural of an iron horse – 8" long – 6" tall.	$ 10.00- 15.00
3721.	GARNIER NAPOLEON ON HORSE (1969) – China figural – 11½" high.	$ 22.00- 28.00
3722.	GARNIER OASIS (1959) – Black china figure and black tree with green plastic palm leaves – 19".	$ 18.00- 25.00
3723.	GARNIER VALLEY QUAIL (1969) – Grey quail perched on a tree – China – 11".	$ 8.00- 12.00
3724.	HARPER, I.W. – Clear – 11½".	$ 2.00- 4.00
3725.	HOBNAIL – Clear with white trimmings – 4½".	$ 8.00- 15.00
3726.	HOUSE OF KOSHU BLUE GEISHA (1961) – Porcelain figural of a geisha girl in blue dress trimmed in orange, pink, and yellow – 13" high.	$ 25.00- 35.00

3725   3750   3751   3760

3727.	HOUSE OF KOSHU RED LION MAN (1959) – Porcelain figural of a Japanese dancer – 9½".	$ 24.00- 28.00
3728.	LUXARDO VENUS DI MILO (1959) – Figural of an Italian goddess – White majolica pottery – Made in Italy – 12¼" high.	$ 15.00- 30.00
3729.	LIONSTONE BARTENDER	$ 15.00- 18.00
3730.	LIONSTONE BELLY ROBBER	$ 22.00- 20.00
3731.	LIONSTONE CAMP COOK	$ 22.00- 26.00
3732.	LIONSTONE CAVALRY SCOUT	$ 15.00- 18.00
3733.	LIONSTONE CASUAL INDIAN	$ 15.00- 16.00
3734.	LIONSTONE CIRCUIT RIDING JUDGE	$ 18.00- 22.00
3735.	LIONSTONE COUNTRY DOCTOR	$ 18.00- 22.00
3736.	LIONSTONE COWBOY	$ 15.00- 20.00
3737.	LIONSTONE FRONTIERSMAN	$ 23.00- 28.00
3738.	LIONSTONE GENTLEMAN GAMBLER	$ 15.00- 18.00
3739.	LIONSTONE GOLD PANNER	$ 20.00- 27.00
3740.	LIONSTONE HIGHWAY ROBBER	$ 23.00- 30.00
3741.	LIONSTONE JESSE JAMES	$ 19.00- 25.00
3742.	LIONSTONE MINIATURES – limited edition of 1,000 of each. Six in a set – PROUD INDIAN – COWBOY – GENTLEMAN GAMBELR – CASUAL INDIAN – CAVALRY SCOUT – SHERIFF – Complete set is	$ 85.00-100.00

3743.	LIONSTONE MOUNTAIN MAN	$ 22.00- 30.00
3744.	LIONSTONE PROUD INDIAN	$ 15.00- 20.00
3745.	LIONSTONE QUAIL – Limited Edition.	$ 30.00- 36.00
3746.	LIONSTONE RAILROAD ENGINEER	$ 18.00- 22.00
3747.	LIONSTONE RENNEGADE TRADER	$ 23.00- 30.00
3748.	LIONSTONE RIVERBOAT CAPTAIN	$ 20.00- 23.00
3749.	LIONSTONE ROADRUNNER – Limited Edition.	$ 35.00- 40.00
3750.	LIONSTONE SHERIFF (1969) – Porcelain – Inscribed on bottom: "Original Lionstone sculptured Porcelain 1969." – Paper label: "Container made in Japan." – Story of Sheriffs on back side of base – 14" high.	$ 16.00- 25.00
3751.	LIONSTONE SHEEPHERDER (1969) – Porcelain – Inscribed on bottom: Original Jeremiah Potts Sculptured porcelain 1969" Paper label: "Container made in Japan." – Story of Sheepherder on back side of base – 12½" high.	$ 24.00- 30.00
3752.	LIONSTONE SOD BUSTER	$ 18.00- 25.00
3753.	LIONSTONE SQUAW MAN	$ 23.00- 28.00
3754.	LIONSTONE STAGECOACH DRIVER	$ 23.00- 28.00
3755.	LIONSTONE STP RACER	$ 19.00- 24.00
3756.	LIONSTONE VIGALENTE	$ 17.00- 21.00
3757.	LIONSTONE WELLS FARGO GUARD	$ 18.00- 25.00
3758.	LIONSTONE WOOD HAWK	$ 22.00- 27.00
3759.	LIONSTONE WYOMING MEADOWLARK	$ 25.00- 30.00
3760.	MARCIALLA WINE – Imported by McKesson & Robbins, Inc., Fort Worth, Texas – Made in Certaldo, Italy – Ceramic Figural masked boy clown bookend – 11¾"...	$ 12.00- 20.00
3761.	MARCIALLA WINE – Imported by McKesson & Robbins, Inc., Fort Worth, Texas – Made in Certaldo, Italy – Ceramic Figural of a masked girl bookend – 11¾".	$ 12.00- 20.00
3762.	MARCIALLA WINE – Imported by McKesson & Robbins, Inc., Fort Worth, Texas – Made in Certaldo, Italy – Glazed ceramic figural of a donkey – 11¾".	$ 7.00- 20.00

3761   3762   3763   3764

3763.	MARCIALLA WINE – Imported by McKesson & Robbins, Inc., Fort Worth, Texas – Made in Certaldo, Italy – Ceramic figural of an Italian guitar – 13".	$ 13.00- 25.00
3764.	MARCIALLA WINE – Imported by McKesson & Robbins, Inc., Fort Worth, Texas – Made in Certaldo, Italy – Ceramic figural of a lantern with a place for a candle – 12".	$ 10.00- 15.00

3765   3766   3767   3768

3765.   MARCIALLA WINE – Imported by McKesson & Robbins, Inc., Fort Worth, Texas – Made in Certaldo, Italy – Ceramic figural of a soldier – 12½ ". .... $ 10.00- 20.00

3766.   MARCIALLA WINE – Imported by McKesson & Robbins, Inc., Fort Worth, Texas – Made in Certaldo, Italy – Ceramic figural of a soldier – 12½ ". .... $ 10.00- 15.00

3767.   MARCIALLA WINE – Imported by McKesson & Robbins, Inc., Fort Worth, Texas – Made in Certaldo, Italy – Ceramic hand painted vase – 10½ ". .... $ 10.00- 15.00

3768.   McCORMICK JUPITER 60 LOCOMOTIVE (1969) – Figural of an old locomotive – 13" long – 7¼ " high. ... $ 15.00- 30.00

3769   3770   3771   3772

3769.   MEXICAN IMPORT – Figural decanter – Violin – Clear – 8" high. .... $ 2.00- 4.00

3770.   MEXICAN IMPORT – Figural decanter – Violin – Royal blue – 8" high. .... $ 2.00- 4.00

3771.   MOHAWK LIQUOR – Light blue china. .... $ 7.00- 10.00

3772.   OLD CHARTER – Clear – Paper label – Gold plastic cap. $ 2.00- 5.00

| 3773 | 3774 | 3775 | 3776 |

3773. OLD CHARTER – DISPLAY DECANTER – Came on rack with 2 decanters – Clear – Metal rack – 9¼". Complete set .... $ 10.00- 20.00
Single decanter .... $ 4.00- 8.00
3774. OLD FORRESTER – Clear – Corked glass stopper – Gold lettering – 11". .... $ 6.00- 12.00
3775. OLD FORRESTER DECANTER – Marigold carnival – Square bottom – Diamond pattern – 10". .... $ 8.00- 20.00
3776. OLD FORRESTER DECANTER – Marigold carnival glass – Round bottom – Thumbprint patterns – 10¾". . $ 10.00- 20.00

| 3777 | 3778 | 3779 | 3780 |

3777. OLD TAYLOR DISTILLERY CO., THE OLD TAYLOR STRAIGHT BOURBON WHISKEY – Ceramic figural of a distillery – 8¼" high – 9" long. .... $ 8.00- 20.00
3778. PIRATE'S MATE – Head serves as stopper – China..... $ 5.00- 7.00
3779. RARE ANTIQUES – FOUR ROSES – Golden amber and amber – China – 9" high. .... $ 6.00- 12.00
3780. SEAGRAM, JOS. E., & SONS – Clear with gold plastic cap – 8" high. .... $ 2.00- 4.00

 3781   3782   3783

3781. SEAGRAM, JOS. E., & SONS – Clear – 9½ ".......... $ 2.00- 4.00
3782. VIOLIN – figural – Light green – Found in various sizes
10" high. .... $ 5.00- 10.00
3783. WEATON NULINE GREAT AMERICAN SERIES –
APOLLO 13 – April, 1970, Wheaton, N.J. – Blue satin –
8¼ ". .... $ 3.00- 6.00

JIM BEAM SERIES

3797

3798

3799

Executive Series

3784. ROYAL PORCELAIN 1955 – The first executive series decanter was issued to commemorate the 160th anniversary of the Jim Beam Distilling Co. The decanter is black porcelain & has a white porcelain stopper. 14¼″ tall. $100.00-185.00

3785. ROYAL GOLD ROUND – 1956 – This circular shaped decanter is decorated with 22-karat gold. The label is supported by a gold chain & is hung around the neck. 12″ tall – Genuine Regal China. $100.00-120.00

3786. ROYAL DI MONTE 1957 – Black & gold trimmed design on a white background – Area set aside for rough edged circular label, is elegantly framed in embossed gold frame. 15½″ tall. Genuine Regal China. . . . . $ 65.00- 85.00

3787. GREY CHERUB 1958 – The entire decanter is embossed with white on grey designs. The lid, spout, border, & base are embossed in a scroll design lined in gold. The neck has three cherubs with golden wings. 12″ tall. Genuine Regal China. $110.00-155.00

3788. TAVERN SCENE 1959 – This circular decanter has embossed tavern scenes on both sides. The scenes are framed with circular 22-karat gold frames. The frames are painted with various colors. 11½″ tall – Genuine Regal China. . . . . $ 65.00- 80.00

3789. BLUE CHERUB 1960 – The label hangs from a gold chain on the neck of the decanter. Cherubs are playing on the body of the bottle. Gold accents the designs on the decanter. 12½″ tall – Genuine Regal China. . . . . $ 75.00- 90.00

3790. GOLDEN CHALICE 1961 – This grey-blue body of the decanter is accented by a gold petal designed skirt. A gold chain is linked around the base of the neck to hold the Beam label. The neck is decorated with two gold bands with an embossed floral design in between the bands. The flower's are colored in a variety of soft colors. 12½″ tall – Genuine Regal China. . . . . $ 65.00- 80.00

3791. FLOWER BASKET 1962 – The oval decanter has a gold base. The decanter is blue with embossed flowers & leaves in the body of the bottle. The stopper is topped by a bulb-shaped design in gold. The label sits on the handle. 12¼" tall – Genuine Regal China. .... $ 40.00- 55.00

3792. ROYAL ROSE 1963 – The base, spout, handle & stopper of the decanter has hand painted roses embossed in a golden frame. The background color on the body of the decanter is light blue. 17" tall. Genuine Regal China. .. $ 50.00- 55.00

3793. ROYAL GOLD DIAMOND 1964 – This decanter is diamond shaped with a circular base. The 22-karat gold is spotted over a background of dull gold. The label is supported by a gold chain hanging around the neck. 12" tall – Genuine Regal China. .... $ 45.00- 50.00

3794. MARBLED FANTASY 1965 – This decanter is divided into seven color sections. The base, central area, neck and the tip of the lid are colored in the marblelized glaze. The remainder of the decanter is in 22-karat gold 15" tall – Genuine Regal China.................... $ 65.00- 85.00

3795. MAJESTIC 1966 – The royal blue background of this decanter allows the golden leaves on the lower portion to stand out. The spout is golden and the stopper is patterned after the decanter. 14½" tall – Genuine Regal China. .... $ 35.00- 40.00

3796. PRESTIGE 1967 – This oval shaped decanter is colored in gold and avocado green. The lower portion of the decanter appears to be an elegant golden bowl. The neck rises from the top of the "bowl." The spout, handle and lower half of the stopper are gold. 12½" tall. Genuine Regal China. .... $ 10.00- 20.00

3797. PRESIDENTIAL 1968 – The bubbles on this decanter are characteristic of the balloons which were present in the political party national conventions of 1968. The body and lid are cobalt blue, and the handle, spout, and a ring around the decanter at the base are gold. 12¾" tall. Genuine Regal China......................... $ 10.00- 15.00

3798. SOVERIGN 1969 – Hand painted yellow roses on front, the remainder of the decanter is light green with white designs and decorated with gold. 12" tall – Genuine Regal China. .... $ 10.00- 15.00

3799. CHARISMA 1970 – 13" tall. .... $ 12.00- 16.00

3807   3801   3804   3808   3809

Club Series

3800. BLUE FOX 1967 – The Blue Fox celebrates the first birthday of the Jim Beam bottle and Specialties Club. The Blue Fox is clothed in a hunter's outfit with a blue coat and white pants. 12¼" tall. – Genuine Regal China. . . . $100.00-120.00

3801. ELKS CLUB CENTENNIAL 1968 – The decanter commemorates the 100th anniversary of the Elks Club. The front of the decanter is embossed with the emblem of the club and a large star. The decanter is golden brown in color. 11" tall – Genuine Regal China. . . . . $ 6.00- 10.00

3802. YUMA RIFLE CLUB 1968 – The Yuma Rifle Club is a duplicate of the Arizona State bottle with the exception that the club bottle has a different decal on the back side. 12" tall – Genuine Regal China. . . . . $ 35.00- 40.00

3803. GOLD NEHRU FOX 1969 – This decanter recognizes the Queen Mary Beam and Specialties Club. Genuine Regal China. . . . . $ 75.00- 85.00

3804. WHITE FOX 1969 – This decanter celebrated the second anniversary of the Jim Beam Bottle and Specialties Club. The fox is wearing a white Nehru jacket and a medallion. 12¼" tall. . . . . $ 35.00- 40.00

3805. ROCKY MOUNTAIN CLUB 1970 – This decanter is in the shape of a grey mountain with the peak serving as the stopper. On the front of the decanter are three mountain scenes encircled and painted gold on it. 9¾" high – Genuine Regal China. . . . . $ 25.00- 30.00

3806. CALIFORNIA MISSION 1970 – This bottle is shaped like a mission with a golden priest and Indian standing in the entrance. 14" tall. Genuine Regal China. . . . . $ 25.00- 30.00

3807. UNCLE SAM 1971 – Honors the National Association of Jim Beam Bottle and Specialties Clubs. Red & white stripe pants, grey and blue coat, black top hat. He holds a lollipop in his left hand, and a replica of the First National Bank bottle behind his back in his right hand. 12¼" high. . . . . $ 15.00- 25.00

3808. CONVENTION 1971 – A U.S. map covered with Beam bottles stretches across the front of this bottle honoring the first Convention of the National Association of Jim Beam Bottle and Specialties Club in Denver, Colorado. . . . . $ 10.00- 20.00

3809. VETERANS OF FOREIGN WARS (of the United States) 1971 – This decanter marks the 50th anniversary of the forming of the VFW in Indiana in 1921. Red, gold, and blue. 9¾" tall. . . . . $ 6.00- 11.00

3812   3813   3814   3815

Trophy Series

3810.   **DUCK 1957** – The green headed mallard duck stands proudly on a grassy pedestal. The decanter is dominantly green with a brown chest and yellow beak. 14½ " tall – Genuine Regal China. . . . . $ 30.00- 40.00

3811.   **FISH 1957** – The sailfish is captured leaping from the water. The fish is blue with black fins and white belly. The water at the base is green. 14" tall – Genuine Regal China. . . . . $ 30.00- 40.00

3812.   **PHEASANT 1960** – Re-issued in '61, '63, '67 & ' 68. Color variations from yellow beak to red circle around the eyes and blue head, to variations of brown feathers to the light blue tail feathers. 15" tall. Genuine Regal China. . . . . $ 8.00- 16.00

3813.   **WOODPECKER 1969** – Bright red head and neck serve as the lid. The red head is glazed china. The black and white body is unglazed. 13½" tall. Genuine Regal China. . . . . $ 7.00- 10.00

3814.   **BLUE JAY 1969** – The plummage of the blue jay decanter is white with black and grey markings. The remainder of the bird has blue feathers. The bird is perched on an oak tree stump and has acorns in with the leaves. 13½ " tall – Genuine Regal China.. . . . . $ 7.00- 10.00

3815.   **CARDINAL 1968** – State Bird of Kentucky, as well as other states. It was created for the home of Jim Beam Company in Kentucky. 13½ " tall. . . . . $ 40.00- 55.00

3817   3819   3820

3816. POODLE 1970 – The Penny Poodle was created in two colors. Each poodle is playing with a ball and has it's left leg extended. Each is also wearing a gold collar. The grey poodle is playing with a white ball with a green stripe. The white poodle is playing with a white ball with a blue stripe. 12″ tall – Genuine Regal China. . $ 7.00- 10.00

3817. HORSES 1961 – Re-issued in 1967 – The horses represent the mustang in a rearing stance. Three differently colored horses were produced. The horses are colored brown, grey, and black. 13½″ tall – Genuine Regal China. . . . . $ 10.00- 25.00

3818. DOE 1963 – Re-issued in 1967 – The doe is brown with white markings on its neck. It is apparently leaping over a huge brown rock. 13½″ tall – Genuine Regal China. . . . . $ 30.00- 37.00

3819. GREEN FOX 1965 – Re-issued in 1967 – The original decanter is clothed in a green and white hunter's outfit. The Fox Series are some of the most popular Beam bottles among collectors. 12¼″ tall – Genuine Regal China. . . . . $ 40.00- 50.00

3820. EAGLE 1966 – The American Bald Eagle is captured in this figural decanter. He has a white head with a yellow beak. His feathers are golden brown and the lower feathers around the legs are white. His yellow claws are gripping on a grey branch. 12½″ tall. Genuine Regal China. . . . . $ 15.00- 20.00

3821. CATS 1967 – The indentically posed cats were produced in three breeds: The grey and white Siamese with blue eyes; The black and white Burmese with yellow eyes; The grey Tabby cat with blue eyes. 11½″. Genuine Regal China. . . . . $ 10.00- 15.00

3822. KENTUCKY CARDINAL 1968 – The beautiful Cardinal decanter was created for, and sold only in, Kentucky. The cardinal is red with black wings and tail feathers and a black mask on it's face. It is posed on a dark brown tree stump. 13½″ tall – Genuine Regal China. . . $ 35.00- 45.00

3823. ROBIN 1969 – The handsome robin is posed on a golden brown tree stump. The bird is various shades of brown with a reddish brown chest. The beak is yellow. Genuine Regal China. . . . . $ 7.00- 10.00

3824. RAM 1958 – The Ram is the most popular of the Trophy Series. He stands boldly in the tall green grass. A 1958 calendar is embedded in the grass and a circular thermometer is captured between the ram's horns and his golden brown body. 12½″ tall – Genuine Regal China. . $100.00-105.00

3825. DOG 1959 – The black and white spaniel is looking up with his paws propped on the stump of a tree. His hind legs are bent to support his body. 15¼″ tall – Genuine Regal China. . . . . $ 55.00- 75.00

3826   3827   3829   3830

Political Series

3826.   **DONKEY AND ELEPHANT 1956** – The 1956 Donkey and Elephant were designed to serve as ash trays when emptied. The tray area on the donkey is the area behind the head of the donkey. The ear serves as the tray area on the elephant. Both are grey and have a screw-on lid. 10″ high. Genuine Regal China. $ 10.00- 28.00

3827.   **DONKEY AND ELEPHANT CAMPAIGNERS 1960** – The campaigners are dressed to attend the national convention. The donkey is wearing grey pants, a black coat, and a tan vest with a gold chain. The elephant is wearing dark grey pants, a brown coat, and a blue vest with a gold chain. 12″ tall. Genuine Regal China. Wrong stopper in picture, it should be a screw-on lid. . . . . $ 15.00- 35.00

3828.   **DONKEY AND ELEPHANT BOXERS** – 1964 – The 1964 political pair are presented in boxing clothes. Each figure is wearing brown boxing gloves, a white T-shirt, black shoes, and a black top hat which has a white band with blue and red stars on it. The elephant is wearing blue trunks and the donkey is wearing red trunks. 12″ tall – Genuine Regal China. . . . . $ 10.00- 28.00

3829.   **DONKEY AND ELEPHANT CLOWNS 1968** – Republican elephant dressed in white costume with a red collar and cuffs and blue polka dots. The Democratic donkey dressed in white costume with blue collar and cuffs and red polka dots. Heads serve as lids. 12″ tall. Genuine Regal China. . . . . $ 13.00- 15.00

3830.   **DONKEY AND ELEPHANT FOOTBALLS 1972** – The decanter is a football, while the figure of a donkey or elephant is the stopper. Each figure has its "fists" doubled, ready to fight the 1972 political game. 10″ tall. . . . . Pair $ 10.00- 12.00

3831.   **SPIRO AGNEW ELEPHANT 1970** – The decanter features an elephant sitting on a pedestal with his right leg lifted and trunk raised into the air. Regal China. . . . . $2,850.00 to 3,000.00

233

3834   3835   3839   3843

State Series

3832. ALASKA STAR 1958 – Re-issue 1964 – This star shaped decanter is light blue and trimmed in gold. The name "Alaska" is embossed and colored in gold across the base of the decanter. 9½" tall. Genuine Regal China. . . $ 40.00- 80.00

3833. COLORADO 1959 – The front is embossed with a mountain scene and a scout riding beside an ox pulled covered wagon. 10¾". Genuine Regal China. . . . . $ 40.00- 50.00

3834. HAWAII 1959 – Re-issue 1967 – Scenes from the islands of Hawaii are embossed on this colorful decanter. 8½" tall. Genuine Regal China. . . . . $ 40.00- 60.00
1967 . . . . $ 50.00- 55.00

3835. OREGON 1959 – This oval shaped decanter has on the front an embossed scene of a fisherman fishing along a stream in a wooded area. The reverse shows an embossed mountain scene. 8¾" tall. – Genuine Regal China. . . . . $ 30.00- 45.00

3836. KANSAS 1960 – This is a circular sunflower decanter. The decanter is yellow with a colored scene of wheat being harvested embossed on the front. 11¾" tall – Genuine Regal China. . . . . $ 30.00- 60.00

3837. IDAHO 1963 – This decanter is in the shape of the "Potato State". On the front is embossed a mountain scene with a skier skiing down the snow covered slope of one mountain. Also on the front, the letters IDAHO are boldly printed in gold. 12¼" tall. . . . . $ 40.00- 67.00

3838. MONTANA 1963 – The Montana is embossed on the front side with a scene showing 2 miners trying to pan gold from a stream. The state trees, the Ponderosa Pine, and state flower, Bitteroot is also shown. The back is embossed with an ox drawn covered wagon, traveling across the prairies with mountains shown in the background. 11½" tall – Genuine Regal China. . . . . $ 40.00- 80.00

3839. NEVADA 1963 – This decanter is circular shaped with a slice taken out of the right side to serve as the handle. The map of the state is embossed in the remainder of the area on the front. In the state is an embossed mountain scene. On the back side is embossed a hunter traveling with his burro. The lettering on the decanter is in silver. 11½" tall. – Genuine Regal China. $ 30.00- 60.00

3840. NEW JERSEY 1963 – This decanter has an embossed outline of the state on the front. The outline of this state, and the lettering on the decanter is lined in gold. 13½" – Genuine Regal China. $ 50.00- 75.00

3841. WEST VIRGINIA 1963 – This decanter has embossed pictures on both sides and each picture is framed by an embossed frame. The front side pictures the Blackwater Falls, and the back pictures the state bird, the cardinal, and an embossed "35" on a star. 10¼" tall – Genuine Regal China. . . . . $ 90.00-125.00

3842. NORTH DAKOTA 1964 – A pioneer family is embossed on the front side and are colored with lifelike coloring. The back side of the decanter is plain. 11¾" tall – Genuine Regal China. . . . . $ 40.00- 80.00

3843. OHIO 1966 – The Ohio bottle was the first Beam to use decals. It is shaped like an embossed map of the state. The front has the colorful seal of the state. The back has decals of the various industries and activities in the state. 10" tall – Genuine Regal China. . . . . $ 7.50- 11.00

3845   3847   3848   3850

3844. KENTUCKY BLACKHEAD 1967 – BROWNHEAD – These decanters are identical except the stoppers are either brown or black and the background on the decanter is either brown or black. The front of the decanter has an embossed outline of the state with decals showing the various industries and recreations of the state. 11½" – Genuine Regal China. . Blackhead $ 6.00- 15.00
Brownhead . . . . $ 6.00- 18.00

3845. NEBRASKA 1967 – The front has a picture of an oxen drawn covered wagon outlined in black. The words "Nebraska . . . where the West begins!!" are in green. The letters on the back are blue, green and gold. 12¼" tall – Genuine Regal China. . . . . $ 6.00- 12.00

3846. NEW HAMPSHIRE 1967 – This decanter is shaped to outline a map of the state. The decanter is white with blue linings. Inside the embossed map of the state are decaled informations about the state – 13½" tall Genuine Regal China. . . . . $ 6.00- 11.00

3847. PENNSYLVANIA 1967 – The "Keystone State" decanter is shaped in the form of a keystone. The decanter pictures the seal of the state in decals. On the back are decal pictures of industries and historic sites. 11½" tall – Genuine Regal China. . . . . $ 7.00- 8.00

3848. ILLINOIS 1968 – The Illinois decanter honors the 150th anniversary of that state. The front of the bottle has an embossed replica of Lincoln's birthplace, a log cabin. The body of the decanter is blue. On the back of the bottle is an outlined decal of the state. 12¾" tall. . . . . . . $ 7.00- 8.00

3849. ARIZONA 1968 – This is a circular decanter with an embossed picture of the Grand Canyon on the front. The back side shows decals of the industry, recreation and scenery of the state. 12" tall – Genuine Regal China. . . $ 5.00- 6.00

3850. FLORIDA SHELL 1968 – 2 colors: Iridescent mother-of-pearl; Iridescent bronze. On the back is a decal map of Florida against a blue world. The words "Sea Shell Headquarters of The World" are in black on a yellow strip. 9¾". . . . . $ 5.00- 6.00

3851. SOUTH DAKOTA 1969 – The front of the decanter is embossed with a picture of the famous Mt. Rushmore. The heads of Washington, Jefferson, T. Roosevelt and Lincoln can be easily recognized. 10½" tall – Genuine Regal China. . . . . $ 5.00- 6.00

3852. MAINE 1970 – Genuine Regal China. . . . . $ 5.00- 6.00

3853. SOUTH CAROLINA 1970 – This decanter has an embossed map of the state on the front. It honors the 300th anniversary of S.C. Genuine Regal China. . . . . $ 5.00- 6.00

3854

3857

3858

3859

Centennial Series

3854. SANTE FE 350th YEAR 1960 – This bottle was issued to commemorate the 350th anniversary of Santa Fe. The front has the "Place of the Governors" embossed on it. The back shows an embossed Indian woman surrounded by baskets. 10" high. $100.00-200.00

3855. CIVIL WAR SOUTH 1961 – This oval shaped decanter pictures the meeting between two generals on horseback on the front. The back of the decanter portrays the meeting of four Southern generals. General Lee's head is pictured on both sides of the stopper. 10¾" – Genuine Regal China. . . . . $ 38.00- 45.00

236

3856. CIVIL WAR NORTH 1961 – The oval shaped decanter pictures a Southern attack on a Northern fort. General Grant's picture is on one side of the stopper, and General Lee's picture is on the opposite side. 10¾" tall Genuine Regal China. .... $ 25.00- 40.00

3857. COLORADO SPRINGS CENTENNIAL 1972 – "1872-1972" is embossed on the front with big "100" between the two dates. The stopper is made in the shape of a building. .... $ 7.00- 11.00

3858. CHICAGO FIRE 1971 – Depicts the Centennial Anniversary of the Chicago Fire. The Sisters of Mercy Hospital, which gave aid to many of the victims, is embossed on the back with its story. 7¾" tall. .... $ 7.00- 16.00

3859. ANTIOCH, ILLINOIS 1967 – The front has an embossed head of a "Sequoit" Indian. The back side has decals picturing a blue and gold diamond honoring the Diamond Jubilee Celebration. 10" high. Genuine Regal China. .... $ 8.00- 10.00

3860   3861   3862   3863

3860. ST. LOUIS ARCH 1964 – Re-issued 1967 – "The Gateway to the West" arch outlines this decanter which commemorates the 200th anniversary of the city of St. Louis. The lettering is gold, the buildings are grey, and the sky and water are blue. On the back is embossed the ferry boat "Admiral". 11" tall – Genuine Regal China. .... $ 20.00- 30.00

3861. ALASKA PURCHASE 1966 – A blue star serves as the stopper for this decanter. The star sits on the top of a decal pictured totem pole. The state flag is shown waving in the breeze on top of Mt. McKinley. Lettering on the bottle is printed in gold. 10" high. – Genuine Regal China. .... $ 10.00- 25.00

3862. CHEYENNE 1967 – On the front of this circular decanter is embossed a buffalo grazing in the grass. The capitol building of Wyoming and a silver rocket can be seen in the background. 11" tall. .... $ 7.00- 12.00

3863. LARAMIE 1968 – This bottle, with embossed scenes of Laramie's history, was issued to help in that celebration of the 100th anniversary of Laramie. The front is embossed with a cowboy riding a bucking bronco. The back is embossed with a locomotive. 10½" tall. Genuine Regal China. .... $ 4.00- 8.00

3865

3866

3867

3864. RENO 1968 – Embossed on the front of the decanter is a skyline of the city toward the base. Toward the top of the decanter is embossed in large characters 100 years with the letters RENO painted on octangles. On the back the letters RENO 100 YEARS are embossed in large characters. An oval is set in the center of the back of the decanter which contians a decal showing high-points of the city. 9¼" tall – Genuine Regal China. . . . . $ 4.00- 8.00

3865. BASEBALL'S 100th 1969 – This bottle is in the shape of a flattened ball. The bold letters, BASEBALL'S 100th are gold. The back of the bottle has a history of baseball on a decal. 10¼" tall – Genuine Regal China. . $ 6.00- 8.00

3866. LOMBARD 1969 – The embossed flowers represent lilacs and are purple with green leaves. The lettering on the emblem is also purple. The body of the bottle is tinted in various shades of green. The back has an em-bossed outline of the state of Illinois. 12½" tall – Ge-nuine Regal China. . . . . $ 5.00- 8.00

3867. SAN DIEGO 1968 – This bottle is gold colored and has on it's front an embossed scene of a Spaniard and a monk. The back is hand painted scenes of the late 18th century common to the San Diego area. 10" tall – Ge-nuine Regal China. . . . . $ 4.00- 5.00

3868. PREAKNESS 1970 – This decanter has an embossed horseshoe on the front and pictures "The Woodlawn Vase." Genuine Regal China. . . . . $ 6.00- 8.00

| 3870 | 3874 | 3879 | 3884 |

Customer Specialities

3869. FOREMOST GREY & GOLD 1956 – FOREMOST BLACK & GOLD 1956 – These 4-sided decanters are tapered from the bottom up to the top. Each of the decanters are rough on the side and have nuggets of gold seemingly implanted in them. 15¼" tall – Genuine Regal China. $100.00-170.00

3870. FOREMOST PINK SPECKLED BEAUTY 1956 – This decanter is shaped like an urn. Pink, black, grey & gold specks cover the decanter and the stopper. 14½" tall. . $150.00-330.00

3871. HAROLD'S CLUB MAN-IN-A-BARREL 1957 – This decanter is a figural of a man in a barrell. He is wearing a shirt collar, a tie, flat-top hat, part of a pair of shoes and a barrel. "Harold's Club" is embossed on the barrel. 14¼" tall – Genuine Regal China. $200.00-415.00

3872. HAROLD'S CLUB MAN-IN-A-BARREL 1958 – The second Man in a Barrel decanter is a near duplicate of the first except that the man does not have a mustache and the "Harold's Club" is embossed on the base of the decanter. 14¼" tall. Genuine Regal China. $150.00-260.00

3873. HAROLD'S CLUB SILVER OPAL 1957 – This decanter is silver glass, painted, with a matching stopper. The Harold's Club identification is represented on a red velvet and silver label. 11" high. $ 18.00- 20.00

3874. MARINA CITY 1962 – The famous twin towers in Chicago are embossed on this decanter. The decanter is blue and has "Marina City" printed in gold down the front of the decanter. 10¾" tall. . . . . $ 35.00- 45.00

3875. HARRAH'S CLUB NEVADA SILVER 1963 . . . . $150.00-300.00
3876. HARRAH'S CLUB NEVADA GREY 1963 . . . . $150.00-300.00
3877. HAROLD'S CLUB NEVADA SILVER 1964 . . . . $170.00-180.00
3878. HAROLD'S CLUB NEVADA GREY 1963 . . . . $160.00-170.00
These decanters are duplicates of the Nevada state bottle with the exception that they have embossed letters on the base of the back of the decanter. The Harrah's Club bottles have "Harrah's--Reno and Lake Tahoe" embossed on the base. The lettering on the Harrah's Silver are painted silver and those on the Grey decanter are unpainted. The embossed letters on the Harold's Club Silver are painted silver and read "Harold's Club Reno". The letters on the Harold's Club Grey are unpainted and read "Harold's Club Reno." 11½" tall. Genuine Regal China.

239

3879. ARMANETTI 1971 – The front says "It's fun to shop Armanetti-Self Service Liquor Store" and has a man pushing a shopping cart. 11¾" high. .... $ 8.00- 12.00

3880. FIRST NATIONAL BANK OF CHICAGO 1964 – This decanter is circular-shaped and blue in color. All lettering and the trim of most of the embossing is in gold. 11½" high. – Genuine Regal China. .... $2,400.00 to 3,000.00

3881. HAROLD'S CLUB PINWHEEL 1965 – This circular decanter is blue and gold. A circle in the center of the decanter reads "Harold's Club Reno." A black ring with evenly spaced gold dots line the outer edge of the decanter – 10¼" tall – Genuine Regal China. .... $ 30.00- 65.00

3882. ZIMMERMAN TWO-HANDLED JUG 1965 – Grapes and grape leaves are embossed on the body of the dark green decanter. The Beam label is set in a circle embedded in the cluster of leaves and grapes. The Zimmerman label is on the base of the decanter. 10¼" tall – Genuine Regal China. $100.00-125.00

3883. HAROLD'S CLUB BLUE SLOT 1967 – This decanter is shaped like a slot machine and is colored various shades of light blue. 10¼" high – Genuine Regal China. .... $ 12.00- 18.00

3884. RICHARD'S NEW MEXICO 1967 – The front is embossed with the famous Taos Pueblo and has a picture of Richard Zanotti, a liquor wholesaler in Albuquerque. Richard says: Discover New Mexico. 11" tall – Genuine Regal China. .... $ 6.00- 8.00

3885. HAROLD'S CLUB VIP 1967 – This decanter is the same as the "Harold's Club Reno" embossed and painted gold on the neck of the decanter. 12½" tall – Genuine Regal China. .... $ 40.00- 55.00

3886. YELLOW KATZ 1967. .... $ 15.00- 26.00

3898

3900

3887. BLACK KATZ 1968. .... $ 8.00- 13.00
These slender decanters are either yellow or black. The tail of the cat serves as the handle. The cat's head, resembling the trademark of the Katz Department Stores of Missouri, serve as the stopper. 14½" tall – Genuine Regal China.

3888. ARMANETTI VASE 1968 – This yellow decanter is embossed with four petal flowers. The flowers are thinly grouped at the top and become grouped thicker as they fall to the bottom. A large "A" is placed near the center of the decanter. 12" tall – Genuine Regal China. ...... $ 8.00- 12.00

3889. HAROLD'S CLUB VIP 1968 – This decanter is a duplicate of the 1968 Executive with 2 exceptions: The blue decanter of the VIP is trimmed in silver instead of gold & "Harold's Club Reno" is printed in an oval on the decanter. 12¾" tall – Genuine Regal China. . . . . $ 35.00- 55.00

3890. ZIMMERMAN CHERUBS 1968 – This decanter is completely embossed. Each decanter has one winged cherub on each side. 11½" tall – Genuine Regal China.
Salmon Cherub . . . . $ 7.00- 8.00
Lavender cherub . . . . $ 6.00- 8.00

3891. CAL-NEVA 1969. . . . . $ 8.00- 11.00
3892. HORSESHOE CLUB 1969. . . . . $ 8.00- 13.00
3893. PRIMADONNA 1969. . . . . $ 8.00- 12.00
The Reno Casino Series are duplicates of the Reno decanter except for the name of one of the casinos being in the oval on the back of the decanter. 9¼" tall – Genuine Regal China.

3894. GOLDEN NUGGET 1969. . . . . $ 40.00- 65.00
3895. GOLDEN GATE 1969. . . . . $ 40.00- 65.00
The Casino Series decanter of Las Vegas Casinos are similar to the Las Vegas decanter. The names of the casinos are placed on the base on an emblem. The back of the decanter gives information, on decal, about which casino the decanter honors. 12½" tall. Genuine Regal China.

3896. HAROLD'S CLUB VIP 1969 – The VIP for 1969 is a duplicate of the 1969 Executive with the exception that Harold's Club Reno is embossed and colored gold on the back. 12" tall – Genuine Regal China. . . . . $ 40.00- 90.00

3897. ARMANETTI AWARD WINNER 1969 – This decanter is in the shape of the number one and has an emblem on the front saying "Armanetti Liquors 1969 Award Winners." The decanter is blue with some of the trimmed in gold. The Chicago skyline is embossed on the back. 10½" tall – Genuine Regal China. . . . . $ 8.00- 15.00

3898. HAROLD'S CLUB COVERED WAGON 1969 – Front embossed with wagon, driver and smiling ox. Front color variations of brown, yellow, white and blue. Back has replica of Harold Smith. Senior's book I Want To Quit Winners is colored red and in the original has a blue background on back and re-issue has light green background. Genuine Regal China. . . . . Original $ 9.00- 12.00
Re-issues . . . . $ 4.00- 6.00

3899. HARVEY'S 1969 – This plain glass decanter has a silver insignia of a wagon wheel with "Harvey's 25th Anniversary printed over the spokes. The decanter has a china stopper which has "Silver 25" printed on it in silver. 11½" tall – Glass. . . . . $ 8.00- 11.00

3900. ZIMMERMAN BLUE BEAUTY 1969 – Blue with gold trimmings on front. The back is embossed with the skyline of Chicago with an arrow pointing to Zimmerman's store. 10" tall – Genuine Regal China. . . . . $ 10.00- 22.00

3901. ZIMMERMAN GLASS 1969 – This plain glass decanter has an insignia in white on the front. The insignia shows a picture of the Zimmerman store with the skyline of Chicago in the background. The bonded Beam information is also in the insignia. The decanter has a china stopper which has a sketch of Max Zimmerman's head. 11¼". Glass. .... $ 6.00- 8.00

3902. ARMANETTI BACCHUS 1970 – This decanter is circular with a rough top. The Bacchus figure is pictured in the circular area. The circular stopper has an "A" in it. Genuine Regal China. .... $ 10.00- 22.00

3903. HAROLD'S CLUB VIP 1970 – This decanter is similar to the 1970 Executive decanter. Genuine Regal China. ... $ 20.00- 50.00

3904. ZIMMERMAN CHICAGO 1970 – Genuine Regal China. . $ 8.00- 18.00

3908   3909   3914   3915

Regal China Specialities

3905. IVORY ASH TRAY 1955 When decanter is emptied it can be laid down on its side and used as an ash tray. The decanter has an indented area for the ash tray, an area to hold the cigarettes, and an area to hold a glass. 12¾" tall – Genuine Regal China. .... $ 20.00- 30.00

3906. SEATTLE WORLD'S FAIR 1962 – This decanter is in the shape of the Space Needle. World's Fair Seattle is embossed on the opposite side. Colorfuk pictures are embossed on all sides. 13½" tall – Genuine Regal China. . $ 20.00- 28.00

3907. MUSICIANS ON A WINE CASK 1964 – This decanter is wood grained olive green in color. The oval body of the decanter rests on a wooden stand. The body has two men playing instruments in a rock walled wine cellar. 9¾" tall – Genuine Regal China. .... $ 8.00- 11.00

3908. NEW YORK'S WORLD'S FAIR 1964 – The world-shaped decanter was created for the 1964 World's Fair. The grey contents are outlined in gold. The lettering is also in gold. The grey lines circling the world represent the paths taken by the first space flights. 11½" tall – Genuine Regal China. .... $ 22.00- 30.00

3909. FIJI ISLANDS 1971 – Depicts the Fiji flag in the center surrounded by "1st Anniversary Fiji Independence Oct. 10, 1971. .... $ 6.00- 10.00

3910. GREEN CHINA JUG 1965 – This vase-like decanter has pussy willows embossed on it's side. The decanter is dark green. 12½" tall – .... $ 6.00- 8.00

3911. OATMEAL CHINA JUG 1966 – This vase-like decanter has leaves embossed around the neck. The stopper repeats the leaf design The "Bonded Beam" label is located on the base. 13¾" tall – Genuine Regal China.. $ 40.00- 50.00

3912. TURQUOISE CHINA JUG 1966 – This vase-like decanter has scrolled stripes and plain stripes. The decanter is turquoise. 13¼" tall – Genuine Regal China. .... $ 7.00- 10.00

3913. BLUE DAISY 1967 – The decanter is blue with three daisies with leaves embossed on a straw-like background. The blue decanter was also issued with Zimmerman paper lables. 12¼" tall – Genuine Regal China. .... $ 6.00- 10.00

3914. REDWOOD 1967 – Triangular shaped green and brown bottle pays tribute to the Redwood forests of northern California. Front side embossed picture of a redwood tree, back side shows a decal picture of the coastal area of Calif. in which the forests are located. 12¾" tall Genuine Regal China. .... $ 10.00- 12.00

3915. YOSEMITE 1967 – The front of this decanter shows famous scenes in the park. The back has a decal map of the park. 11" tall. – Genuine Regal China........... $ 6.00- 10.00

3916   3917   3918   3919

3916. CABLE CAR 1968 – Replica of San Francisco's world famous cable cars. The decanter is embossed with doors, windows, and the wheels. The color is avacado green with red, yellow & black decals. 4½" tall – Genuine Regal China.............................. $ 4.00- 8.00

3917. HAROLD'S CLUB GREY SLOT MACHINE 1968 – The decanter is shaped like a slot machine and is grey in color. 10¼" tall – Genuine Regal China. .... $ 4.00- 8.00

3918. ANTIQUE TRADER 1968 – The bottle is in the shape of a newspaper with red and black lettering. The spout is back with a black and white china stopper. 10½" tall – Genuine Regal China. .... $ 5.00- 10.00

3919. BROADMOOR HOTEL 1968 – The bottle is in the shape of the hotel. The roof sections of the hotel are rust colored and the building is a pinkish tan color. The roof to the tower serves as the stopper for the bottle. 10" tall – Genuine Regal China. .... $ 6.00- 8.00

3920   3921   3922   3923

3920.   HEMISFAIR 1968 – This decanter honors the World's Fair being held in San Antonio & San Antonio's 25th birthday. The bottle pictures scenes of the Lone Star State. 13″ tall – Genuine Regal China. . . . . $ 10.00- 15.00

3921.   PONY EXPRESS 1968 – The embossed front on this decanter shows a pony express rider on his horse. The route of the trail is shown on the reverse on a decal map. Various shades of brown. 11″ tall – Genuine Regal China. . . . . $ 6.00- 10.00

3922.   RUIDOSO DOWNS 1968 – Front embossed with cowboy hat, horseshoe, and "RD" brand. Horseshoe and most lettering painted in silver. Decanter is brown with yellow-lined circle on the front. 12¾″ tall. . . . . $ 5.00- 8.00

3923.   95th KENTUCKY DERBY 1969 – These two bottles honor the "Home of The 95th Kentucky Derby," Churchill Downs. The lettering on the bottle is gold. The front is embossed with a replica of Churchill Downs. The roses on both sides of the bottle are either pink or red. 10¾″ tall. Red Roses . . . . $ 9.00- 10.00
      Pink Roses . . . . $ 4.00- 6.00

3924.   GRAND CANYON 1969 – This decanter is like the Arizona State decanter except that a special decal is on the back to commemorate the 50th Anniversary of the Grand Canyon National Park. 12″ tall – Genuine Regal China. . . . . $ 15.00- 18.00

3925.   HARRY HOFFMAN 1969 – The Harry Hoffman liquor store of Denver, Colorado is embossed on the front of the decanter. The Rocky Mountains rise above the store. The back is embossed with skiiers skiing on ski slopes. 9″ high – Genuine Regal China. . . . . $ 7.00- 8.00

3926.   LAS VEGAS 1969 – The Las Vegas decanter is shaped similar to a football positioned ready for the kickoff. It is embossed with "Las Vegas" and painted gold across the front of the decanter. Embossed scenes and decals are on the remainder of the decanter. 12½″ – Genuine Regal China. . . . . $ 5.00- 8.00

3927.   PONDEROSA 1969 – The decanter is a china replica of the log cabin house in the well-known T.V. series "Bonanza." Painted in blue on the base of the front is "Ponderosa Ranch Nevada." 7½″ – Genuine Regal China. . . . . $ 5.00- 8.00

3928. THAILAND 1969 – The decanter has an embossed picture of an elephant in the jungle on the front. "Thailand" is embossed and painted gold on the front of the decanter. The back pictures a Thai dancer and a map of the nation. 12½" tall – Genuine Regal China. ... $ 6.00- 8.00

3929. AMERICAN VETERANS 1970 – Genuine Regal China... $ 8.00- 10.00

3930. BELL SCOTCH 1970 – This school hand bell shaped decanter is brown and gold. A crest is painted on one side and the identification and information is on the other side. 10½" tall – Genuine Regal China. .... $ 8.00- 10.00

3931. BING CROSBY NATIONAL PRO-AM 1970 – The circular decanter has two golf balls embedded in the base. A Monterrey cyprus tree is embossed on the front and information about the tournament is on the back. 12" tall Genuine Regal China. .... $ 6.00- 8.00

3932. FRANKLIN MINT 1970 – Genuine Regal China. .... $ 8.00- 11.00

3933   3934   3955   3956

3933. GERMANY 1970 – The front of the decanter has an embossed picture of a German man and woman seated at an outside table and a German village in the background. The back of the decanter is embossed with a map of both East and West Germany. 10" tall. .... $ 5.00- 10.00

3934. GERMANY, LAND OF HANSEL & GRETEL 1971 – Designed for the Armed Forces in Germany, has Hansel & Gretel embossed on the front. .... $ 6.00- 10.00

3935. INDIANA SHRINER 1970 – Genuine Regal China. ..... $ 9.00- 10.00

3936. 96th KENTUCKY DERBY 1970 – The decanter is a near duplicate of the 95th Kentucky Derby. It has a different stopper and has red roses. 10¾" – Genuine Regal China. .... $ 8.00- 15.00

3937. INDIANAPOLIS 500 1970 – The rectangular decanter has an embossed scene of a race car speeding past the grand stands. Genuine Regal China. .... $ 6.00- 8.00

3938. KENTUCKY COLONEL 1970 – This blue decanter has an embossed blue, white and gold seal on the front. the seal says, in a circle, "The Honorable Order Kentucky Colonels" and has 2 figures shaking hands embossed in the center. On the back is a scene surrounded by an embossed gold decorated horseshoe. On the base of the back is a quotation. 12" tall – Genuine Regal China. $ 6.00- 10.00

3939. MINT '400' 1970 – The decanter has a stopper that featrues a gold dune buggy. Most of the embossed letters are painted gold. A decal on the back gives information about the race. 13" tall – Genuine Regal China.. $ 8.00- 15.00

3940.	PUSSY WILLOW 1970 – Genuine Regal China.........	$	7.00-	10.00
3841.	SCOTCH BELLRINGER 1970 – Genuine Regal China. . .	$	8.00-	12.00
3942.	SUBMARINE 1970 – The decanter's front pictures a submarine floating on the water. On the back is a quotation. 11½" tall – Genuine Regal China.	$	6.00-	8.00
3943.	TOMBSTONE, ARIZONA 1970 – Genuine Regal China. .	$	6.00-	10.00
3944.	ASTRODOME 1971 – Genuine Regal China.	$	10.00-	15.00
3945.	AUSTRALIA 1971 – Genuine Regal China.	$	9.00-	10.00
3946.	BING'S 30th YEAR 1971 – The decanter is shaped like a captain's bottle with the front and back slashed off. "Bing's 30th" is heavily embossed on the front along with the golfer embossed on the neck of the decanter. Genuine Regal China.	$	5.00-	10.00
3947.	DELAWARE STATE TRAVEL LODGE 1971 – Genuine Regal China.	$	9.00-	12.00
3948.	GUAM 1971 – Genuine Regal China.	$	9.00-	10.00
3949.	97th KENTUCKY DERBY – Genuine Regal China. 1971.	$	9.00-	12.00
3950.	KING KAMEHAMEHA 1971 – Genuine Regal China. ...	$	9.00-	10.00
3951.	LONDON BRIDGE 1971 – Genuine Regal China.	$	6.00-	10.00
3952.	53rd PGA CHAMPIONSHIP 1971 – The decanter has the emblem of the PGA embossed on the front. A palm tree is also embossed on the front. The stopper is in the form of a golfer's cap. Genuine Regal China.	$	7.00-	8.00
3953.	TEXAN RABBIT 1971 – Genuine Regal China.	$	9.00-	10.00
3954.	WISCONSIN MUSKIE 1971 – Genuine Regal China. ...	$	9.00-	10.00
3955.	HAWAIIAN OPEN PRO-AM. 1972 – The upper half of the decanter is a pineapple, using the leaves for the stopper. An airplane is embossed over the pineapple. 10¼" tall.	$	8.00-	15.00
3956.	KASIER INTERNATIONAL 1971 – Designed for the 5th Kaiser International Open held at Silverado California in Napa Valley. There are four golf balls on each side with a ninth ball forming the stopper. 11½" tall.	$	5.00-	10.00

3958

Fantasy Series

3957.	PAUL BUNYAN 1970, '71 – The legendary lumber-jack has one hand on his blue ox, "Babe", and the other on his golden ax. He was the first bottle in the fantasy series, and has "Brainerd, Minnesota 1871-1971 Centennial" on the back. 11¾" tall.................	$	6.00-	10.00

3958. JOHN HENRY, A STEEL DRIVIN' MAN 1972 – The lower half of the decanter depicts the Big Bend Tunnel in West Virginia, where the legend of John Henry originated, and the lower part of John Henry. The stopper is the upper half of his body. 12¾" tall. . . . . $ 25.00- 35.00

3959   3970   3971   3978

Glass Specialities

3959. TALL PIN BOTTLES 1949-1970 – Beginning in 1955, these bottles were furnished with built-in pouring spouts (not on top). Gold top with gold lettering on bottle. Glass – 12" tall. . . . . $ 2.00- 4.00

3960. SHORT PIN BOTTLE 1952 – The short pin bottle was provided with a small wooden stopper and paper lables, 9". . . . . $ 5.00- 10.00

3961. COCKTAIL SHAKER 1953 – The base of the decanter has diamond designs. The upper part of the decanter is embossed with vine-like designs with the exception of a plain strip around the center of the decanter for placing the gold painted Beam identification. 9¼" tall. . . . . $ 4.00- 8.00

3962. ROYAL RESERVE 1953 – The plain decanter has the Beam identification painted on it's side. The decanter has a wooden stopper. These bottles came in various colors of velvet bags. 11¼" tall. . . . . $ 5.00- 8.00

3963. COFFEE WARMERS 1954 – These bottles have the Beam identification painted in gold on the side. A double stripe, one pin stripe and one wide stripe circle the bottles near the neck area. These glass containters are found with either black, gold, white or red plastic wrappings on the entire length of the neck. Wooden stopper is placed on these bottles. 9" high. . . . . $ 7.00- 10.00

3964. DUCKS AND GEESE 1955 – This megaphone shaped glass decanter has painted on white ducks and geese on it's side. A gold plated glass stopper and paper labels are also on the decanter. 13½" tall. . . . . $ 7.00- 10.00

3965. COFFEE WARMERS 1965 – These bottles have four pointed white stars set on white trimmed clear stars. The bottles have black plastic stoppers. Some of the bottles have metal handles & a metal collar around the neck which has black stripes painted on it. The other bottles have plastic handles and a metal collar with imprinted designs – 10" tall. . . . . $ 4.00- 8.00

3966.	ROYAL OPAL 1957 – This circular shaped opal glass decanter has an embossed design on the side. A matching opal glass stopper is on the decanter. 10¾" tall.	$	7.00- 10.00
3967.	ROYAL EMPEROR 1958 – The deep purple glass of this decanter appears to be black. The decanter is in the shape of an urn and has a white Greek figure on both sides – 14" tall.	$	5.00- 10.00
3968.	ROYAL CRYSTAL 1959 – A star burst design appears on both sides and the bottom of this glass decanter. A gold paper label was included to aid the beauty of the decanter. A black stopper is on the decanter. 11½" tall.	$	5.00- 10.00
3969.	OLYMPIAN 1960 – This blue glass decanter is shaped like a Grecian urn. A chariot scene is pictured on both sides of the decanter. A white glass stopper is on the decanter. 14" tall.	$	5.00- 10.00
3970.	GRECIAN 1961 – Light blue glass with white picture on its side. White lid. Glass – 13" tall.	$	4.00- 8.00
3971.	CLEOPATRA RUST 1962 – Deep purple with white figures on a rusty colored background. Stopper (not in picture) is white. 13¼" tall.	$	4.00- 8.00
3972.	CLEOPATRA YELLOW 1962 – This decanter is a duplicate of the Cleopatra Rust except that the figures on the side are yellow with a black background. 13¼" tall.	$	8.00- 16.00
3973.	MARK ANTHONY 1962 – This decanter is a dulpicate of the Cleopatra Rust with the exception that the Cleopatra figure is excluded from the picture. 13¼" tall.	$	15.00- 25.00
3974.	DELFT BLUE 1963	$	4.00- 6.00
3975.	DELFT ROSE 1963	$	7.00- 10.00
	These white glass containers have a sailing ship scene on the front and an embossed tree and windmill scene on the back. They have matching white glass stoppers. The scenes on the Delft blue are painted dark blue. The scenes on the Delft Rose are painted light blue and red. 13".	$	6.00- 8.00
3976.	SHORT DANCING SCOT 1963 – This decanter, like the Tall Dancing Scot, has an indented area in the bottom where a small dancing scot doll can be seen. A music box is applied to the base of the decanter which has a yellow stopper. 11" tall.	$	10.00- 30.00
3977.	TALL DANCING SCOT 1964-1971 – This megaphone shaped decanter has an indented area in the bottom where a scot doll can be seen dancing. A yellow music box applied to the bottom provides the music. Scotch pattern paper labels add color to the decanter. 17" tall.	$	9.00- 10.00
3978.	SMOKED CRYSTAL 1964 – "Geni bottle" Smoky colored glass. 14" tall.	$	7.00- 10.00
3979.	CAMEO BLUE 1965 – This decanter appears to be a beautiful four-sided blue glass vase. The sides have white enameled shepherd at work. A six-sided white stopper is provided for the decanter. 12¾" tall.	$	4.00- 10.00
3980.	CLEAR CRYSTAL 1966 – This decanter has the same embossed designs as the other crystal decanters except that it does not have a sunburst pattern on the bottom. 11½" tall.	$	6.00- 10.00

248

3982

3983

3984

3981. CLEAR CRYSTAL 1967 – This decanter is identical to the other crystal decanters and has sunburst design on the bottom. 11½" tall. .... $ 5.00- 6.00

3982. RUBY CRYSTAL 1967 – Amethyst colored glass, appears ruby red when filled with bourbon. 11½" tall. ... $ 8.00- 10.00

3983. EMERALD CRYSTAL 1968 – The Emerald Crystal is patterned after the Ruby Crystal decanter of 1967 except for the stopper. 11½" tall. .... $ 4.00- 10.00

3984. OPALINE CRYSTAL 1969 – This is a milk glass decanter. 11½" tall. .... $ 5.00- 10.00

3985. BEAM ANNIVERSARY CANNON 1970 – Cannon embossed on glass decanter, barrel extends out to serve as a spout. .... $ 4.00- 5.00

3986 - 3991

3992 - 3995

Collectors Edition

COLLECTORS EDITION VOLUME I, 1966 – Pictured from left to right.

3986. "ON THE TERRACE" .... $ 4.00- 6.00
3987. "BLUE BOY". .... $ 4.00- 6.00
3988. "THE ARTIST BEFORE HIS EASEL" .... $ 2.00- 4.00
3989. "LAUGHING CAVALIER" .... $ 2.00- 4.00
3990. "MARDI GRAS" .... $ 2.00- 4.00
3991. "ARTISTIDE BRUANT" .... $ 2.00- 4.00

COLLECTORS EDITION VOLUME II, 1967 – Pictured from left to right.

3992. "GEORGE GISZE" .... $ 2.00- 4.00

3993.	"THE JESTER"	$	2.00-	4.00
3994.	"NIGHT WATCH"	$	2.00-	4.00
3995.	"SOLDIER AND GIRL"	$	4.00-	5.00
	Not pictured:			
3996.	"NURSE AND CHILD"	$	4.00-	5.00
3997.	"MAN ON A HORSE"	$	2.00-	4.00
3998.	"PORTOLA TREK"	$	4.00-	5.00
3999.	"POWELL EXPEDITION"	$	4.00-	5.00

4000 - 4003   4004   4008 - 4009

COLLECTORS EDITION VOLUME III, 1968 – Pictured from left to right.

4000.	"INDIAN MAIDEN" – (in box).	$	2.00-	3.00
4001.	"ON THE TRAIL"	$	2.00-	3.00
4002.	"WHISTLER'S MOTHER"	$	2.00-	3.00
4003.	"THE KENTUCKIAN"	$	2.00-	3.00
4004.	"AMERICAN GOTHIC"	$	2.00-	3.00
	Not pictured:			
4005.	"BUFFALO HUNT"	$	2.00-	3.00
4006.	"HAULING IN THE GILL NET"	$	2.00-	3.00
4007.	"THE SCOUT"	$	2.00-	3.00

COLLECTORS EDITION VOLUME IV, 1969 – Pictured from left to right.

4008.	"EMILE ZOLA"	$	1.00-	2.00
4009.	"SUNFLOWERS"	$	2.00-	4.00
	Not pictured:			
4010.	"THE BALCONY"	$	1.00-	2.00
4011.	"ZONAVE"	$	1.00-	2.00
4012.	"BOY WITH CHERRIES"	$	2.00-	3.00
4013.	"FRUIT BASKET"	$	1.00-	2.00
4014.	"THE JUDGE"	$	1.00-	2.00
4015.	"THE GUITARIST"	$	1.00-	2.00

COLLECTORS EDITION VOLUME V, 1970 – Not pictured: The red-rust colored decanters include pictures of the artist in addition to the famous works of art.

4016.	"OLD PHEASANT"	$	2.00-	3.00
4017.	"JEWISH BRIDE"	$	2.00-	3.00
4018.	"BOATING PARTY"	$	2.00-	3.00
4019.	"GARE SAINT LAZARE"	$	2.00-	3.00
4020.	"AU CAFE"	$	2.00-	3.00
4021.	"TITUS AT THE WRITING DESK"	$	2.00-	4.00

4022

Beam Imports

4022.   BEAMEISTER WINES – Imported from Germany. They come in five colors: brown, white, light green, dark green. They also come in two sizes: 10½″ and 8½″. Each .... $ 3.00- 6.00

Schroeder's Antiques Price Guide

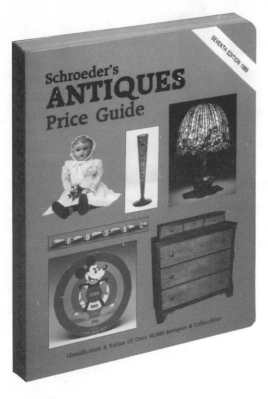

Schroeder's Antiques Price Guide has climbed its way to the top in a field already supplied with several well-established publications! The word is out, *Schroeder's Price Guide* is the best buy at any price. Over 500 categories are covered, with more than 50,000 listings. From ABC Plates to Zsolnay, if it merits the interest of today's collector, you'll find it in Schroeder's. Each subject is represented with histories and background information. In addition, hundreds of sharp original photos are used each year to illustrate not only the rare and the unusual, but the everyday "fun-type" collectibles as well. All new copy and all new illustrations make Schroeder's THE price guide on antiques and collectibles. We have not and will not simply change prices in each new edition.

The writing and researching team is backed by a staff of more than seventy of Collector Books' finest authors, as well as a board of advisors made up of well-known antique authorities and the country's top dealers, all specialists in their fields. Prices are gathered over the entire year previous to publication, then each category is thoroughly checked. Only the best of the lot remains for publication. You'll find the new edition of *Schroeder's Antiques Price Guide* the one to buy for factual information and quality.

No dealer, collector or investor can afford not to own this book. It is available from your favorite bookseller or antiques dealer at the low price of $12.95. If you are unable to find this price guide in your area, it's available from Collector Books, P.O. Box 3009, Paducah, KY 42001 at $12.95 plus $2.00 for postage and handling.